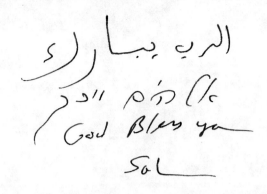

The Land Cries Out

The Land Cries Out

Theology of the Land
in the
Israeli-Palestinian Context

EDITED BY

Salim J. Munayer and Lisa Loden

CASCADE *Books* • Eugene, Oregon

Cascade Books
An Imprint of Wipf and Stock Publishers
199 W. 8th Ave., Suite 3
Eugene, OR 97401

www.wipfandstock.com

ISBN 13: 978-1-61097-335-9

Cataloging-in-Publication data

The land cries out : theology of the land in the Israeli-Palestinian context / edited by Salim J. Munayer and Lisa Loden.

xx + 348 p. ; 23 cm—Includes bibliographical references.

ISBN 13: 978-1-61097-335-9

1. Arab-Israeli conflict. 2. Land tenure—Religious aspects. I. Munayer, Salim J. II. Loden, Lisa. III. Title.

BR115 .L23 L50 2012

Manufactured in the USA.

Contents

Preface

"Your brother's blood cries out to me from the ground."

Gen 4:10 (NIV)

In choosing the title for this book, *The Land Cries Out: Theology of the Land in the Israeli-Palestinian Context*, we wanted to reflect on the fact that, in this place called the Holy Land, much blood has been shed by people with contesting claims to the land based on Scripture. We have justified the shedding of blood, even though the bloodshed belongs to those who were created in God's image, and came from the earth, from the *adamah*. The story of Abel's murder by his brother Cain in Genesis 4 warns us about the severe consequences that result in the shedding of blood, and as we learn from the Scripture, these consequences affect the land as well. Our actions, our moral and ethical behavior, affect the land, for good or for ill. This is critically important to remember as we approach the issue of theology of the land.

All of us approach this question, and approach the Scriptures from our own ethnic, cultural, or religious point of view. This is unavoidable. However, these articles call on us to open ourselves to the possibility of wisdom coming from other perspectives. Our duty is to approach them humbly, and make sure that our theology of the land will not lead us to bloodshed. We need to remember that a person on the other side of the debate, who has a completely different, or even incompatible perspective, may still be as genuine in loving God, as desiring of God's will, and as willing to obey him as we are. Let us listen and learn from one another.

—Salim J. Munayer and Lisa Loden

Acknowledgments

THE EDITORS WOULD LIKE to thank all of the authors who contributed their articles and chapters to this book. Their insights are inspirational and together form a significant contribution to this important discussion.

We would especially like to single out Joshua Korn, Charlotte Williams, and Laura Fabrycky for recognition. Without their tireless work, this book would have never come together, and their editorial work has greatly improved its quality.

We would also like to thank our publisher Wipf and Stock, for their willingness to take on the challenge of publishing a multi-author work, especially one dealing with such a divisive and controversial topic. We would like to thank, in particular, Jeremy Funk and Robin Parry, for their help in getting this manuscript ready for publication.

Finally, we would like to thank God for providing us with the vision, the courage, the discipline, and the means to undertake the task of publishing this book. We pray that it will encourage and challenge those who read it, and further the kingdom of God.

Scriptures labeled NKJV are taken from the New King James Version, Copyright © 1982 by Thomas Nelson, Inc. Used by permission. All rights reserved.

Scriptures labeled NRSV are taken from the New Revised Standard Version Bible, Copyright © 1989, Division of Christian Education of the National Council of the Churches of Christ in the United States of America. Used by permission. All rights reserved.

Scriptures labeled NASB are taken from the New American Standard Bible®, Copyright © 1960, 1962, 1963, 1968, 1971, 1972, 1973, 1975, 1977, 1995 by The Lockman Foundation. Used by permission. (www.lockman.org).

Manfred Kohl's "Towards a Theology of Land: A Christian Answer to the Israeli-Arab Conflict" first appeared in part in *Phronesis* 9.2 (2002) 7–26 and in the *International Congregational Journal* 2.2 (2002) 165–78. Reproduced here with kind permission.

Gary Burge's "Jesus and the Land" is excerpted from *Jesus and the Land, The New Testament Challenge to "Holy" Land Theology*. Grand Rapids/London: Baker Academic/SPCK, 2010, 25–40. Used by permission.

Alex Awad's "A Palestinian Theology of the Land" is excerpted from *Palestinian Memories: The Story of a Palestinian Mother and Her People*. Bethlehem: Bethlehem Bible College, 2008, 249–67. Reproduced here with kind permission.

Contributors

Canon Naim Ateek is a Palestinian theologian who lives and works in Jerusalem. He is the pastor of the St. George's Cathedral and director of Sabeel Ecumenical Liberation Theology Center, Jerusalem. Canon Ateek is also the author of numerous books, including *Justice, Only Justice: A Palestinian Theology of Liberation*.

Alex Awad is pastor of East Jerusalem Baptist Church, as well as Professor at Bethlehem Bible College in Palestine. Awad serves under the General Board of Global Ministries of the United Methodist Church, as the Dean of Students and full-time instructor at Bethlehem Bible College in Bethlehem, and as a charter member of BBC Board of Directors, Commissioned Mission Partner with the General Board of Global Ministries of the United Methodist Church and Pastor at East Jerusalem Baptist Church. Awad is also the author of a number of books, the most recent of which is *Palestinian Memories: The Story of a Palestinian Mother and Her People*.

Ambreen Tour Ben-Shmuel immigrated to Israel from the USA in 2005. She completed her MA in Islamic and Middle Eastern Studies at the Hebrew University of Jerusalem, and has worked for Musalaha since 2008.

Phillip D. Ben-Shmuel is a native Israeli Messianic Jew from Jerusalem. He has been involved in Musalaha since his youth. He is currently working on a degree in Biblical Studies and Comparative Religions at the Hebrew University of Jerusalem and is married to Ambreen Ben-Shmuel.

Gary M. Burge is Professor of New Testament at Wheaton College & Graduate School in Illinois. He has studied at the Near East School of Theology (Beirut, Lebanon), Fuller Theological Seminary, and Aberdeen University (Scotland). He is a frequent visitor to the Middle East as a conference speaker, teacher, archaeologist and researcher. He has written two books on the Israel-Palestinian conflict: *Whose Land? Whose Promise? What Christians Are Not Being Told About Israel and the Palestinians*, and most recently, *Jesus and the Land: How the New Testament Challenges 'Holy Land' Theology*. He has also written books for laity explaining how Middle Eastern culture is a key to interpreting well-known New Testament themes. These include: *The Bible and the Land, Jesus the Middle Eastern Story Teller*, and *Encounters with Jesus*.

Colin Chapman is a former Lecturer in Islamic Studies at the Near East School of Theology in Beirut. He has contributed much to the dialogue concerning the land, especially with his book, *Whose Promised Land?* which continues to be universally recognized as extremely relevant to this ongoing discussion.

John S. Feinberg is chair of the Department of Biblical and Systematic Theology and Professor of Biblical and Systematic Theology at Trinity Evangelical Divinity School in Illinois. Prior to coming to Trinity, Feinberg taught at Western Conservative Baptist Seminary in Portland, Oregon, and Liberty Baptist Seminary and College in Lynchburg, Virginia. Feinberg is also a member of the Society of Biblical Literature. Feinberg has written numerous articles and books, and has dealt with the theology of the land in particular.

Richard Harvey is a Messianic Jew who teaches the Hebrew Bible (Old Testament), Hebrew language, and Jewish studies. He has been involved in planting Messianic congregations and evangelism with Jews for Jesus and Church's Ministry among Jewish People. His writings include *Mapping Messianic Jewish Theology: A Constructive Approach*. Harvey is also a member of the Lausanne Consultation on Jewish Evangelism; European Board Member, Jews for Jesus; Vice-President, British Messianic Jewish Alliance; Board of Reference, Caspari Centre, Jerusalem; Editorial Board, Mishkan (Academic Journal on Jewish Evangelism and Messianic Judaism), Jerusalem. He is a former International President of the International Messianic Jewish Alliance, and teaches the Hebrew Bible (Old Testament), Hebrew language, and Jewish studies at All Nations Christian College in the United Kingdom.

Malcolm Hedding serves at present as the Executive Director of the International Christian Embassy Jerusalem. He holds a Bachelor of Theology degree plus two diplomas in theology. He was ordained as a Minister of the Assemblies of God of Southern Africa in 1975 and for many years discharged a church planting ministry in South Africa. He resisted, theologically, the Apartheid regime that put his life and ministry in danger. Consequently he first came to Israel in 1986 and joined the pastoral team of the Jerusalem Christian Assembly founded by Jim Cantelon and at the same time served as the Chaplin of the International Christian Embassy Jerusalem. He is married to Cheryl and they have three children, all of whom are in Christian ministry.

Munther Isaac is a Palestinian Christian theologian and teacher who serves as a lecturer and assistant Academic Dean at Bethlehem Bible College. He teaches on the topics of the Old and New Testament, and on the Life and Teaching of Jesus. Isaac is currently pursing his Ph.D. at the Oxford Center for Mission Studies on the topic of theology of the land, and is also a regular contributor to the discussion on this subject. Isaac has long been active with Musalaha in reconciliation efforts.

Daniel C. Juster cofounded and directs Tikkun International and has been involved in the Messianic Jewish movement since 1972. He currently resides in Jerusalem, Israel, where he and his wife serve and support the Messianic movement worldwide. Juster has served as the founding president and general secretary of the Union of Messianic Jewish Congregations, the senior pastor of Beth Messiah Congregation, and a cofounder of the Messiah Biblical Institute in several nations. He also holds a B.A. in Philosophy, Wheaton College; M.Div., McCormick Theological Seminary; graduate study, Trinity Evangelical Divinity School; Jewish Studies, Spertus College of Judaica; and Th.D., New Covenant International Seminary.

Yohanna Katanacho is a Palestinian evangelical theologian. He earned his Ph.D. in the Old Testament from Trinity International University and is currently serving as the Academic Dean of Bethlehem Bible College. He has authored two books in Arabic and is now working on a commentary on Proverbs. Katanacho has also translated several religious books from English to Arabic and has published several articles pertinent to Palestinian Theology. He frequently speaks in many churches and conferences around the world lecturing on Palestinian contextual theology.

Manfred Waldemar Kohl was born in Germany during the Second World War, and was educated in Germany, England, and the USA. After serving as a pastor in Massachusetts, he had various leadership positions at World Vision and now serves as VP of Programs & International Development with the Overseas Council International. Kohl writes and lectures frequently on the topic of the theology of the land.

Lisa Loden is a leader in the Israeli Messianic Jewish community. Lisa directed the Caspari Center for Biblical and Jewish Studies in Jerusalem for five years. She has been actively involved with Musalaha since its inception, leading the women's work for many years and currently serves as a member of the advisory board. Lisa heads and is a lecturer in the Department of Leadership Development Studies at the Nazareth Evangelical Theological Seminary. She has also authored many articles on reconciliation issues and frequently lectures on these issues in churches and conferences around the world.

Salim J. Munayer is a Palestinian-Israeli theologian and lecturer at Bethlehem Bible College, as well as the co-founder and director of Musalaha, a ministry that seeks to facilitate reconciliation between Israelis and Palestinians. Munayer has also authored numerous articles and books on the topic of theology of reconciliation, and is invited to lecture on this topic in churches and conferences around the world.

Joseph Shulam is a teacher of the Bible and evangelist. He lectures on the early church in Jerusalem, and is the director of the Netivyah Bible Instruction Ministry. He has established multiple congregations in Israel and is the author of numerous biblical commentaries, including *A Commentary on the Jewish Roots of Romans*.

Stephen R. Sizer is the author of several books on the topic of the theology of the land, and serves as Vicar of Christchurch, Virginia Water. His books on the land include, *Christian Zionism: Road Map to Armageddon?* and *Zion's Christian Soldiers*. Sizer is also a frequent lecturer on the theology of the land and other topics surrounding the theology and politics of the Israeli-Palestinian conflict.

Peter Walker teaches New Testament at Wycliffe Hall, Oxford University, UK. He is the author of a number of books focusing especially on the significance of Jerusalem in early Christian thought, such as *Holy City, Holy Places?* and *Jesus and the Holy City*. His most recent books include *In the Steps of Jesus* and the *Lion Guide to the Bible*. He is a regular contributor to the discussion on theology of the land and has become a well-known figure among both Israeli Messianic Jews and Palestinian Christians.

Introduction

FOR THE CHRISTIAN IN the twenty-first century, there are few subjects as important or as controversial as the theology of the Holy Land. The Israel/Palestine question consistently features in the media around the world. The church today is divided on the question with extreme opinions on all sides of the issue. The majority of Christians would agree that the Bible is the source and final arbiter of truth. Why then is there such a vast array of opinions and interpretations of the same texts?

This book does not attempt to answer this question directly. It does however seek to give the reader a broad perspective on this much-debated subject. To study theology is to enter a complex world. Often there are no simple, unequivocal answers. Ultimately, each person is responsible to seek out scriptural answers for himself. The current struggle in this region of the world has many aspects with theology as an ever-present undercurrent. Issues of land ownership, divine right, conquest, promise, inheritance and justice are only a few of the difficult issues addressed in this book. *The Land Cries Out* is a resource for the serious student as well as for the more casually interested reader.

The Land Cries Out is a collective work that was birthed from a similar book published by Musalaha in 2000, *The Bible and the Land: An Encounter*. Over the past decade, that book was met with much interest. The book was particularly popular among those seeking to understand the theological issues surrounding the Arab/Jewish conflict. *The Bible and the Land* went out of print and during the past ten years much has changed. For these reasons, a decision was taken to update and expand the book.

The editors, a Palestinian Christian man and a Messianic Jewish woman, have attempted to represent all of the significant evangelical points of view related to the issue of the land of Israel/Palestine in the Scriptures. In this collection, you will find articles written from widely different perspectives. Some of them appeared in *The Bible and the Land* and have been expanded or updated. Most of them are new contributions. The authors are Palestinian Christians, Messianic Jews, and Christians from the West. Many of them live in the Holy Land. What all the authors have in common is the questions they are asking and attempting to answer, however different these answers may be.

To give context to the subject, *The Land Cries Out* begins with an overview of the history of the Israeli-Palestinian conflict followed by a look at the hermeneutical issues that influence the discussions and conclusions regarding the theology of the land. The remainder of the book presents various positions on the subject. As previously noted, these chapters are written by scholars from varied backgrounds and perspectives. A number of the chapters offer new ways of looking at the texts and suggest integrative methods of engaging with the issues raised by the texts. Diversity of style is one of the characteristics of the book, and also one of the challenges. In the interest of making the articles as uniform as possible, and accessible to a wider audience, the editors have decided to use the general SBL style of transliteration for Hebrew, Arabic, and Greek.

The chapters do not have to be read according to their order. Each chapter can stand alone. However, when taken together, they present a comprehensive view of the various theological strands and positions on the theology of the land. Having articles and authors from such a diverse array of perspectives and opinions, presented side by side is a unique feature of this book, and one of its strengths. It is a juxtaposition that is both jarring and in keeping with the position of the editors and the ministries they represent, to foster conversations about difficult topics in the context of friendship and love.

Seeing so many different theological positions articulated has the additional benefit of making the reader aware of just how wide the spectrum of opinion (and belief) is. This is very helpful, since it is easy to fall into the trap of thinking that the realm of possibility extends only as far as our opinions reach.

Sadly, this volume is limited in scope, and is far from exhaustive. We have tried to present some of the different theological positions held by those in the local believing community and in the Christian West, but even that is a task that extends beyond the achievable reach of this book. Noticeably absent are Orthodox and Catholic positions, and the views of theologians and thinkers from Asia, Africa, and South America. At issue here is a question of global dimensions, and followers of the Messiah the world over are beginning to articulate their view on this topic. We humbly submit this work as a small contribution towards this discussion, and earnestly hope that it will generate greater interest and further the conversation. Reading over the articles, an encouraging sign is the clear emergence of up and coming young scholars who bring fresh perspectives, critical and contextualized, and have helped breathe new life into this very old debate.

We would challenge you to approach this book with an open mind and heart, seeking understanding as you begin the fascinating journey through the complexities of the theology of the Holy Land against the background of the Arab-Israeli conflict in light of Scripture.

Salim J. Munayer and Lisa Loden,
Jerusalem/Netanya, 2011

An Overview of the Israeli-Palestinian Conflict

Ambreen Tour Ben-Shmuel

There will be a time when "the Jew will not be ashamed to find the Arab part inside of himself, and the Arab will not be ashamed to declare that he is constituted also by Jewish elements. Especially when talking about Eretz Israel in Hebrew and Falestin in Arabic. I am a product of all the cultures that have passed through this land—Greek, Roman, Persian, Jewish and Ottoman. A presence that exists even in my language. Each culture fortified itself, passed on, and left something. I am a son to all those fathers, but I belong to one mother. Does that mean my mother is a whore? My mother is this land that absorbed us all, was a witness and was a victim. I am also born of the Jewish culture that was in Palestine . . ."

—Mahmoud Darwish, Palestinian poet and author[1]

OUR CONFLICT, THE ISRAELI-PALESTINIAN conflict, is painful, complicated, and frustrating. Its roots can be found in both Europe and the Middle East as the concept of modern nationalism arose and influenced perceptions of community, identity, and most importantly,

1. Kimmerling, *Palestinian People*, 416.

1

communal identity. With blood, sweat, and tears, both Israelis and Palestinians forged their national identities. While the conflict pits our two peoples against each other, it is often overlooked that our two identities share much in common. Our shared history has formed us—formed the way we view life, formed the way we view ourselves, formed the way we view one another. Often, Israelis and Palestinians prove to be a mirror to each other; many times, we do not like what we see. We have irrevocably become part of one another's identity. While the conflict has been long, it has not been hopeless. This paper does not focus on the shared identities of our two peoples as much as it does the differences (or is it similarities?) that conflict. We have both made sacrifices, and many continue to do so. These sacrifices, and the sacrifices that must be made for an eventual peace, form the blueprint for our shared future.

I have attempted to present an overview of the roots of identity and conflict, and key events that have shaped our quarrel. It is by no means comprehensive, as the scope of such an article could hardly contain everything that has brought us to where we are now. A disproportionate amount of space is given to the origins and development of this conflict, as they are the formative events. The events closer to the present have yet to be fully analyzed; they are also better known, therefore they are focused on less here.

THE RISE OF ZIONISM

Ever since the Jewish exile from Palestine in the second century of the common era, the Jewish people have maintained an emotional and spiritual connection to the land of Israel, longing for the restoration of their spiritual fortunes and the return to the land of their forefathers. A limited Jewish community remained in the land throughout the years of its people's exile. However, for the majority of the Jewish people, their connection to the land was through the liturgical year as they prayed, hoped, and commemorated their traditional and religious holidays.

The Jewish experience in the Diaspora was marked by discrimination both in Muslim and Christian lands. Between the eighteenth and twentieth centuries Jews were gradually granted legal equality in Europe, America, and the Ottoman Empire. While a number of Jews used their newfound equality to assimilate into the surrounding culture, others held to their Jewish tradition and roots while trying to live in contemporary society. For many, assimilation would be the end of discrimination. But even Jews who turned away from their religious traditions towards secular society were still considered to be Jews, both by themselves and those around them.

Jews were still thought of as the "Other" even as nation-states began to emerge. A number of secular Jewish authors began to write about Jewish nationalism and the Jewish problem, namely, that Jews constituted a nation in and of themselves, but had no home. They argued that Jews were scattered throughout the world and were never fully accepted. This was the point of departure for the nascent Zionist movement.[2]

Beginning in the eighteenth century, small groups of European Jewry began returning to the land of Israel, then situated under the rule of the Ottoman Empire. Jews came to Palestine in waves, often motivated by anti-Semitic violence in their home countries along with some form of religious or socialist ideology. They built new homes and communities, purchasing tracts of land in Ottoman Palestine.

In the late nineteenth century a young journalist named Theodor Herzl was greatly disturbed by the anti-Semitism he saw in "enlightened" France and concluded that even if Jews wished to assimilate and give up their religion and culture, the world would not permit it. In 1896, Herzl published *Der Judenstaat*, in which he advocated founding a Jewish state as the solution to the Jewish problem of anti-Semitism.

In 1897 Zionism was officially established as a political movement with the First Zionist Congress held in Basel, Switzerland. During this meeting, the goal was defined: "Zionism seeks to secure for the Jewish people a publicly recognized, legally secured home in Palestine for the Jewish people."[3] There were differing opinions as to how to achieve this objective. Some advocated promotion of small-scale Jewish settlement and continued land purchase in Palestine, while others, like Herzl, advocated finding a political, legal, and longstanding solution for mass Jewish settlement in the land.[4]

2. Cleveland, *History of Modern Middle East*, 234–37. There are many nuanced definitions of *Zionism*. A relatively neutral definition is presented by historian Walter Laqueur as "the belief in a common past and a common future for the Jewish people." See Laqueur, *History of Zionism*, 589.

3. Laqueur, *History of Zionism*, 106. Quote taken from the First Zionist Congress.

4. Ibid., 84–135.

THE EARLY SOLIDIFICATION OF PALESTINIAN IDENTITY

Over the course of the eighteenth and twentieth centuries, Palestine[5] was subject to the interests and incursions of the French, Egyptians, and British. Palestine was under the control of the Ottoman Empire from the early sixteenth to the twentieth centuries, but the Ottomans briefly lost control of the region in 1831 when Muhammad Ali Pasha of Egypt sent his son Ibrahim Pasha on an expansionary expedition. The modernization of Palestine began with infrastructural and agricultural reforms introduced by Ibrahim, as well as new taxation methods.[6] The local population objected to these changes, but most strongly protested the additional imposition of conscription, reacting in the *1834 Palestinian Revolt*, concentrated primarily in Nablus and Jerusalem. These abhorred reforms proved to unite the diverse population of Palestine from "dispersed Bedouins, rural sheikhs, urban notables, mountain fellaheen, and Jerusalem religious figures against a common enemy. It was these groups that would later constitute the Palestinian people."[7]

While the Ottomans resumed their control of Syria and Palestine by 1840, British and French interests still played an important role in the local economy. As part of their policy of encouraging investment and development, the Ottomans passed laws allowing for foreign purchase of land in the empire, which aided in subsequent Zionist land purchase. In order to export to the European market, peasants had to cease subsistence farming in exchange for cash crops, decreasing their self-dependence. The imposition of new taxes led to poorer families selling their ownership rights to wealthier families and landowners. On the other hand, the economic reforms led to an influx of trade and better medicine, which in turn resulted in a massive increase in Ottoman Palestine's population, which nearly doubled between 1870 and 1914.[8]

In the 1860s, the Ottomans began to reorganize their imperial administration to create a centralized state modeled after European states. Previously, the subprovinces of Beirut and Damascus had been the strongest administrative centers, but due to the economic and social

---

5. At this time *Palestine* refers to the territory that would become Mandatory Palestine, viz., what had been the Ottoman subprovinces of Acre, Nablus, and Jerusalem.

6. Kimmerling and Migdal, *Palestinian People*, 6–13. See also Pappé, *History of Modern Palestine*, 3.

7. Kimmerling and Migdal, *Palestinian People*, 7.

8. Pappé, *History of Modern Palestine*, 3, 24–25.

changes of earlier decades, the Ottomans realized the need to redefine their divisions. The Ottomans wished to form a more "cohesive geographical unit," so they elevated the area surrounding Jerusalem into an independent subprovince.[9] They discussed connecting the subprovinces of Nablus and Acre with the Jerusalem subprovince as these three areas (which would eventually become Mandatory Palestine) shared "its own major dialects . . . customs, folklore and traditions."[10] However, when the land reformers decided against this and included Nablus to the larger province of Beirut extending to the north, there was a great protest resulting in an outbreak of violence in which, reportedly, three thousand people were killed. Historians identify this as an early and significant expression of Palestinian collective unity and identity.[11]

As a result of reforms and Ottoman interaction with Europe, nationalist movements began to emerge within the empire, especially within Turkey itself. Additionally, there were attempts to secularize the empire and separate the religious and secular functions of the state. This led to Arab unease and protest, as their loyalty to Ottoman rule was due (in part) to its Islamic religious authority. The attempts to Turkicize the empire led to the suppression of other national movements, including early Arab nationalism.[12]

Within these dynamics we see the emergence of Palestinian identity and nationalism. The people of Palestine had a strong religious attachment to the Holy Land. Furthermore, there was a strong sense of "urban patriotism" that was evidenced by local loyalty to one's city or village. Although literacy was not high in the early twentieth century, the press played an important role in shaping and reflecting regional identity. The identification of Palestinians with Palestine as an area separate and distinct from surrounding Arab entities solidified prior to the confirmation of the British Mandate.[13]

9. Ibid., 28.

10. Ibid.

11. Ibid., 26, 28.

12. Ibid., 56–57.

13. Khalidi, "Formation," 172–76.

THE BRITISH, THE JEWS, AND THE PALESTINIANS

Britain's interest in Palestine increased over the years, particularly since Palestine served as an entrance to the Middle East through which it could guard British interests in India. As the Ottomans depended on the British to aid them in matters of defense, capitulations were made that allowed for increased British influence and presence in Palestine.

With the beginning of World War I in 1914, the Ottoman Empire aligned with Germany against Britain and its allies. In order to secure a foothold in the Middle East, the British began to court the Arabs and fan their nationalist sentiments. In the 1915–1916 *McMahon-Hussein Correspondence*, the British high commissioner of Egypt, Sir Henry McMahon, promised the sharif of Mecca, Hussein ibn Ali, to support an Arab kingdom in exchange for organizing an Arab revolt against the Ottomans. The British and Hussein did not entirely agree on what would constitute the future Arab kingdom. Both the British and Zionists argued that Palestine was not intended to be included; the Arabs contended that it was.[14] Meanwhile, the British and French began secret talks regarding the division of the Middle East when the Ottoman Empire was defeated, culminating in the 1916 *Sykes–Picot Agreement*. It stipulated that the British would receive present-day Iraq and Jordan, France present-day Syria and Lebanon, and they would share or split Palestine. In 1916, Hussein provided the promised *Arab Revolt*, but it was neither as encompassing nor as helpful as the British had hoped.[15]

The British, keen to maintain alliances with as many parties as could prove useful to them, were also engaging in discussion with the Zionists. There were a number of Jewish groups who allied themselves with Britain at the onset of the war, and their efforts fighting in Palestine on behalf of the British did not go unappreciated or unnoticed, particularly since the Arabs of Palestine allied with the Ottomans. Prior to 1915, many British leaders did not view Zionist presence in Palestine as a strategic interest to them. Yet, due to adjustments in political leadership, this opinion changed.[16] Accordingly, in 1917 the British issued the *Balfour Declaration*, in which the British foreign secretary expressed his support of a Jewish homeland.[17] This declaration was received with great

14. Morris, *Righteous Victims*, 29–70.

15. Ibid., 70–77.

16. Ibid., 71–73.

17. For a copy of the Balfour Declaration, see Laqueur, *Israel-Arab Reader*, 16.

exhilaration. This was the historical opportunity the Zionists had been working for.

Whatever economic and social progress had occurred in Palestine was brought to an abrupt halt with World War I. At first the war was strictly a European affair, but after approximately a year, the hostilities reached Palestine, bringing with it devastation, starvation, and death. Soldiers came to Palestine and set up military camps, Palestinian Arabs were conscripted into the army, and locals were forced to feed and quarter military personnel.[18] The war was a problem for the *Yishuv*—the Jewish community in Palestine—as well. While the Zionist community remained neutral at the start of the war, this did not prevent Ottoman persecution of the Palestinian Jews. In 1915, the Ottomans forbade land sales to Jews, and a number of Zionists were exiled or jailed.[19]

The war ended in late 1918, and although the Allies won and the British were expected to make good on their promises to the Arabs and Jews, all parties felt betrayed. The Zionists were displeased Jewish immigration had been curbed. The Arabs were angry due to the issuing of the Balfour Declaration and the influx of Jewish immigrants.

THE BRITISH MANDATE IN PALESTINE

In the years following the war, a number of significant agreements and events led to the establishment of the British Mandate and the shaping of Europe and the Middle East. During the *Paris Peace Conference* in January 1919, the Allied victors set the conditions for the defeated powers. From this peace conference emerged the June *Treaty of Versailles* that outlined what would happen to Germany and its allies, including the Ottoman Empire. The Ottoman Empire was taken apart, and afterwards split between principal Allied powers.

Although the British had occupied Palestine in 1917, the *British Mandate of Palestine* was only approved in July 1922. The Mandate officially incorporated the Balfour Declaration by legalizing the commitment to establish a Jewish homeland and conferring upon it the approbation of the international community. The Zionist organization wished to retain the eastern bank of the Jordan in their state; the British

18. Pappé, *History of Modern Palestine*, 61–64. See also Morris, *Righteous Victims*, 83; Khalaf, "Effect of Socioeconomic Change," 96.

19. Morris, *Righteous Victims*, 84–87.

disallowed this by detaching Transjordan from the area of Palestine, and by default the area to which the Balfour Declaration applied. The Mandate specifically stipulated the recognition of a Jewish body to govern economic, social, and other affairs and to represent the interests of the Jewish people. No such recognition was guaranteed to the indigenous Arab population.[20]

In the early years of British control, hostilities between Jews and Arabs began to escalate. Some significant events of the following years include the 1920 *Nabi Musa Riots*—also know as the 1920 *Palestine Riots*—in which Palestinian religious leaders incited the population against the Jews resulting in pogroms. The British refrained from extensive punitive measures against the Arab instigators, and subsequently regulated Jewish immigration leading to deterioration in British and Jewish relations.[21] The riots of 1920 were followed by the 1921 *Jaffa Riot* from May 1–7. Clashes between demonstrators resulted in multiple casualties on both sides. Jewish leadership, appalled at its inability to sufficiently protect its own population and horrified by lack of British intervention, concluded that it would have to be self-dependent in matters of defense. In 1921, the *Haganah*, a semi-military force for defense against local aggression, was formed.[22] Subsequently, the British issued the *British White Paper of 1922*, clarifying British policy in Palestine by reaffirming its support of Zionism and a Jewish homeland, but qualifying the policy by reiterating that it was not to be at the expense of the local Arab population, and stating that the Jewish national home would not be in all of Mandatory Palestine.[23]

While violence continued to be a regular occurrence, a particularly violent outbreak transpired in the summer of 1929 when (subsequently disproved) rumors emerged that Jews were attacking Muslims at the al-Aqsa mosque. These rumors reached Hebron and the 1929 *Hebron Massacre* ensued against its unarmed Jewish community, resulting in sixty-four dead. The brutality of the massacre was particularly stomach-turning, shocking the Jews and many Arabs as well. This alarming attack

---

20. Ibid., 30–36. See also Khalidi, "Palestinians and 1948," 12–36.

21. Morris, *Righteous Victims*, 94–98.

22. Tal, "Between Intuition and Professionalism," 887–88.

23. Laqueur, *Israel-Arab Reader*, 25–29.

served to further convince the local Jewish community that dependence on the British for safety and order was futile.[24]

In the background there was a vibrant Palestinian political awakening. In 1936 the Arab Higher Committee (AHC) was established as the national leadership, composed of six political parties. Disgruntled by both the British and Jews, they demanded the establishment of an Arab government, an end to immigration, and a cessation of land sales. The AHC called for a general strike of the Palestinian population.[25] The strike led to general insurrection, and hundreds of villagers all over the country joined in the revolt, establishing armed units throughout Palestine. While the strike lasted from April to October 1936, the violence continued until 1939.

Toward the end, violent internal conflict broke out between the Arab Palestinians, making it easier for the British to suppress the revolt. By the end of the revolt the Palestinian leadership was either in detention camps or exiled. The upper class had fled, and there was no elite, no political system, and no one to guide the people locally or nationally. It is unclear exactly how many Arabs died, but between three and six thousand died in the revolt, and another 4,500 were killed by other Arabs.[26] These events would come to be known as the *1936–1939 Arab Revolt in Palestine*.

The revolt improved the relationship between the British and the Yishuv as they cooperated in their response against the Arab Palestinians. The Haganah became a more professional, experienced fighting force, better trained and armed over the course of the three years. Only a few hundred Jews were killed, and while some property was destroyed, it was of little significance. Due to rising anti-Semitism in Europe and Hitler's rise to power in the early 1930s, the Yishuv absorbed tens of thousands of new immigrants. Additionally, the revolt led the Jews to further their self-sufficiency as they learned to rely less on the Arab Palestinians for food and goods. The Jews gained economically, militarily, and politically. While the Palestinians suffered economically and politically, the revolt served to further forge their national identity.[27]

24. Morris, *Righteous Victims*, 114–20.

25. Abboushi, "Road to Rebellion," 26–27, 38.

26. Morris, *Righteous Victims*, 159–60.

27. Kimmerling and Migdal, *Palestinian People*, 102–31. See also Morris, *Righteous Victims*, 160.

This most recent bout of violence led to the 1936–1937 *Peel Commission* initiated by the British to ascertain what changes should be made in Mandatory Palestine. For the first time the concept of partition came to the fore as it suggested splitting Palestine into two states, and advocated a land and population exchange. The majority of the Zionists were opposed to the commission's proposal, but in the end, accepted it. The Palestinian Arabs rejected it, and insisted that since they were the majority population, they should be the beneficiaries of a state in all of Mandatory Palestine.[28]

Toward the end of the 1936–1939 revolt, Britain issued its *1939 White Paper* advocating one state governed by both Arab Palestinians and Jews. It put a quota on Jewish immigration and land purchase. Both the Jewish and Arab Palestinian communities of Palestine opposed it.

European anti-Semitism was spreading to the Middle East, and the outbreak of World War II in 1939 had implications for Palestine as well. While the Arab Palestinians were not particularly fond of the Germans or Nazi ideology, al-Husseini sided with the Nazis against the British.[29] The Zionists, on the other hand, aided in the British war effort. This proved to be mutually beneficial as it provided further training and fighting experience for the Jewish community, and served to ingratiate the British to them.[30]

With the end of World War II in 1945, the British were faced with a number of difficult issues in Mandatory Palestine. Anti-Zionist demonstrations protesting increased Jewish presence in the region were prevalent throughout the Arab world. The Americans were pressuring the British to allow Jewish immigration to Palestine in light of the war. The Yishuv felt the British were being oppressive by disallowing open Jewish immigration into Palestine, particularly since Western Europe and the United States refused to accept Holocaust survivors. In response to continued British immigration restrictions, a Jewish revolt broke out, initiated by rogue militant groups, but eventually joined by the Haganah. The revolt aimed to oust the British from Palestine.[31]

In February 1947, the British, bankrupt and weary from their economic and physical losses in World War II and Mandatory Palestine,

---

28. Laqueur, *Israel-Arab Reader*, 41–43. See also Morris, *Righteous Victims*, 138–44.

29. Morris, *Righteous Victims*, 162, 166.

30. Ibid., 166.

31. Ibid., 170–81.

announced their lack of interest in continuing the Mandate, and brought the issue to the United Nations. The Arabs were optimistic about this change in events, expecting the UN to act in their favor. The Zionists were unsure of what this move would entail for them.[32]

In May 1947, the UN sent the *United Nations Special Committee on Palestine* (UNSCOP) to look into what should be done. UNSCOP recommended both the termination of the Mandate and the partition of Palestine into a Jewish state and an Arab state with an international trusteeship controlling Jerusalem and Bethlehem.[33]

Apprehensive about the political situation that was emerging on the ground, both the Yishuv and the Palestinian leadership expected imminent war. The Arab League formed the Arab Liberation Army in September 1947 composed of both Arab Palestinians and other Arabs. The Arabs had little faith in the success of diplomatic effort, believing that violence was their only recourse (which had proven to be a self-fulfilling pattern in Palestine throughout the Mandatory period).[34] Al-Husseini was loath to involve other Arab states, fearing they would try and apportion Palestine for themselves.[35]

Until the end of 1946, the military planning of the Yishuv and Haganah anticipated little more than the sort of skirmishes and violence that they had experienced under the Mandate; therefore, they prepared countermeasures of a defensive nature. In late 1946, David Ben Gurion, chairman of the Jewish Agency for Palestine (the prestate Jewish government), changed his strategy. As the British prepared to relinquish the Mandate between May 14 and May 15, 1948, he realized that as long as the British were in Palestine, the Arab world took no action against Jews, but if the British left, they would feel no compunction against taking up arms against the Yishuv. The Yishuv felt little threat from the Arab Palestinian population due to its poor organization and lack of military capability (as a result of the events of 1936–1939). Instead, the Haganah prepared for nationalization upon the departure of the British in order to address the imminent threat from the surrounding countries.

32. Ibid., 180.

33. Ibid., 182–83.

34. Abboushi, "Road to Rebellion, 45": "The Arabs had come to believe, from the failure of diplomacy, that violence was the only way to achieve what they considered to be their rights. Their viewpoint seemed to have been correct. To use the bullet when the ballot was forbidden thus became a firm principle of radical Palestinian Arab nationalism."

35. Morris, *Righteous Victims*, 186–97; Tal, "Forgotten War," 6–9.

As a result of UNSCOP's recommendation and powerful Zionist lobbying, *United Nations Resolution 181*, otherwise known as the UN Partition Plan, detailing the end of the British Mandate and the creation of a Jewish and Arab state in Palestine, was brought to the United Nations General Assembly, passing with a two-thirds majority on November 29, 1947. The Arabs rejected the resolution; they could not accept a recommendation that would apportion Palestine away from its majority indigenous population. They left the General Assembly, stating that the decision would lead to war. While the partition plan gave the Jews less than they had hoped for, they enthusiastically accepted it, as it provided the legal basis for a Jewish state in Palestine, the culmination of years of Zionist work, and the fulfillment of the dream Herzl put in motion.[36]

THE BIRTH OF THE STATE OF ISRAEL AND THE FIRST ARAB-ISRAELI WAR

Jewish rejoicing did not last long. The following day the *1947–1948 Civil War in Palestine* broke out.[37] The civil war was primarily conducted using guerilla tactics.[38] Arab Palestinians as well as volunteer fighters from surrounding countries were on the offensive; the Jews were on the defensive. During the first phase of the civil war, the Jews did not occupy any new territory. By early March, the Arab Palestinian attacks were succeeding. They had a distinct geographical advantage as well as the ability to easily call up additional forces as they passed by villages.[39]

The Haganah realized that its plan of defense was not working and reevaluated its strategy in March 1948. At this time, earlier than anticipated, the British began to evacuate Palestine. As a result, the Haganah devised a new offensive plan with the intent of placing the Haganah forces in the best strategic positions to ward off foreign forces in an imminent Arab war.[40] Additionally, the forces were instructed to begin assuming control of areas evacuated by the British within the boundaries

36. Morris, *Righteous Victims*, 185–86.

37. The opening date of the civil war is debated.

38. Morris, *Righteous Victims*, 191.

39. Tal, "Forgotten War," 12–15.

40. The plan devised at this point is Plan Dalet, or Plan D. This was a controversial plan. Its intent is still being debated by contemporary historians. For more information, see Tal, "Forgotten War," 13. See also section on "The Refugees of the Palestinian Nakba."

of the partitioned Jewish state. In spite of the new policy, the offensive approach was kept to a minimum at this time.[41]

Starting in April 1948, the second phase of the civil war began, and changes in strategy and intent were evident. At this point the Jewish side began to engage in consistent offensive actions. Previously the Haganah would not seize control of the areas where its convoys would pass, but under the new strategy they began to take control of the villages surrounding the roads. This changed their fortunes. Additionally, one of the main commanders of the Arab Palestinian front was killed which led to a breakdown in command and organization.[42]

A critical event during this phase was the *Deir Yassin Massacre* of April 9, 1948 carried out by two small Jewish militia units. This village had good relationships with neighboring Jewish areas and had maintained them from the beginning of the war. Despite no provocation, the units decided to conquer this village and expel its inhabitants. Much of Deir Yassin's population fled prior to the beginning of the battle. In its ascent to the village, the units suffered the loss (by death or injury) of one quarter of its men, enraging the militia. A Jewish militia truck equipped with a loudspeaker called for the population to flee the village, but this order was not heard. Once the units reached the city, the remaining population, including unarmed men, women, and children, were abused and slaughtered by the Jewish forces. The Jewish Agency and Haganah condemned the massacre instantly. While the Haganah was not directly involved in the fighting, it provided backup and ammunition to the smaller militia units. Between 100 and 110 men, women, and children were massacred at Deir Yassin, and while there were other massacres during the war as well, this one stands out as a symbol of Jewish atrocities during the 1948 war.[43]

Refugees fleeing their homes due to expulsion or fear alarmed the surrounding Arab countries and motivated them to provide forces to aid the Arab Palestinians. By the middle of May, the Haganah had seized control of the mixed towns within the Jewish boundaries of partition,

41. On March 23, 1948 General Ismail Safwat, commander of Palestine's campaign for the Arab League, found it interesting that Jews were showing restraint in their attacks, stating, "Until now they have not attacked any Arab village unless provoked by it." See Karsh, "Arab-Israeli Conflict," 39–40.

42. Morris, *Righteous Victims*, 204–14.

43. Ibid., 207–9.

and the Haganah had completed its defeat of the Palestinian Arabs.[44] On May 14, 1948, in the midst of continued fighting, the Yishuv's executive leaders paused in administering the war at 4:00 p.m., and Ben Gurion announced the *Establishment of the State of Israel* in Palestine. The following day, the *1948 Arab-Israeli War* began.

On May 15, armies from Lebanon, Syria, Iraq, Transjordan, and Egypt invaded Israel launching a full-scale conventional war against the newly established state. While the threat was significant (the Haganah anticipated that Israel had a fifty-fifty chance of winning[45]), the makeup of the attacking armies did not tip the chances of winning in the Arabs' favor. The objectives of the invading countries were diverse, uncoordinated, self-interested, and sometimes conflicting.[46] One historian summarizes: "The Arab coalition was one of the most divided, disorganized and ramshackle coalitions in the entire history of warfare."[47] In January 1949, the fighting ceased, ending the 1948 Arab–Israeli War. In the coming months the armistice lines would be set forming what is today known as the *Green Line*, and armistice agreements signed.[48]

THE REFUGEES OF THE PALESTINIAN NAKBA

Historians estimate that between 550,000 and 750,000 Palestinians became refugees as a result of the 1948 Civil War and the 1948–1949 First Arab–Israeli War. Five hundred thirty one villages were destroyed, and eleven urban neighborhoods were emptied of residents.[49] Palestinians refer to this as their national catastrophe: the *Nakba*.

The Nakba can be broken down into a number of stages. The first stage took place from December 1947 to March 1948 and was undertaken

44. Tal, "Forgotten War," 17.

45. Morris, *Righteous Victims*, 215.

46. For a firsthand account of the disorganization, see Nasser and Khalidi, "Nasser's Memoirs." See also Rogan and Shlaim, "Israel and the Arab Coalition," 80–82. In spite of these advantages, Tal explains that Israel lacked qualified military leadership as "none of the veterans had any formal military education or experience in command of combat units." Tal, "Between Intuition and Professionalism," 890. Tal specifically states that "Haganah members were not qualified to command brigades or even companies" (888).

47. Shlaim, "Israel and the Arab Coalition," 82.

48. For more information on Israel's operations see Shlaim, *War for Palestine*, 82–100, and Tal, "Between Intution and Professionalism."

49. See Khalaf, "Effect of Socioeconomic Change," 93; Pappé, *History of Modern Palestine*, 143; Karsh, "Arab–Israeli Conflict," 88; see also Pappé, "1948 Ethnic Cleansing," 7.

by middle-class and upper-class Arab Palestinians. Due to fear of an imminent Jewish attack, approximately 75,000 fled the chaos and rumors of war, just as they did during the turmoil of 1936–1939.[50]

The second stage occurred from April to June 1948, a particularly dire time for the Yishuv and the nascent Jewish state. Politically, the Yishuv found less support than expected from the United States. During this time, expulsion was not commonplace, as many Arabs had already fled upon the arrival of Jewish forces. In this phase between 200,000 and 300,000 Arabs were uprooted from their homes.[51]

The evacuation of Arabs from cities and towns resulted from a combination of the demoralization from the first exodus; of poor leadership, centralization, and administration from local leaders; as well as from fear and failing morale due to Arab flights from nearby towns and cities. This culminated in a sort of domino effect.[52]

The third stage of the Arab exodus from Palestine took place primarily between July 9–18. There was no clear Israeli Defense Force (IDF) policy in place until mid-July, and consequent actions toward conquered populations were varied and haphazard.[53] From mid-July through October, the IDF focused on clearing "potentially hostile" Arab populations, and subsequently, many Arabs were forced to leave.[54] Altogether, the operations of July to October 1948 resulted in the exile of over a hundred thousand Arabs, many of them as a result of forced expulsion.[55]

50. Morris, "Response to Finkelstein," 100, 105. See also Morris, *Birth of the Refugee Problem*, 52–57.

51. In March Haganah leaders instituted Plan D. Intended for use in May once the British left, military leaders decided to implement Plan D earlier to establish territorial continuity between Jewish towns. To achieve this, they saw it necessary to depopulate and destroy many Arab villages. For more information, see Morris, *Birth of the Refugee Problem*, 62. However, Plan D was intended to be defensive, as a response to Arab offenses. See introduction to Plan Dalet: "Plan Dalet." Jewish Virtual Library. Online: http://www.jewishvirtuallibrary.org/jsource/History/Plan_Dalet.html/. For more information on this debated topic, see Morris, *Birth of the Refugee Problem Revisited*, 593. See also, Tal, "Forgotten War"; and Morris, "Response." Ilan Pappé takes Morris's conclusions a step further; see Pappé, *Ethnic Cleansing*. Also, the sheer numbers surprised the Yishuv leadership, leading one to believe that expulsion of this size was unanticipated and unplanned (albeit not unappreciated). See Morris, *Birth*, 128; and Morris, "Response to Finkelstein," 107.

52. For more information on the second wave, see Morris, *Birth*, 61–131.

53. Ibid., 197–98.

54. Ibid., 213.

55. Ibid., 197–216.

A fourth wave of Arab flight resulted from a UN proposal to give the Galilee to the Jews and the Negev to the Arabs. Combined IDF operations in the north and south resulted in the flight of between 100,000 and 150,000 Arabs.[56]

Immediately following the fourth stage, Israeli military and political leaders sought to bolster the security of the new and easily penetrable frontiers by emptying villages in border areas. This policy was implemented along the southern, northern, and Transjordanian-held eastern borders. It is difficult to estimate the number of Arabs expelled and evicted during this period, but the number is somewhere between twenty and thirty thousand, including the Bedouins of the northern Negev.[57] During this time the United Nations General Assembly issued *Resolution 194*, which stipulated, among other things, the return of the refugees to their homes and compensation for loss and damage of property.[58]

It is clear from the sources that there was an ethnic cleansing of approximately seven hundred thousand Palestinians between 1947 and 1949. Parts of it were planned and systematic. However, not all the forced expulsions that took place were premeditated, desirable as they might have been. While some fled due to fear of war, and others were physically forced from their homes, what ultimately defines this series of events as an expulsion is the subsequent disallowal of refugees to return.

THE EARLY YEARS OF ISRAELI INDEPENDENCE

The period following the birth of the state was tumultuous. Israel absorbed seven hundred thousand Jewish immigrants from the Muslim world and resettled them in abandoned Arab neighborhoods and in empty or border areas of the new state.[59] There was international pressure to repatriate the Palestinian refugees, but Israel refused, stating it

56. Ibid., 235–36. In spite of Ben Gurion's desire to expel the Palestinian Arabs of the Galilee, his wishes were not fully carried out. Between 30 and 50 percent of the Galilee's Arabs remained after cessation of operations. See Morris, "Revisiting the Palestinian Exodus," 52–53.

57. Ibid., 237, 251–53. Morris changes this to stage 5, and slightly alters the date to November 1948–1950. Pappé states that "forty Palestinian villages were depopulated between 1949 and 1952, their inhabitants either moved *en bloc* to other villages, driven across the border, or dispersed within the country." See Pappé, *History of Modern Palestine*, 147.

58. Laqueur, *Israel-Arab Reader*, 83–86.

59. Morris, *Righteous Victims*, 260.

had already absorbed refugees from Arab lands, namely the Jewish refugees.[60] Arab animosity toward Israel grew as a result of Israel's intransigence, particularly since the Palestinian refugee issue affected them directly. Most of the refugees were absorbed by Jordan in the West Bank. While Jordan granted citizenship to the refugees under its rule, Egypt, Syria, and Lebanon did not. Humiliated by their failure in the recent war, and infuriated by both a Jewish state and a Palestinian refugee problem, "the Arab countries waged unremitting economic, diplomatic, and propaganda warfare against the new nation."[61]

Persistent anti-Israel propaganda from Arab states caused increased alarm. Israel was also apprehensive that the British (who were present in Egypt) would leave, making it easier for Egypt to begin another war with Israel. Skirmishes between Israelis and Egyptians along their shared border gradually escalated. Egypt eventually closed the Straits of Tiran, blockaded the Gulf of Aqaba, and closed the Suez Canal to Israeli shipping. On October 29, 1956, Israel, Britain, and France attacked Egypt in what would come to be known as the *Suez Crisis* (also known as the Sinai Campaign, or Tripartite Aggression). On November 5, both Israel and Egypt accepted a UN ceasefire, although the quarrel persisted until Israel was assured that its waterways would remain open. By March 1957, Israel had withdrawn from Gaza and Sinai. In short, the war decreased border tensions and infiltration issues as the surrounding Arab countries were afraid of provoking a war with the IDF. However, the war also aggravated an already volatile situation, and the Arab countries began to discuss another war to destroy Israel.[62]

THE POST-1948 FORMATIVE YEARS OF THE PALESTINIAN COMMUNITY

Meanwhile, difficulty of life in United Nations Relief and Works Agency (UNRWA) camps led to despondency. For most of the refugee population, survival was their highest priority. Despairing and hopeless, simply trying to cope with their bleak existence, few were enamored with politics or radical movements forming within their midst.[63] In the 1950s

60. Pappé, *History of Modern Palestine*, 146.

61. Morris, *Righteous Victims*, 259.

62. Ibid., 281–301.

63. Pappé, *History of Modern Palestine*, 152.

the despondency and lack of purpose led to the beginnings of a guerilla nationalist movement. Guerilla activity occurred on the borders with Israel, seeking to take property (sometimes what had been their own property), and occasionally involving attacks on Israelis in border towns. The guerilla fighters were cautious in their activity due to Israel's harsh anti-infiltration policy, but there were still many Palestinian casualties.[64]

The 1950s composed the "'formative years' of the new Palestinian national movement."[65] A number of issues united the Palestinians: the centrality of land, the belief in return to their land, the "politicization of refugee life," and the concept of armed struggle.[66] Disillusioned with the Arab states' unwillingness or inability to obtain their homeland for them, they took it upon themselves to do what others could not.[67] The goals of this emerging national movement were twofold: the liberation of the Palestinians, and the liberation of the homeland. At this point there were nearly two million Palestinian refugees, and only a small minority engaged in guerilla activity. For the most part, the *fida'i* efforts to recruit and rouse nationalist sentiments for the cause were seen as a nuisance and undermined traditional authority structures.[68]

In 1959 two young fighters, Yasser Arafat and Khalil al-Wazir (or Abu Jihad), formed *Fatah* (an Arabic acronym standing for "the Movement for the Liberation of Palestine"). They came from middle-class, educated backgrounds and were very influenced by leftist/Marxist ideologies. In the following years, Fatah was able to rally its forces and increase its influence. In 1964, the *Palestine Liberation Organization* (PLO) was established, its goal being liberation through armed struggle.[69]

Palestinians in Israel came under Israeli military rule in October 1948, and were to remain so until 1966. Although Ben Gurion was responsible for many of the strict policies against Israel's Palestinian citizens, they were given the right to vote and take part in elections. The Israeli government was divided as to whether or not to include its Arab

64. Ibid., 149. Regarding Israel's anti-infiltration policy, see Morris, *Righteous Victims*, 269–75.

65. Shemesh, "Palestinian Society," 89.

66. Ibid., 91–97.

67. Ibid., 91–93.

68. Pappé, *History of Modern Palestine*, 152. Also, see Shemesh, "Palestinian Society," 97.

69. Shemesh, "Palestinian Society," 86–89; Pappé, *History of Modern Palestine*, 149–50; and Morris, *Righteous Victims*, 303.

population (subsequently referred to as Israeli Palestinians) in its conscription policy. In 1954 an experiment was conducted to see if members
of the Israeli Palestinian community would report when conscripted. To
the government's surprise, every individual drafted responded. The government disregarded its attempts, and none of those called up for the
experiment were drafted. While this prevented the possibility of divided
loyalty or asking Israeli Palestinians to do something against their kins-
men that they would be disinclined to do, this negatively affected the
Israeli Palestinian community, as the government subsequently passed
laws to *exclusively* benefit individuals who had served in the IDF. This
policy continues today, as "only people who have served in the army are
eligible for state benefits such as loans, mortgages, and reduced university fees. There is a close link between industry and security in [Israel],
which means that significant sections (almost 70 percent) of industry are
closed to Palestinian citizens because they have not served in the army."[70]

The discriminatory measures against Palestinian citizens came to a
head with the Suez Crisis on October 29, 1956. Prior to engaging Egypt
on Israel's southwestern front, Israel deployed additional forces in Israeli
Palestinian villages along the Green Line as Israel wanted to be prepared
for possible Jordanian aggression in the eventuality that Jordan came
to Egypt's aid in the war.[71] Additionally, Israeli Palestinians were long
considered a hostile presence in Israel.

One of the villages in which Israeli Border Police were deployed
was Kafr Qassem. The Israeli military imposed a curfew on all Arab
villages in Israel the afternoon of October 29, stating that anyone who
was outside, starting that evening, would be punished. Israeli Border
Police were commanded to shoot violators. The workers in most of the
villages had not yet received the word when the curfew was imposed
and were returning home from work after the beginning of the curfew.
In what came to be known as the *Kafr Qassem Massacre*, Israeli forces
killed forty-seven Israeli Palestinians (among them women and young
children) returning home that evening.[72] This event led to a loud outcry,
and those involved were brought to trial. While convicted of murder,

---

70. Pappé, *History of Modern Palestine*, 160.

71. Morris, *Righteous Victims*, 289.

72. Further casualties were prevented in other villages due to local commanders
deliberately disobeying the order to kill anyone violating curfew. Israeli soldiers are
(to this day) told of Kafr Qassem and instructed that they must disobey illegal orders.

all involved were eventually pardoned. This episode evidenced the on-going discriminatory attitude of the establishment toward the Israeli Palestinians living under its rule.[73]

THE SIX DAY WAR

Egypt, Syria, Jordan, and Iraq maintained an interest in another confron-tation with Israel from the end of the First Arab–Israeli War. After 1956, Israel and its neighbors were engaged in an arms race. For Israel, this meant acquiring nuclear capabilities; for the neighboring Arab coun-tries, it meant modernizing their armies and acquiring new weapons.[74]

Egypt initiated the war by bringing troops into no-man's-land in the Sinai Peninsula, advancing toward the Israeli border. Egypt amassed its troops in the peninsula in mid-May, putting Israel on alert. However, when Egypt expelled its United Nations Emergency Force troops that had been present since 1957 and closed the Straits of Tiran, Israel saw this as provocation for war. Israel struck on June 5, 1967 beginning *The Six Day War* (or 1967 War).[75]

Israeli motivation in the war was high; public perception was that they were on the verge of a second Holocaust and fighting for their very survival. Both the Arab and Israeli armies had professional forces, but the Israeli forces, particularly their officers and commanders, were bet-ter trained. While the Arabs were expecting a war, Israel had the element of surprise as it struck first. At the onset of the war, Israel destroyed the Egyptian air force, all of Jordan's air force, half of the Syrian air force, and some of Iraq's as well. Since the Arab armies were unable to offer air support to their ground forces their military capabilities were severely limited. Within two days the IDF had reached the Suez Canal, beginning the Israeli occupation of the Sinai.

Between two hundred thousand and three hundred thousand Arabs escaped from Gaza and the West Bank into Egypt and Jordan, and between 80,000 to 90,000 additional Arabs were expelled from the Golan Heights. As a result of the Six Day War, Israel gained control of the West Bank (which it had debated conquering as Israel assumed it would

---

73. Pappé, *History of Modern Palestine*, 159. See Stern, "President Peres Apologizes," *Ha'aretz* Online, December 21, 2007; also Stern, "50 Years after Massacre."

74. Pappé, *Modern Palestine*, 168, 186–87.

75. Ibid., 302–6.

have to return it to Jordan), Jerusalem (including the Temple Mount and Western Wall), the Golan Heights (which the IDF conquered without orders from the prime minister and cabinet), the Gaza Strip, and the Sinai Peninsula, increasing its size three and a half times, and assuming control of one million new Palestinians.[76] The new territories acquired, specifically the West Bank, East Jerusalem, and the Gaza Strip, came to be known as the *Occupied Palestinian Territories.*

In the immediate aftermath of the war, the Israeli cabinet decided to withdraw to the 1949 borders and return the conquered lands to Egypt (with the exception of the Gaza Strip) and Syria in exchange for peace. Both Egypt and Syria declined the Israeli offer. Israeli defense minister Moshe Dayan stated that he was waiting for a phone call from Jordan to discuss what would happen with the West Bank and East Jerusalem. Due to the obstinacy and hostility Israel felt from these Arab countries, Israel changed its mind. By the end of June, Israel annexed both East Jerusalem and parts of the West Bank, and by October 1967 Israel decided that it would not return to its prewar borders, but would act in the interests of its security needs.[77]

Certain sectors of Israeli society saw the state's acquisition of the West Bank as a sign from God. The settlement movement began quickly. While the majority of people flocking into the newly conquered areas were religiously motivated, others moved there for economic reasons— the land was cheaper, and one could easily obtain grants for living and building. At first the government did not act on the issue, but eventually it sent troops to protect the new settlements and provided basic services such as water and electricity. Over half the land in the West Bank was state owned, and Israel seized it shortly after taking over.[78]

This war was devastating for the Palestinians and reawakened the nightmare of the refugees. Refugees who fled into Gaza and the West Bank during Israel's war for independence were uprooted yet again. UNRWA provided the most basic of services, which were insufficient. Eventually, the PLO began to compete with UNRWA camps outside of Palestine, offering welfare, health, and education services.[79]

---

76. Ibid., 311–29.
77. Ibid., 330–31.
78. Ibid., 331–35.
79. Pappé, *History of Modern Palestine*, 190–92.

There were no civil rights in the Occupied Palestinian Territories, and Israel's occupation was and is the same as all other occupations. Curfews, beatings, humiliations, house arrests, imprisonment without trial, closure of schools and shops, censorship of the press, collective punishment for civil or armed resistance, limitation of movement—these are all characteristics of the Israeli occupation. These oppressive actions prompted a revival of Palestinian nationalism and opened the door for the viability of eventual armed struggle.[80]

On November 22, 1967, the United Nations Security Council passed *UN Resolution 242*, condemning Israel's acquisition of new territory and calling for a "just and lasting peace" based on the principle of land for peace. The Arab countries were called on to recognize Israel's right to exist within "secure and recognized" boundaries, and the resolution also called for a solution to the refugee problem.[81] After this resolution, the UN and United States desisted from pressuring Israel to reabsorb the refugees. While there might have been a chance for Palestinian refugee assimilation into host countries, there was no long-term plan for the refugees. Additionally, even had there been such a plan and attempt, Palestinian refugees dearly hoped for a resolution along the lines of UN Resolution 194, and their sense of nationalism may not have permitted any other offer.[82]

1967–1973, THE RISE OF PALESTINIAN RESISTANCE AND THE CHALLENGE TO ISRAELI INVINCIBILITY

Israel and Egypt engaged in a *War of Attrition* that lasted from 1968 to 1970. It was a rather inconclusive war fought between the two countries, ending with a US-brokered ceasefire. Although Egypt's goal of regaining lost land went unaccomplished, both Israelis and Egyptians viewed the war as a success. Egypt felt it had held its own in the war, and had not suffered defeat. Israelis were satisfied that the status quo was maintained.[83]

By the end of 1967, Fatah networks in the West Bank had been destroyed by Israel. Fatah then moved the bulk of its networks to Jordan, albeit to the chagrin of King Hussein, who tried to prevent such an

---

80. Ibid., 336–43.
81. Laqueur, *Israel-Arab Reader*, 116.
82. Pappé, *History of Modern Palestine*, 189.
83. Morris, *Righteous Victims*, 347–63.

action. Eventually Palestinian resistance developed a "state within a state" in part of Jordan, undermining the state's authority.

Provoked by increasingly inflammatory Palestinian resistance within the state, on September 17, 1970, King Hussein reacted in what is remembered as *Black September*. The Jordanian army ruthlessly attacked the resistance, and hundreds of civilians were killed and wounded. In July 1971 Yasser Arafat, the head of the PLO, declared war on Jordan. Jordan responded by capturing as many guerillas as possible; many of them fled to Lebanon.[84]

The PLO continued its attacks against Israel from southern Lebanon. Many times attacks were carried out against civilians. In 1972 Israel responded to the attacks. The PLO knew that Israel would not relinquish the Occupied Territories without force. The PLO persisted in its activities, desiring to bring media attention to the Palestinian problem. However, Palestinian resistance gained little world sympathy at this time.[85] During the first two decades of occupation, Palestinians were excluded from talks regarding their future as Israel, Jordan, Egypt, and the United States were the main players negotiating what would happen to the Occupied Palestinian Territories.[86] Nevertheless, not all of the PLO's activities were futile. "Given all its difficulties, the PLO, under the control of Fatah, had managed to establish itself as the recognized leadership of the Palestinians. It had nurtured a national mythology of heroism and sacrifice, the portrait of the downtrodden refugee giving way to that of the fed[aʾi]—which in turn became the catalyst for the reconstruction of the national movement. In time, armed struggle would give way to more nonviolent activity, both for the sake of international legitimacy and because of the Israeli abilities to deal with armed threats."[87]

In 1971 Egypt communicated with Israel regarding its desire to regain the Sinai, even going so far as to offer peace in exchange for land. Israel was interested in the offer of peace but would not accept it so long as Egypt stipulated Israeli withdrawal from the Occupied Palestinian Territories. Syria still wanted to repossess the Golan Heights, and when

---

84. Ibid., 365–75.

85. Kimmerling and Migdal, *Palestinian People*, 273. See also Morris, *Righteous Victims*, 386.

86. Pappé, *History of Modern Palestine*, 207.

87. Kimmerling and Migdal, *Palestinian People*, 272.

Egypt's attempts at communicating with Israel failed, Syria and Egypt determined to go to war.

They decided to attack on October 6, 1973—the Jewish holiday of Yom Kippur, a holy day of fasting and prayer. All Israelis would be at home or in synagogue, and all media would be shut down, thus slowing Israeli reaction time. The Arab forces were well prepared for the war. They had the element of surprise on their side, and they engaged in massive media propaganda to lead Israelis to believe they had no interest in war. The Israelis, on the other hand, were overconfident, dismissive of the Arab armies' abilities and competence.[88]

As Israelis were in a lull of overconfidence and concentrated on their holiday, the Egyptians and Syrians attacked, starting the *October War* (or the Yom Kippur War). The Egyptians' war aims were lofty, but brief—"ending the present military inertia, inflicting high casualties and heavy damage on Israel, and liberating the occupied territory in progressive stages."[89] As expected, the Israelis were caught off guard. After difficult and costly battles, Israel was able to push back both Egypt and Syria, even encroaching on Syrian territory. A number of UN calls for ceasefires ended the war, and UN observers were on the borders by the end of the month. The war ended without a clear outcome, but Egypt was satisfied with its achievements. The Egyptians forced Israel to move towards negotiations, and removed their humiliation from previous defeats by successfully catching Israel by surprise and inflicting great damage.[90]

This war was significant for Israel and its Arab neighbors. Israel realized that it would have to make territorial concessions in the future, and that it could not and would not win "stunning victories" in every engagement with its enemies. In the coming years, Israel and Egypt would begin to discuss new agreements, slowly moving toward peace. On the other hand, this war had little to do with the Palestinians and had little effect on what was happening in the West Bank, Gaza, or the refugee camps.[91]

In the following years, a number of important events occurred that would influence the course of an eventual peace process. On November 22, 1974, the United Nations General Assembly adopted *UN Resolution 3236* that recognized "that the Palestinian people is entitled to self-

---

88. Morris, *Righteous Victims*, 387–94.

89. Ibid., 398.

90. Ibid., 387–441.

91. Pappé, *History of Modern Palestine*, 209.

determination," and approved UN dealings with the PLO as the "representative of the Palestinian people."[92] (In 1981 the European Community followed suit; the United States and Israel recognized the PLO in 1988 and 1993, respectively.) In 1974 Fatah issued a "Programme of Stages," a policy document detailing that the primary focus of its activities would be the liberation of the West Bank and Gaza (as opposed to all of Mandatory Palestine). This document signaled a slow shift from violence to diplomacy.[93]

THE ESCALATION OF THE ISRAELI-PALESTINIAN CONFLICT

After 1967, Israel began a process attempting to Judaize the Galilee—a program that was undisclosed until 1976. This process entailed confiscating land in the Galilee for building new Jewish towns.[94] Anger at the policy led to protests, culminating in what is today remembered as *Land Day*. On March 30, 1976, the National Committee for the Defense of Arab Lands called for a strike. Many of Israel's Palestinian citizens joined the protest and were met by thousands of police. Due to clashes, six Israeli Palestinians were killed, and over a hundred more wounded and arrested.[95] Land Day is commemorated to this day. It was a defining moment in the history of Israel's Palestinian citizens. Certain benefits were only given to Jews for years, yet the Arab population had remained a relatively quiet and nonviolent sector of Israeli society. This event awakened their national sentiments, uniting them with the Palestinian Diaspora, as all Palestinians would come to commemorate this day.[96]

During the 1970s, Egypt and Israel continued their discussions regarding Egypt's desire to recover the Sinai Peninsula. The monumental and historic visit of President Anwar Sadat to Israel in November 1977 led to the 1978 Camp David Accords, which resulted in the 1979 *Israel–Egypt Peace Treaty*. The Sinai Peninsula was returned to Egypt, Israel was allowed free passage of its ships in the Suez Canal, and the Straits of Tiran and the Gulf of Aqaba were recognized as international waters,

92. See United Nations, General Assembly Resolution 3236.

93. Pappé, *History of Modern Palestine*, 218–19.

94. Pappé notes that there has never been government-sponsored building of new Arab towns for its Arab citizens. See Pappé, *History of Modern Palestine*, 227.

95. Kimmerling and Migdal, *Palestinian People*, 195–96; Pappé, *History of Modern Palestine*, 228; and BBC News, "Remembering Land Day."

96. Kimmerling and Migdal, *Palestinian People*, 196.

thus fulfilling Israel's desires. Gaza was to remain under Israeli control for a future Palestinian state.[97]

Meanwhile, the PLO still had its base in Lebanon. While there was a ceasefire in effect at the time, Israel was waiting for an excuse to destroy the PLO. On June 3, 1982, there was an assassination attempt against Israel's ambassador to Britain. While it was carried out by an offshoot of the PLO, and not the PLO itself (which certain members of the Israeli government knew), it was used as a justification for war. Israel invaded Lebanon on June 6, 1982, beginning the *1982 Lebanon War* (or First Lebanon War). While the war began under the guise of protecting the Galilee from attacks, defense minister Ariel Sharon wanted to "occupy Beirut, chase out the Syrians, install a Maronite pro-Israeli government in Lebanon, and destroy the PLO."[98] He even deceived prime minister Menachem Begin by allowing him to believe that military operations would not extend beyond southern Lebanon.[99]

Due to US pressure, the IDF withdrew from Beirut in September 1982; however, Israel maintained control of southern Lebanon. For the next few years, Israel tried to counter insurgents in the country, including a Syrian and Palestinian presence, as well as *Hizbullah*, a Shi'ite Lebanese militia that emerged in response to Israel's invasion of Lebanon. There were significant civilian casualties as a result of the war, most of them Palestinian refugees and Lebanese civilians. Although Hizbullah and Syria wanted Israel to leave the country entirely and emphasized this with subsequent violence, Israel withdrew to a Security Zone (a buffer area where Israel left only a few forces) in June 1985. While Israel had achieved its objective of evicting much of the PLO from Lebanon (its headquarters relocated to Tunisia), Syria's influence in Lebanon strengthened, and Hizbullah came onto the scene, later proving to be a thorn in Israel's side.[100]

A solution to the Palestinian problem was consistently sidelined and ignored. The angst and frustration of Palestinians could not be overlooked forever. There was great economic disparity between Israelis and

97. Morris, *Righteous Victims*, 448–55. See also Kimmerling and Migdal, *Palestinian People*, 320. Note that the terms discussed for the Palestinians become significant in 1993 as part of the legal basis for the DOP under the Oslo Accords.

98. Pappé, *History of Modern Palestine*, 222.

99. Ibid., 222.

100. Morris, *Righteous Victims*, 549–60.

Palestinians. Life under occupation was difficult. Increasing settlement incursions into the Occupied Territories infuriated the population, whose national aspirations were constantly thwarted.[101] Many in the Israeli government voiced increasingly hostile opinions toward Israeli Palestinians in the 1980s. There were suggestions to pay them to leave the country, or to forcibly transfer them from their homes. Humiliation was a daily part of Palestinian life in the Occupied Territories. A number of successful guerilla attacks against Israelis boosted Palestinian morale, leading to minor acts of resistance and skirmishes between some Jewish and Muslim worshippers. Islamic resistance groups were rising up alongside secular resistance groups. While they had different goals, they both shared a desire to end the occupation.[102] The young generation felt that "there was little to lose if they broke the rules of the game."[103]

On December 9, 1987, a car accident between Israeli soldiers and some Arab workers resulted in the death of a number of Arabs, leading to rumors that the IDF intentionally hit the car. Palestinians were infuriated, and this was the spark that set off the *First Intifada*.[104] Hundreds of thousands of people began to pour into Gaza's streets, calling for jihad. At that time 35 percent of the Gazan population was unemployed (a third of the population were children).[105] Rioting broke out. People began throwing stones, burning tires, and creating roadblocks. The Arab workers who had been killed were hailed as martyrs, further motivating the population. The rioters boldly faced the IDF with nothing but stones.[106] Very quickly this mass uprising spread from Gaza to the West Bank and East Jerusalem. Women, youth, and children participated alongside the men. The protest against the Israeli occupation was characterized by unarmed protests, strikes, demonstrations, boycotts, and withholding taxes.[107] Palestinians engaged in the intifada at much personal cost, both physical and economic.

---

101. Ibid., 561. See also Pappé, *History of Modern Palestine*, 234; and Lustick, "Writing the Intifada," 567.

102. Morris, *Righteous Victims*, 567–72.

103. Kimmerling and Migdal, *Palestinian People*, 296.

104. Morris, *Righteous Victims*, 573.

105. Pappé, *History of Modern Palestine*, 234–35.

106. Morris, *Righteous Victims*, 574.

107. Ibid., 561–610; see also Lustick, "Writing the Intifada"; and Pappé, *History of Modern Palestine*, 237–39.

On November 15, 1988, the PLO declared the establishment of a Palestinian state. It implicitly recognized Israel and its right to exist as it defined the Palestinian state according to the Green Line. The newly declared state went largely unrecognized by the international community.

In the West Bank, the United National Leadership of the Uprising (UNLU) or Unified National Command rose up, with representatives from the major national groups. It began to take a lead in the intifada (and was supported by the PLO), organizing the days when workers should strike, riot, withhold taxes, and engage in other acts of resistance. Muslim Brotherhood activities in the Occupied Palestinian Territories gave way to the rise of *Hamas*. In 1987 Ahmad Yassin and Abdel Aziz al-Rantissi founded Hamas, an organization whose goals competed with the PLO's secular nationalist goals. One of Hamas's goals was the establishment of a Palestinian Islamic state in Israel and the Occupied Palestinian Territories. Many people were disillusioned with the failure of the more secular PLO to help them during the uprising, and they turned to this distinctly Islamic political movement, which was both nationalistic and religious. Mosques quickly became centers of incitement, and local religious leaders became part of the leadership of the uprising. Since Hamas was a counter-movement to the Palestine Liberation Organization, it initially received Israeli support in an attempt to undermine the PLO, but was quickly abandoned as Hamas took up radical actions and ideology. From the beginning Hamas founder Ahmad Yassin authorized the use of weapons against the IDF and also encouraged terrorism. Hamas's center of control was Gaza, while the UNLU's was the West Bank. The PLO explicitly forbade the use of firearms; it did not want to give Israel an excuse to massacre Palestinians (although it did permit the use of Molotov cocktails).[108] The image the PLO wanted to get across, with the help of the media, was of David versus Goliath, of unarmed Palestinians against the might of the IDF.

As the intifada continued, violence from Palestinians escalated, and Israel was largely unsuccessful in quieting the situation. The IDF was unprepared for riot control. On a number of occasions the IDF's response got out of hand, and some of these incidents were caught in the media—events such as beating blindfolded and handcuffed Palestinians. This caused a huge public relations backlash against Israel.[109]

108. Morris, *Righteous Victims*, 574–80.
109. Ibid., 584.

By October 1991, the Israelis and Palestinians had come to a stalemate. The Palestinians realized they would not be able to eliminate Israel, and Israel realized that it would not be able to get rid of violence, and that a political settlement would be necessary. In September 1993, the intifada officially ended when the PLO and Israel signed their first peace deal in Oslo.

The cost had been high. Tens of thousands of Palestinians were wounded, and some estimates exceed one hundred thousand serious injuries in the first three years of the intifada. Hundreds of homes were demolished, and "one Israeli lawyer estimated that about 25 percent of the Palestinian population passed through the military court system in the first years of the uprising."[110]

THE YEARS OF THE PEACE PROCESS

Secret negotiations between Israel and the PLO began in Oslo in January 1993. In September 1993 Arafat sent a letter to Israeli prime minister Yitzhak Rabin renouncing terrorism, recognizing Israel's right to exist, and accepting UN Resolutions 242 and 338. Subsequently, the Israeli government recognized the PLO. On September 13, Shimon Peres and Yasser Arafat signed the *Declaration of Principles* (DOP)—otherwise known as the Oslo Accords—on the White House lawn. The majority of both populations supported the agreement.[111] The DOP provided the framework for future negotiations between the two peoples. For the first time a Palestinian government (albeit limited), known as the Palestinian Authority, was allowed to govern its own people.[112] It was decided that a peace process would be implemented in stages over the course of five years, and slowly the two sides would build trust and partnership. Palestinians would gain control of territories Israel would relinquish to them, starting with Jericho, Gaza, and in stages, the West Bank. Afterwards, the more controversial core issues such as settlements, refugees, and borders were to be dealt with.

In October 1994, following the signing of the DOP, Israel and Jordan signed the *Israel–Jordan Treaty of Peace*. Jordan and Israel had a

---

110. Lustick, "Writing the Intifada," 566–67.

111. Morris, *Righteous Victims*, 621–22.

112. Kimmerling and Migdal, *Palestinian People*, 316.

special relationship, dating from before the formation of the Israeli state, and for many years the leaders of both countries had desired peace.[113]

While the majority of both Israeli and Palestinian populations initially supported the peace process, terrorist acts from groups such as Hamas attempted to derail the progress. Slowly, right-wing factions on both sides began to radicalize, and rhetoric became particularly vitriolic. Hamas became the primary opposition in both the West Bank and the Gaza Strip, leading to clashes with the PLO and the Palestinian Authority. Hamas's increased violence, which included suicide bombing in the heart of Israel, led to what Israelis termed a policy of "separation" that "involved an intentional reduction in the minimum of contact between the Israeli and Palestinian population, without giving up Israeli military control over the Palestinians."[114] This policy led to further difficulties in the peace process. The peace process slowed toward the end of 1995 when Israeli prime minister Rabin was assassinated by a right-wing religious Jewish student.[115] Shimon Peres, Israel's then foreign minister, succeeded the premiership but lost to Benjamin Netanyahu in subsequent elections. While Netanyahu made further concessions, he succeeded in slowing the peace process considerably.[116]

Ehud Barak became prime minister in May 1999. He was elected due to his promise to completely retreat from Lebanon (which he did in May 2000) and to come to final peace agreements with the Palestinians and the Syrians. In June 2000 Ehud Barak and Yasser Arafat participated in the *Camp David Summit* in which they attempted to reach a final settlement. For the first time, they discussed the core issues that were to be left until the end of the five-year interim period of the Oslo Accords. Ultimately, the summit failed. The Palestinians felt that they were offered a state without a viable West Bank; the Israelis felt that they had made an overwhelming gesture, and the Palestinians made no counteroffer.[117]

---

113. Morris, *Righteous Victims*, 629–32.

114. Kimmerling and Migdal, *Palestinian People*, 372.

115. Morris, *Righteous Victims*, 634–35.

116. Kimmerling and Migdal, *Palestinian People*, 330–34.

117. Cf. Segal, "Palestinian Peace Offer"; and Shyovitz, "Camp David 2000."

COMING TO THE PRESENT

The public was disappointed and disillusioned, feeling that the peace process had been a pipe dream. The opportunity for peace was drawing to a close. The PLO failed to prevent increasing violence against Israelis, leading Israelis to doubt Palestinian sincerity for a peaceful settlement. The years of the peace process led to massive Israeli settlement expansion, proving to the Palestinians that Israel was not serious about peace. Additionally, many Palestinians were angry at the corruption in the Palestinian Authority.

On September 28, 2000, Israeli parliament opposition leader Ariel Sharon visited the Temple Mount with 1,500 Israeli police accompanying him. For Palestinians, Sharon was the symbol par excellence of Israeli domination and oppression.[118] During the Camp David negotiations, the issue of who would control which areas on and around the Temple Mount was a sensitive and controversial matter. Sharon's visit to the Temple Mount capitalized on this controversy by flaunting a sort of Israeli sovereignty over the Temple Mount. This was the provocation needed to set off a disappointed and enraged public. The result was stone throwing and rioting, and the beginning the *Second Intifada* (or Al-Aqsa Intifada).[119]

In the following few days rioting broke out in Jerusalem, leading to clashes between Palestinians and Israeli police, resulting in the death and injury of hundreds of people. The unrest quickly spread to the West Bank and the Gaza Strip. In solidarity, Israel's Palestinian citizens began to protest and strike, leading to the *October 2000 Riots* that included violent clashes with Israeli police. Thirteen Israeli Palestinians were killed by Israeli police. This event stands out, along with the Kafr

118. See "What Started the al-Aqsa Intifada in September 2000?" Palestine Facts reports the number of police with Sharon. Aside from his pro-settlement policy, one particular event earned Sharon the collective contempt of the Palestinian people so that he became a symbol for vilification. During the 1982 Lebanon War, Sharon allowed an anti-Palestinian Lebanese Christian militia to carry out a brutal massacre in Sabra and Shatila, two Lebanese Palestinian refugee camps under his control. Israeli intelligence estimated that between 700 and 800 people were killed—entire families were slaughtered, babies trampled, and women raped. This earned Sharon the contempt and hatred of the Palestinian people. For more on Sabra and Shatila, see Morris, *Righteous Victims*, 543–47.

119. Kimmerling and Migdal, *Palestinian People*, 392.

Qassem Massacre, as a continuation of the discriminatory attitude of Israel towards its Arab citizens.[120]

In a last-minute attempt to salvage the dying peace process, Ehud Barak and Yasser Arafat met at the *Taba Summit* of January 2001 in the Sinai Peninsula. Upcoming Israeli elections projected that Ariel Sharon would succeed Ehud Barak as prime minister, and a right-wing government would take over. While progress was made at the talks, Israelis and Palestinians were not able to come to a conclusion. Government changes in America and Israel did not leave enough time for the Israelis and Palestinians to work out their differences.[121]

Meanwhile, the intifada continued. Although Palestinians engaged in activities similar to those of the First Intifada, such as striking, protesting, and other forms of civil disobedience, this time mass violence broke out. Suicide bombing targeting civilian areas within Israel was a widely used tactic. The PLO, Hamas, and other Palestinian resistance groups engaged in violence against the IDF, settlers, and Israeli civilians. By March 2002 suicide bombings were nearly daily occurrences, targeting Israeli civilians in busy, crowded areas.[122] Palestinians succeeded in wreaking havoc and terror on the Israeli population, and Israel suffered many casualties.

Israel was better prepared to handle riots than it had been in the First Intifada, and it reacted very harshly within days of the intifada's outbreak. Additionally, Israel erected many more checkpoints, and imposed curfews and other restrictions on Palestinians. During the first two years of the Second Intifada, fighting continually escalated. From October 2000 to October 2002, more than 625 Israelis were killed in 14,280 attacks, and 4,500 Israelis were injured. Military forces and settlers killed 1,380 Palestinians, and 19,684 Palestinians were wounded.[123]

In March 2002 the Arab League presented Israel with the *Arab Peace Initiative* in which it offered an end to the Arab–Israeli conflict, the signing of peace agreements with Israel, and normalization of relations between Israel and the Arab world. In exchange, it would require Israeli withdrawal from all occupied Arab territories, including the Golan Heights, and a "just solution" to the issue of Palestinian refugees.

---

120. See Roffe-Ofir, "Families of October 2000 Victims Reject Compensation." See also Ettinger, "Extremism Isn't Growing, but Fear Is."

121. See Matz, "Trying to Understand the Taba Talks."

122. Kimmerling and Migdal, *Palestinian People*, 393.

123. Ibid., 391.

The Palestinian Authority expressed its support of the initiative, while Israeli leaders expressed guarded enthusiasm, apprehension, skepticism, or outright refusal to engage the proposal. The Arab Peace Initiative is still being offered, although threats of withdrawing it have been made.[124]

June 2002 brought a number of significant events. During this month, Israel responded to the intifada with Operation Defensive Shield, in which Israel sent a great number of forces into the West Bank, trying to capture militants and confiscate weapons. The operation succeeded in destroying institutions and infrastructure established by the Palestinian Authority over the past several years, and within several weeks, Israel had destroyed the Palestinian public sector in the West Bank.[125]

The same month, the Israeli government decided to act on the policy of separation it had begun in the 1990s by building a *Separation Barrier* (or the Wall) between the West Bank and Israel. While the barrier is 90 percent fence and 10 percent wall, it is an imposing structure. It is controversial for many reasons—the two main reasons are (1) that it does not follow the Green Line; and (2) that it is built in such a way as to consolidate areas of land recognized by the international community as earmarked for a Palestinian state—the Wall annexes 9 percent of the West Bank to Israel. The Separation Barrier greatly affects the economic livelihood of many Palestinians who are separated from their agricultural land and their work; and at times the barrier cuts through their neighborhoods. The Israeli government argues that the barrier is essential for security. The international community has ruled that the barrier is in violation of international law.[126]

In June 2002, US president George W. Bush outlined his interest in pursuing a plan for peace in Israel and Palestine, a plan that subsequently became the *Road Map for Peace*: a plan supported by the United States, the European Union, Russia, and the United Nations. The plan was to be implemented in phases, and completed by 2005.[127]

---

124. See BBC News, "Text: Beirut Declaration." See also Associated Press and Stern, "Abbas Calls on Obama."

125. Kimmerling and Migdal, *Palestinian People*, 396–97.

126. See B'Tselem, "Separation Barrier." See also "International Court of Justice Ruling on the Israeli Security Barrier," and "Legal Consequences of the Construction of a Wall in the Occupied Palestinian Territory."

127. See Israel Ministry of Foreign Affairs, "A Performance-Based Roadmap." For a transcript of Bush's speech, see MidEast Web, "President Bush Calls for New Palestinian Leadership."

The fighting began to die out in 2004 and 2005. In June 2004, the Israeli government agreed to withdraw from Gaza, which would happen the following year. Yasser Arafat passed away in November 2004. These are two events that marked the end of the Second Intifada.[128] The Road Map was never completed.

The Israelis believed they had no partner for peace; the Palestinians believed that Israel was intent on undermining and destroying any hopes it had for a future. However, reality slowly set in. Israel could not defeat Palestinian violence. Israel could not afford to stay in the settlements. To the shock of Israeli citizens, in August 2005, Ariel Sharon's government unilaterally evacuated all of its citizens from Gaza in what would come to be known as the *Disengagement from Gaza*. While media reports were abuzz with rumors that such an action would lead to a civil war between Israel's Jewish citizens, the disengagement was completed rather quietly. The Palestinians hailed this as a success of their violent struggle. The Israelis claimed it proved they were willing to make sacrifices for peace.

In January 2006, Hamas won the majority of seats in democratic Palestinian elections. The Palestinian population, tired of the games and corruption in Fatah, wanted a change. Becoming part of government forces organizations to tame their rhetoric, and engenders more pragmatism. Upon entering the political arena, Hamas has shown flexibility and willingness to adapt. A number of Hamas documents show that the religious aspect of the organization is gradually being deemphasized, and as it moves toward state building, Hamas has slowly come to terms with the two-state solution.[129]

Following Hamas's victory in the elections, Israel, the United States, and a number of other Western and Western-aligned countries imposed sanctions on Hamas. They refused to release funds to the Palestinian Authority until Hamas recognized Israel's right to exist, renounced violence, agreed to uphold previous agreements made by the Palestinian Authority, and finally, agreed to a two-state solution.[130] The imposition of sanctions was followed by the blockading of the Gaza Strip in June 2007 by both Israel and Egypt. As of this writing, the blockade is still in place. Limited humanitarian aid is allowed into Gaza; the amount of

---

128. See Tenne, "Rising of the Oppressed."
129. See Hroub, "A 'New Hamas.'"
130. See Erlanger, "Hamas Leader Faults Israeli Sanction Plan."

allowable aid is overwhelmingly insufficient considering the needs of the population.[131]

Problems persisted for the new Hamas government as tensions broke out between Fatah and Hamas. By mid-December 2006, Palestinian president Mahmoud Abbas called for new elections, prompting Hamas to decry this call for a coup.[132] Infighting between Fatah and Hamas resulted in over six hundred Palestinian deaths between January 2006 and June 2007. Further infighting still continues, although in a less violent manner at the present.[133] In June 2007, president Mahmoud Abbas dissolved the Hamas-led Palestinian Authority government, leading to a Fatah-controlled West Bank, and Hamas-controlled Gaza Strip.[134]

In July 2006, Hizbullah militants from Lebanon crossed the border into Israel, killing several Israeli soldiers and capturing two, resulting in the *2006 Lebanon War* (or Second Lebanon War). Israel responded with air strikes and a massive ground invasion. Civilian facilities and infrastructure were terribly damaged. The war ended in August with UN Resolution 1701. Israel withdrew. The United Nations Interim Force in Lebanon (UNIFIL) deployed its forces along with the Lebanese, and Lebanon was instructed to disarm Hizbullah. Subsequently there were prisoner exchanges so that Israel could recover the bodies of the two kidnapped soldiers.

The most recent significant event in the Israeli–Palestinian conflict was *Operation Cast Lead* (or the Gaza War) from December 27, 2008 to January 18, 2009. Israel invaded Gaza, stating it wished to stop Hamas rockets from coming into Israel. The short war resulted in significant civilian casualties and destruction of thousands of homes and institutions. As a result of Hamas's kidnapping of Israeli soldier Gilad Shalit in June 2006, Israel wished to prevent the capture of its soldiers during the operation. A tactical decision was made that Israel would minimize the casualties to itself at all costs. Nearly 1,400 Palestinians were killed. Over half of those killed were noncombatants, nearly four hundred of

---

131. See Knickmeyer, "Gaza Straining at Egypt's Door."

132. See Hardaker, "Hamas Accuses Abbas," See also Reuters, "Abbas Calls for Early Elections."

133. See Reuters, "Over 600 Palestinians Killed in Internal Clashes Since 2006."

134. See Fox News and the Associated Press, "Abbas to Dissolve Palestinian Authority Government in Wake of Hamas–Fatah War." See also "Abbas Sacks Hamas-Led Government."

whom were women and children. Five thousand three hundred people were injured, over a third of whom were children. On the Israeli side, nine soldiers were killed and 336 wounded.[135] During the war, both sides committed war crimes and human rights violations.

In the coming years historians will be able to provide analysis and contextualize the more recent events presented here.

We are products of our times, formed by our historical narratives and the stories told to us by our religion and our people. In our specific case, many of our stories focus on the land, conjuring memories of our past, our roots, and our belonging. But our narratives have long been exclusive. We have used our theology and political ideology to marginalize, oppress, and subjugate the very ones we are called to love and live alongside. To go forward, we must look beyond our own community's narrative and see our communities' narrative, the narrative we share together. We must put aside the obstacles of ritual, material, and memory and see the humanity of "the Other" who resides alongside us—who has a narrative, a story, a religion; who are a people just as fiercely bound to this land as we are. Many of our successes and failures have been at the others' expense. Many of the steps taken toward peace have been insincere and insufficient. Our future is dependent on one another, as our humanity, our identity, and our hopes are reflected in each other. In the words of Martin Buber, we need "the ability to put ourselves in the place of the other individual, the stranger, and to make his soul ours."[136] The land is important. The history is important. But it is in the face of the other that we find the image of God.

BIBLIOGRAPHY

Associated Press and Yoav Stern. "Abbas Calls on Obama to Enact Arab Peace Plan as Soon as He Takes Office." *Ha'aretz*. November 22, 2008. Online: http://www .haaretz.com/hasen/spages/1039866.html.

Abboushi, W. F. "The Road to Rebellion: Arab Palestine in the 1930's." *Journal of Palestine Studies* 6:3 (1977) 23–46.

BBC News. "Remembering Land Day." BBC News. March 30, 2001. Online: http://news .bbc.co.uk/2/hi/middle_east/1250290.stm.

135. See Izenberg, "Civilian Deaths." See also United Nations, Office for the Coordination of Humanitarian Affairs, "Field Update on Gaza from the Humanitarian Coordinator."

136. Buber, *A Land of Two Peoples*, 79.

————. "Text: Beirut Declaration." March 28, 2002. Online: http://news.bbc.co.uk/2/hi/world/monitoring/media_reports/1899395.stm.

B'Tselem "Separation Barrier." Online: http://www.btselem.org/english/separation%5Fbarrier/.

Buber, Martin. *A Land of Two Peoples: Martin Buber on Jews and Arabs*, edited by Paul R. Mendes-Flohr. Oxford: Oxford University Press, 1983.

Cleveland, William L. *A History of the Modern Middle East*. 2nd ed. Boulder, CO: Westview, 2000.

Erlanger, Steven. "Hamas Leader Faults Israeli Sanction Plan." *New York Times*. February 18, 2006. Online: http://www.nytimes.com/2006/02/18/international/middleeast/18mideast.html.

Ettinger, Yair. "Extremism Isn't Growing, but Fear Is." *Ha'aretz*. Online: http://www.haaretz.com/print-edition/business/extremism-isn-t-growing-but-fear-is-1.123450.

Fox News and the Associated Press. "Abbas to Dissolve Palestinian Authority Government in Wake of Hamas-Fatah War." Fox News. June 14, 2007. Online: http://www.foxnews.com/story/0,2933,282195,00.html.

Hardaker, David. "Hamas Accuses Abbas of Launching Coup." ABC News. December 17, 2006. Online: http://www.abc.net.au/news/newsitems/200612/s1813233.htm.

Hroub, Khaled. "A 'New Hamas' through Its New Documents." *Journal of Palestine Studies* 35:4 (2006) 6–27.

"International Court of Justice Ruling on the Israeli Security Barrier." Zionism and Israel Information Center. July 9, 2004. Online: http://www.zionism-israel.com/hdoc/ICJ_fence.htm.

Introduction to Plan Dalet: "Plan Dalet." Jewish Virtual Library. Online: http://www.jewishvirtuallibrary.org/jsource/History/Plan_Dalet.html/.

Israel Ministry of Foreign Affairs. "A Performance-Based Roadmap to a Permanent Two-State Solution to the Israeli-Palestinian Conflict." Israeli Ministry of Foreign Affairs. April 30, 2003. Online: http://www.mfa.gov.il/MFA/Peace+Process/Guide+to+the+Peace+Process/A+Performance-Based+Roadmap+to+a+Permanent+Two-Sta.htm.

Izenberg, Dan. "Civilian Deaths in Gaza Op Were Higher." *Jerusalem Post*. September 9, 2009. Online: http://www.jpost.com/Home/Article.aspx?id=154240.

Karsh, Efraim. *The Arab-Israeli Conflict: The Palestine War 1948*. Essential Histories 28. Oxford: Osprey, 2002.

Khalaf, Issa. "The Effect of Socioeconomic Change on Arab Societal Collapse in Mandate Palestine." *International Journal of Middle East Studies* 29 (1997) 93–112.

Khalidi, Rashid. "The Formation of Palestinian Identity, 1917–1923." In *Rethinking Nationalism in the Arab Middle East*, edited by James Jankowski and Israel Gershoni, 171–90. New York: Columbia University Press, 1997.

————. "The Palestinians and 1948: The Underlying Causes of Failure." In *The War for Palestine: Rewriting the History of 1948*, edited by Eugene L. Rogan and Avi Shlaim, 12–36. Cambridge Middle East Studies 15. Cambridge: Cambridge University Press, 2001.

Kimmerling, Baruch, and Joel S. Migdal. *The Palestinian People: A History*. Cambridge: Harvard University Press, 2003.

Knickmeyer, Ellen. "Gaza Straining at Egypt's Door." *Washington Post*. June 18, 2007. Online: http://www.washingtonpost.com/wp-dyn/content/article/2007/06/17/AR2007061701357.html.

Laqueur, Walter, and Barry Rubin, editors. *The Israel-Arab Reader: A Documentary History of the Middle East Conflict*, 6th rev. ed. New York: Penguin, 2001.

————. *A History of Zionism*. New York: Schocken, 1976.

Lustick, Ian S. "Writing the Intifada: Collective Action in the Occupied Territories." *World Politics* 45 (1993) 560–94.

Matz, David. "Trying to Understand the Taba Talks." *Palestine-Israel Journal of Politics, Economics, and Culture* 10:3 (2003). Online: http://www.pij.org/details.php?id=32.

MidEast Web. "President Bush Calls for New Palestinian Leadership." MidEast Web. June 24, 2002. Online: http://www.mideastweb.org/bushspeech1.htm/.

————. "Text of Plan Dalet (Plan D) 10 March 1948: General Section." MidEast Web. Online: http://www.mideastweb.org/pland.htm.

Morris, Benny. "Response to Finkelstein and Masalha," in "Debate on the 1948 Exodus." *Journal of Palestine Studies* 21:1 (1991) 98–114, by Norman Finkelstein, with Nur Masalha and Benny Morris..

————. "Revisiting the Palestinian Exodus of 1948." In *The War for Palestine*, edited by Eugene L. Rogan and Avi Shlaim, 37–59. 2nd ed. Cambridge Middle East Studies 15. Cambridge: Cambridge University Press, 2007.

————. *Righteous Victims: A History of the Zionist-Arab Conflict, 1881–1999*. London: Murray, 1999.

————. *The Birth of the Palestinian Refugee Problem Revisited*. 2nd ed. Cambridge Middle East Studies 18. Cambridge: Cambridge University Press, 2004.

————. *The Birth of the Palestinian Refugee Problem, 1947–1949*. Cambridge Middle East Library. Cambridge: Cambridge University Press, 1987.

Nasser, Gamal Abdul, and Walid Khalidi. "Nasser's Memoirs of the First Palestine War." *Journal of Palestine Studies* 2:2 (1973) 3–32.

Palestine Facts. "What started the al-Aqsa intifada in September 2000?" Online: http://www.palestinefacts.org/pf_1991to_now_alaqsa_start.php.

Pappé, Ilan. "The 1948 Ethnic Cleansing of Palestine." *Journal of Palestine Studies* 36:1 (2006) 6–20.

————. *A History of Modern Palestine: One Land, Two Peoples*. Cambridge: Cambridge University Press, 2004.

————. *The Ethnic Cleansing of Palestine*. England: Oneworld, 2006.

Reuters. "Abbas Calls for Early Elections." ABC News. December 16, 2006. Online: http://www.abc.net.au/news/newsitems/200612/s1813209.htm.

————. "Over 600 Palestinians Killed in Internal Clashes Since 2006." YNET News. June 6, 2007. Online: http://www.ynetnews.com/articles/0,7340,L-3409548,00.html.

Roffe-Ofir, Sharon. "Families of October 2000 Victims Reject Compensation." *Ynetnews .com*. November 20, 2006. Online: http://www.ynetnews.com/articles/0,7340, L-3330476,00.html.

Segal, Jerome M. "The Palestinian Peace Offer." *Ha'aretz*. October 1, 2001. Online: http://www.haaretz.com/print-edition/opinion/the-palestinian-peace-offer-1.70935.

Shemesh, Moshe. "The Palestinian Society in the Wake of the 1948 War: From Social Fragmentation to Consolidation." *Israel Studies* 9:1 (2004) 86–100.

Shlaim, Avi. "Israel and the Arab Coalition in 1948." In *The War for Palestine: Rewriting the History of 1948*, edited Eugene L. Rogan and Avi Shlaim, 79–103. Cambridge Middle East Studies 15. Cambridge: Cambridge University Press, 2001.

Shyovitz, David. "Camp David 2000." Jewish Virtual Library. Online: http://www.jewishvirtuallibrary.org/jsource/Peace/cd2000art.html.

Stern, Yoav. "50 Years after Massacre, Kafr Qasem Wants Answers." *Ha'aretz.* October 31, 2006. Online: http://www.haaretz.com/hasen/spages/780569.html.

———. "President Peres apologizes for Kafr Qasem massacre of 1956." *Ha'aretz.* December 21, 2007. Online: http://www.haaretz.com/hasen/spages/937116.html.

Tal, David. "Between Intuition and Professionalism: Israeli Military Leadership During the 1948 Palestine War." *Journal of Military History* 68 (2004) 885–909.

———. "The Forgotten War: Jewish-Palestinian Strife in Mandatory Palestine December 1947–May 1948." *Israel Affairs* 6:3/4 (2000) 3–22.

Tenne, Ruth. "Rising of the Oppressed: The Second Intifada." *International Socialism* 116 (October 1, 2007). Online: http://www.isj.org.uk/index.php4?id=384&issue=116.

United Nations General Assembly, Resolution 3236, "The Question of Palestine." November 22, 1974. United Nations, Information System on the Question of Palestine (UNISPAL). Online: http://unispal.un.org/UNISPAL.NSF/0/025974039 ACFB171852560DE00548BBE.

United Nations, Office for the Coordination of Humanitarian Affairs. "Field Update on Gaza from the Humanitarian Coordinator." January 20–21, 2009. Online: http://www.ochaopt.org/documents/ocha_opt_gaza_humanitarian_situation_ report_2009_01_21_english.pdf.

❖ 2 ❖

Where Do We Begin?

The Hermeneutical Questions and Their Effect on the Theology of the Land

Lisa Loden

THE LAND OF ISRAEL/PALESTINE is unique in that its ownership and occupancy are matters of theological concern and dispute. In discussions of the subject, neither the simple controversy between two peoples and their rights, matters of justice and morality, nor even the division of spoils of war and occupation, are the issues that determine. Ultimately, it is theology that makes the difference and the division.

The three monotheistic religions—Christianity, Judaism, and Islam —all maintain a strong attachment to the land of Israel/Palestine. It is well known that both the Jewish and the Palestinian peoples claim the right of ownership to the same territory. The Jewish people validate their claim to the land of Israel by appealing to divine promise while the Palestinians base their claim to the same land on the historical fact of their long residence in the land.

Because of the significance of Israel/Palestine as the locus of divine intervention in the affairs of humanity and on account of the events of salvation history that took place (and according to some are still taking place) in this land, both Christians and Jews are concerned with its disposition. Judaism and certain large sectors of Christianity see the land of Israel/Palestine as the land that was promised unconditionally and in perpetuity to the Jewish people (Gen 13:15).

Islam also lays claim to the land of Israel/Palestine, especially Jerusalem. Since the Islamic worldview is all-inclusive, Muslims also have their own "theology of the land." Their veneration of Jerusalem—for them, the third holiest city in the world—is as the site of an important historical event connected with their faith. They evidence passionate devotion to both the city and the "Holy Land." It would appear that on the stage of world affairs, as it touches the small nation of Israel/Palestine, there are few disinterested spectators.

How one views the meaning of the land or thinks about its ownership is conditioned by many factors. History, ancient or modern, and theology are two of the critical factors that affect all discussions of the subject. Since Christians hold to the fact that the God of the Bible is a God who acts in history and for whom history is important, any theology of the land must consider the historical dimension. The modern history of the land is vitally important to the current residents of the land be they Jewish, Christian, Muslim, Israeli or Palestinian.

ROLE OF HERMENEUTICS

In this chapter, we will investigate the role of hermeneutics in the determination of one's theology of the land. Hermeneutical issues will be seen as key factors in the choice of ones theological system and/or bias. The issues themselves are also frequently products of individual background, experience, and bias. No one hermeneutical system will be advocated as "the proper hermeneutic." What will be seen instead is that depending on your starting point, your conclusions follow naturally and will of necessity differ from the conclusions of another who begins at a different point. These things should be obvious. It is, however, an unfortunate fact that in matters where one is personally involved, either as an active participant or as an interested observer, objectivity easily departs or becomes obscured.

While total objectivity is unattainable in any sphere of endeavor, biblical scholars and students need to be as aware of their own prejudices and presuppositions as they are of those of others. Lack of understanding on this level is the source of much conflict and clash of opinion among those who maintain differing theologies of the land. Without an agreed hermeneutical base there is no possibility of ever coming to agreement on theological issues in general and in particular on issues of the theology of the land. If, however, we understand each other's presuppositions, then we can at least have a starting point from which to deal with some of the many conflictual issues that currently divide.

To remain in the realm of "pure theology" is a luxury that those of us who live in the Middle East cannot afford. Theology does not exist in a vacuum and is incomplete without application. It has been said, "The heart of the hermeneutical problem does not lie in the determining of the historical meaning of each passage . . . it lies, rather, in seeing how it applies to you, me, and us at the point in history and personal life where we are now."[1]

In the turbulent Middle East, issues of hermeneutics and theology are often matters of life and death. It is to our peril and at times to the disgrace of the gospel that we neglect a thorough investigation of our presuppositions.

HERMENEUTICAL VIEWPOINT

Hermeneutics, as the science of interpretive principles, should be unbiased. This, however, is not always the case. A cursory glance at theology and the development of doctrine should be enough to convince anyone that historical conditions are major factors affecting one's interpretive framework: "Very often, due to the exigencies of certain historical conditions, polemical or apologetical situations anticipate the truth or value to be discovered and thus dictate the type of exegesis or hermeneutic to be used. The primary goal, however, is to arrive at biblical truths and values by an unbiased use of exegesis and hermeneutics."[2]

Beginning with the text, the task of both the reader and the theologian is to elicit meaning. Biblical scholars work to ascertain "truth" from the texts of the Bible. This hermeneutical task has become critical in the postmodern twenty-first century, particularly with the rise of pragmatism and deconstructionism in hermeneutics.[3] Biblical backgrounds, linguistic analysis, historical context, and literary studies are some of

1. Packer, "Infallible Scripture," 346.

2. Bruce, "Exegesis and Hermeneutics, Biblical," in *Encyclopaedia Britannica* 7:63.

3. Jacques Derrida and Stanley Fish are two of the leading theorists of hermeneutical deconstructionism.

the relevant areas that need to be a part of the process of ascertaining the "truth" of the biblical text. This is the age of contextuality taking precedence over textuality. The context here is multiple, including context of both the human author and the interpreter. "Interpretation in our time is less a matter of what the text says than what the reader does with it, or rather, who the reader is. A person's identity affects and possibly determines the way that person reads. Tell me who you are and I'll tell you how you read. Meaning is neither located in authorial consciousness nor in the structure of the text, but is rather a function of the reader's location."[4]

The question of whether or not the text has meaning in and of itself, if meaning is derived from the interaction between the reader and the text, is a crucial question in contemporary hermeneutical studies. The primacy of the text has been the gold standard of biblical scholarship for decades but is currently under examination and attack.

> The reader, far from being a detached observer, occupies a standpoint that limits and conditions what can be known, not outside history, but within a history that is itself the result of previous interpretations. Gadamer calls such a cultural-historical standpoint a "horizon." One's horizon defines the limits beyond which one cannot see. One's horizon is linked to one's prejudices, to one's habits of looking at the world in particular ways. Readers, in other words, always come to texts with a certain "pre-understanding." At the same time the text also has a horizon, for it too reflects the prejudices of its historical situation. Interpretation, then, is like a dialogue in which the reader exposes himself or herself to the effects of the text, while the text is exposed to the reader's interests and prejudices. Understanding is a matter of fusing the horizons of the text and reader.[5]

A simple reading of the text is insufficient to ensure understanding. Deeper questions of personal and textual context as well as epistemological issues need to be investigated if agreed meaning is ever to emerge from the texts under consideration: "All attempts at a purely biblical perspective are destined to fail. One never reads the biblical text apart from preconceptions drawn from one's own particular historical setting and from some stream of interpretive tradition. That setting and tradition

---

4. Vanhoozer, *Is There a Meaning?*, 149.
5. Ibid., 106.

will shape the questions we address to the text, the concepts and terms we use to answer those questions, and our selection of the portions of the text that speak most directly to our questions and therefore seem to be of the greatest importance."[6]

The importance of one's hermeneutical viewpoint is not confined to matters of biblical interpretation. Hermeneutics are a part of everyone's life, whether or not people are aware of the fact. Actions and thought are in large part determined by the hermeneutical viewpoint one holds: "The question of hermeneutical viewpoint is thus the key issue in life and is not to be thought of solely as the science that informs the interpretation and application of Scripture, although that is one of its major functions for the biblical interpreter. The scope of hermeneutics is all-embracing and serves to disclose the inner patterns of meaning and intention that identify each human being and determine the presuppositions one brings to the interpretation of Scripture."[7]

A current example of the influence of hermeneutical viewpoint is the phenomenon of religious Zionism. Although early Zionism was for the most part secular, there was always a religious component. Religious Jewish Zionism, which interprets the promise of the land of Israel unconditionally and in perpetuity to the Jewish people, has led to a mass settlement of Jews in the land of Israel/Palestine in our day, especially after the events of 1967. It was then that Israel acquired the West Bank (biblical Judea and Samaria), and tens of thousands of religious Jews settled in the occupied/administered territories. These settlers drew inspiration for their settlement from the writings of, among others, Israel's first chief rabbi, Avraham Kook, and his son, rabbi Yehuda Kook.

This movement of immigration and settlement of Jews in the traditional biblical homeland is supported by many evangelical Christians who hold the same hermeneutical viewpoint as many religious Zionist Jews, and has occasioned much practical support for the Jews returning to the land of Israel. The hermeneutical viewpoint (in this case, a literal hermeneutic) has given meaning to the existence of the Jewish people as a whole and has provided direction for the individual who has chosen to act upon the convictions resultant from the application of his hermeneutic.

6. Kinzer, "Scripture and Tradition," 29.

7. Gruenler, *Meaning and Understanding*, xiv.

Another example of the importance of hermeneutical viewpoint is the so-called theology after Auschwitz[8] that developed in regard to Israel and the Jewish people in many Christian circles following the Holocaust. This theology is influenced by a humanistic hermeneutic that cannot come to terms with a God who allows national, ethnic suffering on the scale of the Holocaust. In our day the application of this hermeneutical viewpoint has caused large sectors of the Christian church to abandon mission to the Jews and has led to the development of a two-covenant theology in which there is an alternative way of salvation for the Jewish people that does not require acceptance of Jesus. If this view is embraced, Jewish evangelism then becomes unnecessary and even offensive. As a corollary, many Christians have unilaterally supported the presence and the territorial rights of the Jewish people in the land of Israel//Palestine. Palestinians are seen as having no rights to the land given by God to the Jewish people. In consequence, there is tremendous financial support from Western Christians for the Jewish people and the State of Israel and virtually no such support for Palestinians living in the "Holy Land" that belongs to the Jewish people. Again, history and current events have determined hermeneutical viewpoint and consequent action.

THE BIBLE AS THE SOURCE OF THEOLOGY

For both Christians and Jews the Bible is the source from which they determine theology. How one views the Scriptures, inerrancy, and inspiration (plenary or otherwise), structural analysis, literary genre, and questions of continuity and discontinuity between the two testaments are all factors that affect one's hermeneutic.

> Quite different hermeneutical principles, however, have been inferred from the axiom of biblical inspiration: whereas some have argued that the interpretation must always be literal, or as literal as possible (since God always means what he says), others have treated it as self evident that words of divine origin must always have some profounder "spiritual" meaning than that which lies on the surface, and this meaning will yield itself up only to those who apply the appropriate rules of figurative exegesis. Or again, it may be insisted that certain parts must be treated literally and

8. The term has been widely used since the Holocaust; see Brockway et al., *Theology of the Churches*, 170; Fasching, *Narrative Theology after Auschwitz*; and Mussner, "Theology after Auschwitz."

others figuratively; thus some expositors who regard the allegorical interpretation of the Old Testament histories as the only interpretation that has any religious value maintain that in the apocalyptic writings that interpretation which is most literal is most reliable.[9]

Although the study of the history of hermeneutics is not the subject of this chapter, it is fascinating to see the development of various hermeneutical systems and viewpoints over time. In Judaism, predating the early church, there are several major hermeneutical approaches.[10] These have already been alluded to under the categories of literal and spiritual: "it is well known that in the history of biblical exposition a fourfold scheme of interpretation (comprising the literal, allegorical, tropological and anagogical senses) was long prevalent in church circles. For all practical purposes, however, these four senses amounted basically to two main senses, namely the literal and the allegorical—the literal being the natural or surface sense; and the allegorical the 'spiritual' or deep sense."[11]

Biblical interpreters throughout history continue to struggle with ways of interpreting the sacred texts. At this point in history, interpretive pluralism has become the framework in the wider sphere of Christian hermeneutical typology. The problem with this is that "most interpretive interests are imperialistic—dismissive of other interests."[12]

PALESTINIAN VIEWS

While the question of the theology of the land is vital for those who live in Israel/Palestine, there is much more literature on the subject from within the Messianic Jewish community than from the Palestinian Christian community living in the area. Although the issues are often hotly discussed, there is little written that is reflective of the debates. However, this situation is changing, particularly through the writings of Yohanna Katanacho and the efforts of Naim Ateek and the Sabeel Ecumenical Liberation Theology Center.[13]

9. Bruce, F. F. "Exegesis and Hermeneutics, Biblical," in *Encyclopaedia Britannica*, 7:62.

10. In Judaism there are four traditional methods of interpretation. An acronym for this is "Pardes" or literal, allegorical, homiletical, and mystical.

11. Hughes, "Truth of Scripture," 187.

12. Vanhoozer, *Is There a Meaning?*, 159.

13. See Ateek et al., *Challenging Christian Zionism*.

Within the larger Arab Christian community, the related question of the place of the Old Testament has received some attention. In her unpublished master's thesis, Rana Elfar of Jordan analyzes the Arab Christian writer's use of the Old Testament.[14] She points out that due to cultural, historic, and political factors Arab Christians have numerous difficulties with the Old Testament.

On a cultural level the Old Testament is often viewed as a Jewish book replete with stories of sexual immorality and violence that are abhorrent to the Arab mentality and not in keeping with its conception of a "holy" God. Others view the Old Testament as being on the same level as the mythologies of other ancient Semitic peoples.

Historical and political factors also strongly influence the Arab Christian's view of the Old Testament. The political reality of the modern State of Israel makes it difficult for many Arab Christians, particularly the Palestinians, to even read the Old Testament, much less use it as a source of theology. The Palestinians' current land and rights struggle in a situation of occupation by an Israel who at times uses the Old Testament as justification for occupation renders the use of the Old Testament for the Palestinian and Arab Christian almost impossible.

The results of these factors are seen in the various approaches to the use of the Old Testament by the Arab Christian community. There are those who have stopped using the Old Testament completely and others who use it only selectively. A very few have accepted a literal fundamentalist interpretation of Old Testament prophecy. In some of the liturgies of the historic churches in the Middle East, the biblical texts used have been "de-Zionized" with deletion of references to Israel and Zion. The overwhelming majority of Arab Christians hold to a strongly spiritualized view of the Old Testament, which is the result of a "spiritual" hermeneutic when applied to Old Testament texts.

Ethnic backgrounds and personal and national history all influence the choice of one's hermeneutical method or key. This is especially true in any discussion of the theology of the land between Messianic Jews and Palestinian Christians. Mitri Raheb, a Palestinian Christian, expresses it this way: "The persecuted understand the Bible differently from those who persecute. Those deprived of power interpret it differently from

---

14. Elfar, "Use of the Old Testament in Arab American Churches," 95–105. A summary of her thesis was published as a chapter in the above-mentioned book: *The Bible and the Land*, of which this present volume is a second edition.

those who possess power . . . When a Jewish concentration camp survivor speaks of the promise of land and when an Israeli settler from the United States speaks of the promise of land, the same words have different meanings. The Bible, a book of persecution, has a crucified Lord as its centerpiece. It can only be correctly understood and interpreted when this theme remains in the center; it is our hermeneutic key."[15] Mitri Raheb indicates that he has come to this hermeneutical key in large part due to the fact of his being a member of a suffering minority.[16] This is a case of one's experience informing one's hermeneutic.

Also a Palestinian Christian, Naim Ateek attests to having had his view of the Bible, in particular certain of the Old Testament passages, challenged by current events in the land of Israel/Palestine. He seeks a tool—in this case, a hermeneutic—which will enable him to "identify the authentic Word of God in the Bible and to discern the true meaning of those biblical texts that Jewish Zionists and Christian fundamentalists cite to substantiate their subjective claims and prejudices."[17]

Ateek advocates the adoption of a "new" hermeneutical key—Jesus the Christ. He applies this hermeneutic by asking whether or not the passage under discussion reflects a Christian understanding of God's will that is acceptable in light of the revelation of Jesus Christ. It would appear that Naim Ateek's hermeneutic has been determined in reaction to an unacceptable current situation and has then been used to define what is authoritative from the canon of Scripture. Ateek's conclusions regarding the theology of the land arrive at an inclusive and universalistic view of the land because anything else is repugnant and not reconcilable to his understanding of Christ's inclusive ministry and mission.[18] His hermeneutic appears to be a hermeneutic in progress, developing along a universalizing trajectory.

Palestinian theologian Yohanna Katanacho writes that "Christ is the owner of the land." He does this from the perspective of a Palestinian Christian and he "hope(s) that [his] background might not be an obstacle, but a bridge that will lead us closer to the universal trans-cultural scriptural truth. Although this truth is absolute, its perception is biased; thus

15. Raheb, "Biblical Interpretation in the Israeli-Palestinian Context," 115–16.

16. Ibid., 112–13.

17. Ateek, Justice, 79.

18. Ateek, "The Earth Is the Lord's," 77–80.

we need to consider the same topic from more than one perspective."[19] Like Ateek, Katanacho views Christ as the key for interpreting and, indeed, universalizing the land promises of the Old Testament as they are reinterpreted in the New Testament:

> Paul states that Jesus is the last Adam (1 Cor 15:45). Like Adam, God entrusted him with the whole earth (Gen 1:28–30; Matt 28:18); Jesus dominated the "land," and he was instrumental in filling it. He wanted to fill it with those who are born from God and who are the inheritors of the "land." Several New Testament authors address this issue. Matthew alludes that the inheritance of the fallen land belongs to the resurrected Christ (Matt 28:18–20). John clearly connects his prologue to Genesis 1. He indicates that the earth, including the promised "land" exists by the Logos (John 1:3). Paul teaches in Philippians 2:10 that Jesus Christ is the King of the whole earth. He clarifies that God created the whole earth by Jesus and for him (Col 1:16). The book of Hebrews states that Jesus Christ is the inheritor of the "land" and the whole world (Heb 1:2). Thus it is fair to say that Jesus the son of David the son of Abraham is not only the seed of Abraham that will bless the whole world, but is also the inheritor of the Abrahamic land promises. He is the key to every blessing, even the blessing of the "land."[20]

MESSIANIC VIEWS

Messianic Jews, on the other hand, consistently maintain the Jewishness of the biblical documents (understandably, of course, the Old Testament; but equally the Jewishness of the New Testament is heavily emphasized). Certain Messianic Jews advocate a use of traditional rabbinic approaches to hermeneutics and exposition.[21] The fact that "rabbinic interpretation is in large measure founded on the assumption that Scripture contains potentially unlimited meaning" allows for an exceptionally varied approach to the interpretation of Scripture in certain quarters of the Messianic movement.[22]

19.. Katanacho, "Christ Is the Owner," 3.

20. Ibid., 11.

21. Shulam, "Middle East Peace," 154–57; see also Stern, "People of God."

22. Evans, *Noncanonical Writings*, 116.

It should nonetheless be noted that there is no consensus among Messianic Jews regarding the use of rabbinic sources and interpretation.[23] Much of their theology, however, as it relates to the land, is informed by the fact of their ethnic identity as Jews.[24] A recent survey of the opinions of Messianic Jews living in the land of Israel showed that an overwhelming 95 percent of those surveyed believe that the Bible clearly promises the land to the Jewish people.[25] Those surveyed represented a wide spectrum of theological persuasions, yet on the issue of the possession of the land there was almost absolute consensus.

A typical Messianic Jewish approach to the question of the theology of the land is expressed by David Miller, who unequivocally employs a literal hermeneutic in his article, "Messianic Judaism and the Theology of the Land":

> The history of the Jewish people begins with the call of Abraham ... From that time the national and spiritual history of the Jewish people has been inseparably linked with the land of promise. Throughout the ages the Jewish people have believed that their presence in the land was a result of God's faithfulness to the covenant which he made with Abraham, and when they have been dispersed from the land they have been confident that this same faithfulness would someday restore them. The covenant which God made with Abraham was unconditional, irrevocable, and confirmed with an oath.[26]

Miller by no means stands alone in his understanding. These views are repeatedly expressed by Messianic Jews, whether or not they reside in Israel.[27] One Messianic Jewish author who does live in Israel is David Stern. He expresses his perspective in the following terms: "The promise of the land of Israel is forever, and the plain sense of this is that the Jewish people will possess the land (at least in trusteeship) and live there. To say

---

23. Boskey, "Messianic Use," 25–74.

24. Maoz, *Priorities*, 156.

25. Skjøtt, "Messianic Believers," 75. This survey is of interest as it covers issues of the beliefs and attitudes of Messianic Jews living in Israel towards the land of Israel, Zionism, political affiliations, and relationships with Palestinian believers.

26. Miller, "Messianic Judaism," 31.

27. See, e.g., Urbach, "Land of Israel," 21–30; and Shulam, "The Middle East Peace": "God gave the land of Israel to the seed of Abraham for ever. He promised to bring Israel back to the land after her exile among the nations. (cf. Isa 37, 39:23ff., Isa 60–61) Israel is at present seeing the fulfillment of these promises."

that the New Covenant transforms this plain sense into an assertion that those who believe in Yeshua come into some vague spiritual 'possession' or a spiritual 'territory' is intellectual sleight of hand aiming at denying, canceling and reducing to naught a real promise given to a real people in the real world."[28] Stern is employing a literal or "plain sense" hermeneutic. The approach of Stern is of interest in that he includes not only Israel and the church as those to whom the land is relevant but adds a third element—the Messianic Jewish body of believers, who he sees as being both separate and at the same time fully a part of both groups.

Arnold Fructenbaum, another Messianic Jew, has seriously addressed himself to theological matters. He thoroughly identifies with the dispensationalist agenda regarding the theology of the land. Although he lives in the United States, he expresses the same sentiments regarding the right of the Jewish people to the possession of the land of Israel: "Although the great majority of Jews live outside the land, there is nevertheless a nation which all Jews can call home . . . the promise of the land as a Jewish possession perhaps applies more to the Hebrew Christian than to anyone else."[29]

This would seem to reflect a hermeneutical mix where the promises of the land are viewed literally for the Jewish people with an extra spiritual dimension for ethnic Jews, who are also Messianic followers of Jesus. As in David Stern's understanding, there is a special place for the Messianic Jew or Hebrew Christian[30] in regards to the Old Testament promises to Israel. The remnant theme—ethnic Jews who become followers of Jesus—appears to be a hermeneutical key as issues of land and promise are dealt with in the theology of both Stern and Fructenbaum.

The majority of Messianic Jews uses a "plain sense" hermeneutic. The outcome of the application of this hermeneutic is a physical restoration (return and reestablishment) of the Jewish people to the historic land of Israel. This theological focus on the land of Israel assumes that Israel's restoration is firmly connected to the physical land of Israel. Israel as an

---

28. Stern, "People of God," 4–5.

29. Fructenbaum, *Hebrew Christianity*, 115.

30. The term *Hebrew Christian* has been replaced by the term *Messianic Jew* in recent years and has become the expression of choice for the self-identification of the majority of Jesus-believing Jews. The major reason for the shift in terminology has been a conscious attempt on the part of the Messianic movement to both distance itself from historic Christianity, which is perceived to be anti-Jewish; and to use a term that will not be immediately abhorrent to fellow ethnic Jews.

ethnic and political entity in its ancient land will survive. The Messianic Jewish reading of Scripture sees God himself as having ordained Israel to remain intact until the end of history. For Messianic Jews there is no dichotomy between physical and spiritual survival. Ethnic Israel is the embodiment of God's purposes for the world.[31]

SOME PATRISTIC VIEWS

The theological problems of the land of Israel/Palestine and the place of the Jewish people are not new. It has not become relevant only because of the reemergence of the Jewish people, politically sovereign in the historic "Promised Land." This issue has occupied the thought of a vast number of scholars throughout the ages.

The *Epistle of Barnabas*, dated at the end of the first century, already reflects a spiritualized interpretation of the land.[32] As in the majority of the texts from the period of the first three centuries, the passages that touch on issues of the land and the Jewish people are in the context of an anti-Jewish polemic: "I will tell you concerning the temple how the wretched Jews, wandering in error trusted not in God Himself but in the temple as being the house of God . . . Again it was revealed that the city and the temple and the people of Israel were to be given up. For the scripture saith 'and it shall come to pass in the last days, that the Lord will deliver up the sheep of His pasture, and their sheepfold and tower to destruction. And so it happened as the Lord had spoken.'"[33]

In the third century this issue was debated according to different hermeneutical approaches by Origen, Irenaeus, and Tertullian, each of whom were influenced by the fact of the Jewish people continuing to live in the land of Palestine. For all of them, the continued presence of Jewish people, particularly in the Galilee, presented a theological and exegetical problem. Tertullian and Irenaeus supported a future for the people in their land in the eschatological future, whereas Origen felt that to interpret the prophets in terms of a restoration of Jewish polity

31. Loden, "Messianic Jewish Views," 54.

32. *Barnabas* VI and XVI. Barnabas does not deal with the issue of the land in isolation from the larger context of the fate of Israel and the Jewish people. Throughout his epistle he deals with Old Testament themes in a spiritualized manner. Note his chapter headings: e.g., "The Spiritual Temple of God"; "The False and True Sabbath"; "Christians, not Jews, Heirs of the Covenant"; and "The Red Heifer, a Type of Christ."

33. *Barnabas* XVI.

was to empty the Scriptures of their spiritual content:[34] "Origen's discussion of the principles of biblical interpretation is not simply an essay on exegetical rules in the abstract: his principles of interpretation have an 'anti-territorial edge' to them. They are directed at an alternative exegetical tradition that took the promises in the Scriptures to refer only to the Jewish people and to the restoration of Jewish life in Judea."[35]

Origen was one of the first biblical commentators to grapple with the issues of the importance of the land and the Jewish people from the perspective of the understanding that, with the coming of the Messiah, the messianic age and the prophecies relating to it had already been fulfilled. Hence the Old Testament Scriptures needed to be interpreted in that light.[36] His insistence on a spiritual rather than a political or historical interpretation of prophecy was essential to his hermeneutical agenda. For Origen, the fact that Jesus was the Messiah meant that the messianic prophecies were already fulfilled. All the promises of Scripture must therefore be understood and interpreted in light of this fact.

He saw no future for the Jewish people and the physical, earthly aspect of the land was rendered irrelevant on account of the fact of the "heavenly" having come: "the holy land, which is a 'good land and a large, a land flowing with milk and honey' which promise is not to be understood to refer, as some suppose, to that part of the earth which we call Judea; for it, however good it may be still forms part of the earth which was originally cursed for the transgression of Adam. . . . [B]oth Judea and Jerusalem were the shadow and figure of the pure land, goodly and large, in the region of heaven, in which is the heavenly Jerusalem."[37]

Origen's hermeneutic was a product of his understanding of the all-encompassing work of the Messiah. In its christocentricity it was distinctly spiritual and left no room whatever for literal interpretations.

Eusebius followed in Origen's footsteps, continuing to see the messianic kingdom as already having begun, therefore leaving no room for interpreting the Old Testament, and particularly Isaiah, in terms of a political history for the Jewish people. Further, Eusebius's interpretation of Scripture was influenced by Constantine's conversion and subsequent

34. Wilkin, *Land Called Holy*, 70.

35. Ibid., 69. See ibid., 69–81 for a fuller discussion of Origen's thought on the subject.

36. Ibid., 77.

37. Origen, *Against Celsus* 7:38, 39.

patronage of the church. Eusebius's hermeneutic was partially a product of current events seen through the lens of an already present messianic kingdom.[38] It is of interest to note that both Origen and Eusebius lived in Palestine and had significant contact with the Jews living in the land. These Jews saw the Jewish presence in Palestine as validating the traditional understanding of their claim to the land as the eternal and unconditional inheritance of the people of Israel.

From the time of Eusebius, the patristic view of Israel and her relation to the land was that the Jews were destined for exile from the land until the end of history. The church had become the new Israel. The land of Israel therefore became a place of pilgrimage and "holy" to the Christians by virtue of the events of the incarnation and, in the understanding of some, the anticipated final events of the age.

In this view, the Jews would finally be converted, but without any restoration to the land of Israel.[39] The roots of this stance are apparent in the thought of Origen and Eusebius and have shaped most of the theological thought of the church on the subject of Israel and the land to our day.

It appears that the debate concerning the theology of the land is most acute when Israel as a nation is occupying the land. As there was a hiatus of almost sixteen centuries between the departure of the Jewish people from the "Promised Land" of Israel until their return in the nineteenth century, discussions of the subject in theological studies and systematic theology have been peripheral rather than central. This is so much the case that a contemporary scholar calls "Israelology" the missing link in systematic theology.[40]

CURRENT HERMENEUTICAL CONCERNS

One of the keystones of any evangelical hermeneutic today is the grammatical-historical approach to the Scriptures. Scripture must be seen in context. That context is the linguistic and historical context in which it was written. For the evangelical, the meaning that the Scriptures held for those to whom it was written (or to whom the events happened)

38. Wilkin, *Land Called Holy*, 78–79.

39. Reuther and Reuther, *Wrath of Jonah*, 74. See ibid., 74–91 for a discussion of the history of Christian views regarding Israel and Zionism.

40. Fruchtenbaum, *Israelology*.

is foundational to any interpretation and application of the Scriptures today. For this reason studies of the backgrounds of early Christianity are essential. These studies enable the contemporary student to get in touch with the actual world of the Bible and can be a preventative to an anachronistic interpretative framework.[41]

An example of the importance of this type of study is seen in Davies's study of the rabbinic elements of Pauline theology. Davies has highlighted the tension in Paul's theology between universal and nationalistic themes. He points out what he sees to be the logical inconsistency of Paul's stance in Romans 11 that, on the one hand, gives priority to Israel as a nation while, on the other hand, emphasizes the universalization of the gospel.[42] That these issues touch the theology of the land is self-evident. Within the Judaism of Paul's day, it would have been utterly inconceivable to divorce the people of Israel and their future from the territorial dimension of the land of Israel. It was an unquestioned assumption of first-century Judaism that even if there was a trancendentalized sense of the land, it existed together with the territorial element.

Contemporary scholars continue to deal with the same issues that occupied earlier generations. The New Testament itself struggles with the interpretation of the Old Testament texts in ways that seem remarkably current. The New Testament allows for a variety of interpretative methods in its use of Old Testament texts, and rabbinic methodology can frequently be seen in the New Testament's discussion of Old Testament material. The church has indeed inherited many things from Judaism, and its methods of interpretation are certainly part of that heritage.

As children of any age, we are products of numerous factors and forces that are particular to that age and are the result of cumulative developments in areas as diverse as theology, philosophy, science, technology, and perhaps most important, politics. It is an illusion to think that we can maintain an uninterrupted link to the biblical past, independent of history and cultural developments. This is as true for us today as it was Paul, the church fathers, and the Reformers in their respective times. The different hermeneutical approaches we see employed today are only more refined or contextualized developments of trends that originated in the early church.

41. For a fascinating view of the influence of the rabbinic context of Paul's theology, see Davies, *Paul and Rabbinic Judaism*. See also Danielou, *Theology of Jewish Christianity*, and Skarsaune, *Jewish Roots*.

42. Davies, *Paul and Rabbinic Judaism*, 58–85.

DANGER OF HERMENEUTICAL SELFISHNESS

The shift in hermeneutical thinking since the Enlightenment has had many repercussions in the area of biblical interpretation. Gruener, in *Meaning and Understanding: The Philosophical Framework for Biblical Interpretation*, states: "Kant's Copernican revolution in the realm of critical thought and hermeneutics replaced the authority of Scripture with the autonomy of the human mind, making experience and reason the focus of authority in the quest for understanding the meaning of the world and human existence"[43]; and "philosophical hermeneutics that impact biblical interpretation in the twentieth century remain deeply ingrained by a Kantian dualism that accords priority to the autonomous self, not only in the sphere of religious experience but also in the scientific sphere of inquiry where nature and history are interpreted."[44]

Today, at the beginning of the twenty-first century, the focus of humanity, particularly in the Western, developed world, has to a great degree become the self. In the realm of biblical interpretation, the danger also exists of interpreting the Scriptures for the benefit of oneself or one's people group without reference to the context and backgrounds of the biblical record. Baruch Maoz warns of the "danger of hermeneutical selfishness . . . that chooses to understand Scripture as if particularly directed at the historical moment at which any interpreter happens to stand."[45] This warning is necessary and should be heeded.

The importance of context cannot be underestimated. This includes the original social, political, geographical, linguistic, and cultural context as well as the multiple contexts the contemporary reader or theologian brings to the text. This has been discussed earlier in this chapter by the comments relating to the hermeneutical "horizons."

When dealing with the theology of the land, there are many components to be reckoned with: election and calling, prophecy and promise, Israel and the church, millennial questions, eschatology, dispensationalism, the Holy Land, the Promised Land, ownership, tenancy, covenant, morality, justice, ethical issues, and the kingdom of God. These are all subjects that compose any comprehensive theology of the land. I have chosen not to deal with these themes specifically, or to show the exegesis of selected key Scriptures, or even to outline the various theological

43. Gruenler, *Meaning and Understanding*, 22.

44. Ibid., 67.

45. Maoz, *Priorities*, 6.

systems and their underlying hermeneutical systems. That work has been done by many able scholars in a plethora of books. Moreover, the authors of those books are adept at pointing out the erroneous hermeneutic of those who differ from them. The contemporary theologian would do well to remember Augustine's counsel towards charity in matters of interpretation: "What happens when Christians hold conflicting interpretations of the Bible? . . . Augustine commends charity. His chief hermeneutic maxim is to 'choose the interpretation that most fosters the love of God and neighbor.' Augustine's principle of charity offers a salient correction to the present situation, in which the conflict of interpretations all too often disguises a conflict of interests and of powers."[46]

CHALLENGES FOR THE PALESTINIAN CHRISTIAN AND THE MESSIANIC JEW

Examining the views and literature coming from within the Messianic Jewish and Palestinian Christian community regarding issues of the land and theology, certain patterns become apparent. The theological focus of each group tends to be particular to the needs and life situation of their respective communities. For the Palestinian, issues of justice and righteousness prevail; and for the Messianic Jew, promise and prophecy are ascendant. The Palestinian Christian sees in Jesus the one who universalized the story of the chosen people in the chosen land from the particular reference of localized Israel to the wider community of the world and all its peoples, whereas the Messianic Jew sees continuation and fulfillment of the story and destiny of Israel living once again in its ancient, Promised Land. The Palestinian Christian focuses on the mercy and love of God for the oppressed and suffering, while the Messianic Jew focuses on the faithfulness of God towards his ancient people, the Jews.

When it comes to issues of the land and promise, the theology of the Arab church is largely drawn from the New Testament whereas the Messianic Jew, on the same issues, situates himself almost totally within the context of the Old Testament. For the Arab Christian, particularly the Palestinian, the person and teachings of Jesus are the key to understanding and interpreting Scripture. This has resulted in a serious neglect of the Old Testament. Jesus in his various roles (e.g., Suffering Servant, Liberator, coming King) is often the hermeneutical key. The Messianic

46. Vanhoozer, *Is There a Meaning?*, 32.

Jew, on the other hand, draws theological buttressing for his view of the land from the Old Testament promises and prophecies. Israel (as the Eternal People of God, the Remnant) has become a hermeneutical key for many. To the concerned observer, this difference is both striking and alarming. Challenges exist for all: Palestinian, Jew, and Christian, separately and together.

The Palestinian Christian should be ready to examine the backgrounds of the New Testament and the Jewish roots of his faith. At the same time, he should seriously deal with the Old Testament and, in particular, the prophetic texts. He should not allow his cultural conditioning to become an obstacle to a thorough examination of the Old Testament Scriptures. Any less than a full appraisal of the two testaments impoverishes one's understanding of the God of the Bible and will inevitably lead to error. Much of the character of God is expressed and revealed in the Old Testament. If the Palestinian Christian disregards these texts, his faith will be diminished and is in danger of becoming shallow. In addition, the Palestinian Christian should acquaint and familiarize himself with the history and narrative of his Messianic Jewish brother.

Messianic Jews must engage in the struggle to understand what the "newness" of Jesus really meant. Was this "newness" intended to be a radical break with the past and the inauguration of something completely new—for example, the kingdom of God on earth as opposed to the territorial dimension of Israel? Was the "newness" Jesus embodied meant to change and reform the existing structures while leaving them basically intact, or was it intended to augment by bringing fulfillment and completion to an already existing tradition? As regards the Old Testament, the Messianic Jew should not focus on promise to the exclusion of the ethical message of the prophets, neglecting matters of justice and righteousness as they touch issues of the land. Only by a serious and thorough evaluation of the New Testament, in the context of the Old, can the Messianic Jew safeguard his theology from narrow parochialism and theological arrogance given his unique situation of being both ethnically Jewish and spiritually Christian. In addition, Messianic Jews, particularly those living in Israel, need to acquaint and familiarize themselves with the context and narrative of their Palestinian Christian brothers and sisters.

Both groups need to be careful not to make too much of the relative absence of New Testament texts that deal *directly* with issues of the land.[47] Diametrically opposed conclusions have been drawn from the same dearth of texts. Arguments from silence speak with many and conflicting voices, ultimately signifying nothing.

The Palestinian Christian and the Messianic Jew should continue in theological dialogue, maintaining attitudes of openness and sensitivity to their respective cultural and national situations. The theological discussion needs to be broadened beyond narrow textual considerations to include matters of culture, context, language, and structure. At present, the Messianic Jew and the Palestinian Christian live in the same land and share a marvelous biblical heritage and inheritance. Together—yet retaining their ethnic and cultural uniqueness—they are members of the "one new man" in Messiah. Both have been reconciled to God and each has received an ongoing ministry of reconciliation that is first of all to be realized in reciprocal relationship. The fact of belonging to the Body of Messiah is not dependent on individual ethnic or national identity but rather on individual commitment to Jesus. Issues of love and reconciliation, ethical behavior, justice and morality are of far greater importance than territorial considerations. This is true regardless of one's status as occupier or occupied. However important, when taken in light of the implications of Jesus's sacrificial love, territorial considerations are secondary.

Western theologians who concern themselves with issues of the land should exhibit attitudes of sensitivity and tolerance, taking care not to become polarized and radicalized by the high passions on both sides. If they are able to maintain their theological and emotional balance, the potential exists for Western theologians to be used as peacemakers who can bring perspective into an area that is all too often clouded by excessive subjectivity and personal theological agendas.

CONCLUSION

My purpose in this chapter has simply been to point out that one's hermeneutic is the decisive factor that determines one's eventual theology of the land. Different keys unlock different doors. Theology is never done in a vacuum. We bring to our studies our unique personal, ethnic, and national history; our culturally determined predilections; our

---

47. For a thorough discussion of New Testament attitudes and texts regarding these issues, see Walker, *Jesus and the Holy City*; and Davies, *Gospel and the Land*. Walker beautifully highlights the imperative of considering the biblical triad of land, Jerusalem, and temple when dealing with the larger issue of the land in the New Testament.

individual bent of character, and our viewpoint. There is no such thing as a pure theology, however hard we may try to rid ourselves of bias and prejudice. Our discussions need to be conducted in a spirit of honor and respect; we must remain cognizant of the fact that regardless of our differences, each one is personally a member of Messiah's body and is indwelt by the same Spirit of Truth. Our status in God is one of equality. Let us therefore be the first to remove the beam from our own eye before we attack the mote in our brother's eye (Matt 7:4–5).

Any discussion of the theology of the land being done by active participants in the drama of life in contemporary Israel/Palestine needs to be done in a spirit of humility and brotherly love, in the recognition that (1) there is "nothing new under the sun" (Eccl 1:9, KJV) and (2) "We see . . . dimly and we know in part" (1 Cor 13:12, KJV). If this be so, let us labor to "keep the unity of the spirit in the bond of peace" (Eph 4:3, KJV) "*until* we come to the unity of the faith" (Eph 4:13, KJV).

BIBLIOGRAPHY

Ateek, Naim. *Justice, and Only Justice: A Palestinian Theology of Liberation*. Maryknoll, NY: Orbis, 1989.
———. "The Earth is the Lord's: Land, Theology and the Bible." *Mishkan* 27 (1997) 75–80.
Ateek, Naim et al., editors. *Challenging Christian Zionism*. London: Melisende, 2005.
Barnabas, Epistle of. In *The Apostolic Fathers*, 1:210–43. Grand Rapids: Eerdmans, 1986.
Berkof, Louis. *The History of Christian Doctrines*. Edinburgh: Banner of Truth Trust, 1937.
———. *Systematic Theology*. Edinburgh: Banner of Truth Trust, 1939.
Boskey, Avner. "The Messianic Use of Rabbinic Literature." *Mishkan* 8/9 (1989) 25–64.
Brown, Wesley H., and Peter F. Penner, editors. *Christian Perspectives on the Israeli-Palestinian Conflict*. Schwarzenfeld: Neufeld, 2008.
Brockway, Allen R. et al. *The Theology of the Churches and the Jewish People: Statement of the World Council of Churches and its Member Churches*. Geneva: WCC, 1988.
Bruce, F. F. "Exegesis and Hermeneutics, Biblical." In *Encyclopaedia Britannica*, Macropaedia, vol. 7 (1978) 63.
Buber, Martin. *The Prophetic Faith*. Translated by Carlyle Witton-Davies. New York: Macmillan, 1949.
Carson, D. A., and John D. Woodbridge, editors. *Scripture and Truth*. Grand Rapids: Zondervan, 1983.
Chapman, Colin. *Whose Promised Land?* London: Lion, 1983.
Clouse, Robert G. editor. *The Meaning of the Millennium: Four Views*. Downers Grove, IL: InterVarsity, 1977.
Cohen, Abraham. *Everyman's Talmud*. New York: Schoken, 1975.
Crombie, Kelvin. *For the Love of Zion: Christian Witness and the Restoration of Israel*. Seven Oaks, UK: Hodder & Stoughton, 1991.
Danielou, Jean. *The Theology of Jewish Christianity. History of Early Christian Doctrine before the Council of Nicaea 1.*Philadelphia: Westminster, 1978.

Davies, W. D. *Paul and Rabbinic Judaism: Some Rabbinic Elements in Pauline Theology.* Philadelphia: Fortress, 1980.

———. *The Gospel and the Land.* Sheffield: JSOT Press, 1994.

Elfar, Rana. "The Use of the Old Testament in Arab American Churches." In *The Bible and the Land: An Encounter,* edited by Lisa Loden et al., 95–105. Jerusalem: Musalaha, 2000.

Elgvin, Torleif, editor. *Israel and Yeshua.* Jerusalem: Caspari Center, 1993.

Epp, F. H. *Whose Land Is Palestine? The Middle East Problem in Historical Perspective.* Grand Rapids: Eerdmans, 1970.

Evans, Craig A. *Noncanonical Writings and New Testament Interpretation.* Peabody, MA: Hendrickson, 1992.

Fasching, Darrel J. *Narrative Theology after Auschwitz: From Alienation to Ethics.* Minneapolis: Fortress, 1992.

Ferguson, Everett. *Backgrounds of Early Christianity.* Grand Rapids: Eerdmans, 1993.

Fruchtenbaum, Arnold G. *Israelology: The Missing Link in Systematic Theology.* Tustin, CA: Ariel Ministries, 1989.

———. *Hebrew Christianity: Its Theology, History and Philosophy.* Grand Rapids: Baker, 1974.

Gruenler, R. G. *Meaning and Understanding.* Grand Rapids: Zondervan, 1991.

Heschel, Abraham J. *God in Search of Man: A Philosophy of Judaism.* New York: Farrar, Straus & Giroux, 1955.

Hughes, Philip Edgcumbe. "The Truth of Scripture and the Problem of Historical Relativity." In *Scripture and Truth,* edited by D. A. Carson and John B. Woodbridge, 173–94. Grand Rapids: Zondervan, 1983.

Islamic Council of Europe. *Jerusalem, The Key to World Peace.* London: Islamic Council of Europe, 1980.

Jocz, Jakob. *The Covenant: A Theology of Human Destiny.* Grand Rapids: Eerdmans, 1968.

Loden, Lisa. "Messianic Jewish Views of Israel's Rebirth and Survival in the Light of Scripture." In *Christian Perspectives on the Israeli-Palestinian Conflict,* edited by Wesley Brown and Peter F. Penner, 43–55. Schwarzenfeld: Neufeld, 2008.

Kaiser, Walter C. *Toward Rediscovering the Old Testament.* Grand Rapids: Academie, 1987.

———. "The Promised Land, A Biblical-Historical View." *Bibliotheca Sacra* 138 (1981) 302–12.

Katanacho, Yohanna. "Christ is the Owner of Haaretz." *Christian Scholar's Review* 34 (2005) 425–41.

Kinzer, Mark. "Scripture and Tradition." In *Voices of Messianic Judaism: Confronting Critical Issues Facing a Maturing Movement,* edited by Dan Cohn-Sherbok, 29–38. Baltimore: Lederer, 2001.

Maoz, B. *Priorities in Eschatology.* Rishon L'Zion: Hagefen, 1991.

Miller, David. "Messianic Judaism and the Theology of the Land." *Mishkan* 26 (1997) 31–38.

Mussner, Franz. "Theology after Auschwitz: A Provisional Program." Paper presented at a conference of the International Catholic–Jewish Liaison Committee, Prague, September 3–6, 1990. Online: http://www.jcrelations.net/en/?item=771.

Origen. *Against Celsus,* vol. 4. Grand Rapids: Eerdmans, 1989.

Packer, J. I. "Infallible Scripture and the Role of Hermeneutics." In *Scripture and Truth,* edited by D. A. Carson and John D. Woodbridge, 325–58. Grand Rapids: Zondervan, 1983.

Raheb, Mitri. "Biblical Interpretation in the Israeli-Palestinian Context." In *Israel and Yeshua*, edited by Torleif Elgvin, 109–17. Jerusalem: Caspari Center, 1993.

Reuther, Rosemary Radford, and Herman J. Reuther. *The Wrath of Jonah: The Crisis of Religious Nationalism in the Israeli-Palestinian Conflict*. New York: Harper & Row, 1989.

Ryrie, Charles C. *The Basis of the Premillennial Faith*. New York: Loizeaux, 1953.

Shulam, Joseph. "*The Middle East Peace, Teaching from Zion—the Middle East Peace Talks—Oslo*, 2003. Online: http://www.Netivyah.org.il/English%20Web/TFZ/ME %PeaceTalk.htm. When this article was written, this link was correct. Both quotation and link no longer exist on the website.

Skarsaune, O. *The Jewish Roots of the New Testament*. Jerusalem: Caspari Center, 1997.

Skjøtt, B. F. "Messianic Believers and the Land of Israel: A Survey." *Mishkan* 26 (1997) 72–81.

Stern, David H. "The People of God, the Promises of God, and the Land of Israel." Paper presented in conference on Theology of the Land, Droushia, Cyprus, 1996.

———. *Restoring the Jewishness of the Gospel*. Jerusalem: Jewish New Testament Publications, 1988.

Stevenson, James. *A New Eusebius*. SPCK Large Paperbacks. London: SPCK, 1975.

Terry, Milton S. *Biblical Hermeneutics*. Grand Rapids: Zondervan, 1974.

Tirosh, Yousef, editor. *Religious Zionism: An Anthology*. Jerusalem: World Zionist Organization, 1975.

Urbach, Chaim. "The Land of Israel in Scripture." *Mishkan* 26 (1997) 22–30.

Vos, Geerhardus. *Biblical Theology: Old and New Testaments*. Grand Rapids: Eerdmans, 1948.

Vanhoozer, Kevin. *Is There a Meaning in this Text? The Bible, the Reader, and the Morality of Literary Knowledge*. Grand Rapids: Zondervan, 1998.

Walker, P. W. L. *Jesus and the Holy City: New Testament Perspectives on Jerusalem*. Grand Rapids: Eerdmans, 1996.

———, editor. *Jerusalem Past and Present in the Purposes of God*. Carlisle, UK: Paternoster, 1994.

Wilken, Robert L. *The Land Called Holy: Palestine in Christian History and Thought*. New Haven: Yale University Press, 1992.

❖ 3 ❖

A Messianic Jew Looks at
the Land Promises

Daniel C. Juster

SOME INTRODUCTORY COMMENTS

Followers of Yeshua, the Messiah Jesus, embrace many and various positions on the issue of the status of the land of Israel. Some affirm the continual election of the Jewish people along with the literal promises of the land, while others think that all of the promises connected to the land of Israel are now to be spiritualized and applied to the everlasting inheritance of the church, which is seen as the new and true Israel—a position that is known as "replacement theology" or supersessionism, based on the premise that the church has replaced or superseded Israel. Luther, a notorious expounder of punitive supersessionism, famously wrote that, "all the Gentiles who are Christians are the true Israelites and new Jews, born of Christ, the noblest Jew."[1]

In her article, "From Jesus to Shylock: Christian Supersessionism and the *Merchant of Venice*," Susannah Heschel explores the historical role of Christian supersessionism, which climaxed in the Nazi race theories

---

1. Luther, *Word and Sacrament I*, 288. The NIV (New International Version) is used for all Scripture quotations.

of the 1930s.[2] Although the subject of much debate, it is largely agreed that these were partly brought on by the confusion within Christian theology regarding the contemporary role of the Jewish people. She argues that this confusion is exemplified in the figures of Jesus and Shylock. Jesus is the model of goodness, but not because he is Jewish; and Shylock is the model of evil, precisely because he was Jewish. Both figures negotiate the presence of Judaism in the Christian realm in which questions regarding the ethnic and social status of Jews who come to faith in the Messiah arise. Can a Jew convert to Christianity? In what way can ethnic Judaism be transformed through Christian conversion? In this context conversion to Christianity was tantamount to assimilation into the Gentile world. Herschel believes that it is supersessionist teachings which are at the heart of this confusion, with its representation of Judaism as Israel "in the flesh" and Christianity as Israel "in the Spirit." This strikes at the core of Christian Platonic metaphysical dualism in which the flesh is considered bad and the Spirit good. In Shakespeare's *The Merchant of Venice*, Christianity is understood to have begun with the shedding of Jewish blood—the blood of Jesus—which indicates a conversion through crucifixion: The Jewish body is destroyed in order to become Christian. When Shylock requests a pound of flesh from Antonio, it is from his breast and so enacts the Christian fantasy of the Jew stabbing Christ in the heart.

The historical "Christian" narrative of the relationship between Jesus and Judaism has been wrought with anti-Semitism from which Christianity is only beginning to emerge post-*Shoah*. Pope Paul VI in his "Declaration on the Relation of the Church to Non-Christian Religions" did much to counter centuries of anti-Jewish teaching and began to build bridges with the Jewish people stating, "Since the spiritual patrimony common to Christians and Jews is thus so great, this sacred synod wants to foster and recommend that mutual understanding and respect which is the fruit, above all, of biblical and theological studies as well as of fraternal dialogues. True, the Jewish authorities and those who followed their lead pressed for the death of Christ; still, what happened in His passion cannot be charged against all the Jews, without distinction, then alive, nor against the Jews of today."[3]

Yet even from this positive position, he later categorizes the church as the "new people of God," and so falls back on classical formulations

2. Heschel, "From Jesus to Shylock," 407–31.

3. Paul VI, *Nostra Aetate*, para. 4.

of replacement theology. There are likewise other contemporary theologians who attempt to disassociate themselves from traditional replacement theology by affirming a continued election of the Jewish people, and yet at the same time who reject the literal promises of the land to the Jewish people (e.g., as several Puritan writers do). These are issues that have a direct impact on believers living in the land of Israel.

Some who repudiate replacement theology and hold to the continued election of the ethnic Jewish people also hold that the promises concerning land should not now be taken in a carnal and literal way. We see in this that replacement theology and the rejection of a still literal promise of the land are not always held together.

In recent seminar in Israel, Rowan Williams, the Archbishop of Canterbury, submitted a paper that argued that ethnic Israel was still elect and that this election could not be disassociated from the promise of the land, although conditions applied: "The Israel of Scripture is a community whose identity is bound up with a calling to show wisdom and justice, a calling which successive modes of government for the people fulfil in very varying degrees; the land of Israel is not a gift given in the abstract to the Hebrew tribes: it is a territory given as the necessary backdrop of stability for a law-governed community to flourish."[4] One important factor or condition was justice for the Palestinians. Given to a Christian audience in Israel, the archbishop's paper provoked a strong reaction from both local and international visitors, and served to highlight the fact that these issues are very much contemporary issues that often bring disunity between Arab and Jewish followers of Yeshua. There are many Christian Zionists and Messianic Jews who look at the present return of the Jewish people to the land with such rose-colored glasses that their counsel for Israel's political leadership is to take the Promised Land and to dispossess anyone that stands in the way. We need to reflect more deeply about the meaning of the Jewish return to the land of Israel and the meaning of the resistance to this return from the Palestinian Arab population and the surrounding Arab nations, not to mention the larger Muslim world.

This chapter will therefore seek to address how Messianic Jews should interpret the Bible with regards to the promises concerning the land, the importance of building and maintaining familial relationships

---

4. Williams, "Holy Land," 295.

with Arab Christians and non-believing Jews, and will address the concept of justice within the contemporary social and political climate.

THE HERMENEUTICAL ISSUE

It is important that I express my approach to biblical interpretation. I believe in a contextual, historical, and grammatical approach to every text in context, where we seek to understand the intent of the original human author and the understanding of his original audience. This method should dominate our understanding wherever possible. In this regard, I am in accord with Walter Kaiser, president emeritus of Gordon-Conwell Theological Seminary.[5] Any other approach to texts leads to subjectivity. The original intent is the primary meaning of the text. Any other approach to the text shows itself to be an escape from this authority. Much has been written concerning the New Testament reinterpreting the meaning of the Hebrew text. If by reinterpretation we mean additional applications by analogy that are prophetically given by the New Testament writer, I have no objection, but rather believe that this is part of New Testament revelation. If, however, we mean a change of meaning from what the original author intended to be understood by his targeted audience, then I beg to strongly disagree.

In this regard, even a cursory reading of the Hebrew Bible reaffirms the election of ethnic Israel as an everlasting election (Isa 45:17). It is not an election that can be fulfilled by another but analogous Israel that becomes the true meaning of Israel and inherits the promises given to Israel. The biblical writer and his audience would and could not entertain such a notion in their worldview. The comfort and promise given by the prophets is that Israel will eventually get it right, will eventually fulfill their destiny and forever walk in fellowship with God. This is a corporate promise to the surviving nation—the remnant—and does not include all Jewish individuals without discrimination. We might see the church as analogous to Israel with analogous promises, but supersession or replacement is impossible for anyone who takes the biblical texts with any degree of straightforward contextual meaning.

In this regard, it is impossible to justly disassociate election from the land promises. These promises, some of which we shall summarize, do have conditions for their ultimate fulfillment, but that Israel will fulfill

5. Kaiser, "Single Meaning."

these conditions and come into their destiny of righteousness in this land is affirmed again and again. This is why Archbishop Williams asserted that it is not feasible to affirm ethnic Israel's election and separate this from the promise connected to the land.

WHAT IS JUSTICE?

One of the factors that muddies understanding of this issue is the permeating influence of secular humanism. Many in the West, since the Enlightenment, have understood justice as a leveling equality.[6] While equality functions as part of justice in limited and defined ways in the Bible, it is never the primary meaning of justice. There is equality before the courts for crime, punishment, and restitution for all people, who are equally created in the image of God. However, this leveling aspect of equality is counterbalanced by God giving differing gifts, talents, and callings to different individuals and peoples. *Justice then, is that order of righteousness whereby individuals and peoples can fulfill their God intended destinies.* As a result, humanity participates in a divine-human social order that allows every individual to move towards fulfilling his and her God-given purpose. Differences of roles between men and women are also to be comprehended within the idea of divine order. Such destinies are not only individual but also corporate; in God's vast transcendence of human time, such purpose and destiny meanings may span centuries or millennia. For God, such durations are insignificant. *Biblical justice begins with God's declared will for Israel and the nations.* It is rooted in his covenant with Abraham and his choice, for whatever good reasons may be known to him (Gen 12:1–20). Biblical justice begins with God's macrocosmic declarations, and righteousness begins with conforming our understanding and actions to his declarations.

Unbiblical humanistic justice begins with the microcosmic situation of the peoples in the Holy Land. It begins with the issue of empathy for the displaced Palestinian Arabs, who, in some cases, have had roots in the land for generations. It also begins with empathy for the Jews, who understandably need a homeland after so much suffering and persecution. How do we balance the claims of the Palestinian population and the refugees against the claim of the Jews, who have ancient roots in

---

6. On the failure of secular reasoning to deal properly with the subject of justice, see Alasdair Macintyre, *Whose Justice? Which Rationality?*

this land but have only returned in significant numbers over the last hundred-plus years—in some cases after being forced from Arab lands without any compensation for their loss?

My contention is that although these types of reasoning will dominate the councils of the unredeemed institutions of the nations, such reasoning must not dominate those who embrace biblical faith.

Unbiblical humanistic reasoning also majors on the sufferings of the Palestinians and the Jews and the relative merits of their pleas for justice on this basis. While the suffering of human beings is biblically important, the root cause of such suffering must be subjected to biblical analysis. Indeed, this analysis must include how people treat one another according to biblical ethical standards, but it must also include that consequences result from failure to submit to the revealed will of God. Much Palestinian and Jewish suffering can be traced to the root of not being willing to submit to God's declared will on many levels.

For example, if the Jewish people do not submit to the law of God and are instead a lawless people, or if they replace God's law with human laws which contradict that law, they will find themselves suffering and resisted by God himself. By the same rule, if Palestinians refuse to recognize what God says about the Jewish people and their connection to the land of Israel, then suffering will result.[7]

One important consideration is the answer to the question, "Whose land is this?" The Bible tells us that this land belongs to God. I will argue that the land belongs to Yeshua, Jesus. Until Arabs and Jews admit that the land belongs to Jesus, not to Mohammed, we will not have lasting peace and resolution. Do we ever consider that the statements on the mosque that God has no Son and the denial of Yeshua by the first-century Jewish community are still root causes of the problem we see today? Is it possible that the conflict of Jews and Arabs over the land today is part of God's purpose to bring that acknowledgment of his Son without which lasting peace will remain elusive—not only for the Middle East but for the whole world? Sometimes I am amazed that Christians who seek justice in the Middle East counsel nonregenerated Jews and Arabs to live out the Sermon on the Mount with each other.

---

7. I should note in passing that suffering is sometimes a result of righteousness. Peter tells us that one can suffer both for the sake of righteousness and because of sin (1 Pet 2:19–20).

MOHAMMED'S LAND OR YESHUA'S LAND?

The great nineteenth-century classic by W. E. Hengenstenburg, *The Christology of the Old Testament*, argued that the many passages where God appears in the Old Testament are pre-incarnate revelations of Yeshua.[8] This includes the One who argued with Abraham before the destruction of Sodom and Gomorrah, the One who appeared to Moses in the burning bush, the Angel who was in the cloud and pillar, the One who wrestled with Jacob, and the One who appeared to Menoah before the birth of Samson. The Holy Land belongs to him. This should give pause to anyone who would think that the ultimate control of the land should be forever ceded to those who deny Yeshua and his ownership. This could look as if we are returning to the theology of the Crusades when it was argued that the Christians who acknowledge Jesus should have control of the Holy Land and the holy places. The reason that this medieval interpretation was wrong was that it was steeped in replacement theology where the church was said to be true Israel. The Crusaders failed to read the biblical texts utilizing this natural hermeneutic, which clearly illustrates that it is the Lord's will that this land be given to the Jewish people. This ultimate destiny in the land is connected to his kingship over Israel and all the earth. Peace in the land for the Jews and peace in the whole world is contingent on acknowledging him to be the King of Israel and the Lord of the whole world.

There is currently a large threat from Islamic fundamentalism, which teaches that it is the will of God for a political system of *sharia* law to govern all national states. When we see the effects of Islam, especially in the Arab world, the terrible oppression of women, the destruction of Christian communities like the Copts, Assyrians, and Christian Arabs of Bethlehem, can any Christian seriously desire that this land be ruled under Mohammed and the present revival of fundamentalist, radical Islam? When we think of the right of religious liberty and the right of people to choose their own religious beliefs, or to change their religion, we are even more alarmed at the prospect of Islamic rule in the Holy Land.

It is this spiritual wrestling between Islam and God's will that is physically manifested in the Israeli-Arab conflict which I believe is the primary root of the situation and the failure of the parties involved to acknowledge the Kingship of Jesus over this land. It is his land, not Mohammed's!

8. Hengenstenburg, *Christology*.

Will Arabs who confess Jesus have a place in the land in the days of fulfillment? No doubt. The Bible predicts that there are special ones among the Gentiles who will live in the land with the Jewish people. There are special promises to the nations of the Middle East as well (cf. Isaiah 19). The biblical picture is that when Israel comes into their Promised Land, the nations will also attain to their inheritance in lands promised to them:

- When the Most High gave the nations their inheritance, when he divided up all mankind, he set up boundaries for the peoples according to the number of the sons of Israel (Deut 32:8).

- From one man he made every nation of men, that they should inhabit the whole earth; and he determined the times set for them and the exact places where they should live (Acts 17:26).

- He will judge between the nations and settle disputes for many peoples (Isa 2:4).

Many peoples in the world occupy land that they took from others. Sometimes this is God's judgment, and sometimes it is unjust. The history of the prophets and their words to Assyria, Babylon, and the other nations make this quite clear. Ultimately, God will provide a place that is according to his will for all. Until then we have temporary human decisions that hopefully will mitigate suffering.

THE BIBLICAL PATTERN OF EXILE AND RETURN

I should also note that the Bible lays out a clear pattern of expectation. When Israel is obedient to God, she will be blessed in her land. When she is disobedient, she may be oppressed by foreigners in her land, or even scattered into exile. When she repents, she will be brought back to her land. It is the general consensus of Christians that Israel has not repented. Messianic Jews largely agree. Therefore, she is said not to meet the conditions for being in the land. However, as we shall see, those conditions are not of such easy application. Northern Israel was within the land for centuries in a largely unrighteous state before being exiled. In addition, Judah was only sporadically more righteous, but years passed before her exile a century after the northern tribes. Other passages indicate that a return to the land before transformation and righteousness is envisioned (Ezek 36:24–38). Such considerations lead us to the next section of this paper.

THE PROMISE OF THE LAND TO ISRAEL

Just what are the promises of the land to Israel or the Jewish people? What are the conditions to inhabit the land? What is the ultimate destiny of the Jewish people in this land? Lastly, do the New Covenant Scriptures affirm the promise of the land to the Jewish people? While this last question is significant, as a Messianic Jew, I do want to emphasize that this last question does not have the same weight that it might have for Christians. Why? It is because for Messianic Jews the Hebrew texts in their context stand on their own. If the New Testament reinterpreted those texts in a way that they were not true to the original intent, then I as a Jew would be duty bound to reject them on the basis of the principle that later revelation must be in accord with earlier revelation (Deuteronomy 18). However, a reaffirmation of the promises to Israel in the New Testament would be significant.

The texts that promise an everlasting connection of the Jewish people to the land of Israel and her eventual, lasting fulfillment in this land as a New Covenant people are too numerous to quote in their entirety, but we will explore a few of them here.

1. *"I will plant Israel in their own land, never again to be uprooted from the land I have given them, says the Lord your God"* (Amos 1:15). Does this verse speak to the ethnic-national people or a metaphorical future people from all nations who will inherit the eternal kingdom that is metaphorically the land? Would this be a comfort to faithful ancient Israelites?

2. *"Judah will be inhabited forever and Jerusalem through all generations. Their bloodguilt, which I have not pardoned, I will pardon. The LORD dwells in Zion"* (Joel 3:20). This passage comes after the description of a severe world judgment of the nations that are described as invading Israel. It is hard to see how this can be the church. This has not yet happened.

3. *"Is it too small a thing for you to be my servant to restore the tribes of Jacob and bring back those of Israel I have kept? I will also make you a light for the Gentiles, that you may bring my salvation to the ends*

of the earth" (Isa 49:6). There is no legitimate way to confuse the meaning here. The promise is to Israel and includes the salvation of the nations. A new Israel of Jew and Gentile replacing Israel cannot be the interpretation. It is not in the text at all.

4. *"Can a mother forget her nursing child and have no compassion on the child she has borne. Though she may forget, I will not forget you. See, I have engraved you on the palms of my hands; your walls are ever before me. Your sons hasten back and those who laid you waste depart from you. Lift up your eyes and look around; all your sons gather and come to you . . . Though you were ruined and laid waste, now you will be too small for your people, and those who devoured you will be far away. The children born during your bereavement will yet say in your hearing, This place is too small for us; give us more space to live in.*

    "See I will beckon to the gentiles, I will lift up the banner to the peoples; they will bring your sons in their arms and carry their daughters on their shoulders. Kings will be your foster fathers, and their queens your nursing mothers" (Isa 49:15–23). Can this be the situation after the first return after Babylonian captivity? No, for this glorious turning of the nations to favor Israel to this extent has not yet happened. Indeed, the "first return" was a small minority. The Jews of the first century were a minority as well, less than one-third of Jewry. Israel has since remained under foreign domination except for one brief and corrupt period.

5. *"Arise, shine, for your light has come, and the glory of the LORD rises upon you. See darkness covers the earth and deep darkness is over the peoples, but the Lord rises upon you and his glory appears over you. Nations will come to your light and kings to the brightness of your dawn. Lift up your eyes and look about you: All assemble and come to you; your sons come from afar, and your daughters are carried on the arm. Then you will look and be radiant, your heart will throb and swell with joy; the wealth of the seas will be brought to you, to you the riches of the nations will come . . .*

    "Surely the islands look to me, in the lead are the ships of Tarshish, bringing your sons from afar, with their silver and gold, to the honor of the LORD your God, the Holy One of Israel, for he has endowed you with splendor. Foreigners will rebuild your walls and kings will serve you. Though in anger I struck you, in favor I will show you compassion. Your gates will always stand open; they will

never be shut, day or night, so that men may bring you the wealth of the nations, their kings led in triumphal procession. For the nation that will not serve you will perish; it will be utterly ruined . . .

"The sons of your oppressors will come blowing before you; all who despise you will bow down at your feet and will call you the City of the Lord, Zion of the Holy One of Israel . . . You will drink the milk of nations and be nursed at royal breasts, then you will know that I, the LORD, am your Savior, your Redeemer, the Mighty One of Jacob. Instead of bronze I will bring you gold, and silver in place of bronze, and iron in place of stones . . .

"No longer will violence be heard in your land, nor ruin or destruction within your borders, but you will call your walls Salvation, and your gates Praise . . .

"[T]he LORD will be your everlasting light, and your days of sorrow will end. Then will all your people be righteous, and they will possess the land forever. They are the shoot I have planted, the work of my hands, for the display of my splendor" (Isa 60:1–6, 9–12, 14, 16–17, 18, 19b–21). Of course, we would not deny that this has application to all the people of God, but is this the primary meaning? It cannot be, for this is a comfort to the nation going into exile. It is a comfort to know the future glory of Jerusalem in spite of the current destruction. The glory predicted here has never been fulfilled. The sons of the oppressors who come are those nations who oppressed the ethnic Israel, the Jewish nation. It is not about the persecution of Christians, though God may certainly speak from these verses to their hearts. Context makes it abundantly clear that this is about the ancient nation.

6. *"For Zion's sake I will not keep silent, for Jerusalem's sake I will not remain quiet, till her righteousness shines out like the dawn, her salvation like a blazing torch. The nations will see your righteousness and all kings your glory . . . for the LORD will take delight in you and your land will be married"* (Isa 62:1–2a, 4b). Here the Jews of exile are comforted by the promise of the restoration of Jerusalem, not comforted by a spiritual, metaphorical Jerusalem from heaven. This would not have been such a comfort.

7. *"So then, the days are coming, declares the LORD, when people will no longer say, As surely as the LORD lives, who brought the Israelites up out of Egypt, but they will say, 'As surely as the LORD lives, who*

brought the descendants of Israel up out of the land of the north and out of all the countries where he had banished them. Then they will live in their own land" (Jer 23:7–8). Can this be the church? No, the church was not banished. Can this be the return from Babylon? No, this was a small remnant that returned and, five hundred years later, was still a minority of the Jewish people, perhaps less than a third. Never has there been such an all encompassing and comprehensive return that this language could describe until, perhaps, today. There is still more to come from this verse. This return is to yet make the exodus pale by comparison. This has to be a prophetic word about the literal, national, ethnic people.

8. *"'The time is coming,' declares the Lord, 'when I will make a new covenant with the house of Israel and with the house of Judah' . . . 'I will put my law on their minds and write it on their hearts. I will be their God and they will be my people' . . . 'They will all know me, from the least of them to the greatest,' declares the Lord. 'For I will forgive their wickedness and will remember their sins no more.'*

   "This is what the Lord says, he who appoints the sun to shine by day, who decrees the moon and stars to shine by night, who stirs up the sea so that its waves roar, the LORD Almighty is his name. 'Only if these decrees vanish from my sight,' declares the LORD, 'will the descendants of Israel ever cease to be a nation before me.' This is what the LORD says, 'Only if the heavens above can be measured and the foundations of the earth below be searched out, will I reject the descendants of Israel because of all they have done declares the LORD'" (Jer 31:31, 33b, 34b, 35–37). Here is food for thought. The New Covenant is made with national/ethnic Israel. It includes the promise of the forgiveness of their sins and that they will all know God. It includes the promise of their ethnic-national preservation.

   When Christians hear the words "New Covenant," this context of meaning is hardly in their minds. So how is it that Christians are part of the New Covenant? It is by the fact that the salvation of the Gentiles is part of the Abrahamic Covenant; the New Covenant enables its implementation. However, this covenant has only been partially fulfilled. It includes, as an essential component, the restoration of the Jewish people. The affirmation to the physical, ethnic seed in this passage could not be clearer. There is no way that the church can be read as the intended subject of the last part of the quote above.

9. *"For I will take you out of the nations, I will gather you from all the countries and bring you back into your own land. I will sprinkle clean water on you, and you will be clean. I will cleanse you from all your impurities, and from all your idols. I will give you a new heart, and put a new spirit in you; I will remove from you your heart of stone and give you a heart of flesh. And I will put my Spirit in you and move you to follow my decrees, and be careful to keep my laws. You will live in the land I give your forefathers, and you will be my people, and I will be your God. I will save you from all your uncleanness"* (*Ezek 36:24–29*). In this passage on the New Covenant—parallel to Jeremiah 31—we have an amazing promise to the ethnic/national people that has not yet been fulfilled. The meaning is plain. The promise of being born again is connected to the return to the land, and there is a national conversion. Certainly Paul had many passages in mind, including this one, when he wrote, looking forward to this national conversion in Romans 11.

10. I will not quote it here, but Ezekiel 37 is the famous "dry bones" passage that repeats the promise of Ezekiel 36 of the people coming back to the land and receiving the Spirit. They will be one nation under one King. This is happening and will continue to happen.

11. *"Jerusalem shall be an immovable rock for all the nations. All who try to move it will injure themselves . . .*

    "A day of the Lord is coming when your plunder will be divided among you. I will gather all the nations to Jerusalem to fight against it, the city will be captured, the houses ransacked, and the women raped. Half of the city will go into exile, but the rest of the people will not be taken from the city.

    "Then the LORD will go and fight against those nations as he fights in the day of battle. On that day his feet will stand on the Mount of Olives, east of Jerusalem and the Mount of Olives will be split in two from east to west, forming a great valley . . . then the Lord My God will come, and all the holy ones with him.

    "Then the survivors from all the nations that have attacked Jerusalem will go up year after year to worship the King, the LORD Almighty, and to celebrate the Feast of Tabernacles" (*Zech 12:3b, 14:1–4, 5b, 16*).

RETURN BEFORE REPENTANCE AND TRANSFORMATION

It is important to make further comments on the Ezekiel and Zechariah passages. While there are many passages that describe the order of repentance leading to return, here we have verses that speak of return and then repentance. Therefore the idea that there is a return to the land as part of the process of bringing Israel to repentance and to her ultimate destiny is well established by these passages. In Zech 12:10, Israel looks on the One they pierced after the last days' war. Then all will repent.

The passages I have summarized here are only a selection from many that repeat the same basic promise. In the light of these many passages, I think it is stunning—even breathtaking—to note how replacement theology simply collapses all these passages into Yeshua being Israel, and the land promises now referring to the spiritual inheritance of those who follow him.[9] No one reading these passages could come up with any anticipation of such a meaning. Jewish people especially find such interpretations to be perverse and offensive. Were this really the teaching of the New Covenant Scriptures, Jewish people would be duty bound to reject the New Covenant Scriptures as false Scriptures that did not cohere with previous revelation. While milder, those interpretations that affirm the election of Israel and dissociate it from the promise of the land simply avoid taking the promises of the covenant according to their contextual meaning.

INTERPRETING ROMANS 9–11 AND THE PROMISE OF THE LAND

The continued election of ethnic Israel—the Jewish people—is now an overwhelming consensus in New Testament interpretation. That election is the inescapable conclusion for honest exegesis in light of Romans 11:11–31. The affirmations are enormous. They include that there will be a full acceptance of ethnic Israel that will lead to life from the dead; that the Gentile believers are called to work to see some of Israel saved because of this ultimate promise; and that Israel will receive the promised remission of sins and will enter final and lasting fellowship with God for, "All Israel will be saved." The last is generally understood as the conversion of the nation at the end of this age. In my view, Romans

9. See, e.g., Horner, *Future Israel*.

11:28–29, however, is the most noteworthy of all the verses, for it asserts that though the Jewish people are enemies of the gospel, they remain elect and beloved for the sake of their fathers, "for God's gifts and call [to Israel] are irrevocable." The Roman Catholic Catechism itself affirms these verses in a clear and solid way.[10]

The question of the gifts and call are not mysteries that have not been revealed. Israel still plays a role in the redemption of the world. Romans 9 summarizes the gifts and call in terms of Israel's priestly functions and the glory that is promised. The chapter also says that to Israel still belong the promises, this in the present tense. What are the promises? It is obvious to me that they are the very promises that are found in the Hebrew Bible, and that Paul is here encouraging us to simply embrace the truth that the promises of God to Israel still hold. Two promises are repeated more than any others. One is that Israel will repent and be forgiven and will come into everlasting fellowship with God that will never end. The other is that Israel will return to her land, never again to be plucked up, or removed in judgment and war.

When some Hellenistic or Gnostic antimaterial interpretations on the Scriptures make the promises of the land unimportant, or as some carnal thing to be transcended, *they show themselves unable to submit to the clear, intended, and contextual meaning of the text.* When they affirm an election for Israel but without the land, they empty Paul's words of meaning when he states that to them belong the promises.

Some hold that the land promises cannot be in effect because the New Testament does not emphasize them. From their places of influence in seminaries and graduate schools, these interpreters teach that the New Testament writings are situation-specific and only address concerns that have arisen from within the communities of the New Covenant. They are not systematic theological texts. Yet such teaching goes by the way when they expect the New Testament to emphasize the land. Why would it emphasize it? For one thing, this was not at issue in apostolic days since the Jewish people were occupying the land. Paul's affirmation of irrevocable promises is more than adequate since we can simply turn to the Hebrew Scriptures to find out what these promises and covenants are. Lastly, the approach we are refuting is woefully disrespectful to the Hebrew Scriptures as if clear Hebrew texts somehow have less authority than the New Testament texts. Yes, the

10. Konstant, *Catechism of the Catholic Church*, para. 674.

New Testament is God's highest revelation, but by biblical standards it must be consistent with the revelation already given.

ADDITION THEOLOGY, NOT REPLACEMENT THEOLOGY

It is true that the New Testament applies terms and promises given to Israel to Christians. There is *no evidence that this is meant in a replacement way.* Replacement is pure assumption. Since Christians are now also the seed of Abraham by faith and share in a complementary priesthood, *the promises of God have analogous meaning for Christians.* The meek shall inherit the earth, and the Bride of Messiah shall rule and reign with him. These new analogous applications are in addition to the promises to Israel, not in replacement, as Romans 9 and 11 make clear with finality.

THE PAINFUL PRESENT SITUATION

However, all of the exegesis above does not fully answer the pain and suffering that is associated with the present and complex situation in the land of Israel. To introduce this section, I think it is important to review Deuteronomy 19:8–9: "If the Lord your God enlarges your territory as he promised on oath to your ancestors, and gives you the whole land he promised them, because you carefully follow all these laws I command you today —to love the LORD your God and to walk always in obedience to him."

I believe that this passage applies beyond the original context and presents us with a continuing principle. This passage shows us that the full possession and population of the land is contingent on faithfulness and obedience to God. If Israel is obedient she will attain to the promised borders. If she is not obedient, however, she will find resistance from God expressed as opposition and resistance by other nations, which will prevent the attainment of the promised borders and control in the land. Some Christian Zionists forget this passage and others parallel to it, and give idealistic counsel unrelated to Deuteronomy 19 and to today's realities. So while the promise remains—and we are assured that Israel will attain it as she comes into repentance and righteousness—the attainment is conditional.

Conditional attainment is related to the reality that the majority of Israelis today have no intent to submit to God and his standards of righteousness. All this is without even touching on the topic of the Jewish embrace of Yeshua!

Some have made a great deal of the treatment of the Palestinians as a reason why Israel has lost its right to attain the possession of the land. However, this is a double-edged sword. If righteousness is submission to the declared will of God, we have to begin with what God has declared about the land. Contrary to a humanistic understanding of justice, God has different destinies for different people. The years of one people's occupation or another people's occupation are not the determining matters. Justice is not humanistic equality or leveling. Justice in regard to the land requires that there be a submission to what God has declared about this land. The attainment of the Jewish people to their destiny in this land opens the way for all nations to attain their inheritance. This is connected to Israel's priesthood. So if the Palestinians do not acknowledge God's promise, they are foundationally unjust and are themselves resisted by God and lose their rights in this land. This resistance spreads to the other nations of the world, particularly to those that are involved in resisting God's purposes for the land, resulting in judgment for all the nations and a general blockage for all to obtain their inheritance.

However, is there resistance from God toward Israel due to Israel's treatment of the Palestinians? This is an issue of righteousness. In many ways Israel has not lived up to biblical standards in its treatment of Palestinians, especially Palestinian Christians. In ways not necessary to her national defense, she has alienated those who could have been her friends. On the other hand, the texts on how to treat strangers in the land assume that those who fit this category embrace the legitimate reality of God's promise that this land is intended as part of Israel's destiny.

Here is a list that shows the issue of the land to be complex.

1. The attainment of the promise of the land by Israel is contingent on her submission to God and his righteous standards, though the promise itself is unconditional and will eventually be fulfilled.

2. The treatment of strangers in the land is one of those standards of righteousness.

3. The strangers in the land must acknowledge God's declared will with regard to the land and his sovereign right to allocate it as he wishes.

4. The ultimate fulfillment of the promise of the land is connected to Israel's repentance, submission to God and the conversion of the nations of the world.

These complexities make any counsel of idealism foolish. Israel's government in the present situation may be forced to navigate through the present reality that may include seeking coexistence with a Palestinian state. In addition, this includes acting with real justice toward Israeli Arabs, including spending money on infrastructure and education. Israel must also negotiate the dangerous waters of protecting their people from a form of Islam that is increasingly violent and oppressive, making a peaceful two-state solution even more unlikely. Israel's government is ultimately secular and seeks secular solutions. While such solutions may give temporary respite, we do know that lasting peace will be attained only when all acknowledge that Yeshua, Jesus, is king over this land! This brings us back to the Mohammed or Jesus question: whose land is it? It is the land of Yeshua!

PRESENT-DAY ISRAEL AND FULFILLMENT

Is it possible that the present conflicts and impossibilities are an opening for evangelism for Jews and Palestinians? I personally believe that evangelism is the most important thing that we can do to further peace. The existence of Jews who do not submit to God and Yeshua—and of Muslim Arabs who increasingly embrace radical Islam—make lasting peace seem quite unlikely. Yet can we believe in a real movement of the Spirit where Jews and Arabs become one in Yeshua? In the ultimate fulfillment, will a Jewish majority share this land with Arabs as brothers and sisters in Yeshua? I do believe so.

The present situation is disappointing to the Jewish people. This seems much more like a most pressured situation to bring Israel to God. We all should be able to agree that Zionism, without God and Yeshua, cannot be the answer for the Jewish nation. Certainly Arab Christians should not think that God intends the land of Israel to be under the banner of Islam. So may we see Yeshua, Jesus, lifted up and his kingdom extended over Israel and the nations.

THE NEW HEAVENS AND NEW EARTH

What about the ultimate promise of inheritance in Revelation 21–22? In this wonderful picture all are in their transformed and everlasting spiritual bodies. Due to the fact that we believe in the resurrection of the body and not the immortality of the soul, there is still a place of dwelling. Some interpreters who do not embrace a literal future millennium still maintain that the new heavens and new earth are the present heavens and earth fully restored. They take the images of destruction as of this world order. Others think of a new creation completely. The promises of Israel and the land are for as long as the sun and the moon endure. However, in that day where we read there is no sun, there are still distinct nations and peoples, all with their distinct glory. God has a destiny and a place for all the redeemed peoples, and the God who loves variety preserves distinct cultures. Only in that everlasting age will we say as Richard Lovelace, the church historian, said to me in personal conversation, that the promises of God will be fulfilled in the letter or in the better. For me, the eventual destiny of Israel in the land, never to be plucked up, leads to a future literal millennium on earth. However, beyond that age, we are happy for God to determine the places for all his people in that everlasting time when there will be no more death!

BIBLIOGRAPHY

Hengenstenburg, W. E. *The Christology of the Old Testament*. Grand Rapids: Kregel, 1970.

Heschel, Susannah. "From Jesus to Shylock: Christian Supersessionism and the *Merchant of Venice*." *Harvard Theological Review* 9 (2006) 407–31.

Horner, Barry. *Future Israel*. Nashville: B & H Academic, 2007.

Kaiser, Walter C. "Single Meaning, Unified Referents: Accurate and Authoritative Citations of the Old Testament by the New Testament." In *Three Views on the New Testament Use of the Old Testament*, edited by Kenneth Berding and Jonathan Lunde, 45–89. Grand Rapids: Zondervan, 2008.

Konstant, David, editor. *The Catechism of the Catholic Church*. London: Burns & Oates, 2004.

Luther, Martin. *Luther's Works: Word and Sacrament 1*. Edited by E. Theodore Bachmann. Luther's Works 35. Philadelphia: Fortress, 1960.

MacIntyre, Alasdair C. *Whose Justice? Which Rationality?* Notre Dame, IN: University of Notre Dame Press, 1988.

Paul VI, Pope. "Declaration on the Relation of the Church to Non-Christian Religions: *Nostra Aetate*." (1965). Online: http://www.vatican.va/archive/hist_councils/ii_vatican_council/documents/vat-ii_decl_19651028_nostra-aetate_en.html.

Williams, Rowan. "Holy Land and Holy People." In *Challenging Christian Zionism: Theology, Politics and the Israel-Palestine Conflict*, edited by Naim Ateek, et al., 293–303. London: Melisende, 2005.

❖ 4 ❖

Toward a Messianic Jewish Theology of Reconciliation in the Light of the Arab-Israeli Conflict

Neither Dispensationalist Nor Supersessionist?

Richard Harvey

INTRODUCTION

TO WHAT EXTENT ARE Messianic Jews equipped to engage theologically and politically with their Arab Christian brothers and sisters, and develop their theological thinking and political involvement to resolve the Middle East conflict? This contribution will explore from a Messianic Jewish perspective the potential for interaction with other Christian voices and stakeholders in the conflict. It will then survey the implications for peacemaking of the different Messianic Jewish theologies of the land and the future of Israel. By examining how Messianic Jews respond to other voices in the debate, and examining the different views they hold, it invites a discussion between Messianic Jews and others. This discussion challenges Messianic Jews to address the difficult questions, not only of their own identity and theology, but also of the need for justice, peace, and reconciliation in the midst of a deeply rooted conflict for which no easy resolution is in sight. In conclusion the author's own perspective will be offered.

The present article does not claim to speak for all or even any particular segment of Messianic Jewish thought.[1] However, it is generally true that Messianic Jewish theology is based on two "epistemic priorities"—the Messiahship of Yeshua (Jesus) and the continuing election of Israel (the Jewish people).[2] This chapter attempts a preliminary survey of Messianic Jewish theology on the subject of reconciliation, with a particular focus on Messianic Jewish perspectives on the future of Israel. We note the present state of Messianic Jewish eschatologies and their implications for engagement in political action and reconciliation ministry with our Palestinian Christian brothers and sisters. Messianic Jews, in addition to their belief in Yeshua as Messiah, owe a fundamental loyalty to and identification with the aspirations of the Jewish people that have been achieved in the establishment of the State of Israel. They show a concern for security and peace that largely reflects current Israeli and Jewish political views but are not united in their analysis of the situation, their programs for change, or their theological interpretation of the present conflict. Neither are they, with a few rare exceptions, experienced in or equipped to engage with other Christian perspectives on the conflict; they have often developed their thinking within a vacuum or a strongly Christian Zionist perspective. This essay makes a plea for a broader and more realistic engagement with some hard questions. In what way is it possible to work for peace, reconciliation, and restorative justice while still affirming the ongoing election of Israel (the Jewish people), which includes the promise of the land of Israel to the descendants of Abraham, Isaac, and Jacob?

ENGAGEMENT WITH OTHER VOICES

Messianic Jews are but one small and minority voice that is found on the continuum of Christian approaches to the conflict.[3] Other representative voices that speak into the politics and theology of the conflict include:[4]

1. For a general survey of Messianic Jewish theology, see Harvey, *Mapping*, 264–76. NKJV (New King James Version) has been used for all Scripture quotations.

2. For a fuller discussion of how these epistemic priorities are defined and held in tension, see Harvey, *Mapping*, 262–84.

3. Merkeley, *Christian Attitudes*.

4. For the summary of other views, see Harvey, "The Need for a Bridging Narrative."

- Christians campaigning for justice for the Palestinians (Ben White, Stephen Sizer, Colin Chapman, Christian Aid)[5]
- Palestinian liberation theologians (Naim Ateek)
- Israeli-Palestinian Ubuntu/reconciliation perspectives (Elias Chacour, Musalaha)
- Peacemakers and observers (Mennonites, Quakers, and Concordis International)
- Pro-Israel lobby groups, including Christian Zionists (International Christian Embassy, John Hagee)

A Messianic Jewish theology of reconciliation will need to engage with these different stakeholders and the positions they hold. This must be done at the level of both public engagement and theological reflection. Messianic Jews both in Israel and the Diaspora find this a challenge for several reasons. Their loyalty to the Jewish people and the State of Israel is already under suspicion because they believe in Yeshua as Messiah. This problematizes their rights as citizens, their status as immigrants, and their ability to speak into the political debate.

What is also problematic is that Messianic Jews generally situate themselves on one side of what Robert Rotberg characterizes as the "double helix" of narratives regarding Israel-Palestine—two contradictory perspectives on the conflict that both portray the opposite "side" as guilty and itself as the victim. In this context there is a vital need for Messianic Jews and others involved in the conflict to construct a "bridging narrative" that can begin to bring together the various understandings of the history of the conflict and construct workable options for the short and long-term future.[6]

How can Messianic Jews respond to the voices of others? A brief interaction with each approach is given before addressing different views within Messianic Judaism itself.

1. Christians Campaigning for Justice for the Palestinians

Christians campaigning for justice for the Palestinians, often labeled "Christian anti-Zionists,"[7] meet with significant disagreement from

---

5. See White, *Israeli Apartheid*; Sizer, *Zion's Christian Soldiers?*; Chapman, *Whose Promised Land?*

6. See Rotberg, *Israeli and Palestinian Narratives of Conflict*.

7. For the usage of the term "Christian anti-Zionism," see Ye'or, "Christian Anti-Zionism," para. 1; and Nerel, "Anti-Zionism."

Messianic Jews. Their historical analysis, political loyalties, and theological interpretation are called into question as delegitimizing the rights of the Jewish people to the land of Israel. They are seen as supersessionist in their attempt to deny the Jewish people today any continuity with the Israel of the Old Testament Scriptures, either physically and politically or in terms of salvation history.[8]

Stephen Sizer is a prominent spokesman for Christian anti-Zionism, and his work is polemical in its deconstruction of dispensational premillennialism and Christian support for the State of Israel on the grounds of the particular fulfillment of prophecy in the return of the Jewish people to the land and the establishment of the State of Israel. Sizer counterposes "covenant theology," which sees the promises to Israel (land, covenant, temple, etc.) as being fulfilled in Christ, as the alternative to "dispensationalism/restorationism," which takes "literally" the ongoing physical fulfillment of such promises.[9] Needless to say, such a dichotomy oversimplifies complex issues of theological interpretation.

Many Messianic Jews would affirm the critique of his views as expressed by orthodox Jewish Israeli Faydra Shapiro:

> *Zion's Christian Soldiers* never pretends to be the work of objective scholarship and should not be thought of as such. The author has a very strong opinion that is anti-Israel and highly critical of Christians (or presumably anyone) who support Zionism. Sizer's passionate anti-Zionism and anti-Judaism give this work a great deal of energy, yet they harm any scholarly aspirations this book might have. Sizer writes in the preface that the "fear of being labeled an anti-Semite is a powerful disincentive" to challenging Christian support for Israel. Rather than simple anti-Semitism, his work expresses something more complex, deeper, and ultimately more terrifying—a sincere, theological, Christian anti-Judaism. In several instances the reader hardly knows whether to laugh or cry.[10]

8. For discussion of supersessionism, see Soulen, *The God of Israel*. In this chapter I use the term *supersessionism* employed by Soulen as the structural supersessionism that rereads the biblical metanarrative omitting the election of Israel as a key stage in the history of salvation and that sees no continuing relevance of the Jewish people outside of the new covenant in Christ. "Replacement theology" is a more popular and emotionally laden term that lacks the theological precision of Soulen's discussion; therefore, it is not used in this chapter.

9. See Sizer, *Christian Zionism*, 255–64.

10. Shapiro, "Review of *Zion's Christian Soldiers*."

Shapiro models a response to Sizer with which most Messianic Jews would concur. Sizer's views are as polemical as the Zionist position he attacks. They are interpreted by Messianic Jews as the product of overt or implicit Christian anti-Judaism, and while Sizer is at pains to deny the charge, they are understood as an expression of anti-Semitism.[11] Aaron Abramson voices similar misgivings, noting his critique of Sizer's "uneven approach to theology and politics of the Middle East conflict." Abramson writes:

> His theological method consistently employs emotive and polemic language. Pejorative labels are associated with dispensationalism and other theologies that espouse Restorationism. His aggressive methodology has been recognized as a form of "negative campaigning," which tarnishes the reputation of others while lacking personal reflection and criticism. Such an approach has been more accurately described as "anti-Christian Zionism" or "anti-dispensationalism," rather than "Covenant theology" . . . Furthermore, his research suffers from inadequate personal theological reflection. Instead he relies upon the views of other "covenantalists" which are insufficiently presented in his thesis. Sizer's dualistic theological approach ultimately shapes his New Covenant views and his eschatological understanding of Israel . . .
>
> Similar weaknesses are perceptible in his political readings of the Middle-East conflict. He expresses ample concern for suffering Palestinians, but fails to seriously consider the anti-Semitism and Jewish suffering which has plagued Jewish identity. As previously argued, his method is polemicized and polarized against the State of Israel. Such a reading is unbalanced and Manichean in outlook.[12]

While the accusation of Manichaeism may be overstating the case, it is clear that the critique of Sizer's position is strongly adversarial. In fact, a dispute rages on the Internet between Sizer and his opponents, which at the level of blog and counter-blog is as polarized and hostile as the conflict on the ground.[13]

11. Heated exchanges between Sizer and his critics have led to a series of accusations and counteraccusations, police investigations, and claims about the suppression of free speech. The present writer has attempted to mediate between the parties, with little success. See blog posts, e.g., Weissman, "Anglican Group Intimidating"; and Sizer, "Seismic Shock: One Year On."

12. Abramson, "Stephen Sizer's," 23.

13. See, e.g., Sizer, "Are Israel and Apartheid South Africa Really Different?"; and http://seismicshock.wordpress.com/ for the campaign against Sizer.

However, there needs to be a more open and less antagonistic engagement with those who hold such strongly charged political and theological positions. The present writer has had several debates and dialogues with Colin Chapman, another writer whose work argues a strong Palestinian reading of the history of the conflict. Chapman sees a future spiritual restoration of the Jewish people to their Messiah in his reading of Romans 9–11. But his interpretation of the New Testament's understanding of Jesus as the fulfillment of the Old Testament types of land, temple, and nation leaves no room for a continuing theological significance for the land of Israel. Over several years discussions have revolved around the understanding of the history of the Middle East conflict, the injustices of land deprivation and humanitarian suffering of the Palestinians, and the theological interpretation of this history. Below are some recent questions posed by Chapman (italicized) and my responses.[14]

1. I'd like to know some of the points in my survey of the history that you feel are biased or inaccurate. I fully understand that there are huge differences between the Jewish and Palestinian narratives, the ways they tell their stories. But I don't think there is a great deal of doubt about the bare facts—the increase in the numbers of Jewish immigrants from 5 percent in 1880 and the increasing tensions as a result of the perceived goals of the immigrants, etc. The main sources for my telling of the story are Jewish, and I don't think that all the new Israeli historians like Tom Segev, Benny Morris, Avi Shlaim, and Ilan Pappé can be dismissed as being revisionist and therefore unreliable.

"I disagree with the way you tell the narrative. While I read critically and with interest the 'revisionist historians,' many of the details they report are matters of heated debate, such as Ilan Pappé's defense of the account of one of his students of the alleged massacre in the Palestinian village of Al-Tantura during the war in 1948. Your use of terms such as 'ethnic cleansing' for the policies of the IDF is polemical

14. Chapman, e-mail correspondence with author, December 13, 2009, which reveals the mutual regard developed between us over thirty years of discussions: "Dear Richard, many thanks for the session on Thursday! It's always good to be able to disagree in public, though I always feel frustrated at the end that we haven't had enough time to engage with each other or to engage with the participants in the course. So I thought I would set down a few points about our discussion partly to clarify my own thinking and partly to try to move the discussion between us forward. I sometimes feel that you and I are going round in circles, going over the same ground again and again and not actually moving forward very much! These are the main areas I would want to explore further with you . . . "

and inflammatory. The 'bare facts' have to be set in the broader context of the politics of the region, the way that both Arab and Israeli positions were used to further the interests of the Imperial powers. I factor the psychological impact of the increasing Jewish population from 1880 with the suffering of the Jewish people escaping the *pogroms* and holocaust in Europe, and am moved by the suffering of my people as much if not more. In terms of a moral calculus of 'who suffered more,' it would be invidious to make a judgment."

2. I would love to sit down with you and go through my statements of the two different starting points and find out which particular sentences/ phrases you do and do not accept. I understand your unwillingness to be pushed into a box and own the labels of "Restorationism" or "Covenant Theology." But I find it difficult to understand that you say that you don't accept either of the two starting points and want to own a third position. Could you articulate your own starting point in the same way that I have attempted to articulate the starting points of the Restorationists and Dispensationalists on the one hand and Covenant Theology on the other? Would it be a mixture of the two positions I have given or something completely different?

"My starting point for a Messianic Jewish theology of election is a non-supersessionist biblical metanarrative. Both the 'restorationist' and 'covenantal' alternatives you propose have been framed in the light of, and in reaction to, the wider Christian tradition. Following R. Kendal Soulen's *The God of Israel and Christian Theology*, I see the history of the Church's understanding of the election of Israel as superseded by the new Israel, the Church, as fundamentally flawed by a misreading of the Scriptures in the light of Christian anti-Judaism. The building blocks of this metanarrative are creation; fall; the election of Israel to be a means of blessing for the nations and preparation for the coming of the Messiah; redemption through the death and resurrection of the Messiah; restoration and the consummation of all things. This means that Israel (the Jewish people) has an ongoing election, in partnership with the nations grafted in to an enlarged and renewed Israel. The election of Israel (the Jewish people) carries the covenantal privilege and responsibility of righteous stewardship of the land of Israel."

3. I have great difficulty in understanding what you mean by your accusation that I am functioning with a kind of "Aristotelian dualism" which makes a distinction between the literal and the spiritual. My approach is that the NT writers see Jesus as the fulfillment (a very biblical concept) of everything in the OT—the Abrahamic covenant, the Davidic kingship, the temple, the priesthood, the sacrificial system, the coming of the kingdom of God, etc.—and also the land. The incarnation is a physical incarnation—there's no Docetism—so we're not talking about something purely spiritual. The NT writers see the coming of the kingdom of God in the incarnation of Jesus as the real, the substantial fulfillment of all these themes of the OT that were very physical. I feel that "spiritualizing" is a very slippery term and is probably overused, and the distinction between "literal interpretation" and "spiritual interpretation" isn't always clear or helpful. The letter to the Hebrews sees Jesus as the fulfillment—the real, substantial, fulfillment—of so much in the OT, and even relates the very physical theme of the Promised Land to the present experience of every believer in the Messiah (Heb 4). If this is labeled as "spiritualizing," then so be it; but isn't this the main way—even the only way—the writer attempts to interpret the significance of the coming of the Messiah? Is there any suggestion that the writer secretly still holds to another way of interpreting the OT—a literal way—which is different from the one he has developed? The only Zion and Zionism that he is interested in is "the city of the living God, the heavenly Jerusalem" (12:22). I cannot see anything in the NT to suggest that the Jewish disciples continued after the Resurrection to hold onto their earlier understanding that the coming of the kingdom of God would mean the establishment of a sovereign independent Jewish state in the land.

"Like you, I am unhappy with the overuse of the distinction between 'literal/physical' and 'spiritual.' But for me this means both the 'physicality' and the 'spirituality' of the land promises are held together. I look for a redeemed Israel back in the land, living in peace and justice alongside her neighbors. I do not want to separate the heavenly Zion from the physical Jerusalem, but rather to see the spiritual truth of Yeshua's teaching lived out in the physical reality of the Old City today. What you see as an argument from silence, I see as an assumed position—that the land of Israel, the people of Israel, and the kingdom of God, would eventually be restored."

4. I have said many times that I do not accept the charge that I am teaching either supersessionism or replacement theology. I recognize without hesitation that this has been a dominant view for centuries and one that has led to some disastrous consequences. I have said that it was a sad day when Christians started describing the Church as "the new Israel."

So, if I say that the Church is Israel—but Israel renewed and restored in the Messiah (using the language of [N. T.] Wright and many others)—I don't see how you can possibly accuse me of teaching that the Church has taken the place of biblical Israel, that the Church has superseded Israel or replaced Israel. In Paul's analogy in Romans 9–11, Gentile believers are grafted into biblical Israel and Gentile believers come to inherit all the covenant promises that were given to Abraham and his descendants. In this context Paul can say that the Jewish people, biblical Israel, "are loved for the sake of their forefathers" (present tense); but he also says that those of them who do not believe are "cut off because of unbelief." There is a real tension here, but it seems that Paul was able to live with the two sides of the tension—that the covenant promises are still available to all who see themselves as the physical descendants of Abraham, but that they are cut off and no longer share the benefits of that covenant because of their unbelief. I have constantly tried to distance myself from replacement theology and supersessionism, and I hope you can see the difference between what I and others are saying and what supersessionists have unfortunately been saying and are still saying.

"I realize that you wish to distance your position from the historical supersessionism of church history. But I regard Tom Wright's position as continuing this supersessionist position. See the criticism leveled at him on this by Douglas Harink in *Paul among the Postliberals*.[15] When you say that Paul lives with two sides of the tension, the ongoing election of Israel (the Jewish people) and their unbelief in Yeshua cutting them off from the benefits of the covenant, I do not agree with this reading. They are still within the one covenant (in which the nations are also incorporated through the Messiah), and their election has not been substituted with the election of others. Yes, they do not enjoy all the benefits of this election (faith in Messiah, forgiveness of sins, new life in him), but they have not forfeited this election either."

5. I long to hear more from you about the realities of what is happening on the ground in the West Bank and Gaza and how you respond to these situations. I hear your strong plea for reconciliation and for new ways of doing theology. When strongly pressed, you do seem to support the idea of a Palestinian state within the '67 borders, over against Chawkat Moucarry, who argues for the one-state solution. But I wonder what your theology encourages you to think about the Jewish settlers on the West

---

15. Harink, *Paul among the Postliberals*, 189.

Bank who, according to yesterday's Times *[12 Dec 2009], are demonstrating against Netanyahu's partial freeze on settlements and burning Korans? According to the report, the banners of these demonstrators say: "Obama wants us frozen, God wants us chosen" and "God's Bible gave us this land." Does your interpretation of the Hebrew Bible allow you to challenge their interpretation, or do you support it? I want to see more of how your theology relates to the present, painful realities on the ground, remembering our starting point on Thursday that the whole discussion needs to be seen in the context of our witness to the Gospel in the Muslim world.*

"My theology challenges racism, xenophobia, and Islamophobia, so I oppose the burning of the Koran just as I would oppose the burning of the Talmud or the New Testament. I personally favor a two-state solution, as my theology allows for the negotiability of territory in the search for peace. This challenges the settler movement's ideology. My interpretation of the Hebrew Bible is not factored through Rabbi Kook[16] and his disciples' mystical re-interpretation in the light of political Zionism, but through a different messianic redemption that has come through the Messiah Yeshua. However, I do not rule out of the scope of redemption the land of Israel itself."

Such responses show the challenges to Messianic Jews of engaging with the views of Sizer, Chapman, and others, but they cannot be avoided.

2. Palestinian Liberation Theology (Naim Ateek and Sabeel)[17]

Naim Ateek's "Palestinian liberation theology" has not met with a welcome from most Messianic Jews, who see in it neo-Marcionite[18] tendencies to downplay the significance of Israel in the Hebrew Bible as a product of a liberal hermeneutic and a strong political agenda that leaves little room for constructive engagement.

16. For Rabbi Kook's development of a religious justification for Zionism that became the ideology of the settler movement see Goldberg, *To the Promised Land*, 148–57.

17. For surveys of different approaches, see Houston, "Towards Interdependence."

18. Marcion was a second-century Christian heretic who was excommunicated for denying the compatibility of the action of God of the Old Testament with the teachings of Jesus, repudiating the Hebrew Bible and much of the New Testament. *Neo-Marcionism* is the term used to describe "bypassing, relegating or even rubbishing the Old Testament on the ground of the novelty of the New Testament revelation." See Nichols, *Lovely, like Jerusalem*, 3. See Olsen, "Going Deeper" (http://www.ignatiusinsight.com/features2007/anichols_interview_july07.asp). In this context it is used as a label for this who see no relevance for New Testament understanding of the significance of Israel in the Hebrew Bible.

De-Judaization of the Bible is seen, for example, in the liberation theology of Naim Ateek, who writes, "As a Christian, I cannot begin my study of the Bible from Genesis . . . What God did for the world in Christ far exceeded the best that the prophets predicted and anticipated."[19] Gershon Nerel describes Sabeel's website as "one of the most aggressive in its anti-Zionist and anti-Israel campaign. It gives the reader the impression of a serious religious site, aimed toward intellectuals who espouse liberation theology."[20] Nerel also critiques the thinking of other Palestinian Christian voices. He sees views articulated by the Lutheran pastor Mitri Raheb as no less explicit: "Israel failed because it laid claim to election as law, according to Paul. But Christ has put an end to all law (Rom 10:4). In him the law has achieved its real purpose and election its original meaning."[21] For Raheb and Ateek, then, Israel's election and God's covenant with Israel in the Old Testament, which includes divine promises related to the land, are null and void after the coming of Christ and Israel's rejection of Christ.[22]

Given such a strongly adversarial perspective in Palestinian liberation theology to that of Messianic Jews, Messianic Jews have demonstrated little interaction with the underlying concerns of the Palestinian liberation theologians—concerns for justice and recognition of the Palestinian cause. Instead, Messianic Jews have responded with an equally polemical justification of their own position. Nerel's position is common among Messianic Jews, but not all would concur with his position. However, it demonstrates why there has been little occasion for direct discussion between those of radically different perspectives on the conflict, and its political and theological interpretation.

3. Israeli-Palestinian Ubuntu/Reconciliation Perspectives (Musalaha)[23]

While a fully developed theology and praxis of reconciliation has yet to be articulated by Musalaha, the possibility of engagement with this

19. Ateek, "Putting Christ at the Centre," 57; see Nerel, "Anti-Zionism," 8, 77–87.

20. Ibid., 8. A Hebrew version of this paper appeared in *Mahanaim: A Review for Jewish Thought and Culture—Between Jews and Christians: Contemporary Issues* 15 (2003) 77–87; and Nerel, "Spiritual *Intifada* of Palestinian Christians and Messianic Jews," in *Israel: His People, His Land, His Story*, 205–19.

21. Raheb, *I Am a Palestinian Christian*, 68.

22. Nerel, "Anti-Zionism," 25.

23. See Loden et al., *The Bible and the Land*; Munayer, *Seeking and Pursuing Peace*; Munayer, *In the Footsteps of Our Father Abraham*.

significant ministry is a challenge to Messianic Jews. Judy Houston's master's thesis examined the theory and practice of Musalaha's ministry in the light of Desmond Tutu's Ubuntu theology and that of Miroslav Volf.[24]

Houston positions the theology of Musalaha as an alternative to dispensationalism and Christian Zionism, to the covenant theology of Sizer and Chapman, and to Palestinian liberation theology. She argues for an inclusive, interdependent theology that draws on the insights and participation of those who address each other from across the barricades. To use Volf's terms, it is in the "embrace" of the "excluded" that true reconciliation comes.[25] There is significant material for Messianic Jews to address here, as it touches their own conflicted roles and identities, as Jews, believers in Jesus, and those engaged in the geo-political conflict. How this relates to their theology of the land of Israel will be addressed below.

4. Peacemakers and Observers (Mennonites, Quakers, and Concordis)

External peacemaking agencies and reconciliation facilitators have attempted to engage interested parties on both sides of the Arab-Israeli divide in consultations and joint activities. Messianic Jews have been involved in these consultations, and have contributed to the final outcomes of their reports. They serve as working examples of the peacemaking and reconciliation process, although Messianic Jews have yet to articulate a clear theology and praxis of such encounters.[26]

5. Pro-Israel Lobby Groups, Including Christian Zionist (International Christian Embassy, John Hagee)

Messianic Jews are aware of the strengths and weaknesses of the Christian Zionist position.[27] While offering friendship and political support for the State of Israel and the Zionist cause, the Christian Zionist can take an uncritical and polarized view of the conflict, in the light of a particular hermeneutic of Scripture and a reading of contemporary political events.

24. Houston, "Towards Interdependence."

25. Volf, *Exclusion and Embrace.*

26. Dixon, *British Churches.*

27. For articles strongly critical of Christian Zionism, see Maoz, "Christian Embassy"; and Zaretsky, "International Christian Embassy."

Some Christian Zionists are reluctant to identify and stand alongside Messianic Jews for fear this may jeopardize their attempts to build friendship and trust with the Israeli authorities, and with Jewish people who do not believe in Jesus. Some Christian Zionists, such as John Hagee, incline to universalism in their soteriology, so strong is their desire to affirm the election of Israel (the Jewish people).[28]

Having briefly surveyed the context in which Messianic Jews need to formulate their approach to peacemaking and reconciliation, we will now examine the various perspectives they have on the significance of the land of Israel, and the implications for practical involvement in the reconciliation process.

5. Messianic Jewish Views on the Land

Messianic Jews are uniquely placed when it comes to a theology of the land of Israel. They locate themselves geographically, spiritually, and eschatologically within what is "sacred space" to them. Their identity as Jews and as Jewish believers in the Messiah is tied to their sense of the land of Israel and the people of Israel as fundamental to their worldview and *Sitz im Leben*. Therefore, it is difficult to conceive of the land of Israel in neutral terms, much less as something to be traded for peace and security. It is also difficult to balance consideration of the plight of the Palestinians in their demands for restorative justice and peace with the key concerns of security and identity that often take priority for Jewish believers in Jesus. When we consider views put forward on the significance and future of the land of Israel, Messianic Jews have generally borrowed the systems of eschatology of Protestant conservative evangelicalism and have done little to wed their eschatologies to engaged activity in Palestinian-Israeli dialogue, the politics of the peace process, or the work of reconciliation.

Bodil Skjøtt surveyed Israeli Messianic Jewish beliefs on the land of Israel.[29] Ninety-four Messianic Jews of mixed age, gender, and education living in Jerusalem, the West Bank, and throughout Israel were asked a series of questions to ascertain their views on what the Bible teaches about the land and the Jewish people, on the significance of the return of the Jews to the land, on its proper boundaries, on how Messianic Jews

28. Harvey, "Implicit Universalism."
29. Skjøtt, "Messianic Believers," 72–81.

should relate to Palestinian Christians, and on how Messianic Jews relate to the Palestinian people and their demand for a state. While small, the survey sample represents a significant proportion of Messianic Jews in the land.[30]

Skjøtt found that the majority of respondents believe that the biblical promises of the land apply to the Jewish people forever, and this was an important part of the teaching of Jesus.[31] However, while 95 percent understood that the Bible clearly promised the land to the Jewish people, only 20 percent saw this as an essential part of the teaching of Jesus. Only one in five saw the message of the gospel as incomplete without a clear statement of the right of the Jewish people to the land. While the eternal validity of the promises of the land to the Jewish people was accepted by 90 percent, it was not regarded as an essential element of the gospel.

The majority of respondents saw the return of the Jews to the land as the fulfillment of God's promises, and understood Zionism not just "as a secular movement but rather as a necessary instrument in the fulfillment of prophecies and in God's program to bring the Jewish people to faith in Jesus."[32] However, this percentage varied among male and female respondents (72 percent and 62 percent respectively), and only 57 percent believed that the Jewish people would never again be exiled from the land; one in twelve disagreed with the statement, and a third were unsure.

As regards the boundaries of the land of Israel, 76 percent saw Judea and Samaria—the Occupied Territories—as included within the State of Israel. Fifty-nine percent included the Golan Heights, and a surprising 49 percent believed areas to the east of the Jordan River should also be part of the State of Israel. Skjøtt suggests that this view is derived from the respondents' eschatological scheme that sees the boundaries of Israel in the "last days" as extending beyond those of the present state, although only 50 percent believed that the Bible gives clearly defined borders. Skjøtt also suggests that most respondents, from the confused

---

30. According to Kjær-Hansen and Skjøtt, 94, respondents represent 3 percent of Israel's Messianic Jewish congregational members. See Kjær-Hansen and Skjøtt, *Facts and Myths*.

31. Skjøtt, "Messianic Believers," 75.

32. Ibid., 76.

nature of their responses to this question, "are not sure whether we are living in the last times."[33]

As regards relationships with Palestinian Arab Christians, 94 percent thought that there should be more fellowship between Messianic Jews and Arab Christians, and 85 percent believed that developing this fellowship was more important than land issues. On the political rights of the Palestinians, the majority of respondents believed that Palestinians living in the land have as much right as Jews to remain there, but nearly half the respondents did not wish to grant Palestinian refugees the right of return to the land in which they or their family had once lived.[34]

The survey found areas of uncertainty amongst Messianic Jews, particularly on the borders of the land and the right of Palestinians to return. These levels were higher among women and those under 35. The most agreement was found on the biblical teaching on the rights of the Jews to the land, and on the need for fellowship with Palestinians. As Skjøtt wryly comments, "Presumably, in order to achieve greater fellowship, someone is going to have to back down on the question of ownership of Judea and Samaria/West Bank."[35]

Skjøtt interprets the results as showing that Messianic Jews inconsistently support the peace process with a willingness to share the land, on one hand, and also maintain, on the other hand, the claim of ownership of the West Bank. While the majority of Messianic Jews in the survey upheld the promises of the land to the Jewish people as permanently valid, this did not necessarily affect whether they voted for a particular political party whose program was to hold on to all land. Nor is it straightforward how the biblical promises of the land are to be interpreted and applied in the contemporary situation. "The certainty with which the Bible speaks is not easily translated into a clear understanding of the present political situation in which we all have to act and react."[36]

Skjøtt concludes by noting that while respondents agreed that the teaching of the Bible on the land was clear, they disagreed as to the importance of the land in the teaching of Jesus. Messianic Jews could be taking this in one of two ways. Either its lack of prominence in the teaching of Jesus has little significance, as Jesus did not "negate or nullify

33. Ibid., 77.
34. Ibid., 78.
35. Ibid., 79.
36. Ibid., 80.

the promises," or else the lack of importance it had to Jesus should lead his followers to "look at the question through the teachings of Jesus and not put emphasis on issues that Jesus did not speak about, perhaps even avoided."[37] While Messianic Jews choose the first option, Skjøtt, whose aim in doing the survey was to "provide a tool for positive and constructive self-evaluation" that would "provide direction and inspiration" for the building up of the Messianic community in Israel, clearly implies that they should also consider the second.

Building on Skjøtt's findings and anticipating future trends in the Messianic movement in Israel, Kai Kjær-Hansen observed continuing millennial "fever" and a strengthening of right-wing political attitudes strongly tied to dispensational premillennialism.[38] "I have to say that I consider the end-times fever—all other things being equal—much more dangerous and destructive for Jewish believers in Israel and for a sound development of the Messianic movement than, for example, a tightening of the anti-mission legislation or increased harassment, opposition or downright persecution of Jewish believers in Israel . . . Jewish believers in Israel would do themselves and the rest of us an enormous favour if they disassociated themselves from this day's speculative prophecy teachers!"[39]

Kjær-Hansen reviews the trend of eschatological speculation, recognizing it as an unhelpful focus when it distracts from the practical realities of living in the land, relating with other Messianic believers and engaging in the quest for peace, justice, and reconciliation with the Palestinians. "I also hope that the movement as such will not become so much involved in the eschatological drama of the future that it does not take the present challenges seriously."[40]

Dan Cohn-Sherbok summarizes the eschatology of Messianic Judaism along the lines of Christian Zionism: "Because of the centrality of Israel in God's plan . . . Messianic Jews are ardent Zionists. They support Israel because the Jewish State is viewed as a direct fulfillment of biblical prophecy. Although Israel is far from perfect, Messianic Jews believe that God is active in the history of the nation and that the Jews

37. Ibid.
38. Kjær-Hansen, "Upside-Down."
39. Ibid., 1.
40. Ibid., 15.

will never be driven out of their land again. While God loves the Arabs, he gave the Holy Land to his chosen people."[41]

While this is a fair assessment of those streams of the movement influenced by dispensational premillennialism and historical premillennialism, there are alternative voices within the Messianic movement who articulate less dogmatic and more speculative proposals. Rich Nichol's amillennialist position, Baruch Maoz's studied agnosticism, and Mark Kinzer's reconceptualizing of eschatology in line with the Jewish covenantal theology of David Novak are illustrations of dissatisfaction with the dominant influence of dispensationalist thought.[42]

Arnold Fruchtenbaum's dispensational premillennialist system pays due attention to the continuing place of Israel and the role of Jewish believers.[43] It preserves the distinction between the church and Israel rather than concede to supersessionism or a bilateral ecclesiology. Such a view holds attractions to the Messianic movement, preserving its own distinctive place and identity as belonging to both Israel and the church. Messianic Judaism has a special role to play as an expression of the believing remnant. The land of Israel—both as the original evidence of God's covenantal promises with the patriarchs, and as the place of dénouement for the final outcome of God's purposes—still has significance. While Fruchtenbaum is wary of spelling out the contemporary political implications of his scheme, it is clear that he sees negotiation of territory for peace as a ploy of the conspiracy against Israel and not something to be contemplated. His reluctance to deal with the issue of the Palestinian refugees is also to be noted.

Baruch Maoz challenges the assumptions and methods of such a hermeneutic, retaining the complexities of the biblical material, which Fruchtenbaum carefully systematizes.[44] His own eschatology may be labeled as "studied agnosticism." Maoz recognizes and critiques the hermeneutic of dispensationalism that emerged within the particular set of historical conditions of rationalism, romanticism, and nineteenth-

41. Cohn-Sherbok, "Introduction," xi.

42. See Nichol, "Are We Really at the End," 203–10; Kinzer, "Beginning with the End"; Novak, "Beyond Supersessionism"; and Harvey, *Mapping*, esp. chap. 9 for full expositions of these views.

43. See Fruchtenbaum, *Israelology*; Fruchtenbaum, *Footsteps of the Messiah*; Fruchtenbaum, "Eschatology and Messianic Jews," 211–19.

44. Maoz, "A Review of Premillennialism."

century positivism.[45] If Messianic Judaism disassociates itself from dispensationalism, it would render less dogmatic some of the assertions of the movement and would open itself to a broader range of theological influences within Judaism and Christianity. Maoz's views on the politics of the Arab-Israeli context are not expounded. It is clear he has deep reservations with the Christian Zionist position, but he adopts a Zionist left-of-center politics linked to a Protestant Reformed position in which the relationship between contemporary and Old Testament Israel is one of both continuity and discontinuity.[46]

Both dispensational and historic premillennialism emphasize the land of Israel as the locus for the fulfillment of prophecy, and recognize God's continuing purposes for the people of Israel. Her re-gathering in unbelief, eventual salvation, and future role in the millennial kingdom are all affirmed by both systems, which are more closely linked than their various advocates might suppose. It is likely that the consensus in the Messianic movement will remain among the two types of premillennialism. Despite the exegetical, hermeneutical, and theological limitations of the dispensationalist position, it continues to be held as the majority view. The radical reconceptualization of Kinzer and Nichol and the studied agnosticism of Maoz are theologically venturesome but at present lack popular appeal. Daniel Juster's historic premillennial position, with its more nuanced exegetical base and hermeneutical framework, provides an alternative option for those arguing for God's continuing purposes for Israel without dispensationalist features.

Nichol critiques the negative otherworldly tendencies of dispensationalism, and Kinzer explores the proleptic eschatological aspects of traditional Jewish life to give an understanding of this-worldly life as indicative of the days to come. Kinzer and Nichol explore dimensions of Jewish eschatological thinking that are new to the Messianic Jewish movement. The Messianic movement has yet to engage with the Jewish mystical tradition of which the signs of the Messiah's coming to inaugurate the redemption of Israel are so strong a theme.[47]

What is needed is an authentic and coherent eschatology to emerge from within the Messianic Jewish movement that does not rely wholly

45. Cf. Rausch, *Zionism*; and Cohn-Sherbok, *Politics of Apocalypse.*

46. Maoz, "Jerusalem and Justice."

47. See, e.g., Cohen, "Eschatology," 183–88; Cohn-Sherbok, "Afterlife," 456–60, and Cohn-Sherbok, *The Jewish Messiah*; Scholem, *The Messianic Idea.*

on the Christian (or Jewish) thinking that preponderates the discussion. To achieve this, a more robust engagement with the biblical material is needed, with greater awareness of the assumptions that are brought to the texts by the various schools of thought.[48]

The future of Israel, as part of the eschatological map, relates to the broader issues of a theology of land and the land of Israel in particular. A vital task for Messianic Jewish theology is to link eschatology with a practical theology of reconciliation with Arab Christians and the Arab population in the light of the Israel-Palestine conflict.[49] This has yet to be attempted by those who expound a specific eschatological scheme, and it is to be hoped that the present volume of essays will provide a significant stimulus to such an undertaking. Those who see the State of Israel as a fulfillment of prophecy must still give opportunity for self-critical reflection on present issues of justice, peace, and reconciliation whatever their understanding of the future.

What would such an eschatology—with an emphasis on justice and reconciliation—look like? It would hold together the materiality and specificity of God's promises to his people that recognize their re-gathering, restoration to the land, and restoration to the Messiah are all part of his sovereign purposes. But in addition, as a people called to be a light to the nations, Israel is to be a means of justice, peace, and reconciliation with her neighbors. This means sharing her resources, welcoming the stranger, and seeking peace actively. Repentance and restoration must be a part of such a process, as must recognition of the sins of the past, and the ongoing corrosive nature of the conflict in the present. Such a Messianic Jewish theology of reconciliation has yet to be written. My prayer is that the present volume of essays may aid us in that process.

BIBLIOGRAPHY

Abramson, Aaron. "Stephen Sizer's *Christian Zionism: Road-map to Armageddon*: A Critique." Online: http://www.jfjonline.org/Sizer.doc.

Ateek, Naim Stifan. *Justice, and Only Justice: A Palestinian Theology of Liberation.* Maryknoll, NY: Orbis, 1989.

———. "Putting Christ at the Centre: The Land from a Palestinian Christian Perspective." In *The Bible and the Land*, edited by Lisa Loden et al., 55–63. Jerusalem: Musalaha, 2000.

48. For a historical survey of the doctrine of eschatology in Christianity, see Doyle, *Eschatology*.

49. Houston, "Towards Interdependence."

Ateek, Naim, et al., editors. *Jerusalem: What Makes for Peace! : A Palestinian Christian Contribution to Peacemaking.* London: Melisende, 1997.

———, editors. *Faith and the Intifada: Palestinian Christian Voices.* Maryknoll, NY: Orbis, 1992.

Chapman, Colin. *Whose Holy City? Jerusalem and the Israeli-Palestinian Conflict.* Oxford: Lion, 2004.

———. *Whose Promised Land? The Continuing Crisis over Israel and Palestine.* 5th rev. ed. Oxford: Lion, 2002.

Cohen, Arthur A. "Eschatology." In *Contemporary Jewish Religious Thought: Original Essays on Critical Concepts, Movements, and Beliefs,* edited by Arthur A. Cohen and Paul Mendes-Flohr, 183–88. New York: Scribner, 1987.

Cohn-Sherbok, Dan. "Introduction." In *Voices of Messianic Judaism: Confronting Critical Issues Facing a Maturing Movement,* edited by Dan Cohn-Sherbok, ix–xx. Baltimore: Lederer, 2001.

———. "The Afterlife." In *Judaism: History, Belief, and Practice,* 456–60. London: Routledge, 2003.

———. *The Jewish Messiah.* Edinburgh: T. & T. Clark, 1997.

———. *The Politics of Apocalypse: The History and Influence of Christian Zionism.* Oxford: Oneworld, 2006.

Concordis International. "British Churches and the Israeli-Palestinian Conflict," Concordis International Consultation Report (September 2009). Online: http://www .concordis-international.org/files/pdfs/2009_September_Consultation_Summary _ISR-PAL_Cambridge.pdf.

Dixon, Peter, editor. *The British Churches and the Israeli-Palestinian Conflict.* Cambridge: Concordis Papers, 2010.

Doyle, Robert C. *Eschatology and the Shape of Christian Belief.* Carlisle, UK: Paternoster, 1999.

Fruchtenbaum, Arnold G. *Israelology: The Missing Link in Systematic Theology.* 2nd ed. Tustin, CA: Ariel Ministries Press, 1993.

———. *Footsteps of the Messiah: A Study of the Sequence of Prophetic Events.* San Antonio: Ariel Ministries Press, 1982.

———. "Eschatology and Messianic Jews: A Theological Perspective." In *Voices of Messianic Judaism: Confronting Critical Issues Facing a Maturing Movement,* edited by Dan Cohn-Sherbok, 211–19. Baltimore: Lederer, 2001.

Goldberg, David J. *To the Promised Land: A History of Zionist Thought from Its Origins to the Modern State of Israel.* London: Faber & Faber, 2009.

Harink, Douglas. *Paul among the Postliberals: Pauline Theology Beyond Christendom and Modernity.* Grand Rapids: Brazos, 2003.

Harvey, Richard S. "Implicit Universalism In Some Christian Zionism and Messianic Judaism." In *Jesus, Salvation and the Jewish People,* edited by David Parker, n.p. Milton Keynes, UK: Paternoster, 2011.

———. *Mapping Messianic Jewish Theology: A Constructive Approach.* Milton Keynes, UK: Paternoster, 2009.

———. "The Need for a Bridging Narrative." In *The British Churches and the Israeli-Palestinian Conflict,* edited by Peter Dixon, 20–21. Cambridge: Concordis Papers, 2010.

Houston, Judy. "Towards Interdependence, Remembrance and Justice: Reconciliation Ministry in the Israeli/Palestinian Context." MA diss., All Nations Christian College, 2006.

Kjær-Hansen, Kai. "Upside-Down for the Sake of Yeshua: Challenges and Pressures on Israeli Jewish Believers in Jesus." Paper presented at the Seventeenth North American Consultation of the Lausanne Consultation on Jewish Evangelism, Atlanta, Georgia, March 13–15, 2000. Online: http://www.lcje.net/papers/2000/Kjaer-Hansen.pdf.

Kjær-Hansen, Kai, and Bodil F. Skjøtt. *Facts & Myths about the Messianic Congregations in Israel.* Jerusalem: United Christian Council in Israel, 1999.

Kinzer, Mark S. "Beginning with the End: The Place of Eschatology in the Messianic Jewish Canonical Narrative." Paper presented at the Fourth Annual Hashivenu Forum, Pasadena, California, February 2002.

Loden, Lisa et al., editors. *The Bible and the Land.* Jerusalem: Musalaha, 2000.

Maoz, Baruch. "The Christian Embassy in Jerusalem." *Mishkan* 12 (1990) 1–12.

———. "Jerusalem and Justice: A Messianic Jewish Perspective." In *Jerusalem: Past and Present in the Purposes of God,* edited by P. W. L. Walker, 151–73. Cambridge: Tyndale House, 1992.

———. "A Review of Premillennialism." Paper presented to the Elders of Grace and Truth Christian Congregation, Rehovot, December 2003.

Merkeley, Paul Charles. *Christian Attitudes towards the State of Israel.* McGill-Queens Studies in the History of Religion, Series 2. Montreal: McGill-Queen's University Press, 2001.

Moucarry, Chawkat. *Faith to Faith: Christianity & Islam in Dialogue.* Leicester, UK: InterVarsity, 2001.

Munayer, Salim. *Seeking and Pursuing Peace: The Process, the Pain, and the Product.* Jerusalem: Musalaha, 1998.

———, editor. *In the Footsteps of Our Father Abraham.* Jerusalem: Musalaha, 2002.

Nerel, Gershon. "Anti-Zionism in the 'Electronic Church' of Palestinian Christianity." *Mahanaim* 15 (2004) 77–87.

———. "Anti-Zionism in the 'Electronic Church' of Palestinian Christianity." *Analysis of Current Trends in Anti-Semitism* 27 (2006). The Hebrew University of Jerusalem: Vidal Sassoon International Center for the Study of Antisemitism

———. "Spiritual *Intifada* of Palestinian Christians and Messianic Jews." In *Israel: His People, His Land, His Story,* edited by Fred Wright, 205–19. Eastbourne, UK: Thankful, 2005.

Nichol, Richard C. "Are We Really at the End of the End Times? A Reappraisal." In *Voices of Messianic Judaism,* edited by Dan Cohn-Sherbok, 203–10. Baltimore: Lederer, 2001.

Nichols, Aidan. *Lovely, like Jerusalem: The Fulfillment of the Old Testament in Christ and the Church.* San Francisco: Ignatius, 2007.

Novak, David. "Beyond Supersessionism." *First Things* 81:3 (March 1998) 58–60.

Olsen, Carl E. "Going Deeper into the Old Testament: An Interview with Aidan Nichols, OP, Author of *Lovely Like Jerusalem.*" Online: http://www.ignatiusinsight.com/features2007/anichols_interview_july07.asp

Raheb, Mitri. *I Am a Palestinian Christian.* Translated by Ruth C. L. Gritsch, with a foreword by Rosemary Radford Ruether. Minneapolis: Fortress, 1995.

Rausch, David A. *Zionism within Early American Fundamentalism, 1878–1918: A Convergence of Two Traditions.* Texts and Studies in Religion 4. Lewiston, NY: Mellen, 1979.

Rotberg, Robert I., editor. *Israeli and Palestinian Narratives of Conflict: History's Double Helix.* Indiana Series in Middle East Studies. Bloomington: Indiana University Press, 2006.

Shapiro, Faydra L. "Review of *Zion's Christian Soldiers? The Bible, Israel and the Church*, by Stephen Sizer." *Review of Biblical Literature* (2009). Online: www.bookreviews .org/pdf/6781_7345.pdf.

Scholem, Gershom. *The Messianic Idea in Judaism, and Other Essays on Jewish Spirituality.* New York: Schocken, 1971.

Sizer, Stephen R. *Zion's Christian Soldiers? The Bible, Israel and the Church.* Nottingham, UK: InterVarsity, 2007.

————. *Christian Zionism: Road Map to Armageddon?* Downers Grove, IL: IVP Academic, 2004.

————. "Are Israel and Apartheid South Africa Really Different?" Stephen Sizer's blog, January 7, 2010. Online: http://stephensizer.blogspot.com/2010/01/are-israel-and-apartheid-south-africa.html.

————. "Seismic Shock: One Year On." Stephen Sizer's blog, September 18, 2009. Online: http://stephensizer.blogspot.com/search?q=seismic.

Skjøtt. Bodil F. "Messianic Believers and the Land of Israel—a Survey." *Mishkan* 26 (1997) 72–81.

Soulen, R. Kendal. *The God of Israel and Christian Theology.* Minneapolis: Fortress, 1996.

Stuart. "Anglican Group Intimidates Another Blogger." *Seismic Shock* blog, January 28, 2010. Online: http://seismicshock.wordpress.com/2010/01/28/anglican-group-intimidates-another-blogger/.

Volf, Miroslav. *Exclusion and Embrace: Theological Exploration of Identity, Otherness and Reconciliation.* Nashville: Abingdon, 1996.

White, Ben. *Israeli Apartheid: A Beginner's Guide.* London: Pluto, 2009.

Wright, N. T. *Jesus and the Victory of God.* London: SPCK, 1996.

Zaretsky, Tuvya. "The International Christian Embassy in Jerusalem: Christians for Whom and What?" *Mishkan* 12 (1990) 34–36.

Ye'or, Bat. "Christian Anti-Zionism and Dhimmitude." Online: http://www.dhimmitude .org/d_today_christian_antizionism.html.

❖ 5 ❖

Dispensationalism and Support for the State of Israel[1]

John S. Feinberg

IN THE DEBATE AMONG many Christians about Palestinian and Israeli rights and their respective treatment of one another, pro-Palestinian Christians often complain that their pro-Israeli Christian counterparts have been infected by the malady of dispensationalism, and that is why they seem to support everything the modern State of Israel does, regardless of how unjust and oppressive it is to Palestinians. Pro-Israeli Christians often complain that if their pro-Palestinian Christian counterparts properly understood Scripture's end time prophecies, they would not reject what *God* has done in the land of Israel during the twentieth century and has planned for the future. And they would not complain when Israelis take various steps to secure their hold on the land God gave them thousands of years ago.

Many who listen to this debate conclude that the ultimate culprit is dispensationalism and its alleged misunderstanding of end time prophecy about Israel and the nations. Unfortunately, some non-believers hear bits and pieces of this debate and conclude that the problems in

1. Originally presented as a paper at the "Christ at the Checkpoint" conference in Bethlehem, West Bank, March 12–17, 2010. All Scripture quotations taken from the NASB (New American Standard Bible).

the Holy Land could be greatly assuaged if not for these fundamentalist dispensationalists. Non-believers understand neither fundamentalism nor dispensationalism, but these labels (and the views they supposedly represent) become convenient weapons to use against Christianity. They think these two "-*isms*" are at least part of the reason so many conservative Christians seem to turn a deaf ear to the plight of the Palestinians and do not seem particularly disturbed that the peace process in the Middle East moves interminably slow, if at all.

In the midst of such complaints, does it ever occur that the characterization of dispensationalism in view might not be what the position actually requires its proponents to hold? That possibility seems seldom, if ever, even considered.

Even so, might dispensationalism be innocent of the charges lodged against it? Is it really true that dispensationalists are logically bound to support everything the modern State of Israel does, regardless of how oppressive and unjust its actions are? Does dispensational understanding of end time prophecy tie the hands and shut the mouths of believers who would otherwise protest injustice and oppression? The answers to such questions are biblical, theological, and moral; but their implications are very practical and personal, especially for people living in the land of Israel. How should we address such issues?

In this chapter I propose to argue for two theses that address the issue of dispensationalism's support for the modern State of Israel. The first thesis centers on an ethical rule grounded in Scripture. Scripture teaches that neither governments nor private citizens should engage in social, economic, or political oppression and injustice. Hence, my first thesis is that no evangelical theology, including dispensationalism, should support social and political oppression and injustice. Second, even though there are varieties of dispensationalism, core biblical and theological commitments common to dispensational*isms* do not require—i.e., logically entail—supporting governments or people when they commit social and political injustice and oppression.

In what follows, I plan to look at each thesis, explain it, and offer support for it. Thesis two will require the most explanation and defense. Before turning to thesis one, however, I must clarify what I mean by "support" of Israel and "support" of the Palestinians, as I will be using these ideas in this chapter.

THE MEANING OF SUPPORT FOR PALESTINIANS AND ISRAELIS

When discussing whether one should support Israel and/or the Palestinians, there are a number of things one might have in mind. For the sake of this paper, I want to define three types of support and clarify which is at issue. An initial sense of "support" is that one supports the right of individuals to live and not be killed when they have done nothing meriting loss of life. The foundation of this kind of support is that all humans bear the image of God and innocent human life must not be taken. This right has been violated in regard to many Jews throughout history and most notoriously in the Holocaust of the twentieth century. But history shows that this right has also been violated on various occasions when Arabs—guilty of no crime—have lost their lives. In this sense of "support," both dispensational and non-dispensational evangelical theologies support both Israelis' and the Palestinians' right to life. Adopting a biblical account of ethics requires this type of support, and I strongly affirm it.

A second sense of "support" agrees that there is a right (political, legal, and/or moral) for a people to exist as a nation with its own government. As this relates to the Israeli–Palestinian conflict, it involves having the right to be a nation in the Holy Land. Talk of such rights and support, of course, escalates the emotion involved in this debate, because it raises questions about who owns the land, how they are to acquire and possess it, and what happens to those who do not own it but live in it. So what is my position on this kind of support?

I affirm initially what all Christians should—namely, that the whole earth, including the Holy Land, belongs to God, and he is free to do with it as he chooses. As we shall see later, God gave it to Abraham, Isaac, and Jacob, and their descendants. As we shall also see, end–time prophecy predicts that the people of Israel (in the end times) will have their own government, but it also shows that when Jesus reigns from Jerusalem, Jews and Arabs alike will possess the land in peace and harmony. I shall explore this more later. But, given biblical teaching, all evangelical Christians should support the right of Israel to have its own government in the land.

But, that is not the end of the story, because we must speak briefly about what happened during the twentieth century. After World War I, Britain was entrusted with the Mandate of Palestine. Before the Mandate began, the Balfour Declaration (November 2, 1917) expressed the British government's willingness to provide a homeland for the Jews in Palestine. The Balfour Declaration, however, said nothing about political control of the land by Jews, but it did not forbid it either. It did say, however, that if Palestine became a homeland for the Jews, "nothing shall be done which may prejudice the civil rights of existing non-Jewish communities in Palestine, or the rights and political status enjoyed by Jews in any other country."[2]

After World War II the United Nations (UN) voted in November 1947 to partition the land into a Jewish state and an Arab state. Jerusalem was to be an international city, belonging to everyone. In 1948, the State of Israel was born. The birth of an Arab state, given the UN vote of 1947, would also have been in order, but Jordan annexed the West Bank territory, which was to have been a major portion of an Arab state. In 1988 King Hussein of Jordan relinquished his claim to the West Bank, but in the Six Day War of June 1967, Israel captured the West Bank and still holds it today. By 1988 when King Hussein gave up Jordanian claim to the West Bank, the international will to create a distinct Arab state in Palestine had ebbed to the point that it is still an unrealized dream for Palestinians.[3]

Let us assume for the sake of argument that the UN in November 1947 actually had the legal and political right to partition Palestine into two distinct states. If one agrees, then in addition to a divine right granted by God's decision to give Israel the land, there is also a political and legal right conferred by the UN to have an Israeli state in Palestine. But, because of the UN's 1947 resolution, there is also a legal and political right for Palestinians to have a separate state in the Holy Land. Moreover, as I shall explain later, Scripture also teaches that in the end time Arabs and Jews will live in the land together in peace. Hence, there is a biblical expectation that Arabs will have access to the land in the end times.

So, because of biblical teaching, and if one accepts the UN's right to partition Palestine in 1947 and sanction both an Arab and Israeli state in the land, one can support both Israel's and the Palestiniass's rights not only to live in the land, but to have political control over their respective peoples in nation-states. Of course, this says nothing about whether one

---

2. Quoted in Brown, "A Historical Overview," 15.

3. For more of the history of the Palestinian-Israeli conflict during the last hundred years, see Burge, *Whose Land? Whose Promise?*, esp. 38–39, 48.

has to support the boundaries of a partitioned Palestine that the UN drew up, or the boundaries of the State of Israel as they have emerged through many wars since 1948. But neither dispensational nor non-dispensational theology logically precludes the kind of support I have just mentioned.

There is a third sense in which someone might claim to "support" the modern State of Israel, and this is clearly the most controversial. It is also the focus of this paper. According to this sense of "support," one holds that it is necessary (or at least acceptable) to approve of every action Israel takes with respect to its own people, the Palestinians, and other nations of the world. The rationale for such support is typically taken to be the belief that Scripture promises a distinctively blessed future for Israel not only spiritually, but materially as well, and the belief that this is predicted by a proper understanding of end time prophecy.

Now, it is this third kind of support for Israel that most rankles her opponents (Christian and non-Christian), and it is this kind of support that dispensationalism supposedly not only allows but requires. According to my second thesis, I reject this sort of support when it involves approving of oppression and injustice. I shall argue that dispensationalism or any other form of evangelical theology does not require such support. But, let me turn now to my first thesis.

THESIS ONE: REJECTION OF SOCIAL AND POLITICAL OPPRESSION AND INJUSTICE

A hallmark of evangelical theology is its commitment to the full inspiration and inerrancy of Scripture. That means that Scripture is not mere human opinion but rather the very word of God. God is omniscient, and so God cannot be wrong about anything he thinks. He is also morally perfect and so would never lie about anything. Hence, whatever he affirms as true matches the way things actually are. As evangelicals, we believe, thus, that whatever Scripture teaches must be true and that lives must be lived in accordance with Scripture's teachings. Scripture's moral dictums bind all people, regardless of whether they think they are obliged to follow such rules.

So what does Scripture teach about social and political oppression and injustice? Thankfully, it is easy to find the answer. Scripture clearly forbids both individuals and nations, along with their governments, to treat anyone—citizen or not—unjustly and oppressively. A notable example of God's distaste for injustice is found in God's indictment of

Isaiah's Israel as recorded in Isaiah 5. But this is hardly the only passage relevant to my point (see also Deut 23:15–16; 24:14; Ps 10:17–18; Isa 1:16–17; Jer 7:5–7; 22:13–17; Amos 4:1–3; Habakkuk 2).[4] Even though Isaiah 5 and many of the other passages are written about ancient Israel, nothing in Scripture suggests that it applies only to her. Any nation or person who oppresses others is committing sin, and needs to stop (Deut 16:18–20; Ps 82:1–4; Prov 1:3; 21:15; Isa 26:7; and Amos 5:7–15).[5] Jesus himself said that we are to love our neighbors as ourselves (Mark 12:31), and the Apostle Paul explained how we should treat our enemies (Rom 12:17–20). Though Jesus and Paul speak of interpersonal relationships, it is hard to imagine that they would not want us in some way to apply these commands to groups of peoples, even to neighboring nations or to other ethnic groups that live within a state's national borders.

Hence, we can say unequivocally that Scripture forbids social and political oppression and injustice. Since evangelical theology is committed to the inspiration and truthfulness of Scripture and is, therefore, bound to approve whatever it teaches, it should be clear that no theology can qualify as evangelical if it affirms that it is morally acceptable to break Scripture's moral laws. That also means that no *evangelical* theology can approve of social and political oppression and injustice and at the same time be internally logically consistent.

Friends and foes alike think of dispensationalism as an evangelical theology. If it is, then from what I have said, it cannot remain internally consistent if it supports anyone or any nation that treats people unjustly or oppressively. Still, some critics believe that dispensationalism's fundamental tenets commit it to unwavering support for the State of Israel, even when Israel acts oppressively or unjustly. Is this complaint true or unfounded? The best way to decide is to clarify the nature of dispensationalism and then to see whether its core principles explicitly or even implicitly sanction oppression and injustice by Israel.

THESIS TWO: CORE PRINCIPLES OF DISPENSATIONALISM AND SOCIAL AND POLITICAL JUSTICE

Though many of dispensationalism's opponents believe it is a uniform set of beliefs, this is not so. Not all dispensational*isms* are created equal!

---

4. Linder, "Oppression," 473.

5. Ibid.

And, not everything associated with dispensationalism is one of its core principles. Elsewhere I have written in detail about my understanding of the core tenets of dispensationalism.[6] I cannot discuss them in detail here, but I can briefly mention what I consider the six core principles common in one way or another to all forms of dispensationalism.

First, dispensationalists understand terms like "seed of Abraham," "Jew," and "Israel" to be used in multiple senses in Scripture. They are used sometimes in 1) an ethnic, biological sense; at other times in 2) a spiritual sense to refer to anyone spiritually saved; sometimes in 3) a political sense to refer to the kingdom or nation of Israel (this use is common in the OT); and in 4) a typological sense to connect something in the OT (an event, ritual, etc.) with something in the church. Whereas non-dispensationalists typically see these terms used in the NT only in a spiritual or typological sense, dispensationalists argue that all four senses can be found in both testaments. Thus, when many NT passages speak of Israel or Jews, they refer specifically to those who are ethnically, biologically Jewish, not to the *spiritual* descendants of Abraham—i.e., the church, which is composed of both Jews and Gentiles.[7]

A second essential dispensationalist principle is an understanding of literal hermeneutics. For example, dispensationalists typically argue that one must understand the meaning of OT prophecies about Israel's future in their own OT context, rather than reinterpreting these prophecies in light of how some NT writers apply them to the church. Hence, dispensationalists typically argue that the general rule for relating the testaments is that if God has said something once (OT), it is still in force later (NT), unless God either explicitly or implicitly reveals that the prior teaching is cancelled. Dispensationalists further argue that proper interpretation of the NT shows that promises about Israel's future blessings are neither explicitly nor implicitly nullified in the NT. In fact, some NT passages clearly affirm that those promises are still to be fulfilled.

One outcome of such hermeneutics is that if a NT passage takes an OT promise to national Israel and applies it to the church (as with Peter's handling of Joel 2 on the day of Pentecost, recorded in Acts 2), that means the prophecy must have more than one fulfillment—one to the church (because the NT says so), and another to Israel (because the OT demands

---

6. See Feinberg, "Systems of Discontinuity," 63–88.

7. Ibid., 71–73.

it). While there is more to dispensational hermeneutics than what I have mentioned, these items capture at least some key essentials.[8]

A third dispensational distinctive is an understanding of the great OT covenants made to Israel. Here the Abrahamic, Davidic, and New Covenants are especially in view. Dispensationalists specifically believe four things about these covenants: 1) They were addressed to those who are ethnically, biologically Jewish; 2) They contain promises that include spiritual blessings for ethnic Israel, but also social, political, and economic blessings. In addition, 3) these covenants are made with Israel unconditionally. That means that though blessing under a covenant is always conditioned on one's obedience, if the covenant itself is unconditionally ratified, God will fulfill it to some generation (an obedient one) of Jews. And finally, 4) dispensationalists maintain that the covenant blessings and prophetic promises that grow out of them have never all been conjointly, simultaneously fulfilled to ethnic Israel in the way the covenants demand (for example, forever!).[9]

Consistent with this understanding of the great OT covenants is dispensationalism's fourth distinctive. Dispensationalists believe that both the OT and NT affirm that there will be a distinctive future for ethnic Israel as a nation. This means Israel will be restored both spiritually and materially, and that includes possession of the land promised to the patriarchs. As to everything involved in this distinctive future, individual dispensationalists may disagree somewhat, but there is still the belief that God will deal with Israel in the future to bless them as a corporate, national entity. One way this distinctive manifests itself is that dispensationalists hold that the millennial kingdom of Christ will contain both saved Jews and Gentiles, but the kingdom will have a distinctively Jewish flavor to it.[10]

A fifth dispensational essential is the belief that the church is something distinctly new in the NT era. This is not to say that no one before the church began was saved or had a relationship with God. Rather, the point is that the defining characteristics of the church include more than being a group of spiritually saved individuals. They include such things as being baptized into the body of Christ and being indwelt with the

8. For a fuller discussion of dispensational hermeneutics see Feinberg, "Systems of Discontinuity," 73–79; and also Feinberg, "Hermeneutics of Discontinuity," 109–30.

9. Feinberg, "Systems of Discontinuity," 79–81.

10. Ibid., 81–83.

Holy Spirit—events that only began occurring on the day of Pentecost. They also include the church as a group of believers to whom the Holy Spirit has given spiritual gifts. According to Paul, the giving of spiritual gifts comes from Christ through the Holy Spirit *after* Christ ascended on high, following his resurrection (Eph 4:8). And, the distinctives of the church also include having Christ as head of this body of believers in which Jews and Gentiles alike are on equal spiritual footing. According to Paul again, Christ was not made the head of the church until after his resurrection and ascension (Eph 1:20–23), none of which happened in the OT era.[11] There are other defining characteristics of the church according to dispensationalists, but those mentioned here give some of the flavor of this dispensational distinctive.

A sixth core principle of dispensationalism focuses on its philosophy of history. For non-dispensational systems, the key idea is that God is using history to save men and women. History is to be seen as salvation-history, and other things God is doing with our world are of lesser import. Dispensationalists also think that God is calling out from the Jews and Gentiles alike a body of people to be redeemed. But this is only part of what God is doing with history. Most fundamentally, God's plan is to implement the kingdom of God. That kingdom, of course, has a spiritual basis, but it also involves social, political, and economic—i.e., material—things. The establishment of God's kingdom does not happen all at once, but God's hand is in the affairs and events of peoples and nations as he works out his plan for history.[12]

These six items, I believe, are at the heart of dispensational thinking. That means that other beliefs that some dispensationalists have held are, at most, applications of one of these six principles. In many cases, I think those applications are wrong, but unfortunately, some dispensationalists have publicized them loudly enough so that non-dispensationalists conclude that it is imperative to hold these views as a dispensationalist. Here I refer to beliefs like the notion that the Sermon on the Mount is not at all for the current age, that the church is a parenthesis (almost an afterthought) in God's main plan (for Israel), and that Israel and the church must be so distinct in all things that there must actually be two New Covenants—one for the church, because Jesus institutes the Lord's

11. Ibid., 83–84.
12. Ibid., 84–85.

Supper with such language, and another for Israel, one that she will enter into as a nation in the future.

These beliefs about the Sermon on the Mount, two New Covenants, etc., are possible applications of dispensational distinctives, but I think they are wrong applications. Nonetheless, they are not what dispensationalism is actually about at its core. The six distinctives I have set forth are.

DO DISPENSATIONAL DISTINCTIVES LOGICALLY REQUIRE SUPPORT FOR THE STATE OF ISRAEL?

Now that I have enumerated what I see as the six distinctives of dispensationalism, we must first ask whether any are even relevant to the question of my paper. If not, then it cannot logically entail support for the State of Israel.

The first two dispensational distinctives relate to hermeneutics. They help us to understand how to interpret certain biblical terms and how to understand how the Old and New Testaments relate. Given the nature of the terms and the testaments, we can say that these points are relevant to Israel, but the hermeneutical points *per se* do not even address the question of whether one should support the State of Israel. So, the first two dispensational distinctives are broadly relevant, but not specifically relevant to the topic before us.

Principle 5 about the church as a distinctive organism is even less relevant to our topic. I do not mean that how the church relates to Israel is irrelevant, but only that the matter of the defining characteristics of the NT church say nothing about the church's relation now or later to national Israel. From this distinctive it is hard to see how one could conclude much of anything about dispensational or even non-dispensational support for the modern State of Israel.

Since the kingdom of God (principle 6) relates to all of reality, it must broadly have something to do with Israel, the Palestinians, and all other people. But to say that God is establishing his kingdom and that it has spiritual and material elements is to say nothing about the particulars of either. Nor does it *per se* say anything specifically about Israel's exact role in that kingdom.

Given this evaluation of principles 1, 2, 5, and 6, I do not see how any of them can logically entail anything about support or non-support of the State of Israel. On the other hand, principles 3 and 4 do appear relevant to Israel's role in God's plans and his plans for the future. Principle 3 is about OT covenant promises made to Abraham, Isaac, and Jacob, and their descendants. It promises blessings to the whole world through them, but it also promises specific blessings to Israel. In addition to promising a right spiritual relationship with God, Israel is promised a kingdom with both spiritual and material elements to it. This kingdom is said to be never-ending (Dan 7:14, 27) and, ultimately, to include all people. Part of these covenant promises includes the promise of land. As noted when discussing the covenants, dispensationalists believe that these covenant promises were addressed to ethnic Israel and are about her, and they also believe that all of these promises have never been conjointly fulfilled. So there is reason to expect a fulfillment of these covenant promises and any prophecies that grow out of them.

Clearly, this third dispensational distinctive is relevant to the question of this paper, and the fourth distinctive is as well. When dispensationalists hold that there will be a distinctive future for Israel as a nation, they mean that God has a plan for Israel and that plan has not yet been fulfilled. Details of the plan are broadly sketched in the great OT covenants, and further details are clarified in various end time prophecies about Israel. Given the nature of these promises and prophecies, it is hard to imagine that they are not also relevant to other nations and peoples, including Palestinians.

In sum, only principles 3 and 4 of dispensationalism are even relevant to our topic. But, what picture do those principles paint of the end times in particular, and does any of this logically require that dispensationalists must approve of everything the State of Israel does? To those matters we now turn.

A DISPENSATIONAL SKETCH OF WHAT OT COVENANTS AND END TIME PROPHECIES REQUIRE

Above I noted four key features about the great covenant promises made to Abraham and David and also found in the New Covenant. Here I note some specifics of these covenant promises.

An initial point has to do with the blessings promised to Abraham. God told Abraham to leave his homeland and go to a land that God would show him. So Abraham left, not knowing where he was going (Gen 12:1; Heb 11:8). But, we learn in Genesis 15 that God ratified his covenant with Abraham. In Gen 15:18–21 God gave Abraham the dimensions of the land he was to inherit and a list of the peoples who at the time of the promise lived in the land. Most specifically, the Promised Land extended from the river of Egypt[13] on the west and south to the Euphrates River on the north and east (15:18).

During the reign of David, Israel existed as a kingdom with David as king. David was a man of God and wanted to build a house for God. But because David was also a man of war, God said it would fall to David's son Solomon to build God a house. But, God promised David that he would establish David's ruling house as head of the kingdom of Israel forever. That is, God promised that there would never lack a son to sit on the throne of David (2 Samuel 7). Kings come and go, but as Scripture moves into the NT, it becomes clear that the everlasting king is none other than David's greater son, Jesus—the Messiah of Israel, Savior of all, and ultimate King of an everlasting kingdom. Various OT prophecies about Israel's future speak of the material aspects of that kingdom in such a way as to predict that it would not only be spiritual in nature, but a material kingdom with various social, political, and economic blessings (detailed below).

So, the great OT covenants with Israel promised a king and a kingdom with a specific land. These God promised unconditionally. (Note his unilateral ratification of the Abrahamic Covenant twice, recorded in Genesis 15 and 17.) In Gen 17:7–8 God tells Abraham that the covenant is to be an everlasting one, and the promise of the land is also everlasting. That God promises unconditionally means that he guarantees that he will do this. Of course, the specific generation of Abraham's seed that receives all that is promised is the one properly related to God. As the apostle Paul teaches in Romans 9, Israel's election to privilege (Rom 9:1–6) is not the same thing as election to salvation. Merely being Jewish biologically and ethnically does not save one spiritually, and it does not necessarily include one in the fulfillment of all of the promised national blessings. One must be spiritually saved to get those blessings.

Because OT covenant promises were made unconditionally to Israel, dispensationalists maintain that they must at some time be fulfilled to national Israel. Moreover, dispensationalists also note that these promises include a whole matrix of spiritual and material blessings, and that Israel

13. Commentators are divided as to whether this is the Nile or the *Wadi el Arish*, the seasonal riverbed on the Sinai Peninsula.

has never experienced the fulfillment of all of those blessings conjointly. Since God is not one to renege on his promises, and since Israel has yet to receive all of these blessings as a nation, there is reason to believe that OT covenant promises and the prophecies of end time blessings that grow out of them are still to be fulfilled as promised.

Of course, the nation of Israel as a whole rejected her Messiah when he first came; so many Christians believe that Israel forfeited the promises. If not, we need some NT evidence that God still plans to fulfill them to national Israel. The apostle Paul wrote to the Romans well after the Jews as a nation had rejected their Messiah. In Romans 11 Paul directly addresses the question of whether God has irrevocably cast off his people Israel, since in Christ's day and in Paul's, most Jews rejected Jesus. Paul exclaims emphatically that God has not cast off his people Israel (Rom 11:1). He then proceeds to offer three reasons why God is not finished with Israel. His final proof appears in Rom 11:25–27 where Paul explains that after the "fullness of the Gentiles" has come in, God will then save all of Israel. To underscore his point that God has not forgotten or annulled his promises to Israel, Paul writes that "the gifts and calling of God are irrevocable" (Rom 11:29). In the context of Romans 9–11, this cannot mean anything other than that the great OT covenant promises made to Abraham, David, etc., and the promises of blessing for Israel that grow out of those covenants, are still going to be fulfilled! God's promises can be trusted—even if most Jews since the time of Jesus until now have rejected their promised King, Jesus.

Because of the nature of the OT covenants and Paul's affirmation that they are still to be fulfilled, dispensationalists believe that the promises to Israel, including ones about land and a kingdom, are not cancelled. But since dispensationalists insist that those blessings have never conjointly been fulfilled to Israel, there must still be in store a distinctive future for ethnic Israel as a nation (dispensational principle 4). So, dispensationalists have a lot to say about end time prophecies and the role of Israel as depicted in them. Here I cannot cover all end time prophecies, but I want at the very least to mention those that relate to Israel as a national entity and to the Promised Land.

First, there are various prophecies that suggest that after dispersion from the land, God will bring Israel back to the Holy Land. Since the whole matrix of prophesied blessings has not been fulfilled yet, dispensational scholars believe that Israel will return to the land in the end times.

This does not rule out the possibility that she might come back before the end time; the point is that she will have a presence in the land at the end time. Scripture also says, however, that when she returns at the end time, it will be in unbelief. Here one thinks of Ezek 37:1–14 and its vision of the valley of dry bones. In the vision the bones lie scattered in a valley, but then come together and muscles and skin form upon them. Ezekiel tells us that this means that God will bring Israel back to the land. But, the vision shows that though the bones come together and form the figure of a man, there is no life in them. Later, breath comes into the form, and the man comes alive. Ezekiel explains that this means that Israel will not fully come to life until God puts his spirit in Israel. That is, Israel will return to the land and have a semblance of life (Ezek 37:8, 12–13), but will only come to life when God saves her spiritually (Ezek 37:9–10, 14). For a time, then, she will be in the land, but in unbelief.

Will the people of Israel be back in the land at the end time under the authority of another country, or will they have their own national identity and government? This brings me to a second point about Israel in the end time. In dispensational thinking Dan 9:24–27 is a key passage about the course of history for Israel—viz., the vision of the seventy weeks. It predicts the future from the perspective of Daniel's time onward, and the things predicted relate to Daniel's people and his holy city, Israel and Jerusalem (9:24). According to the vision, the first sixty-nine weeks (literally, heptads; i.e., groups of 7) will conclude with the coming of the Messiah (9:25). After the sixty-ninth week, the Messiah will be cut off and the city of Jerusalem and the temple will be destroyed (9:26). While one would initially think these last two events come during the seventieth week, Dan 9:27 teaches otherwise. It speaks of the seventieth week and the events that come after the death of the Messiah and the destruction of Jerusalem and the temple.

From our perspective, we can roughly date the coming of the Messiah and his death, and we know exactly when the fall of Jerusalem and the temple occurred—AD 70 under the Romans. While you might expect the seventieth week of Daniel's vision to begin immediately after the sixty-ninth week, or at least after the events of AD 70, we must see what Daniel 9:27 says about the seventieth week. In 9:26 an individual is introduced who is referred to as "the prince of the people who will come." Verse 27 says this prince will make a covenant with the people (meaning Israel) for one heptad (or, the seventieth week; a seven-year period). Exegetes presume that this is a covenant of peace, which he will break in the middle of the seven-year period and will stop sacrifices, presumably in the temple. He will bring abominable things that make desolate, but he will ultimately be completely destroyed himself.

It is very hard to fit the predictions of Dan 9:27 with anything that happened after AD 70. Moreover, in Matt 24:1–3, we read that Jesus walked out of the temple and pronounced doom and destruction on it. His disciples were troubled and asked him when this would happen and what would be the sign of his coming and of the end of the age. In Matthew's account of Jesus' answer, the latter two questions get the most attention. Jesus details events that run the course of the tribulation era, the seven-year period yet to come at the end of the age.

What is crucial is that Jesus links what he is saying with Dan 9:27. In Matt 24:15 Jesus says that when those living at the time of the events predicted in Matthew 24 see the abomination of desolation standing in the holy place, they should flee, for the time of intense tribulation is beginning. But Jesus says even more. If we are not sure what the abomination of desolation refers to, Jesus says it is the one spoken of by Daniel the prophet (24:15).

Daniel refers to the abomination of desolation in three passages: 9:27, 11:31, and 12:11. I agree with commentators who see 11:31 as fulfilled by Antiochus Epiphanes. Since the events of Antiochus's life were past history from Jesus' perspective, when he speaks of something future to himself, he cannot be referring to Dan 11:31 when Jesus speaks the words of Matt 24:15. Dan 9:27 and 12:11 can be seen as future events to Jesus' day. In fact, the events of Dan 9:27 and Matthew 24 have not yet occurred, for the Lord has not returned at the end of the tribulation (Matt 24:30).[14]

As do many others, I believe that Dan 9:27 and 12:11 are referring to the same time period—the tribulation, Daniel's seventieth week. I think as well that Jesus in Matt 24:15 is most directly referring to Dan 9:27, and he tells us more explicitly what the willful prince of Dan 9:26–27 will do that is so abominable, and where he will do it (the temple). Remember, Jesus is responding to his disciples' questions about the sign of his coming and of the end of the age. His disciples, raised in Judaism, would be familiar with Dan 9:24–27 and the broad outline

14. For more details on Daniel's portrait of the events and people of the seventieth week see Daniel 7, especially verses 23–28.

of the course of Israel's history it sets forth. If they truly believed Jesus was the long-awaited Messiah, they would know that the first sixty-nine weeks had concluded, and they would wonder about the events after the sixty-ninth week (Dan 9:26) and those of the seventieth week (9:27). Jesus' reference to the abomination of desolation and his linkage of it with Daniel suggest that Jesus and Daniel are talking of the tribulation period—the end of Daniel's seventy-weeks vision.

Regardless of whether one agrees with such an interpretation, my purpose in mentioning these passages and events is two-fold. One is to present a typical dispensational understanding of the tribulation period and to show some of the biblical basis for it. The other is to note what these things teach about the condition of Israel during the end times, specifically during the tribulation. For one thing, Dan 9:27 says that the seventieth week begins by the willful prince making a covenant (presumably of peace) with Israel. But, if Israel is in the land but not in control of its people politically, no treaty of peace can be formalized with Israel, or so it would seem. Hence, it seems that when Israel is in the land at the end time, she will not only be physically present but will also have political control of the nation, i.e., there will be an Israeli government that can make such a treaty.

Another point to be gleaned from what Daniel and Jesus say is that during the tribulation there will be sacrifices made in the temple in Jerusalem. The willful prince (many refer to him as the Anti-Christ and/or the Roman Beast—see Daniel 7 and the first beast of Revelation 13— he is the world-wide political leader during the tribulation) will stop sacrifices in the temple and will set up there the abomination of desolation. If these things are to happen during the tribulation, there must be a functioning temple in Jerusalem. Currently, that is not the case. Hence, it is reasonable to believe that the temple must be rebuilt at the latest in time for these events to happen. Some believe it must happen before the tribulation starts. Perhaps, but the key is that it is functioning by the mid-point of the tribulation, and that could happen even if the temple is not rebuilt until the early years of the tribulation.

Because Jesus speaks of the tribulation as a horrible time (Matt 24:21–22) and thereby confirms the teaching of OT prophets about it (e.g., Jer 30:7; Joel 2:1–2; Zeph 1:14–15), dispensationalists expect things to get worse as the tribulation moves toward its end. Often portions of Revelation (e.g., 14:14–20; 16; 19:11–21) are noted as predicting widespread death and destruction during this time and persecution of any who would take a stand for God against the Anti-Christ (see Rev 13:11–18).

By the end of the tribulation, Israel will be surrounded by a confederation of nations from the whole world whose aim is to blot her out once and for all. This climactic battle is most specifically identified in the NT as the battle of Armageddon, but OT prophecies give many details as well. In particular, Zechariah 12 and 14 teach about this battle. According to Zech 14:1–2, the battle at its outset will be going poorly for Israel. Things will look altogether hopeless, but as Zech 12:4–9 shows, God will go forth to fight for Israel. He will strengthen Israel to fight as never before, and he will also confound the enemy. Rev 19:11 ff. shows the Lord riding out of heaven followed by the armies of heaven to do battle with his enemies. He will utterly destroy them (see Joel 3; Rev 14:14–20), but more than that will happen. When he returns at his Second Advent, he will be seen by all that day. Zech 12:10 predicts that in the midst of the destruction of Israel's foes, the Holy Spirit will be poured out on Israel, and he will move them to repent. But why? Because they will look upon him whom they have pierced and mourn for him. Undoubtedly, many will think that now would be the right time for Messiah to come, if there ever were a right time! And then he does come! But it is none other than Jesus whom they have for so long rejected (see also Matt 24:30, where Christ returns and the tribes mourn). At the Second Coming Israel's reaction to the Lord will not be rejection, but repentance and trust in him. It is here that we begin to see how Paul's prediction in Rom 11:26–27 can be fulfilled.

Following the Second Advent will be the Judgment of the Sheep and Goats (Matt 25:31–46). The Goats will be the losers at this judgment; they will be destroyed. The Sheep are those alive who remained faithful to Christ during the tribulation or who turned to him in faith at his Second Coming. They are told to inherit the kingdom. It is then, dispensationalists believe, that the thousand-year rule of Christ will begin (Rev 20).

Dispensationalists believe that the redeemed of all ages will be present to enjoy the kingdom (some in resurrected, glorified bodies, and others in natural bodies), but they also expect this kingdom to have a special Jewish flavor to it. That is, OT prophecies speak of a time of unparalleled peace and prosperity for Israel (e.g., Isa 60; 11:1–10; Zech 14:10–11; Zeph 3:13–20). These passages also teach that during the kingdom even more Jews will return to the land. It is at this time that

Israel will enter fully into the blessings of the New Covenant because she will at last be right with God (Jer 31:27–40). And, Jesus will be ruling physically and visibly from Jerusalem (Isa 2:1–4). Jerusalem will become the throne of the Lord (Jer 3:17). The results will be staggering. Isa 2:1–4 teaches that the Lord will make just laws and enforce them. He will arbitrate disputes among the nations, and will do that so equitably that there will be nothing left to fight about. Hence, the nations will disarm, and—the Hebrew text says—they will not even know how to make war anymore. When righteousness itself is enthroned in the person of Jesus the King, all of Jerusalem and Israel will be holy. Even the most mundane things like the pots in the temple and the bells on the horses' necks will be holiness unto the Lord (Zech 14:20–21).

Long-held animosity toward Israel will cease, and in its place there will be respect and admiration (Zeph 3:13–20). There is also good news for the nations of the world. God always intended for Israel to be a light to the Gentiles, a blessing in their midst, and OT prophecies about the kingdom show that when Israel is in her proper place spiritually with the Lord, all the nations will be blessed. For one thing, they will be saved as well and will flourish in the kingdom.

Especially meaningful is the promise in Isa 19:16–25, where Isaiah predicts that a day will come when Israel and Egypt will no longer be enemies, but rather partners in serving the Lord. Even more, Assyria will be a third partner in this alliance of holiness and service to the Lord. If Isaiah is thinking of the Assyrian empire as he writes, it included countries that we know today as Iran, Iraq, Jordan, Syria, and Lebanon, as well as Israel and Egypt. What an incredible prophecy! How could this possibly happen unless the peoples of these nations turn to Christ in saving faith? How could it happen prior to the millennial kingdom? Dispensationalists, then, see the course of this age leading ultimately to the millennial reign of Christ, the absolute monarch. His reign will result in peace and prosperity for Israel and the nations.

DISPENSATIONAL PRINCIPLES 3 AND 4 AND SUPPORT FOR ISRAEL

The preceding is a brief description of dispensational understanding of the OT covenants God made with Israel and of some events of end time prophecies. It is now time to face squarely whether these intellectual commitments mandate that anyone holding dispensationalism must approve of what the State of Israel does, regardless of what it does. We have seen something of what the promises and prophecies predict and of how they need to be fulfilled. But it is a long way from promises and prediction to fulfillment, and Scripture does not explain all the steps it will take to get there—"there" being the fulfillment of these things. Some are so excited about things to come, that they unfortunately think they can somehow bring them to pass sooner, rather than later—at least they want to try. Some well-meaning American Christians have even talked of sending rock and stone to help in rebuilding the temple. If there is anything not needed in Israel, it is more rock and stone. Even if there were such a need, contributing money to fill that need will not make the end times come any sooner than God has planned. Unless you happen to be the Anti-Christ, there is probably little you can do to make these events happen. No one can move God's sovereign timetable one moment faster or slower than he wants.

But how does a dispensational understanding of the OT covenants and of end time prophecy relate to support for the State of Israel? I believe it is helpful to answer by addressing three distinct, yet not totally unrelated, questions. They are: 1) Are any events of the last hundred years as they relate to Israel fulfillment of any end time prophecies described above? 2) Do dispensational principles 3 and 4 require (or even legitimize) attempts to "make the end times happen"? and 3) Do dispensational principles 3 and 4 logically entail that one must approve of everything the modern State of Israel does, no matter what it is?

I believe that answers to the first question are often where things start to go wrong in our understanding of whether one must support the current State of Israel. Put simply, many dispensationalists would say that the return of Jews to the Holy Land and the founding of the State of Israel during the twentieth century are fulfillments of end time prophecies. And, if that is right, the argument continues, we dare not disrupt or interrupt what God is doing as he moves us toward the end of the age. It is true that in Israel most Jews are unbelievers, but end time prophecies predicted that Israel would return to the land in unbelief. That is, because God has a distinctive future planned for ethnic Israel as a nation, including political control of the land, that means that if at any time in our day or the future Israel gets political control of the land, then we must be in the end times and Israel's political control of the land must fulfill prophecy. That being so, Christians should support the State of Israel in what it does, because it is a fulfillment of end time prophecy.

Note that this line of reasoning contains two basic assumptions. The first is that what happened in the twentieth and now the twenty-first century to Israel fulfills end time prophecies. The second is that if something fulfills prophecy, we must affirm what happens, because we do not want to disrupt God's plans.

In response, I think the reasoning just sketched is wrong. That is so at least in part because the second assumption is false, and we do not yet actually know that the first is true. Let me explain. I begin with the second assumption because it is the easier one to handle. This is the assumption that if something fulfills prophecy, we must leave it alone and affirm what has happened and will happen as a result of prophecy being fulfilled. I trust that it is obvious that this assumption is false. Someday, someone will be the Anti-Christ and will do the various horrible things Scripture predicts. Because he and his deeds fulfill prophecy, should everyone just let him alone and applaud whatever he says and does? That suggestion is patently absurd, but then, so too is the general assumption that if something fulfills prophecy, we must rejoice and support whatever happens next, regardless of what it is.

Now, I doubt that if you put the point to a dispensationalist the way I have just made it, he would disagree. But, when dispensationalists are not thinking as clearly as they should, they may tacitly think the assumption has merit. I am relatively sure that many non-dispensationalists think dispensationalists hold this assumption, especially when they hear no critique from dispensationalists when Israel does something unjust or oppressive. Nonetheless, many dispensationalists do not hold this assumption, and there is nothing in dispensational understanding of prophecy as I have described it earlier in this article that requires its advocates to believe that if someone or something fulfills a prophecy, we must applaud it and in no way inhibit its doing whatever else it chooses to do.

As noted, I am not really convinced that many dispensationalists actually hold this second assumption, though at times some seem to. But, the "touchier" issue is the first assumption about the events of the last century fulfilling prophecy. Certainly, there are people, including some dispensationalists, who use such language about the birth and growth of the State of Israel. Of course, making such claims sensationalizes headlines in the newspapers, sells books (fiction or non-fiction), makes for entertaining movies, and generates interest in parts of Scripture—at least for a time. However, our understanding of biblical prophecy should not depend on the daily newspaper headlines, stories, or movies.

My major contention is that we do not actually know that the events of the last century fulfill prophecy. Why is that so? The reason is that end time prophecies involve a lot of different events, and prophecies about blessings for Israel involve blessings that are spiritual and ones that are material. At this point in history, there are just too many details of end time prophecies that need to be fulfilled in order to confirm that we are in fact in the end times to be sure that what has happened during the last hundred years fulfills biblical prophecy. In particular, we noted that during the tribulation there would be sacrifices in the temple—currently that at least requires that it be rebuilt so that it could function in that way. But, even more specifically, we noted that Daniel's seventieth week—the tribulation—begins with the signing of a seven-year peace pact between Israel and the Anti-Christ (the willful prince of Dan 9:26–27). Once that happens, it will be a very good sign that the tribulation is beginning, but until it does and until sacrifices can be made in the temple, we cannot be certain that Israel's return to the land and the birth of the State of Israel fulfill end time prophecy.

Though many do not like to think this, it is still possible that God might again disperse Israel from the land, only to bring her back five hundred to a thousand years later, and then bring the end. Such suggestions will not sell many books, but they are within God's sovereign right to do. I believe recognizing this is a more responsible way to understand God and his plans, and end time prophecy, than to say that we *know* prophecy is being fulfilled. Even if what has happened in the last century does fulfill end time prophecy, assumption two about having to support everything that follows is simply false. If it does not fulfill prophecy, then both assumptions are wrong, and the reasoning that is used to support is quite suspect.

So, we may not in fact be living in the end times, though some feel certain that we are. Let me just say reverently that given various conditions in our world today, if God does not use the current situation to wrap up his end time plans and institute the kingdom, he is missing a very good chance. At the very least, what has happened over the last hundred years should convince everyone that, despite appearances for a long time in history, God is fully capable of bringing to pass whatever he has prophesied. I should also add that even if the two assumptions we have been considering are false, that would not mean dispensationalism in general, or its six core principles I have set forth, are false. Dispensationalism's understanding of the events of the end time can still be right, even if some dispensationalists are wrong about whether events in our day fulfill prophecy.

But, what about question two? Apart from whether what has happened in the last hundred years fulfills end time prophecy, do dispensational principles about the covenants and a distinctive future for ethnic Israel require us to do something to "make the end time events happen"? The answer here is both simple and obvious. If we are not certain that we are in the end time, how can we be sure that whatever we do would make the end times come to pass? Even if we are in the end times, what can we do to make these events happen, unless we happen to be the Anti-Christ, for example? Since no true believer, dispensationalist or not, is the Anti-Christ, it is hard to see what we can do. But, more to the point, principles 3 and 4 obligate individual Christians to do nothing! The covenants will be fulfilled by God in his relation to Israel, not by us. The only part we might have in that is to plant the gospel seed in Jewish hearts. But, even if they respond and accept Christ, that does not mean we have made end time events happen or even come sooner. As you think about dispensational principle 4, it involves a number of end time events, none of which individual Christians have any control over. So, it is hard to see how that principle can require those who hold it to try to "make end time events happen." The answer to our second question, then, is a resounding "no!" You are not obligated to try to make these things happen, and most of it, if not all, you cannot make happen anyway. Dispensational essentials agree on my answer to the second question.

This brings us to the third question: Do dispensational understandings of OT covenant promises to Israel and its understanding of end time prophecies require approval of anything that the current State of Israel does? No, they do not, but I must explain why not.

Let us consider initially the promises made in the great OT covenants. Some will quickly note that Abraham was promised the land with very specific dimensions (Gen 15:18–21), so they have a divine right to it. Moreover, the UN resolution also granted them certain rights to the land. But, what does that entail? When God made the promise of land to Abraham, he did not say how Abraham's descendants would acquire it, or how they were to maintain control over it. When God told Moses, Aaron, and later Joshua to go in and possess the land, he told the Israelites to wipe out the Canaanites in the process. But, that was then, and even then they did not get the whole land promised to Abraham, so it was clear that more land was to come. God certainly has not revealed that the current State of Israel was to take and is to hold onto the land by any means whatsoever. And, given the UN resolution in 1947, if Israel had not been attacked by its Arab neighbors after declaring statehood in 1948, there would not have had to be a war to establish the Israeli government as legitimately in command of the land given them by the UN resolution.

The main point here, however, is that God's promise of the land to Israel and her own political control of the land in no way says anything about how they are to acquire these things or maintain them. They certainly do not give Israel the right to do anything whatsoever, including unjust and oppressive measures, to maintain their hold on the land. Some may reply that Israel is only fulfilling what God planned for them when he promised the land to Abraham and a kingdom to David.

Assuming that what has happened over the last hundred years actually fulfills those promises, the fact of being God's instrument to bring about his will does not mean one can do that any way one chooses. Let me illustrate this point. In Isaiah's day God predicted that because of Israel's evil, he would send the Assyrians to punish Israel (Isa 7:17–20), and he did so. The Northern Kingdom was swept away. Assyria served as God's instrument to accomplish his will, but that did not mean God sanctioned everything the Assyrians did to overthrow the Northern Kingdom. The Assyrian army committed many atrocities in its war of conquest of Israel. God did not respond by saying that the atrocities were fine, because Assyria was only doing God's bidding. On the contrary, God was angry at the way Assyria waged this war of conquest, and God responded by promising Assyria's punishment and downfall.

Similarly, even if Israel, in taking and protecting the Holy Land for herself, serves as God's instrument to bring to pass what he has promised to do for Israel in relation to possession of the land and having their own government, that does not legitimize anything and everything Israel does in serving as God's instrument to bring these things to pass. Those who act unjustly and oppressively as they rule Israel and hold onto the land can expect to be punished by God when and how he sees fit. Nothing essential to dispensationalism disagrees with what I am saying on this point.

Still unconvinced, some may reply that the great covenants promise Israel many material blessings, so what has happened and continues to happen in Israel in our day is merely a case of Israel holding on to what God has promised her. However, here is where it is essential to underscore the dispensational point that the covenants promise material blessings for Israel *in conjunction with* spiritual blessings that require her salvation. Too often, non-dispensationalists focus only on the spiritual aspects of the covenant promises and forget the material. The opposite error is to focus only on the material blessings and ignore the spiritual ones.

Dispensational understanding of the covenant promises requires that one take all aspects of the promises—the material and the spiritual —seriously. Hence, even though the things that have happened over the last hundred years may begin to fulfill some of the material blessings, the spiritual change that is required by the covenants has not happened. The nation as a whole does not have a saving relationship to Jesus, and Jesus is not King of Israel. Most of the people in the land and in the government are non-believers. Even if the government were composed of all evangelical Christians, that would not mean everything they would do would be right. People in non-glorified bodies (saved and unsaved) can and do sin. Thus, we cannot simply say that anything the current government does is acceptable, because God has promised Israel so many blessings. Not all of those blessings have yet been bestowed be-cause much of the nation and its government are spiritually far from God. People without God (and even non-glorified saints) cannot simply be trusted to do the right thing, so there can be no blanket approval of everything the Israeli government and people do, regardless of what it is. Remember that when Israel does come to possess all of these blessings, her government will be an absolute monarchy with Jesus as the King. Since he is morally perfect, at that time it will make sense to approve of whatever he does. But, we cannot give such approval to the current government, and dispensational understanding of covenant promises does not require that we do.

Some may still be unconvinced, for Israel is still God's chosen people, his elect nation. Does that not give them certain rights and privi-leges in the way they conduct their business as a political entity? Not really, but I must explain. Here we get much help from the Apostle Paul in Romans 9. Paul begins the chapter by noting that Israel is God's elect nation. But, from verses 1–6, we can see that it is an election to privilege.

Immediately following these verses, Paul underscores the critical point that election to privilege is not election to salvation, nor does it guarantee it. Salvation is not merely secured by virtue of ethnic Jewish heritage.

So, people elected to privilege are still abject sinners without a saving relationship to God. But, for our purposes, there is another point I must make about this election. The underlying assumption in the imagined objection about Israel as God's chosen seems to be that if one is a member of God's elect, that legitimizes anything you might do. This is absolutely false! Being elected to privilege no more justifies a people to engage in political and social oppression of those under its authority than being elect to salvation sanctions those elect people to engage in as much sin as they want to commit. That is, being a member of God's elect—regardless of the nature of the election—does not free you to sin with impunity! And nothing about dispensational distinctives says otherwise!

In sum, nothing about dispensational understanding of God's OT covenant promises to Israel requires dispensationalists to approve of Israel when she acts unjustly and oppressively. But, what about dispensational understanding of end time prophecies and the distinctive future for Israel as a nation that dispensationalists espouse? Here again, I must affirm that there is nothing in that understanding of end time prophecies that requires approval of everything Israel does. Let me explain.

As argued earlier, one can support Israel's return to the land, the establishment of her own government, and even, when it happens, the rebuilding of the temple. None of these events in and of themselves require any acts of political or social oppression and injustice. If, of course, in the process of rebuilding the temple, for example, Israel engages in political and/or social oppression, we cannot support those acts of injustice, even if we in general can be positive about the temple being rebuilt. If the temple can be rebuilt without treating Israelis and non-Israelis unjustly, that would, of course, be preferable. But, nothing in dispensational belief about these end time events requires approval of acts of political and social injustice at any time.

What about the rest of end time events yet to come? Does a dispensational understanding of the events of the tribulation, the battle of Armageddon, the Second Advent, and the salvation of Israel require approval of Israel's actions involving these events or events of other times besides the end times, even if some of those actions are socially and politically unjust? Not at all.

During the tribulation, there will be much persecution of Jews and Israel. Nothing in end time prophecy says that Israel will be attacked militarily only at Armageddon; there may be other military strikes earlier in the tribulation. Though it is not an essential of dispensationalism, and not all dispensationalists hold it, I favor just war theory (though I recognize its limitations, especially in a nuclear age). Just war theory requires a just cause in order to go to war. Self-defense when attacked is considered a just cause. So, if at any time during the tribulation, Israel is attacked, she has the right to defend herself.

However, just war theory also talks about just actions in conducting the war. Specifically, a nation's actions during a war are not considered just if there is not non-combatant immunity. That is, civilians not engaged in the war are to be free from harm. If, in the course of defending oneself, a nation not only attacks enemy armies but also harms civilians who live in the enemy's country, it is morally unacceptable. Whether the war comes during the tribulation or before it, it cannot be just if it is waged unjustly, and killing innocent civilians is unjust. Nothing inherent to dispensationalism disagrees. That is, dispensationalists do not believe or hold anything that entails believing that killing non-combatants in war is morally permissible.

The Second Advent of Christ and his establishment of the millennial kingdom will in no way be unjust. Scripture is clear that when Christ is King, there will be justice and peace for all. We have already mentioned passages that teach this. Israel's special place in the millennium will be brought about not by Israel's deeds, but by the gracious work of the Lord. Since it is the Lord who does this, it is not Israel's work, and hence there can be no question of whether Israel is acting justly or unjustly. The only question is whether the Lord has acted justly in giving Israel prominence. Since the Lord is morally perfect, his special blessing of Israel as an act of divine grace can in no way be unjust! Dispensational understanding of Israel's future, as laid out in end time prophecies, in no way involves approving of *Israeli deeds* of political and social injustice whenever they occur, because the Second Advent, the salvation of Israel, the establishment of the kingdom, Jesus' just reign and Israel's prominence are not *Israeli* acts. They are *God's* acts, so believing these events will happen does not commit anyone to approving of Israel's acts, just or unjust.

Therefore, nothing involved in a dispensational understanding of Israel's future trials and blessings and the end time prophecies that predict them requires anyone to approve of Israel today or in the future when she commits acts of political and social oppression and injustice.

CONCLUSION

In this chapter I have clarified the essentials of dispensational thinking. I have also examined whether any of them require that dispensationalists approve of social and political injustice and oppression when done by Israel. Despite what some may think, nothing essential to dispensationalism requires that kind of support for Israel. One can believe everything dispensationalism is really about and still insist that the Israeli government treat its own citizens with justice and do the same for Palestinians living in the land. And, it is a good thing that this is so, because at the very beginning we saw that no evangelical theology should approve of social and political oppression and injustice. And dispensationalism is a form of evangelical theology!

In closing, I must add that disapproval of unjust and oppressive deeds applies not only to Israel, but to the Palestinians as well. When Palestinians or military organizations claiming to represent them unjustly kill via rocket attacks, suicide bombings or whatever, Israeli civilians who are not attacking them, no form of evangelical theology can approve of those acts as morally right either.

In the current struggle between Israelis and Palestinians, there is plenty of blame to be shared by all sides in this struggle. Nothing about dispensationalism, or any other form of evangelical Christian theology, requires supporting acts of sin done by anyone. Hopefully, dispensational and non-dispensational theologians, as well as just ordinary Christians, will understand the theological points I am making, and will turn their attention from vilifying one form of theology or another to focusing on meeting the needs of the many suffering people who are victims of this ongoing conflict. While it is proper to work and pray for peace, only Jesus as King is the ultimate answer to these problems. Even so come Lord Jesus—quickly!

BIBLIOGRAPHY

Brown, Wesley H. "A Historical Overview of the Israeli-Palestinian Conflict and Christian Responses." In *Christian Perspectives on the Israeli-Palestinian Conflict*, edited by Wesley H. Brown and Peter F. Penner, 14–42. Schwarzenfeld, Germany: Neufeld, 2008.

Burge, Gary M. *Whose Land? Whose Promise?* Cleveland: Pilgrim, 2003.

Feinberg, John S. "Systems of Discontinuity." In *Continuity and Discontinuity*, edited by John S. Feinberg, 63–88. Westchester, IL: Crossway, 1988.

Feinberg, Paul D. "Hermeneutics of Discontinuity." In *Continuity and Discontinuity*, edited by John S. Feinberg, 109–30. Westchester, IL: Crossway, 1988.

Linder, Robert D. "Oppression." In *Baker's Dictionary of Christian Ethics*, edited by Carl F. H. Henry, 472–73. Grand Rapids: Baker, 1973.

❖ 6 ❖

The Biblical Concept of Inheritance

Joseph Shulam

W ORD STUDIES ARE OFTEN technical, and it is easy to manipulate them to fit one's own point of view. They are not my favorite kind of study. However, at times word studies are essential for understanding the text. Words are like cups. They have a bottom and sides but only very rarely do they have a cover. For this reason, they can hold different meanings in different contexts. For example, when I was in New England recently, I was looking for a shop called "Radio Shack." I asked a shop owner where it was located and he replied, "You go up to the Rotary and turn right." Well, the only Rotary I knew was the "club" kind, so I proceeded to look for the Rotary Club, which happened to be on the other side of this small town. Eventually, after some frustration, I found out that "rotary" in New England means what we in Israel call a "circle" and what the English call a "roundabout!"

When we study ancient documents like the Bible, we must try as much as possible to look at the words within their original context and historical setting. This is much harder to do than one would expect. Many Christians filter their understanding of the biblical text, wittingly or unwittingly, through their own particular denominational creed and theology. In the following article we shall endeavor to review some of the relevant biblical texts in order to look at them afresh and possibly re-evaluate the significance that they have traditionally been attributed. So please be patient as we survey the biblical concept of "inheritance." Since the analysis cannot be exhaustive because of the limitations of space, we shall bring those biblical citations that are necessary to elaborate the point we are endeavoring to make.

One way to define inheritance is the passing of property at the owner's death to those entitled to succeed him. The first aspect of the concept of inheritance is legal, where the idea is applied to the physical land; most of these references occur in the OT legal books. Another is theological and is applied in a spiritual sense. This is the sense most often used by Jesus within the NT. However, the legal and spiritual usages can be found in both testaments alike. Sometimes they are also used simultaneously, which introduces a third category for analysis. In addition, we shall briefly examine two further terms that, used in a biblical sense, add considerably to our understanding of the term "inheritance." These terms are "possession" and "forever."

INHERITANCE AS A LEGAL TERM

Unlike ancient Near Eastern society, which conferred the legal status of son or daughter through adoption of a stranger, with the consequent right to inherit from his adopted parent, Israelite law only recognized family relationships of blood kinship. In addition, the patriarchal structure of Israelite society was based upon the "agnatic" family in which only blood relatives on the father's side were entitled to inherit.

Most of the biblical legislation governing inheritance is embedded in the material dealing with the territorial division of the land of Canaan according to tribes, clans, and families at the time of the original conquest of the land (i.e., the thirteenth to twelfth centuries BC). However, we also find several injunctions that deal with family inheritance and the transfer of property.

In regard to inheritance within the family, the most important ruling is found in Numbers 27:8–11, which explicitly sets out the hierarchical structure which governed Israelite families:

1. If a man dies and leaves no son, turn his inheritance over to his daughter.
2. If he has no daughter, give his inheritance to his brothers.
3. If he has no brothers, give his inheritance to his father's brothers.
4. If his father has no brothers, give his inheritance to the nearest relative in his clan, that he may possess it.

For daughters who inherit from their father, an added restriction to this ruling exists: "They may marry anyone they please as long as they marry within their father's tribal clan" (Num 36:6).[1] Sons received special attention in the biblical legislation. The father was prohibited from transferring the right of the firstborn to a younger son (Deut 21:16), although this had been a prevalent practice in the patriarchal period (Gen 21:10, 27:37; cf. Gen 48:18–20, 1 Chr 5:1). Furthermore, the right of the firstborn to inherit a double portion of his father's possessions (i.e., twice as much as that received by each of his brothers) was also established by legislation (Deut 21:1, 7).

Brothers still shared their father's inheritance during the NT period, as the following verse illustrates: "Someone in the crowd said to him, 'Teacher, tell my brother to divide the inheritance with me'" (Luke 12:13). Although Jesus answered by warning the gathered crowd to avoid greed, the passage witnesses to the fact that in Jesus' day the legislation regarding brothers sharing their father's inheritance was still valid.

The non-legal literature portions of the Bible contain other scattered references to inheritance customs. For instance, it is not clear how the status of the mother affected her son's right to inherit. On the one hand, there is evidence that the sons of a concubine did not inherit (Gen 25:5–6; cf. Judg 11:1–2). Yet at times, such sons seem to have been considered equal to the sons of the wife (Gen 35:23–26). Perhaps the right of the sons of a concubine are dependent upon the wishes of the father. This would accord well with the Code of Hammurabi (170–71), which states that if a father legally recognized sons born to him by a slave girl, they were to be counted among his heirs. However, if the father failed to acknowledge them, they had no claim to any share in his estate.

One of the biblical examples of this idea occurs when Abraham's wife confronts him saying: "Get rid of that slave woman and her son, for that slave woman's son will never share in the inheritance with my son Isaac" (Gen 21:10). Sarah came from a society (Haran) in which the sons of a concubine could inherit together with the sons of the wife. Sarah's fear was that Isaac, her son, might have to share the vast wealth of Abraham with Ishmael, the son of Hagar (Abraham's concubine). She anxiously besought her husband, Abraham, to exile both the slave woman and her son. This theme is taken up in the NT. In Galatians, Paul draws on the idea that inheritance is through the son of promise, Isaac, and not by the

---

1. All Scripture quotations taken from the NIV (New International Version).

slave woman's son, Ishmael. He states, "But what does Scripture say? Get rid of the slave woman and her son, for the slave woman's son will never share in the inheritance with the free woman's son" (Gal 4:30).

The right of daughters to inherit along with their brothers is mentioned in the book of Job, whose setting is non-Israelite (Job 42:15). Rachel and Leah also seem to expect to inherit from their father's estate: "Do we not still have any share in the inheritance of our father's estate?" (Gen 31:14). We realize, however, that they are also from the land of Haran.

The legal aspect of inheritance can also be found in the NT: "See that no one is sexually immoral, or is godless like Esau, who for a single meal sold his inheritance rights as the oldest son" (Heb 12:16). Esau, the older twin son of Isaac, exchanged his rightful inheritance of his father's physical estate with Jacob, his younger twin brother, "for a mess of potage."

The reason behind this legislation now becomes clearer: "No inheritance in Israel is to pass from one tribe to another, for every Israelite shall keep the tribal inheritance of their ancestors" (Num 36:7). This concept is again reinforced: "No inheritance may pass from one tribe to another, for each Israelite tribe is to keep the land it inherits" (Num 36:9). The primary purpose of these biblical laws was to preserve the territorial integrity of the tribes, clans, and families as established at the time of the conquest and settlement of the land of Canaan (cf. Num 36:7). The right to inherit and transmit one's patrimony continued to be strongly advocated, at least well into the monarchical period and probably much beyond. We read, for instance, that Ahab, king of Samaria, sought to buy Naboth's vineyard, but Naboth replied: "The Lord forbid that I should give you the inheritance of my ancestors" (1 Kgs 21:3).

This attitude may also explain the intense attachment that the peoples of the Near East feel for their land to this day. This bond is not easily understood by the Western nations, where land is often sold from hand to hand with no accountability to family, clan, or tribe.

INHERITANCE AS A THEOLOGICAL TERM

In addition to its legal usage, the term "inheritance" is also used in theological contexts to affirm the spiritual relationship between God and his people, the Israelites.

Following the incident of the golden calf, Moses pleads before God for the Israelites as he returns to Mt. Sinai to present God with the second set of tablets for the inscribing of the commandments. "'Lord,' he said, 'if I have found favor in your eyes, then let the Lord go with us. Although this is a stiff-necked people, forgive our wickedness and our sin, and take us as your inheritance'" (Exod 34:9). Moses asks God to take the people of Israel as his inheritance. This is a spiritual concept: The people of Israel are now to be God's portion. In the subsequent verses God lays down his conditions for doing as Moses requests in the Mosaic covenant. Obedience to the specified commands and injunctions is necessary so that the Israelites may live long in the land and enjoy its benefits (Deut 11:13–25).

A similar spiritual inheritance is applied to Aaron and the Levites. Aaron and his family do not receive any land as an inheritance: "The Lord said to Aaron, 'You will have no inheritance in their land, nor will you have any share among them; I am your share and your inheritance among the Israelites'" (Num 18:20). The Lord, not land, is to be Aaron's inheritance. The next verse addresses the Levites and their service: "I give to the Levites all the tithes in Israel as their inheritance in return for the work they do while serving at the tent of the meeting" (Num 18:21). Thus the Levites' inheritance is also to be a spiritual one—the tithes offered by the Israelites to the Lord. To emphasize this legislation, the text continues: "Instead, I give to the Levites as their inheritance the tithes that the Israelites present as an offering to the LORD. That is why I said concerning them: 'They will have no inheritance among the Israelites'" (Num 18:24).

In the NT we find numerous uses of the term inheritance in its spiritual context: "For of this you can be sure: No immoral, impure or greedy person—such a person is an idolater—has any inheritance in the kingdom of Christ and of God" (Eph 5:5). Likewise: "Whatever you do, work at it with all your heart, as working for the Lord, not for human masters, since you know that you will receive an inheritance from the Lord as a reward. It is the Lord Christ you are serving" (Col 3:23–24). Paul also says: "Now I commit you to God and to the word of his grace, which can build you up and give you an inheritance among all those who are sanctified" (Acts 20:32).

INHERITANCE USED SIMULTANEOUSLY AS A LEGAL AND SPIRITUAL TERM

Inheritance can also be used in both a spiritual and a physical context simultaneously. An examination of two passages from both the OT and NT will illustrate this point. In Moses' address to the Israelites in the Arabah desert, he says: "But as for you, the Lord took you and brought you out of the iron-smelting furnace, out of Egypt, to be the people of his inheritance, as you now are. The Lord was angry with me because of you, and he solemnly swore that I would not cross the Jordan and enter the good land the Lord your God is giving you as your inheritance" (Deut 4:20–21). The people of Israel are God's inheritance, a spiritual concept and, conversely, the land is their inheritance from God! This plainly shows that inheritance can carry dual significance.

This idea is amplified in the NT where we see that inheritance again deals with the land, although most commentators interpret the particular passage in question in a spiritual context. As Jesus is teaching in the temple, he uses a parable to instruct the chief priests and the elders: "But when the tenants saw the son, they said to each other, 'This is the heir. Come, let's kill him and take his inheritance'" (Matt 21:38). In a physical sense the tenants are not only murderers but are also blindly rejecting the laws of inheritance. There is very little possibility of them actually taking the son's vineyard and possessing it for any length of time. Even Jesus' listeners respond to his question by stating that the owner "will bring those wretches to a wretched end . . . and will rent the vineyard to other tenants" (Matt 21:41).

INHERITANCE AND THE "FOREVER" PROMISES

Many Christians frequently view the "forever" promises of the Old Testament as having been made obsolete with the advent of the New Covenant or Testament. We need to analyze this position carefully.

A central passage which deals with this follows the incident of the golden calf. God wishes to destroy the Israelites and tells Moses: "Now leave me alone so that my anger may burn against them and that I may destroy them" (Exod 32:10). Moses pleads, "Remember your servants Abraham, Isaac and Israel, to whom you swore by your own self: 'I will make your descendants as numerous as the stars in the sky and I will give your descendants all this land I promised them, and it will be their inheritance forever'" (Exod 32:13). In this passage, Moses pleads with God for the survival of the Israelites—descendants of the patriarchs Abraham, Isaac, and Jacob—reminding him of his promises to Abraham. God swore these promises with the highest of all oaths, the holiness of his own self. These promises are that Abraham's seed will be as the number of the stars in the sky, and that the Israelites will inherit the land forever.

To say that "forever" in the OT does not mean *forever* risks inferring that God changes his mind. If "forever" does not actually mean "forever" in the OT, why should it do so in the NT? In both Old and New Testaments, the "forever" promises must be held to be "forever." Nothing less will do!

Isaiah especially emphasizes this prophetically: "Instead of your shame you will receive a double portion, and instead of disgrace you will rejoice in your inheritance. And so you will inherit a double portion in their land, and everlasting joy will be yours" (Isa 61:7). Why does God promise a double portion to his OT people, the Israelites, together with everlasting joy, if this is not to become reality in God's timing?

This is a key passage. It is the prophetic text that Jesus read in the synagogue at the very start of his ministry. As it is recorded in the Gospel of Luke, Jesus read the first verses of this chapter and closed the book, stating, "Today this Scripture is fulfilled in your hearing" (Luke 4:17–21).

A question of interpretation arises at this point: Did Jesus stop reading at this specific place because he fulfilled only the words which he read, or is his reading of that portion a prelude to the fulfillment of the whole messianic scheme? The common practice during Jesus' lifetime was for a person to read the Torah portion of the week and the accompanying passage from the Prophets and then to refer only to a specific verse or verses from the text. I propose that, considering the messianic implications of Isaiah 61 and their fulfillment in Jesus, the text relating to the inheritance of a double portion of the land in Isa 61:7 should also be understood as a promise that is yet to be fulfilled.

INHERITANCE AND POSSESSION

Having established that from a biblical perspective inheritance can be used in both a spiritual and physical sense, either separately or simultaneously, we now need to examine the term in the light of what the Bible says about "possession."

King David gives us a very clear example of the distinction between inheritance and possession: "So now I charge you in the sight of all Israel and of the assembly of the Lord, and in the hearing of our God: Be careful to follow all the commands of the Lord your God, that you may possess this good land and pass it on as an inheritance to your descendants forever" (1 Chr 28:8). In this passage David is speaking to the people of Israel following the conquest of a large portion of the land that God promised the Israelites under Moses and Joshua. He repeats the Mosaic injunction that if the people wish to possess the land in order to pass it on to their descendants as their rightful inheritance, the people must obey the commandments and injunctions given to them prior to entering the Promised Land. Disobeying these commands and injunctions will result in exile from the land.

This does not mean, as events proved, that they would be disinherited! The Israelites, when disobedient to God, temporarily lost possession of the land and were exiled. Yet they never forfeited their inheritance of the land from God! Far from it; the inheritance given to Abraham is a "forever" promise from God.

In his review of Israel's history prior to being stoned to death, Stephen, speaking about Abraham, says that God gave him no inheritance: "He gave him no inheritance here, not even a foot of ground. But God promised him that he and his descendants after him would possess the land, even though at that time Abraham had no child" (Acts 7:5). From this, we must understand that Abraham never possessed his inheritance. But, of course, Stephen affirms that God promised Abraham's descendants that they would possess the land. Once again, the NT presents this idea as a prophecy still to be fulfilled.

On the plains of Moab by the Jordan across the river from Jericho, the Lord spoke to Moses and said: "Take possession of the land and settle in it, for I have given you the land to possess" (Num 33:53). Later, Moses exhorts the Israelites: "You are about to cross the Jordan to enter and take possession of the land the Lord your God is giving you. When you have taken it over and are living there, be sure that you obey all the decrees and laws I am setting before you today" (Deut 11:32). We know that the tribes of Israel did not conquer all the land God promised, neither were they obedient to God. Likewise, despite his many victories, King David did not succeed in possessing the whole land. Even today, Israel as a state does not possess the land as delineated by God.

Therefore, both historically and to date, the total territorial appropria-
tion of the land of Canaan given as an inheritance to Abraham and his
descendants to possess has not yet come to pass. This promise should
therefore be considered as a prophecy yet to be fulfilled in the fullness
of God's time.

CONCLUSION

We have established that the primary purpose of the laws of inheritance
was to preserve the territorial integrity of the tribes, clans, and families
as established when Joshua divided the land of Canaan (cf. Num 36:7).
The biblical right to inherit and to transmit one's inheritance continued
to be strongly advocated through the monarchical period (1 Kgs 21:3),
while the sharing of the inheritance by sons was still the custom in Jesus'
time (Luke 12:13).

Under normal conditions a people's pattern of behavior over a period of time establishes their society's culture. The Israelites, however,
are a separate people. As we have seen, God first establishes their patterns of behavior, through his commandments, laws, and ordinances.
The culture then develops as directed by God's legislation. Obedience to
this covenantal legislation develops a culture that is blessed; disobedience leads to cursing and possibly exile from the land.

This obedience to God's statutes, including the laws of inheritance,
may well explain the intense attachment to the land that the people of
Israel exhibit to this day. The Western world has no such inheritance-
culture, and land is bought and sold with little, if any, accountability to
family, clan, or tribe.

As we have seen, the people of Israel are God's inheritance and the
land is their inheritance from God. The term possesses both a spiritual
and a physical dimension. We have endeavored to demonstrate that even
in the OT "inheritance" is not used solely in the physical dimension relating to the land but is also used in a spiritual dimension, in relation
to God: Inheritance can be directed both towards God and towards the
people of Israel. This reinforces God's promises of the people's inheritance of the land.

The use of the term inheritance in the NT mirrors its usage in the
OT. It is therefore more than possible that the inheritance of the land by
the people of Israel remains a "forever" promise, especially because God
took an oath to this effect on the holiness of his own name (Exod 32:10).

The question remains: How do we deal with the "forever" promise of this inheritance of the land in the light of Jesus' command in the NT: "My command is this: Love each other as I have loved you" (John 15:12)? Until possession of the land is effected by God, and in his timing, both Arabs and Jews must live together in some form of harmony.

❖ 7 ❖

Hagshamah

A Theology for an Alternate Messianic Jewish Zionism

Phillip D. Ben-Shmuel

THE PURPOSE OF THIS article is to demonstrate that it is possible for Messianic Jews to hold to an authentically Israeli Zionism that is also genuinely Christ-like and Christ-centered. The article will focus on the way such a Zionism relates to the land of Israel/Palestine as well as the "Other" we encounter in the land, and will posit a Zionist approach that is redemptive and inclusive. Therefore, this article is directed toward three audiences. First, toward those both within and outside Palestine who believe the term Christian Zionism to be intrinsically oxymoronic and irredeemable, I hope to show that this does not have to be the case. Second, toward those who ascribe to the current State-Zionism that is prevalent in Israel and among "Christian Zionist" circles in the West, I hope to demonstrate that holding to such an exclusive form of Zionism, which tramples upon the dignity of the Palestinian nation, is simply irreconcilable with true allegiance to the Messiah. I will challenge them to make the crucial turn from "Christian Zionism" to Christ-like Zionism. And third, and perhaps most importantly, I address fellow Israeli followers of the Messiah who, like myself, desire to subject them-selves to the kingship of Yeshua, and his radical vision of the kingdom of God without watering down their Zionist Jewish identity. I hope I will be able to concisely articulate a theological paradigm in which this is possible, and advocate a more inclusive form of Zionism based on historical precedents.

Throughout the article the key word will be *hagshamah*—a Hebrew word that can mean realization, fulfillment (as in the fulfillment of a hope or a prophecy), and enfleshment (from the Semitic root *g-sh-m*, which means body/flesh). This word can be used to translate the Latin *incarnatio* to Hebrew, pointing to the Messiah both as the enfleshment of God and as the fulfillment of the Torah and the Prophets. Coincidently, this term acquired an almost mythical status in early Zionist writings where it was used in the sense of realizing the Jewish national spirit in the land of Israel. Therefore, the central question of this article is: What does Christ-centered *hagshamah* look like in this land today? How do we—the Body of the Messiah—incarnate the Word here and now?

Since I am seeking to articulate a particular perspective on the land, my methodology can be likened to painting a landscape, a process that includes several stages. In the first stage I will draw charcoal sketches of the land that will determine the composition of the painting, sketches of the biblical text that will establish the theological paradigm and framework for the article. In the second stage I will set the canvas aside and begin mixing pigments on my palette, finding the materials and colors that will "enflesh" the landscape on the canvas and give it life. In this case the pigments I will use are the culture and language of Israeli Zionism. In order to prepare them properly, I will explore the writings of Martin Buber, a prominent Zionist thinker, focusing especially on his approach to the land and to the "Other," thus finding precedents within Zionism that can be applied to my theological paradigm. Finally, in the third stage, I will begin the painting itself by applying the pigments to the composition one layer at a time. The result should be a landscape image of a Christ-like and Christ-centered Zionism.

STAGE ONE: DRAWING THE INITIAL THEOLOGICAL SKETCHES

Like the charcoal sketch that precedes the painting, the first stage consists of determining the paper's perspective and arranging its composition. I will begin by outlining the hermeneutic with which I will approach the biblical text, followed by an exploration of the major themes in the Hebrew Bible that relate to the land. I will then consider how these themes are incarnated or realized in the person of Yeshua of Nazareth. Out of this there will emerge a defined theology of the land that can be applied to contemporary Zionism.

The Hagshamah *Hermeneutic*

Many of the theological disagreements concerning Zionism and the land of Israel/Palestine are rooted in the different hermeneutical approaches with which we read Scripture. Therefore, before exploring the biblical text, it is important to define the hermeneutic with which the Scriptures are approached. When discussing the "plain meaning"—or *pshat*, as Jewish exegetes call it—there are two possible extremes of approach: secular reductionism and literalism. On one hand, secular reductionists do not recognize the divine nature of Scripture, opting for a hermeneutic that quite obviously neuters the potency of biblical prophecies, promises, and admonitions concerning the land. On the other hand, literalists fail to account for the human dimension of Scripture. The literalist approach does not take into account the human horizon of the passage, or in other words, the historical, social, and literary context in which the scriptural passages were written. In the name of the dogma known as the "inerrancy of Scripture," the literalist approach wishes to view the entire Bible as one homogeneous and static eternal truth dictated by God. The great irony of this approach is that a literalist reading of a passage is almost never a literal reading. Instead of considering each passage in its original context, it is forced into a preconceived theological paradigm (e.g., Darbyist dispensationalism), thus maintaining the illusion of a homogeneous text.

One can avoid these pitfalls by recognizing the dual-nature of Scripture—seeing Holy Writ as the eternal Divine Word written in human words through human worldviews. Such an approach calls for a contextualized understanding of the "plain meaning" [*pshat*] of each passage, taking into account the literary genre and historical setting, but also faithfully hoping and trusting in the divine promises and commandments. However, this alone will not suffice to explain the way the New Testament authors read the Hebrew Bible. We find that the apostles employed a hermeneutic of radical *midrashic* re-reading of the ancient texts designed around the person of the crucified and risen Lord. *Midrash* is a Jewish method of interpreting the holy Scriptures that deliberately penetrates beyond the *pshat*, and reads the text imaginatively by using word play, allegory, and general inventiveness, allowing the text to speak into new situations and address new needs. However, this *midrashic* approach is not without rules; there is not a sense that "anything goes." Instead, in the case of the New Testament authors, the text of the covenant is redefined specifically around Yeshua of Nazareth: his words, actions, and nature. He is the Archimedean point for any understanding of the Scriptures.

This hermeneutic will also seek to realize and incarnate the Christ-centered reading of Scripture within the "here and now"—in our case, within the current situation in Israel/Palestine, and in the indigenous Zionist culture. Therefore, this paper's hermeneutic—combining contextualized *pshat*, Christ-centered *midrash*, and contemporary application—may be called the *hagshamah* (or incarnational) hermeneutic.

Torah, People, and Land in the Hebrew Bible

It has long been recognized within Jewish circles that the Hebrew Bible revolves around three major themes: the Torah, the people of Israel, and the land of Israel. These three are intractably interconnected through the divine covenant. The covenant with YHWH is upheld only as long as these three divinely ordained institutions remain in proper relationship with each other. In other words, in the Hebrew Bible, the relationship between Israel and God depends on obedience to the Torah, which includes proper treatment of the land, and is rewarded by the land being a source of blessing for Israel. Even though these three themes are drawn out in their clearest form within the Sinai covenant between Israel and YHWH, they exist in nascent form from the very beginnings of the biblical narrative.

The story of the Garden of Eden in Genesis 2–3 lays the narrative foundations for the relationship between mankind [*adam*] and the soil [*adamah*] from whence it was created (Gen 2:7). It is the story of a community (Adam and Eve) that is bound to a place (Eden) through a divine mission (to till/serve it and keep/guard it).[1] It is also the archetype for future failures in this relationship between man and the land, since

---

1. *L'ovdah ulshomrah* (Gen 2:15); the NRSV translates "to till it and keep it," but the Hebrew verb *'avad* can also be rendered as "work," "serve," or "worship," depending on the context. *Shamar* can also be rendered "guard" or "observe," as in observing a commandment. These verbs are used in conjunction only in this verse and when referring to the service of the Priests and Levites in the Tabernacle and temple of YHWH (e.g., Num 18:1–7).

Adam breaks YHWH's commandment; thus the soil [*adamah*] is cursed because of him (3:17). The discord between the human community, the land, and the divine commandment results in a series of exiles—the banishment from Eden (3:24), the wandering of Cain (4:14), and the scattering of the nations (11:8).

The divine response to this state of exile is YHWH's covenant with Abraham. Abraham receives a divine promise which contains three aspects: a land, a posterity, and a global blessing.[2] This three-fold promise is most explicit in the initial calling of Abram in Genesis 12:1–3, but the three elements are repeated with variations throughout the story of Abraham, especially in Genesis 15 and 17. First, Abraham is required to go to the land YHWH will show him (12:1) and there he is given the promise that it will be his everlasting possession (15:7; 17:8). Second, Abraham is promised to become a great nation (12:2), and his innumerable offspring are to have an everlasting covenant with YHWH marked by the commandment of circumcision (15:5; 17:9–14). Finally, Abraham is promised that through him all the families of the earth [*adamah*] shall be blessed (12:3). This blessing of the *adamah* implies a reversal of the curse that Adam brought on the *adamah*.[3] In other words, Abraham's promise is no less than a global return to an Edenic condition. The global scope of the promise is further accentuated in Genesis 17:4–6, when YHWH promises Abraham that he will be the father of *many* nations. The story of Abraham establishes the relationship between God and the people of God as revolving around the three aforementioned themes: a nation, a land, and a covenantal commandment. Yet the scope of the promise is not to remain national—it is ultimately global; all the nations will be blessed by God. By extension, truly biblical Zionism will not be concerned only with the relationship between the Jewish people and the land of Israel, but rather with encouraging *all* nations to come to a proper relationship with God and the earth.

These promises begin to be fleshed-out through the Exodus event and the Sinai covenant: YHWH redeems the children of Israel from Egypt and makes them a people, he promises them the land of their fathers, and he commands them with his Torah.[4] All the detailed stories,

2. See Williamson, "Promise and Fulfillment," 17–18.

3. See Alexander, "Beyond Borders," 44–45.

4. The close connection between the Torah, the people, and the land is a recurring theme throughout the Pentateuch. See, e.g., Deut 4:1–8; Israel is promised to be

commandments, promises and warnings of the Pentateuch are intended to define the proper relationship between the Torah of Moses, the
People of Israel, and the land they are given. This is a continuation of
the theme of exile and return that begins with the fall from Eden and
the calling of Abraham. The horizon of the Sinai covenant is obviously
national, but beyond the horizon there lies the promise that Israel's
inheritance of the land is in fact a return to Eden and therefore, the
beginning of a global blessing.

There are many aspects to the land and to the way Israel is to relate
to it. Within this article the focus is on three major themes: holiness,
justice, and peace. The land is holy because the Tabernacle (and later,
the temple) of YHWH dwells in it. The presence of YHWH in the land
through the Tabernacle/temple sanctifies it as a sacred place. Moreover,
scholars have drawn many parallels between the descriptions of the
Tabernacle/temple of YHWH and the descriptions of the Garden of
Eden.[5] Even the verbs most commonly used to describe the actions of
the Priests and Levites in the sanctuary ['*avad* and *shamar*] are the verbs
that describe Adam's mission in Eden—to serve it and keep it (Gen 2:15;
Num 3:7–8; 8:26; 18:1–7). '*Avad* is also the verb used to describe the
tilling of the soil [*adamah*], and so the Israelite who tills the soil may be
described as serving the land.[6] The '*avodah* [worship] of YHWH in the
sanctuary is deeply connected to the '*avodah* [tilling] of the land: they
are both a service and a divine mission. Therefore, Israel's inheritance of
the land and the establishment of a sanctuary for YHWH are the beginning of the return to Eden.

renowned as a *great nation* and to possess the *land* YHWH is giving them if they heed
to the statutes and ordinances of the *Torah*.

5. Prominent examples: (1) Both Eden and the sanctuaries of YHWH are entered
from the east and are guarded by cherubim (Gen 3:24; Exod 25:18–22; 26:31; 27:13–16;
1 Kgs 6:23–29); (2) The *mnorah* (lamp stand) with its distinct floral design is probably
meant to represent the Tree of Life that was in Eden (Gen 2:9; 3:22; Exod 25:31–35);
and, (3) The prophet Ezekiel's description of Eden as being covered in gold, onyx, and
every precious gem is reminiscent of the Tabernacle/temple and especially of the High
Priest's garments (Ezek 28:13–14; Exod 25:7, 11, 17, 31; 28:9–28; cf. Gen 2:11–12). For
a more detailed account of the similarities and symbolisms, see Wenham, "Sanctuary
Symbolism," 19–25.

6. This insight was important in Buber's philosophy of the land and the Hebrew
nation's relationship with the land. Cf. Buber, "A Letter to Gandhi (February 1939),"
122–23.

The holiness of the land is evident also by the fact that it can be defiled by sin, especially by idolatry, sexual immorality, and murder (Lev 18:1–30; 20:1–22; Num 35:33; cf. Ezek 36:17–18).[7] Israel is warned that if they defile the land [eretz] in this way, the land will vomit them out just as it vomited out its previous inhabitants (Lev 18:25, 28). Upon closer examination, we find that the land is defiled by any action that desecrates the image of God. Idols attempt to replace God's true image (humanity) with false images, while sexual immorality and murder desecrate the human body. The defilement of adam causes the defilement of the adamah. Even failing to properly bury a broken human body can be a curse that defiles the land (Deut 21:23). Such language is not merely metaphorical. According to the Torah, sin tangibly pollutes the land and not just the people.[8] The only thing that can redeem the land that was polluted by murder, other than the death of the shedder of blood, is the death of the High Priest (Num 35:22–34). The High Priest represents all of the people of Israel, whose names he bore upon himself, and his death could make expiation for the land.[9]

The fact that the land can be a victim of human sin points to the second theme—justice. Justice is given not only to the land, and to those who inherit the land, but also to the landless sojourning upon it. One of Israel's great tasks is to care for the landless—for the poor (Exod 23:6), for the widow and orphan (Deut 24:19–22), and for the alien (Exod 23:9).[10] Since the land is meant to be a source of justice, when the cause of justice is neglected, the land becomes defiled. The call for justice in the land is related to the holiness of the land and its ability to be polluted by sin that does not honor the image of God. The land is the place of social and ecological justice ordained by YHWH, which is further exemplified by the Sabbatical principles that are associated with the land:

7. Notice that Judaism later treated idolatry, murder, and sexual immorality as the three sins that one must never transgress, even at the pain of death; cf. Babylonian Talmud, Sanhedrin, 74A.

8. This is evidenced by the assertion in Num 35:22–34 that if the land is polluted by murder it must be redeemed by the blood of the murderer. If the murder was unintentional, the slayer can flee to a city of refuge and he must remain there till the death of the high priest. Even if the family is willing to accept a ransom for the death of their kin, the slayer is not allowed to leave the city of refuge, for his presence in the land pollutes it.

9. This insight was shared in a lecture by professor Israel Knohl of the Hebrew University, Jerusalem.

10. See Brueggemann, The Land, 61.

the release of slaves in the seventh year (Exod 21:2–6; Deut 15:12–18), the practice of *shmitah*, in which Israel would let the land rest every seven years (Exod 23:10–11; Lev 25:1–7), the returning of the land to its original owners on the year of Jubilee (Lev 25:8–55), and the remission of debts every seventh year (Deut 15:1–11).

These Sabbatical practices are also an expression of the third theme connected to the land—peace. Peace in the land is expressed by the promises of rest and of abundant blessing.[11] One expression of rest in the land is the Sabbath. In Deuteronomy's version of the Decalogue, the command to rest on the Sabbath is explicitly said to reflect Israel's redemption from slavery in Egypt, and therefore, implicitly, the inheritance of the land (Deut 5:15).[12] Thus, the Sabbath rest is not only a sign of the covenant of Sinai, but also an expression of the rest in the land. The land is intended to be a source of peace and blessing for Israel. YHWH not only calls Israel to come into their inheritance [*nahalah*] but also into their rest [*mnuha*], with the promise of security from all their enemies (Deut 12:9–10). Peace in the land is expressed both by rest from warfare and also by the social, economical, and ecological rest embodied in the different Sabbatical practices. The practice of letting the land rest every seven years demonstrates that the land is not only a rest for Israel—the land *itself* requires rest. As Old Testament scholar Walter Bruegemann puts it: "Land has its own rights over against us and even its own existence. It is in covenant with us but not totally at our disposal."[13] The land

---

11. The land is a source of blessing and therefore a place of rest. It is described as full of bountiful fields, springs of water, and hills rich in iron and copper (Deut 8:7–9). The abundance of the land is expressed by the oft repeated phrase "a land flowing with milk and honey" (e.g., Exod 3:8, 17; 13:5; Lev 20:24; Num 14:8; 16:13–14; Deut 6:3; 11:9; 26:9, 15; 27:3). Moreover, Israel inherited a land already "fully furnished," as it were, with vineyards and olive groves they did not plant and cisterns they did not hew (Deut 6:10–11). This demonstrates that the land is a pure gift (see Brueggemann, *The Land*, 46). Even so, this peace and blessing are not entirely unconditional: They are the result of abiding by the covenant. Israel is reminded that the land they are entering is not like Egypt from whence they were redeemed. This land has no Nile on which they can rely for their agriculture; this is a land utterly dependent on the merciful rains of YHWH, whose eyes are always on it. Only if Israel heeds the covenantal commandment to love and to serve their God with all their hearts and all their souls, then the land will be a blessing to them. But if Israel is seduced to worship other gods, the land will yield no fruit (Deut 11:10–17). The land is the playing field where both Israel and YHWH must express their faithfulness to the covenant.

12. See Alexander, "Beyond Borders," 38–39.

13. Brueggemann, *The Land*, 59.

is a defined and tangible place where Israel is to encounter and practice holiness, justice, and peace; thus, bearing witness to the global promise given to Abraham that in him all the families of the earth [*adamah*] will be blessed.

However, these three interlocking and interlacing themes were never truly realized throughout the Hebrew Bible; they never reached their fulfillment or *hagshamah*. The divine promise of the land did not come to perfect completion in the days of Joshua since there was no permanent peace, as is demonstrated throughout the book of Judges. Moreover, this peace was dependant on loyalty to the covenant (see Deut 11:10–17), and therefore the promise was never fully actualized, not even in the golden age of Solomon whose very name means peace and rest (cf. 1 Chr 22:9).[14] Actually, it was Solomon, the head and representative of Israel, who polluted the land with his sexual immorality (1 Kgs 11:1–3), idolatry (4–8), and oppressive injustice (12:1–11). The renewed cycle of rebellion and punishment led to an ever-growing threat of exile from the land, which culminated in the destruction of YHWH's temple in Jerusalem and the exile of YHWH himself from the land (Ezek 10). The promise of a restored Eden never seemed further from fulfillment.

However, in the midst of exile, Israel's prophets spoke of a day in which YHWH would gather his people back to the land of Israel and re-turn himself to reign from Zion (e.g., Ezek 43:1–7; Isa 40:9–11; 43:5–7; 52:7–10). Israel indeed returned to the land but they were still waiting for the *hagshamah* of the covenantal promises. They were still waiting for the day when all the families of the earth would come to Zion to worship YHWH as king so that their lands could be blessed (Zech 14:9, 16–19). Israel physically returned to the land, but they continued to be subjugated by the Persians, by the Hellenists, and then by Rome. This was summed up best by the cry of Ezra: "Here we are, slaves to this day—slaves in the land that you gave to our ancestors to enjoy its fruits and its good gifts" (Neh 9:36). Yet Israel was still hoping for holiness, justice, and peace at a time when all three seem scarce, still hoping for the day when "Zion will be redeemed by justice [*bmishpat*]" (Isa 1:27). It is into this reality of oppression and expectation that Yeshua of Nazareth was born.

---

14. Cf. Williamson, "Promise and Fulfillment," 30–32.

Yeshua of Nazareth

After sketching out the general lines of the composition, it is now time to shadow and shade the sketch in order to give it body; it is, in fact, the body of Yeshua of Nazareth. The gospel accounts imply that Yeshua's understanding of his own vocation is that he himself embodies YHWH's return to Zion, a vocation that culminates with his passion week in Jerusalem.[15] It is along the same vein of thought that John the Evangelist affirms that Yeshua is God "enfleshed" (John 1:1, 14)—the very incarnation [*hagshamah*] of YHWH. Therefore, Yeshua fulfills in himself Israel's deepest hope for the return and kingdom of YHWH. In this following section I wish to demonstrate that the New Testament authors (and Yeshua himself) view Yeshua not only as the incarnation of God, but also as the fulfillment of the Torah, of the People of Israel, and of the Promised Land. Because Yeshua is the *hagshamah* of the land, it is in him that Israel finds holiness, justice, and peace, and through him the land is redeemed.

It is commonly asserted that Yeshua is the fulfillment of the Scriptures, since he himself testifies: "Do not think that I have come to abolish the law or the prophets; I have come not to abolish but to fulfill" (Matt 5:17). Yeshua's embodiment of the Torah is described most potently by John's use of *logos* to describe the eternal identity of the Messiah (John 1:1–18). Yeshua is the "enfleshment" of God's spoken word, which he spoke from the beginning. If Yeshua is indeed the embodiment of YHWH's return and kingdom, then surely the words of the prophets become "enfleshed" in his person. This does not mean that Yeshua supersedes the prophecies of YHWH's return, but rather that those prophecies are now reinterpreted around the Messiah. This is the *hagshamah* hermeneutic in practice.

Likewise, the New Testament authors describe Yeshua as the representative of Israel, as king, priest, and sacrifice; in all these ways he embodies the whole community of Israel in himself.[16] Just as in the case of "the law and the prophets," to say this is not to claim that Yeshua supersedes or abolishes Israel, but that he fulfills Israel's vocation to the world. In that sense Paul can rightfully redefine the promised heir of

15. For a detailed study of Yeshua's vocation as the embodiment of YHWH's return to Zion, see Wright, *Jesus and the Victory*, 612–53.

16. For a thorough discussion on Yeshua as the messianic king and the focal point of the true, returning-from-exile Israel, see Wright, *Jesus and the Victory*, 477–539.

Abraham as being the Messiah himself, and therefore all who are in the Messiah are Abraham's heirs (Gal 3:13–16). This is not the "Christian supersessionism" of Israel by "the Church," but rather the Christ-centered inclusion of the nations into Israel. Through Yeshua all the families of the earth are blessed. Consequently, this redefinition of the Word of God and of the People of God has major implications for the land.

The New Testament authors draw parallels between Yeshua and the temple; he is the dwelling place of God where one finds holiness, purification (Matt 8:1–4), and forgiveness of sins (Mark 2:5). This is perhaps most explicit in the Gospel of John in which Yeshua proclaims that the Father is in him and he is in the Father (10:38), and in which Yeshua calls his body "this temple" (John 2:19–22).[17] Also in the Apocalypse of John, the Lamb is said to be the temple of New Jerusalem (Rev 21:22–23). In Hebrews Yeshua is described as the great High Priest who removes sin by the sacrifice of himself (4:14–15, 9:24–28). As we have seen, in the Torah the death of the High Priest makes expiation also for the land. Therefore, the author of Hebrews can say that the blood of Yeshua speaks "louder than the blood of Abel" which cries out from the earth (Heb 12:24). In the New Testament, Yeshua is interpreted to be the true source of the land's holiness. Through him, the curse is removed from the land, and through him the land will be restored to its Edenic state.

Furthermore, Yeshua is the source of justice in the land. In Mary's *Magnificat* she sings that "[the Lord] has brought down the powerful from their thrones, and lifted up the lowly; He has filled the hungry with good things, and sent the rich away empty. He has helped his servant Israel, in remembrance of his mercy, according to the promise he made to our ancestors, to Abraham and to his descendants forever" (Luke 1:52–55). Through Yeshua the rich will be sent away and the hungry and landless will inherit the land. "For everyone who exalts himself will be humbled, and he who humbles himself will be exalted" (Luke 14:11), and "the meek . . . will inherit the earth" (Matt 5:5).

Finally, Yeshua, the "Prince of Peace" (Isa 9:6), is also the source of rest and peace in the land. In Matthew's narrative, Yeshua invites the weary to come to him so that he may give them rest (11:28) and

17. Compare this passage in John with the references in the Synoptic Gospels to the false witnesses' accusation against Yeshua that he claimed to be able to destroy the temple of God and to build it in three days (Matt 26:61, 27:40; Mark 14:58, 15:29). Cf. also Matt 12:6 in which the Messiah claims to be one greater than the temple.

shortly afterwards declares himself to be the lord of the Sabbath (12:8). In the Epistle to the Hebrews, this Sabbath theme is further developed as the author exhorts the believers to enter into the promised rest (Heb 3:16—4:16), a clear reference to the inheritance of the Promised Land. This land is now interpreted as "the city that is to come" (Heb 13:14), and the rest is achieved only through the Messiah, the great High Priest. It is Yeshua who fulfills the purpose of the land to be a place of holiness, justice, and peace.

In his oft-quoted study, W. D. Davies claims Paul viewed the land as being "christified" so that the believers' inheritance is no longer the land, but rather the risen Lord.[18] In some sense I want to affirm this, for as we have seen, Yeshua is the *hagshamah* of the land. But this does not mean that land, in the sense of actual soil, is done away with.[19] Indeed, Paul often speaks of those who are in the Messiah as being "heirs" (Rom 8:12–25; Gal 3:27; 4:1–7). That which is to be inherited is the *cosmos*, which was promised to Abraham and to his descendants (Rom 4:13), God's creation set free (Rom 8:19–23). Surely our inheritance is re-imagined around the person of Yeshua and made global (as already promised to Abraham), but this is still an unveiled reference to *land*. In fact, it cannot be interpreted otherwise unless we use an otherworldly hermeneutic that looks toward a disembodied future—an approach reminiscent of Gnosticism. Nor can we say that the promise of land is only for the eschatological future unless we ignore passages that speak of the kingdom of God as being also a present reality (e.g., Luke 20:21). Though we are landless sojourners in the present age and hope in "the city that is to come" (Heb 13:14), we must continue to insist on the land being treated correctly today.

This proper treatment of the land is not only demanded of individuals, but also of nations. As Paul proclaimed to the Athenians: "From one ancestor he made all nations to inhabit the whole earth, and he allotted the times of their existence and the boundaries of the places where they would live, so that they would search for God and perhaps grope for him and find him" (Acts 17:26–27). The God of individuals is also the God of nations; and the God of history is also the God of land. Already in the Torah and Prophets, YHWH asserts that his concern for nations and land extends beyond Israel, for he is the God that brought "Israel up from the

18. Davies, *The Gospel and the Land*, 213.
19. See Brueggemann, *The Land*, 165–69.

land of Egypt, and the Philistines from Caphtor, and the Arameans from Kir" (Amos 9:7) and gave lands as an inheritance to the nations (Deut 2:9; 19; 22–23). Therefore, as the ecclesial community that embodies the Messiah in the land, we must speak prophetically to the nations, calling them to serve and keep the land as a place of holiness, justice, and peace as exemplified by Yeshua himself. This has political, social-economical, and ecological implications that we will draw out in the next two stages, particularly as they relate to the land of Israel/Palestine.

In summary, the Hebrew Bible is concerned with three major themes: the covenant with YHWH, the people of God, and the Promised Land, which is a place of holiness, justice, and peace. All these themes are fulfilled through the person of the Messiah and redefined around him, so that their scope becomes global, as previously promised. Based on this theological analysis, truly biblical and Christ-centered Zionism cannot be concerned only with the redemption of Israel in their land, but rather with the redemption of all the families of the earth. This can be referred to as "general Zionism," because it looks towards the establishment of New Jerusalem. In Jewish terms, this active pursuit of the kingdom of heaven on earth is called *tikkun 'olam*—the restoration of the *cosmos*.

If we stay consistent with the *hagshamah* hermeneutic, then Zionism cannot be merely a general abstract concept, but it must concern itself with the particular "here and now." The liberation of the Jewish people and of *Eretz-Israel* [the land of Israel], by bringing them into a proper relationship with each other and with their God, can be referred to as "particular Zionism," which is the prototype for "general Zionism" [*tikkun 'olam*]. Zionism's inherent particularity does not by any means infer exclusivity. From the theological analysis above, it is clear that a Christ-like and Christ-centered Zionism must be inclusive and redemptive toward all peoples, including the Arab Palestinian nation that has its rightful place among "the families of the earth." In the following section we will find precedent for such an inclusive form of Zionism within the writings of a prominent Zionist thinker.

STAGE TWO: MIXING THE PIGMENTS OF ZIONIST THOUGHT

In the first stage the theological outline and composition was established. Now it is time to set aside the theological canvas and begin mixing the pigments on our artist's palette, finding the colors of Zionism that can incarnate the theological paradigm in the current reality. In studies regarding the intersection of Zionism and Christian theology, it is too often neglected that Zionism was not (and is not) a monochrome and homogeneous phenomenon. Instead, it is a greatly variegated movement, both in thought and in praxis, which is precisely why it is capable of being either destructive or redemptive. It is important to differentiate between the different forms of Zionism and sift through them in order to find a Zionist paradigm which may be appropriated to a Christ-centered Messianic theology. Due to the constraints of this paper, the focus will be primarily on one Zionist thinker and activist—Martin Buber, and how the Zionism he promoted can inform a Christ-centered form of Zionism.

Martin Buber is most well known for his philosophical writings, but there is no doubt that he was also a committed Zionist. Buber, who was born in Austria and immigrated to Jerusalem in 1938, became an official member of the Zionist movement in 1898 when he was a young man. He testified that even then he sided with the "practical" tendency in the movement over the "political" tendency. The practical Zionists hoped to establish a great, productive Jewish community of pioneers (*halutzim*) in Palestine and to bring about a *renaissance* of Jewish culture.[20] Buber was particularly fascinated by the cultural Zionism espoused by Ahad Ha'Am, the goal of which was spiritual and cultural revival and which had little concern for the establishment of a Jewish state, especially if this was done at the expense of true revival.[21] This was contrary to the political Zionism spearheaded by Theodor Herzl who believed the goal of Zionism was to establish the *Judenstaat* ["Jew State"] that would serve as a safe refuge for Jewry who suffered from anti-Semitic persecution. Therefore, the political Zionists claimed that working towards Jewish cultural and spiritual renewal was not an integral and obligatory part of Zionism. They focused instead on diplomatic negotiations with the Ottoman Empire and the other Great Powers.

In contrast, Buber was of the opinion that Zionism was prompted and intensified by modern anti-Semitism, but not caused by it. Even though the external impetus for Zionism was persecution and pogroms, the deep inner motivation was the desire of the people of Israel to renew its relationship with the land of its earliest beginnings. The nation of Israel desired to perfect the land so that the land could perfect the nation.

20. Buber, *A Land of Two Peoples*, 289–93.

21. See Ha'Am, "The Spiritual Revival (1902)," in *Selected Essays*, 253–305.

In other words, the roots of Zionism lie in the connection between the people of Israel and the land of Israel, and in their divine mission to create a just society here. Buber saw this mission as the prototype for any aspiration toward the "Kingdom of God on earth" among the Christian peoples. He also saw Zionism as *athalta dge'ulta*,[22] the beginning of the eschatological redemption. Jews could survive as a people in exile only because they had the hope of returning to the land and fulfilling their mission. Therefore, the purpose of modern Zionism was the reunion between the Jewish people and the soil of Palestine centered in just and voluntary village communities—the *kibbutzim*.

Therefore, Zionism as conceived by Buber had three irreducible demands that together formulated the concept of "a national home":

1. The freedom to acquire land in sufficient measure so that Jews could be a cultivating nation once more—but without ousting any Arab Palestinian peasants.

2. A permanent influx of young settlers that would keep the Zionist restoration from slipping into stagnation—but without harming the economic conditions of the Arab Palestinians and without aspiring towards a Jewish majority.

3. Self-determination of the Jewish community in Palestine—but not necessarily a sovereign Jewish state.[23]

He strongly believed that the Jewish nation had the right to come to Palestine/*Eretz-Israel* and to settle in the land as an autonomous community for three reasons: 1) because of the ancient connection and covenantal bond between the people of Israel and the land of Israel; 2) because the Zionists served, developed, and fertilized the land; and 3) because the *kibbutzim* that the Zionists established were communities committed to social justice and personal freedom, and therefore offered the entire world hope for a future captive neither to the Western capitalist nor the Soviet communist imagination.[24] Buber recognized that when a nation is in Diaspora, without any growing home center, without a "piece of earth wherein one is in the midst of an ingathering and not in dispersion," then this dispersion becomes dismemberment. Therefore, the Jewish destiny

22. Buber, *A Land of Two Peoples*, 194–202.

23. Ibid., 179–84.

24. Ibid., 81–91.

is "indissolubly bound up with the possibility to ingather" in Palestine/ *Eretz-Israel.*[25]

Even so, Buber did not view Zionism simply as another national-ist movement. Buber believed that true Zionism works toward justice for all nations. He believed it is characteristic of Zion that it "cannot be built by 'every possible means' but only *bmishpat* (Isa 1:27), only in justice," because the nature of the means must be like that of the goal.[26] Buber insisted that "it is a false teaching that the rebirth of a people can be accomplished by violent means. The way of violence does not lead to liberation or healing but only to renewed decline and renewed enslavement."[27]

Therefore, for Buber, Zionism without justice is not true Zionism, because the purpose of Zionism is the rehabilitation of the Jewish per-son.[28] In reaction to Zionist excitement about the Great Powers' com-mitment to the establishment of a Jewish homeland in Palestine after World War I, Buber remarked, "If this were the day of Zionism, Zionism would not be a movement of Jewish liberation. Can Jewry be truly liber-ated so long as Judaism's unswerving demand for justice and truth for *all* nations is shouldered out of the way?"[29] Buber held that "the moment national ideology makes the nation an end in itself, it annuls its own right to live; it grows sterile."[30]

Buber understood the biblical truth that the purpose of the prom-ise to Abraham was to bless all the families of the earth. Therefore, we can conclude that the liberation of Israel is ultimately concerned with the blessing of the world. The *telos* of Zionism could not be Jewish sov-ereignty for sovereignty's sake. Buber had no desire for a Jewish state because he was highly critical of the very concept of nation-states and their development in the enlightenment era: "[The emerging nations] did not try to establish themselves *as peoples*, that is, as a new organic order growing out of the natural forms of the life of the people. All they

25. Ibid., 117.
26. Ibid., 100–106.
27. Ibid., 189–91.
28. Ibid., 169–73.
29. Ibid., 38–41.
30. Ibid., 47–57.

wanted was to become just such states, just such powerful, mechanized, and centralized state apparatuses as those that had existed in the past."[31]

Buber believed both Jews and Arab Palestinians were in need of autonomy in Palestine, but one's autonomy did not have to come at the expense of the other, for neither needed an independent state. The demand for a state (whether Jewish or Arab) constituted political "surplus," or the desire to achieve more than what was truly needed. Instead, Buber advocated for a bi-national socio-political entity that he hoped would eventually become part of a federation of Arab states, all the while ensuring the Jewish right of immigration in accordance with the country's capacity to absorb them.[32]

Buber saw it as a great contradiction for Zionists to work towards building a true communal life for the Jewish community in the land, while at the same time excluding the other inhabitants of the country from participation—inhabitants whose lives and hopes were also dependent on the future of this country.[33] This inclusive form of Zionism was seen by Buber to be the central mission of Judaism and the Jewish people. He saw Zionism as the *hagshamah*, the incarnation, of Israel's prophetic proclamation of peace within the reality of the nation's life and deeds "here and now."[34] Buber was highly critical of abstract Messianism and believed instead that "fulfillment in a [future] Then is inextricably bound up with fulfillment in the Now."[35] Thus the Jewish people in their national renewal proclaimed the oneness of their God, who has the same ethical standards for nations as he does for individuals:

> The atheist does not know God, but the adherent of a form of ethics which ends where politics begin has the temerity to prescribe to God, whom he professes to know, how far his power may extend. The polytheists distribute life and the world among many powers. As far as they are concerned, Germany has one god and France another; there is a god of business, and a god of the state. Each of these domains has its own particular code of laws and is subject to no superior court. Western civilization professes one God and lives in polytheism . . . What is wrong for the individual cannot be right for the community; for if it

31. Ibid.
32. Ibid., 194–202.
33. Ibid., 81–91.
34. Ibid.
35. Ibid., 100–106.

were, then God, the God of Sinai, would no longer be the Lord of peoples, but only of individuals.[36]

Buber was the prophetic voice in the wilderness who recognized that the world of politics is dominated by an evil spirit of "great powers" who try to exploit conflicts among smaller nations to their own interest, while the smaller nations then try to exploit the exploitation to their own advantage. For there to be hope, nations must instead embody the spirit of truth, justice, and peace in relations between peoples.[37] Therefore, Buber called on his fellow Zionists to reject the policies and patronage of the imperialist European States. Instead, he insisted that there is room for a joint Arab-Jewish national policy in Palestine/*Eretz-Israel* because both peoples love the land and seek its future welfare.[38] Buber felt that there were two good foundations for active cooperation between Jews and Arabs: a common ancestral, cultural, and linguistic origin as well as a shared task—the desire for their beloved homeland to flourish.[39] Buber distinguished between the Western model of "expansive colonization" and the Jewish model of "concentrative colonization," in which the colonizer is tied indissolubly to the land. The Zionist error was to adopt the scheme of Western colonial policies that created two distinct parties—those that were engaged in colonization and those that suffered from it. Instead, Buber advocated the creation of a covenant with the Arabs of the Middle East rather than relying on the Great Powers of the West. Since the Arabs were not interested in such a covenant at that time, he proposed a land policy: "[We must] direct all of our efforts, to the limit of our powers to the upbuilding of the land of Israel, not simply to building our nation within the land, nor only to the extent that is necessary for the success of our nation, but rather to building the land truly for its own sake . . . I say 'Land Policy' but it would be more truthful to say 'Love of the Land.'"[40] Buber believed that the Jewish settlers were not like Western colonialists that made the "natives" do their work for them. They themselves "set their shoulders to the plow" for they believed in the great marriage between man and earth, *adam* and

36. Ibid.
37. Ibid., 194–202.
38. Ibid., 78–80.
39. Ibid., 194–202.
40. Ibid., 70–72.

adamah. The Jewish peasants wanted to cultivate and "serve" the land. Therefore, a true Zionist asks not to rule over his Arab brothers, but to serve together with them.[41]

Buber insisted that Zion cannot remain merely some ethereal idea or eschatological hope; it was a real place in the "here and now."

> A land about which a sacred book speaks to the sons of the land is never merely in their hearts; a land can never become a mere symbol. It is in the hearts because it is the prophetic image of a promise to mankind; but it would be a vain metaphor if Mount Zion did not actually exist. This land is called "Holy"; but this not the holiness of an idea, it is the holiness of a piece of earth. That which is merely an idea and nothing more cannot become holy; but a piece of earth can become holy just as a mother's womb can become holy.[42]

Buber admired the Palestinian *fellahin's* [peasants'] organic connection to the land and sought to learn from them.[43] He believed in serving the land for its own sake, truly loving it instead of lusting after it. Knowing that the land was destined by God to be a place of holiness, justice, and peace, he desired for the freedom of both nations on the land and therefore abhorred the struggle for demographic superiority.[44] He stated: "[W]e love this land and we believe in its future; and, seeing that such love and such faith are surely present also on the other side, a union in the common service of the land must be within the range of the possible. Where there is faith and love, a solution may be found even to what appears to be a tragic contradiction."[45] And he said "the ploughshare must remain our only weapon, the ploughshare without fear. We need fearless hoers of the soil and not throwers of bombs."[46]

Buber was very critical of how most "Zionists" actually treated the local Arab population. He believed the problem emerged when Jews began to return to the land, acting as if it were empty of inhabitants, or worse, as if the people they saw were of no consequence to them.[47] The

41. Ibid., 111–26.
42. Ibid. 116–17.
43. Ibid., 81–91.
44. Ibid., 78–80.
45. Ibid., 120.
46. Ibid., 134.
47. Ibid., 130–34.

great mistake Zionists made was that *halutziut* [Jewish pioneering] was not accompanied by cooperation with the Arabs. Because of historical developments in Europe, the Jewish community in Palestine began to absorb large numbers of Jewish refugees escaping anti-Semitism instead of a smaller number of ideological *halutzim*. Consequently, the Arabs became fearful and felt threatened.[48] Thus Buber lamented:

> Alas, it has transpired that in any fundamental sense, we have not lived nor do we now live "together *with*" the Arabs, but merely "alongside" them. And the consequence of this situation is that this "alongside" had been rendered an "against." Had we been prepared to live in genuine togetherness with the Arabs, the latest events [the Arab riots of August 1929] would not have been possible . . . The "alongside" has been rendered an "against," and we are not free from blame for the fact that this "against" found expression in the form of religious fanaticism.[49]

Buber was very much aware of the tension between how he and his associates conceived of Zionism, and the State Zionism the majority of Jews in the land were advocating. He attributed this to two different interpretations of national rebirth:

> One tendency was to comprehend that concept as the intention of returning and restoring the true Israel, whose spirit and life would once again no longer exist beside each other like separate fields, each one of which was subject to its own law, as they existed during the nation's wandering in the wilderness of exile, but rather the spirit would build the life, like a dwelling, or like flesh. Rebirth—its meaning is not simply the secure existence of the nation instead of its present vulnerability, but rather the experience of fulfillment [*hagshamah*] instead of present state of being, in which ideas float naked in a reality devoid of ideas.[50]

In contrast to the Zionism which sought such a *hagshamah* [or incarnation] of the national spirit in a just and spiritually fruitful community connected to the land, there was a second tendency to interpret rebirth as normalization. Buber viewed the desire to be a "normal" nation, to be "like the nations," as no less than national assimilation, which was even more dangerous than individual assimilation for it threatened

48. Ibid., 289–93.
49. Ibid., 92–95.
50. Ibid., 220–23.

the spiritual core of the whole people. Of this Buber said: "This sort of 'Zionism' blasphemes the name of Zion." Overtaken by the desire for a state, these "Zionists" frivolously sacrificed the redemption of the land; true national freedom was traded in for the sake of administrative "sovereignty." Therefore, Buber was very concerned by Israel's declaration of independence in 1948. He prophetically warned that the geopolitical reality would force the new state to become highly militarized. Buber feared that a Jewish victory in the war would actually signify the downfall of true Zionism and its permanent substitution with militant nationalism.[51]

Indeed, from the very beginning, Buber was a radical voice of self-awareness and self-critique in the Zionist movement. Even as early as 1918, Buber wrote in a personal letter to a friend: "We must face the fact that most leading Zionists (and probably also most of those who are led) today are thoroughly unrestrained nationalists (following the European example), imperialists, even unconscious mercantilists and idolaters of success. They speak about rebirth and mean enterprise."[52] Buber claimed that official State Zionism did not achieve the Zionist ideal as it claimed to, for immigration and independence were merely means to an end. The purpose of Zionism, in Buber's view, is national rehabilitation and regeneration. In 1949, he wrote: "We are told that the goal has been reached. Yes, a goal has been reached, but it is not called Zion. Not for that goal did Israel, yearning for Redemption, set its path . . . We have full independence, a state and all that appertains to it, but where is the nation in the state? And where is that nation's spirit?"[53]

Despite the fact that Buber hoped for a different outcome, he accepted the State of Israel that emerged after the war and had no qualms identifying as an Israeli. He believed that the continuing redemption of the people and the land must start therefore from the state, but he still hoped that one day the circumstances would change so as to favor some form of Jewish-Arab confederation.[54] Buber believed that the verse "Zion shall be redeemed in justice" (Isa 1:27) was a prophecy of truth, and therefore amidst the pain of that time, he believed their mission was not over, but merely entering a new stage.

51. Ibid.
52. Ibid., 37.
53. Ibid., 250.
54. Ibid., 289–93.

Buber vehemently spoke against transferist rhetoric and defended the right of those who cultivated the land to remain on the land, and this put him at odds with David Ben-Gurion and other Zionist leaders who defended the decision to deny the right of Arab refugees to return to their lands with *realpolitik* reasoning.[55] In the early years of the state, Buber lobbied Ben-Gurion to take the initiative on solving the Palestinian refugee problem caused by Israel because the leaders of the state must set a moral example for its citizens.[56] Until his death in 1965, Buber continued to work for the cause of justice; he did this by strongly protesting against expropriation of Arab lands[57] and by continually calling for a just resolution to the Palestinian refugee problem.[58]

Normative Israeli Zionism leans heavily on the legacies of David Ben-Gurion and Ze'ev Jabotinsky. The two leaders had very different concepts of Zionism. Ben-Gurion was the leader of the socialist practical Zionists, and Jabotinsky founded the capitalist and imperialist Revisionist Zionism. Therefore, the two leaders and their followers often clashed with one another. However, they are also similar, since they were both, ultimately, State Zionists who believed the goal of Zionism is the establishment and maintenance of a Jewish state. In practice, this has always taken on an exclusivist form which ensured Jewish hegemony over the Arab inhabitants of the land. This type of State Zionism is indoctrinated in Israel via the school systems and the public media through ceremonies that constitute a form of civil religion. (The most potent examples are the corporate mourning on "Holocaust Day" and "Memorial Day" followed by the national celebration of independence; these ceremonies are equipped with rituals, myths, and creeds that are designed to form Israelis into a coherent community.)

Israeli State Zionism and civil religion have had great influence on Israeli Messianic Jewish identity.[59] Unfortunately, many Messianic Jews hold to a state-oriented Zionism which is grounded in a literalist understanding of Scriptures and nourished by Israeli civil religion. The

55. Ibid.,169–73.

56. Ibid., 239–44.

57. Ibid., 261–63.

58. Ibid., 269–72.

59. See Warshawsky, "Returning to Their Own Borders," 8–79, 213–14. Warshawsky is somewhat critical of the way Israeli civil religion influences Messianic identity because it attempts to secularize Judaism, but she does not address the political implications of this influence.

literalist reading of biblical prophecies and promises allows the believer to separate the issue of land from the person of Yeshua, who is theologically "set aside" from the land until his eschatological return. Moreover, liberty is erroneously confounded with sovereignty, and so Zionism as a liberation movement is lost; the land is conceived as something to be owned as capital rather than cherished and shared as gift; it is seen as something to dominate as a possession rather than to be in a covenantal relationship with. State Zionism, which has only the goal of preserving the State of Israel as a Jewish state, becomes a sacred tenet of the faith, thus allowing the believer to justify all means to that goal—war, occupation, land-theft, and even expulsion. Thus, ironically, some Messianic Jews seemed to have adopted a Crusader-like paradigm in regard to the land, in which the name of Yeshua is retained mostly as a logo and as a fig leaf to cover the nakedness of imperial greed.

The legacy of Martin Buber offers the Israeli an alternative form of Zionism, which is not stuck in the deathly cycle of the state's self-perpetuation through military violence, capitalist possession, and consumerism. Buber's inclusive Zionism was a direct consequence of his moral philosophy of dialogue that sought to truly encounter the "Other" in an "I-Thou" relationship, a relationship in which the "Other" ceases to be "It," "He," or "She," and is genuinely embraced as "Thou."[60] Buber's Zionism can therefore be described as "the politics of embrace" and named "*hagshamah* Zionism," for it seeks to incarnate God's justice and truth "here and now." Unlike State Zionism, which demands only allegiance to the state apparatuses, *hagshamah* Zionism demands love for the land, for the "Other," and for God. *Hagshamah* Zionism, therefore, does not rely on the *State* of Israel for its existence, and hence it is not threatened by the idea of a one-state solution in Israel/Palestine; indeed it might welcome such a solution if the freedoms of both peoples were ensured. This type of Zionism dovetails, of course, with Yeshua's politics of love, and his fulfillment of holiness, justice, and peace in the land. In the following and final section of my paper, I will draw out what a Christ-centered theology of Zionism might look like through a synthesis of Buber's teaching on Zionism and the theological paradigm explored in Stage One. Now is the time to pick up the paintbrush and paint, layer upon layer, of holiness, of justice, of peace, and of return.

60. Buber's most important and best-known philosophical treatise on this subject is *Ich und Du.* See Buber, *I and Thou.*

STAGE THREE: PAINTING THE LANDSCAPE OF MESSIANIC HAGSHAMAH ZIONISM

Encountering the Holiness of the Land

The holiness of the land was fulfilled by the Messiah, the true temple of God. The very fullness of that holiness is promised to the believer in the expectant New Jerusalem. However, we have already discovered that the holiness of the land is no mere metaphor for some spiritual reality or disembodied future. As Buber put it, "That which is merely an idea and nothing more cannot become holy; but a piece of earth can become holy just as a mother's womb can become holy."[61] The holiness of God's future New Creation bursts into the "here and now" in the form of the Messiah's body and blood present to us in the Eucharist—in the bread that was brought forth from the earth and in the fruit of the vine. The early Zionist *halutzim* [forerunners, pioneers, *avant-garde*] came to the land in order to redeem and prepare it for the nation. Yeshua is the great *halutz* [forerunner] who crossed through the veil of death into the Holy of Holies of New Creation (cf. Heb 6:19–20), and he brings us back a taste of what is to come in the form of his body and blood, incarnated in the fruit of the land. The Lord can therefore be likened to the spies whom Moses sent into the Promised Land before Israel entered their inheritance, who brought back the fruits of that future land to the people in the wilderness (Num 13:23–26).[62]

In an early church document known as the Didache, we find one of the earliest Eucharistic liturgies:

> And concerning the broken bread:/We give You thanks, our Father,/for the life and knowledge/which You have made known to us/through Jesus, Your servant;/to You be the glory forever./ Just as this broken bread was scattered upon the mountains/ and then was gathered together and become one,/so may Your Church be gathered together/from the ends of the earth into your kingdom;/for yours is the glory and power through Jesus Christ forever.[63]

This prayer accentuates the connection between the Body of the Messiah, manifested as the ecclesial community, and the Body of the Messiah,

61. Buber, *A Land of Two Peoples*, 117.

62. Wright, *The Meal Jesus Gave Us*, 55–58.

63. Didache 9:3–4.

manifested as the Eucharist. It stresses the oneness of the community that shares in the one bread (cf. 1 Cor 10:17–18), the hope of the future kingdom that is present in the Eucharist, and also the "earthiness" of the Eucharistic bread that "was scattered upon the mountains." The Eucharist comes from the land, and speaks of the land's future redemption.

The sacramentality of the Eucharist testifies to the potential and anticipated sacramentality of the *adamah* [earth] and of the *cosmos*. However, for the Jewish people and for the Palestinian people, it is particularly *this* land—Israel/Palestine—that is holy. This is due to the fact that we, these nations, are particularly in covenant with *this* land, the land of our forefathers, which has been called holy more than any other. By this I am not suggesting that Israel-Palestine is *exclusively* made holy, for we have seen that the entire *cosmos* shall be made holy, but rather that this land is *particularly* made holy for these particular peoples. Therefore, when we, Jewish and Palestinian followers of the Messiah, share together in the Eucharist, the fruit of this land, we encounter together the crucified and risen Lord who is truly present in, through, and as the Eucharist, and are reconciled as one. Moreover, by sharing together bread and wine, we also share the *land* that we both love. As Buber taught us, it is precisely this shared love for the land that is the foundation for any and every Jewish-Arab cooperation. Therefore, it would be wise for any such work of cooperation that is done in a Christ-centered context to be organized around the sharing of the Eucharist.

Messianic Zionism, therefore, will seek to bring the Jewish and the Palestinian peoples to a covenantal relationship with the land. As was discovered earlier, the verbs used to describe Adam's mission in Eden (*'avad* and *shamar*) are the verbs that describe the vocation of the Aaronic Priests in YHWH's holy temple. In respect to the land, they are often translated "tilling" and "keeping," but they can more literally be rendered service and guardianship. The nations of this land are its servants and guardians, and if we live in the land according to this vocation, every daily act upon it becomes a sacrament, an act of *tikkun 'olam* by which the land is redeemed.

Meeting the Land's Demand for Justice

As was explored previously, the land's holiness also speaks of its vulnerability to pollution (spiritual and physical), and thus to its demand for justice. The land cries out for a three-fold justice: 1) justice for the landless sojourning on the land, 2) justice for the "Other" who belongs to the land, and 3) justice for the land itself. This can alternately be described as socio-economic justice, political justice, and ecological justice.

The Torah instructs us to care for the landless (i.e., the poor, the orphan, and the alien) and the Messiah proclaims "just as you did it to one of the least of these . . . you did it to me" (Matt 25:40). Therefore, we cannot claim to belong to the Messiah if we do not care for the landless on the land—the single mothers, the unemployed citizens, the asylum-seeking refugees, the migrant workers, the homeless Gazans. The Messianic community should be known as a community that fights for the rights of the disenfranchised, especially when it is unpopular to do so. Currently, with the rising number of asylum-seekers pouring into Israel from Africa, the forced expulsion of migrant workers and their children, and the ghettoization of the destroyed Gaza strip, Messianic Jews must offer themselves as a voice for the voiceless and cry out for justice together with the land.

However, the Palestinian people cannot properly be seen as truly landless, for they belong to *this* land, the land of their fathers. They deserve to be treated with justice and to be recognized as belonging to the land, no less than the Jews belong to the land. True *hagshamah* Zionism works towards justice for all nations, including the Palestinian nation. Zion can be redeemed only *bmishpat* (Isa 1:27), only in justice, and therefore a Zionism that excludes the Palestinian people from full participation in the spiritual and political life of the land is not a biblically based Zionism, but rather a manifestation of fascist nationalism. Therefore, as long as the Palestinians are denied equal political rights in the land as a whole, the land will continue to be polluted spiritually. This cannot be achieved through separation, but only through reconciliation, and therefore justice will not be fully restored by establishing a sovereign Palestinian state, but only by both nations serving and guarding the land together, whether in two states or in one.

Moreover, one cannot work for political justice while ignoring socio-economic justice or vice versa. The *adamah* demands justice for every *adam*, because each person is an image of God, whether she is a single Jewish mother living in poverty, a politically marginalized Palestinian, or a Darfurian refugee seeking asylum. Likewise, the *adamah* demands justice also for its own sake. Justice for those who sojourn on the land and for those who belong to the land is inextricably bound to ecological justice for the land itself, as demonstrated by the Sabbatical practices commanded by the Torah. As the *Ecclesia* community, we must be deeply concerned with matters of ecological stewardship: sustainable production of energy, sustainable use of resources, and sustainable cultivation of the land, as well as humane treatment of animals, preservation of the beauty of nature, and the curbing of pollution.

As Zionists, we already have a model for justice-oriented, land-cultivating communities in the form of the *kibbutzim*. Instead of observing the corruption and disintegration of this uniquely Zionist form of village life, the Messianic community can imaginatively re-apply this social model in a Christ-centered way to our twenty-first-century condition, both in a rural and urban context. Not everyone should escape from the cities into the country, but one could reconnect to the land and to creation also in an urban context, in *kibbutz* communities that voluntarily share the physical and spiritual wealth of the sisters and brothers who inhabit them. The urban *kibbutzim* would stress the importance of serving the land and of small-scale agriculture inside the cities. They will also have unique advantages over rural *kibbutzim* in the opportunity to serve the disenfranchised communities that exist only in the urban centers.

Such Messianic *kibbutzim*, rooted in the sacramental holiness of the land and in unity with the Palestinian Christian community, could spearhead the national mission of Israel to restore justice to the land, to the land's inhabitants, and to the landless. These would be communities engaged in *tikkun 'olam* on a daily basis, through sharing the holy Eucharist and through sharing profane *mammon*, through sustainable agriculture and through sustaining prayer, through studying the Word, and through embracing the marginalized.

Entering the Peace of the Land

As we have seen, the Messiah is the source of peace and rest in the land, a peace we will fully experience when all creation is renewed. However, the writer of Hebrews admonishes us to "make every effort to enter that rest" (Heb 4:11) "today" (4:7). As heirs of New Creation and the restored Eden, we are called to seek peace and reconciliation in the land. Yet there can be no peace without holiness and justice. We, as Israeli Messianic Jews, cannot honestly embrace the Arab Palestinian Christians as brothers and sisters in Christ without simultaneously dealing with the sin and injustice that pollutes the land of Israel/Palestine. We cannot dictate the terms of "peace" and continue to deny the Palestinian national center in Jerusalem or the right of Palestinian refugees to return to their land. Nor can we relegate these issues of justice to the realm of "secular politics" as if they have no bearing on our unity in the Messiah. Final peace will come only when the Messiah returns to his New Creation. However, this hope energizes us to "enflesh" God's peace here and now, since we ourselves are a foretaste of God's New Creation.

It is this author's opinion that Buber was correct in calling for a bi-national federation in this land, and that even today this may be the best paradigm for peace. That however, is secondary. Whatever political paradigm is chosen, we must continue to insist that the nations (and the *Ecclesia* community) will not be divided into powerful and powerless, haves and have-nots. Instead we proclaim that "every valley shall be lifted up, and every mountain and hill be made low; the uneven ground shall become level, and the rough places a plain" (Isa 40:4) and "Let justice roll down like waters, and righteousness like an ever-flowing stream" (Amos 5:24). Peace can never be based on separation, only on reconciliation; it is not enough to live "alongside," lest the "alongside" again be rendered into an "against." We must live "together-with" the "Other," aspiring not to mere "coexistence" but to genuinely reciprocal "inter-existence." How else can we love our neighbor? And if we do not see God in our brother's face (cf. Gen 33:10), how can we say we love our God? (cf. 1 John 4:20)

One of the central aspects of the mission of the Messianic *kibbutz* would be to actively create spaces in which true reconciliation could occur between the Jewish and Palestinian peoples. Reconciliation comes through the Messiah and by the power of the Spirit, but this does not mean peace will not come until all the inhabitants of the land have converted to Christianity. The Messiah taught us that we must choose to be the neighbor who loves, rather than choosing who qualifies as our neighbor before we love her. Therefore, instead of promoting another crusade, let us humbly embrace the "Other" and the enemy, as the Messiah did.[64] The Messianic *kibbutz*, would thus be a true example of

---

64. It is interesting that in Yeshua's popularly quoted parable on neighborly love (Luke 10:29–37), he chose to speak of a Samaritan—a member of a competing ethno-religious group that also belonged to the land and worshiped the God of Abraham; this is not unlike the Muslim Palestinians today. Throughout this article, when the Palestinian nation's connection to the land is referred to, this naturally includes the Muslim majority. The need for reconciliation in the land is between the entire Jewish

halutziut [pioneering], boldly making the desert of separation bloom into reconciliation. Only thus can we enter into the rest which was created for us.

Return Now!

When Yeshua of Nazareth began his ministry in the Galilee, he proclaimed the gospel that the kingdom of God has come near, and called his brothers and sisters to repent. Yeshua called out these words in Jewish Aramaic, not in Greek; he could not have only been calling for *metanoia*, in the sense of an internal religious change of heart, but rather for *tshuvah*—"returning" unto YHWH. Just like in the Torah and the Prophets, the Messiah's call to return to God is deeply connected to the promise of returning to the land.[65] Yeshua's proclamations of God's kingdom cannot be separated from the New Testament hope in God's New Creation; the kingdom of God is the means through which all the nations will "return to the land," the restored Eden. As was previously explored, this return must be understood not only as an eschatological hope, but as a current political agenda for all nations who are to be in covenant with God and with the land. Zionism—the return of the Jewish people to the land of Israel—is therefore an expression of *tikkun 'olam*—the "restoration of the *cosmos*"—and it goes hand-in-hand with *tshuvah*—"returning" to YHWH in repentance. This Jewish return to the land is called *kibbutz galuyot*, the ingathering of the exiles, a phrase that lies below the surface of every use of the word *kibbutz*, which can also simply mean community.

It is important to note that Zionism's particularity does not justify exclusivity. Instead, *hagshamah* Zionism demands justice, peace, and freedom for all nations. Therefore, the biblical prophecies of returning to the land, which literally, at the level of *pshat*, referred to the Jews returning from Babylon in the sixth and fifth centuries BCE, and which are *midrashically* applied to the current return of the Jewish nation from the Diaspora, could just as legitimately be applied to the Palestinian refugees' *haqq al-'auda* [right of return] to their lands. It is important to recognize

---

nation and the entire Palestinian nation (and the Arab world), and not exclusively between those who are "in the Messiah."

65. For an excellent discussion on the Messiah's call of repentance, see Wright, *Jesus and the Victory*, 246–58.

that the Palestinian refugees' connection to the land is particularly localized. They view themselves as belonging to a particular town or village,
and until they have the freedom to reconnect to that particular plot of
land in a covenantal relationship, justice will not be restored. This does
not mean that all, or most, Palestinian refugees will return to the precise
plot from whence their fathers departed, only that they should have the
freedom to do so. *Tshuvah* [repentance], *kibbutz galuyot* [Jewish ingath-
ering], and *'auda* [Palestinian return] are all interconnected with each
other in the framework of Messianic *hagshamah* Zionism. Whatever
political paradigm is chosen, it must ensure that the entire Jewish nation
is allowed to be in covenant with all of *Eretz-Israel* and that the entire
Palestinian nation is allowed to be in covenant with all of Palestine. As
the two peoples begin to live in positive and reciprocal "inter-existence"
we can move away from the concept of Israel/Palestine (as an "either/
or") and co-create the concept of Israel-Palestine (as a "both-and").

CONCLUSION

In the newly formed painting one discovers a new Zionist *kibbutz* at the
center of which is the Messiah. This community seeks to embody the
ideal of *halutziut* by incarnating YHWH's future redemption of the *cosmos*, the expectant *tikkun 'olam*, in their particular location in the land.
Thus the Messianic *kibbutz* is the *hagshamah* of God's promise of return
to the land, of *kibbutz galuyot*. This community (whether it is in a rural
setting or an urban setting) treats every action as a sacrament—from the
taking of the Eucharist to the tilling of the earth. Though celebrating its
particularity, it is radically inclusive, embracing all those most marginalized, the last and the least of these. It is actively engaged in safeguarding
a sustainable environment, in defending the economically marginalized,
and in liberating the politically oppressed. It is faithful in its *'avodah*
[work, tilling, service, worship] but also in its *mnuhah* [rest] as it actively
enters its rest by creating spaces for the Messiah's peace to come, even to
the troubled land of Israel-Palestine.

As we observe the landscape painting, we see that it can also be
viewed as a portrait. It is a portrait of the Messiah himself incarnated
in the land and in the *Ecclesia* community. More than a portrait, this
landscape is an *eikon* through which we see our Lord, "enfleshed" in the
midst of the reciprocal covenant between *adam* and *adamah*, a covenant

that can last only if YHWH stands in the center of it. Some who look at this portrait may feel encouraged, others convicted, still others enraged.

To those who will accuse this work of being post-Zionist, I can only send you back to Buber and to his radical vision of Zionism grounded in the Hebrew Bible and even more importantly, to the Messiah and to his radical example of love. If the views I shared in this article are post-Zionist, then so were many of the early Zionists themselves. I urge you to examine your allegiances: Do they belong to the kingdom of Caesar with its "cannons, flags, and military decorations,"[66] or do they belong to the kingdom of God, where the last will be first and the first will be last? It is time to shed the *realpolitik* imagination of the state and to prophetically imagine the kingdom of God into existence.

To those who are frustrated that I referred to the Jews as having an equal stake in the land as the Palestinians, I encourage to check yourself for any latent xenophobia or rejection of the claims of the land-less (as the Jewish people were for far too long). I set out to incarnate the theological paradigm in an Israeli context and therefore frequently used Hebrew words and Zionist terminology. The Palestinians must do the same in their own cultural context and through the richness of the Arabic language and the wealth of their liturgical heritage. I surely did not mean that the Palestinian Christians should live in *kibbutzim* or use Jewish terminology (though we definitely can learn from each other). Instead, the Palestinian Christians must reclaim the Old Testament as it has been interpreted in their own traditions and rediscover their promise of return.

And finally, to those who are encouraged by this old-new conception of Zionism, do not let it remain an interesting idea in your heads. Zionism has always been a movement of dreamers who were willing to be foolish enough to realize those dreams. Following the crucified and risen King consists of faith in the rationally impossible, hope in the seemingly inconceivable, and love towards the absolutely unlovable. The Messiah imagined the impossible into the world. So fulfill the holiness, "enflesh" the justice, incarnate the peace; by the grace of God, bring this painting to its *hagshamah*.

66. Ibid., 35–37.

BIBLIOGRAPHY

Ahad Ha'Am. *Selected Essays by Ahad Ha'Am*. Edited by Leon Simon. Philadelphia: Jewish Publication Society of America, 1912.

Alexander, T. Desmond. "Beyond Borders: The Wider Dimensions of the Land." In *The Land of Promise: Biblical, Theological and Contemporary Perspectives*, edited by Philip Johnston and Peter Walker, 35–50. Downers Grove, IL: InterVarsity, 2000.

Buber, Martin. *A Land of Two Peoples: Martin Buber on Jews and Arabs*. Edited by Paul R. Mendes-Flohr. New York: Oxford University Press, 1983.

———. *I and Thou: A New Translation with a Prologue "I and You" and Notes by Walter Kaufmann*. New York: Scribner, 1970.

Brueggemann, Walter. *The Land: Place as Gift, Promise and Challenge in Biblical Faith*. 2nd ed. Overtures to Biblical Theology. Minneapolis: Fortress, 2002.

Davies, W. D. *The Gospel and the Land: Early Christianity and Jewish Territorial Doctrine*. Berkeley: University of California Press, 1974.

Warshawsky, Keri Zelson. "Returning to Their Own Borders: A Social Anthropological Study of Contemporary Messianic Jewish Identity in Israel." PhD diss., Hebrew University, Jerusalem, 2008.

Wenham, G. J. "Sanctuary Symbolism in the Garden of Eden Story." *Proceedings of the World Congress of Jewish Studies* 9 (1986) 19–25.

Williamson, Paul R. "Promise and Fulfillment: The Territorial Inheritance." In *The Land of Promise: Biblical, Theological and Contemporary Perspectives*, edited by Philip Johnston and Peter Walker, 15–34. Downers Grove, IL: InterVarsity, 2000.

Wright, N. T. *Jesus and the Victory of God*. Christian Origins and the Question of God 2. Minneapolis: Fortress, 1996.

———. *The Meal Jesus Gave Us*. Louisville: Westminster John Knox, 2002.

❖ 8 ❖

The Earth Is the Lord's

Land, Theology, and the Bible

Naim Ateek

U NDOUBTEDLY, THE MOST CRUCIAL aspect in the political conflict over Palestine is that of the land. This is the bottom line of the conflict. The whole peace process is very much dependent on the land question. *To whom does the land belong?* Does it belong to the Jewish people or to the Palestinians? How can their claims be reconciled? Is peace possible between them? The answers we give, as people of faith, to these questions and many others depends on one's theology of land.

At its inception the Zionist movement was not religious. Most of the Zionist fathers were not interested in religion. In fact, religious Jews at the time were anti-Zionist. Subsequently and due to a number of historical and political factors most of them were won over to Zionism. Since 1967, there has been a shift in Zionism from secular to more religious. Today, the strongest and most ardent Zionists are religious. For many Zionists today the religious argument for Zionism has become the most convincing. This argument uses religious language and bases itself on the biblical promises regarding the land. A theology of land has become mandatory as a result. On it depends the future of peace in the region. This is especially true when one considers that Jewish religious parties are a strong component of the successive Israeli governments.

THE CENTRALITY OF CHRIST

Although many Christians might differ in their understanding of revelation and inspiration, they believe that the Holy Spirit was active in guiding the writers as they recorded the story of salvation that God accomplishes in Jesus Christ. In other words, there is a crescendo in the biblical books that reaches its climax in the coming of Christ. From this perspective, the biblical material is not viewed in a horizontal way as having the same authority and the same theological or spiritual value. What God has done in Christ for the redemption of the world is more authoritative and has greater value for the believer than anything else.

The heart of the Bible is, therefore, Jesus Christ. From a Christian perspective, Christ stands at the center of history. History is the story of God's love for the world in Jesus Christ to bring justice, healing, peace, salvation and liberation to all. The Israelites are enjoined "to do justice, to love kindness, and to walk humbly with God" (Mic 6:8).[1] Apart from Christ, this world is an enigma. Christians can understand the meaning of history when they view it through what God has purposed for it in Christ. The Old Testament is very much a part of that background. However, it cannot stand on its own, nor can it be understood apart from the New Testament. It cannot be fully comprehended apart from its completion and fulfillment in Christ. In fact, without the New Testament, many parts of the Old Testament are, in today's language, Zionist and racist. Without Christ, the Old Testament is not only incomplete; it can be, in some of its parts, a very dangerous document that calls for ethnic cleansing and can produce fanatical actions by fanatical people. We value the Old Testament because of Christ. On its own it is not sufficient for salvation.

For me as a Christian, Christ is the heart of the Bible, and he is its hermeneutic. He is the criterion for its interpretation and understanding. As a Christian, I cannot begin my study of the Bible from Genesis. I must begin with what God in Christ has done and then move into the Old Testament in order to understand the background of the faith. *As I do this, I find that the outcome was not precisely what some of the Old Testament writers envisage.* What God did for the world in Christ far exceeded the best that the prophets predicted and anticipated. The

---

1. NASB (New American Standard Bible) is used for all Scripture quotations in this article.

best illustration is the resurrection of Christ. It is possible to discover certain hints of the resurrection here and there in the Old Testament as the early church did, but the event itself far exceeded anything that they had imagined. It was God's great surprise.

In other words, in order to understand any issue in the Bible, I have to understand it in light of its fulfillment in Christ. The whole Bible is a progressive revelation of Christ. For example, if I want to study the topic of choseness or election, my points of departure are Christ and the New Testament. What the New Testament teaches about election becomes authoritative for me because, in Christ, I have received the full picture. What was said of election before Christ might be interesting for study, but if it differs from its point of completion in Christ, it cannot be authoritative for me. I will adopt and embrace the New Testament version because it is the completed and fulfilled version. From this foundational understanding of the centrality of Christ, let me go on to reflect on the issue of the land.

A THEOLOGY OF THE LAND

It is clear to me from the Synoptic Gospels that Christ was interested in the issue of the kingdom of God and not the land. In fact, it is interesting to point out that in the Old Testament the word or words designating "the land" appear more than 1,600 times while in the New Testament less than 50 times. However, it is interesting to note that in the Old Testament, God states that he is the final owner of the land (Ps 104:24). At the same time the expressions "the kingdom of God" or "the kingdom of heaven" are frequently on the lips of Jesus and are recorded more than 100 times in the Synoptics. The concept of the kingdom in the New Testament is the counterpart to the concept of the land in the Old Testament, with one major difference: a consistent stress on the inclusive nature of God's kingdom. It does not differentiate between gender, race, or ethnicity. It is for the entire world and all peoples. Jesus practiced what he preached in his attitude to Jews, Romans, Greeks, Canaanites, and Phoenicians as well as to men and women. The New Testament has abundant illustrations to attest to this (Matt 8:5–3, 15:21–28; Mark 7:24–30; Mark 10:2–12; Luke 17:11–19; John 4:4–42).

Jesus did not appear to be interested in the issue of the land. Indeed, he always tried to stretch his disciples' understanding away from the narrow conception of God and the land. He always tried to shatter any narrow nationalism that they exhibited (Matt 15:21–28; Luke 9:51–56, 24:13–27; Acts 1:6–8). The whole spirit of the ministry of Christ in the Gospels puts us on a different ground from that of the Old Testament. Ethnocentricity is opposed, ethnic arrogance is challenged, and any superior feeling is discouraged and shattered (Matt 20:1–16; Mark 12:1–12; Luke 20:9–19).

According to Luke 24:13–33, even after the resurrection, the two disciples on the road to Emmaus said to him that they "were hoping that it was he [Jesus] who was going to redeem Israel." Jesus started to help them understand the Scriptures: "Then beginning with Moses and with all the prophets, he explained to them the things concerning himself in all the Scriptures" (24:27). Jesus Christ is the clue and the focus, not Israel. In him, the redemption of Israel, as well as other people, has been accomplished.

In the Gospel of John, *all* those who believe in Jesus Christ have become children of God, "born, not of blood nor of the will of flesh nor of the will of man, but of God" (John 1:13). It is no more the law that Moses gave to the children of Israel that governs, but rather God's grace given through Christ to the entire world. "For God so loved the world . . . " (John 3:16)—not only the children of Israel or *Eretz-Israel*. Jerusalem and Gerizim are no longer theologically important. "God is Spirit, and those who worship him must worship in spirit and in truth" (John 4:24).

At every point and turn, the focus now is not on one land (the land of Israel), or one people (the Jewish people), but on what God will do, or indeed, is doing for the whole world and for all the people of the world in Christ. The land of Palestine is only the launching pad for God's activity in and for the world. That is why in the early church, the land of Palestine was not perceived as theologically important.[2]

Rather, the focus was on Christ and the importance of preaching the gospel to the world. It was only after the fourth century that the land began to be perceived as holy, and Christian pilgrimages to the land ensued. Indeed, for the early church, the destruction of the temple was an indication of the disappearance of the old order (the temple sacrifice) and the old Abrahamic covenant (land) and of the dawning of the new covenant (the church as the Bride of Christ). For the early Christians it reflected the displeasure of God with those Jews who did not accept the

2. See Walker, *Holy City, Holy Places?*

Messiahship of Jesus. Christ has replaced the temple, and the believers in Christ have become themselves temples of the Holy Spirit of God (1 Cor 3:16; 6:19; 2 Cor 6:16). Faith in Christ has shattered the importance of any geography and can no longer be limited in one locale.

The same basic theology is present in almost every one of the New Testament writings. God's purposes for the world have been revealed in Christ, and they are inclusive of all people. Any narrow understanding of God or the land is shunned. One of the most telling examples is Stephen's sermon in Acts 7. Stephen drove home the fact that the temple did not represent the original plan of God. God had given instructions for the tabernacle that was not bound to any one geographic location and symbolized the universal presence of God (7:44). Solomon was permitted to build the temple later, but when it was dedicated, God made it clear that he would not be limited to it (7:48–50). God never limited himself to one land. No one land as such was holy. It is neither the land nor the temple; it is Christ who is the focal point.

The New Testament then reinterprets the promises of the land in light of Christ. So Paul in Rom 4:13 says something very revolutionary: "For the promise to Abraham or to his descendants that he would be heir to the world [cosmos] was not through the law, but through the righteousness of faith." Nowhere in the Old Testament was such a promise specifically given to Abraham. Paul understands the promise in the light of the coming of Christ. Christ is the true seed of Abraham (Gal 3:16), and in his coming he brought salvation and redemption for the whole world. In light of their universal fulfillment in Christ, the narrow Old Testament promises regarding the land take on a very transitory and provisional meaning. They are time bound and, in view of their completion in Christ, become theologically obsolete.

The New Testament does not only reinterpret the Old Testament, it de-Zionizes it. One can illustrate this by comparing, for example, what Jesus said in John 1:51 and its antecedent in Gen 28:12–13. In the latter passage, we read: "[Jacob] had a dream, and behold, a ladder was set on the earth with its top reaching to heaven; and behold, the angels of God were ascending it and descending on it. And behold, the Lord stood above it and said, 'I am the Lord, the God of your father Abraham and the God of Isaac; the land on which you lie, I will give it to you and your descendant.'" In John, Jesus says to Nathanael, "I say to you, you will see the heavens opened and the angels of God ascending and descending on the Son of Man." Jacob's ladder was set on the earth. The land was seen as important, and the promise to inherit the land was reiterated to Jacob. In John the land is no longer important. Jesus the Christ replaces it. The angels in John are ascending and descending not on the land but on the Son of Man. I believe this represents a definite attempt at de-Zionizing the faith. It is no more Israel or the land. The focal point is Jesus Christ.

There is plenty of Zionist material in the Old Testament where the land is exclusively claimed and the Jewish people are glorified and set above others, and where non-Jews are despised. The New Testament shatters this exclusivity at every turn. One of the classic examples is found in Jesus' sermon in Nazareth. According to Luke 4:16–30, Jesus read from Isaiah 61. I believe he intentionally stopped where he did to omit all the Zionist materials against other nations, viz., "and the day of vengeance of our God" (v. 2b); also, "Strangers will stand and pasture your flocks, and foreigners will be your farmers and your vinedressers. But you will be called priests of the Lord; you will be spoken of as ministers of our God, you will eat the wealth of nations, and in their riches you will boast" (vv. 5–6). That kind of racism has no place in the kingdom of God. Jesus' reference to the widow of Sidon and to Naaman the Syrian expressed clearly where God stood in his concern and love for all lands and people.

It is in light of this theology that centers on Christ that we can then evaluate the Old Testament concept of land. It moves from a generally exclusive theology in the Pentateuch to a more inclusive one after the exile. Yet within the exclusive material, it is possible to find some gems breaking through and reflecting a more inclusive view. For example, Lev 25:23 is one of them: "The land, moreover, shall not be sold permanently, for the land is mine; for you are but aliens and sojourners with me." Ps 24:1 is another: "The earth is the Lord's, and all it contains, the world, and those who dwell in it."

It is only after the exile that one begins to see a gradual shift towards a more inclusive understanding of God and the land. The experience of exile must have stretched the people's understanding of God. One of the most exciting books in the Old Testament that reflects this inclusive theology is the book of Jonah. The story must have been written by a Jewish liberation theologian who was rebelling against the traditional view of God and the land. It is clear in this book that God's care is shown to people other than Israelites, even to their most hated enemy, the Assyrians, and to a land other than the land of Israel.

In this movement towards inclusiveness, Ezek 47:21–23 reflects a new realism where the land belongs to both the Israelites returning from exile as well as to the people who were already living in the land. Although the vocabulary used is still discriminatory by calling the people of the land "aliens," its theology is far more advanced than the language that is found in some parts of the Torah where the people of the land must be totally exterminated (Num 21:1–3, 31–35; 33:51–52; Deut 7:1–2, 22–24). Undoubtedly, the experience of exile forced them to understand God more universally and to become much more open to people of other nations. Yet within the writings of these postexilic prophets, one can still find a good amount of material that reflects a very exclusive theology of land. However, the shift to a more inclusive theology had started. It is picked up again in the New Testament and finds its truest and clearest expressions in Christ and his inclusive concept of the kingdom of God.

CONCLUSION

What are the implications of an inclusive theology of land for peace in the land? Simply put, it is this: The land of Palestine/Israel is part of God's world. It belongs to God. God is its creator and owner as God is the maker and owner of the whole world. Today, God has placed both Palestinians and Jews to live on it. They must share the land under God and become good stewards of it. It does not belong to either of them exclusively. They must share it equitably and live as good neighbors with one another. Both nations must do justice, love kindness, and walk humbly with God (Mic 6:8). Once the demands of justice have been satisfied, a good measure of peace will be achieved and security will be enjoyed by all throughout the land. "The work of righteousness will be peace, and the service of righteousness, quietness and confidence forever" (Isa 32:17).

BIBLIOGRAPHY

Walker, P. W. L. *Holy City, Holy Places? Christian Attitudes to Jerusalem and the Holy Land in the Fourth Century*. Oxford Early Christian Studies. Oxford: Clarendon, 1990.

❖ 9 ❖

Jerusalem Is the City of God

A Palestinian Reading of Psalm 87

Yohanna Katanacho

LUTFI LEHAM SAYS THAT in Jerusalem Jews represent the 17 million Jews, Muslims represent the 850 million Muslims, and Christians represent the 1300 million Christians around the world.[1] Even if we disagree with the accuracy of Leham's statement, we have to admit that Jerusalem is very important in the eyes of many Muslims, Jews, and Christians. It is known that Jerusalem is the third-most holy city in Islam. According to an Islamic *hadith*, the prophet of Islam said that if a Muslim prays the five daily Islamic prayers in Jerusalem, he will become sinless just like the day he was born.[2] Dr. ʾamru summarizes the feelings of most Muslims when he says that Muslims cannot give up one inch of Jerusalem because it is a sacred Islamic city.[3] In addition, Bishop Leham rightly affirms that Jerusalem is the spiritual capital of many Christians.[4] It is the city ͺof the resurrection and of Pentecost. Also, according to Jewish tradition, Jerusalem is the center of national life since its conquest by King David. It is the city in which Abraham

1. Leham, "Al Quds," 62.
2. ʾamru, "Al Quds," 19.
3. Ibid., 25.
4. Leham, "Al Quds," 47.

181

offered Isaac, David ruled as king, and Solomon built the temple of God. Indeed, Jerusalem is an important place, and we hope in this essay to contribute to the discussion related to the holy city by providing a detailed study of Psalm 87, which presents a vision of Jerusalem in which enmity and bloodshed are terminated and its citizens uphold justice and righteousness. We shall argue that Psalm 87 provides a new understanding of Davidic theology. A restorative eschatology of the "Jewish" city of King David could no longer serve the people of God who were in exile. Instead, the psalmist presents a servant David who advocates a multiethnic Jerusalem. Only then would Jerusalem be a blessing, not a curse. The following article will elaborate my claims by a close study of Psalm 87. [5]

THE STRUCTURE OF PSALM 87

At the risk of oversimplification, one can present the various views concerning the structure and coherence of Psalm 87 in three groups. The first group questions its coherence and rearranges its verses, producing dozens of possibilities. [6] Kraus, for example, describes Psalm 87 as badly injured, claiming that its half verses have been torn apart and "senselessly coordinated." [7] Beaucamp reconstructs the psalm by dividing it into two main parts: the oracle (vv. 1–4) and its commentary (vv. 5–7). [8]

The second group accepts the order of the Masoretic Text but differs on dividing it. Weiser, VanGemeren, Perowne, and Kidner divide it into three units. Weiser and VanGemeren divide it into vv. 1–2, 3–6, and 7, while Perowne and Kidner split it into vv. 1–3, 4–6, and 7. [9] Booij differs from them in seeing v. 7 connected to v. 6. He divides the psalm as 1–2, 3–5, and 6–7. [10]

The third group highlights the significance of the order of the Masoretic Text. Gladly, Tate, Smith, and Terrien pay more attention to the unity of the psalm. Terrien divides it into six sections, including four

5. My interpretation of the psalm focuses on its *Sitz im Text*. As a result, it differs from those of several scholars who tend to interpret Psalm 87 by focusing on its spatio-temporal components, Gattung, and/or *Sitz im Leben*.

6. For a list of reconstructions, see Booij, "Some Observations," 16.

7. Kraus, *Psalms 60–150: A Commentary*, 184–85.

8. Beaucamp, "Psaume 87," 279–88.

9. VanGemeren, "Psalms," 561; Perowne, *Commentary on the Psalms*, 136–38; Kidner, *Psalms 73–150: A Commentary*, 314–16.

10. Booij, "Some Observations," 16–21.

strophes (vv. 2–3, 4, 5, and 6), a prelude (v. 1b), and a postlude (v. 7).[11] Smith sees vv. 1–2 as a thematic preface followed by a "concentric pentacolon" that unifies the psalm—i.e., A: *bakh* (v. 3), B: *sham* (v. 4), C: *bah* (v. 5), B': *sham* (v. 6), and A': *bakh* in (v. 7).[12] In light of Smith's concentric pentacolon, it is better to see vv. 4–6 as a unit in which v. 5 is the center, and vv. 4 and 6 mirror each other. Indeed, it is hard to claim that the structure of Psalm 87 is ambiguous.[13] In fact, we agree with Tate, who argues that placing *bah* at the center, followed by "a statement of the Most High's establishment of Zion (5c) is striking and makes the rearrangement of the verses dubious."[14] It seems that the third group has provided sufficient evidence for the coherence of the present order of Psalm 87.[15] Consequently, our interpretation of the psalm rejects its reconstruction and respects its skillful composition.

INTERPRETING THE PSALM

It seems that Psalm 87 is not only skillfully composed, but it might also be intentionally placed after Psalm 86. Consequently, we suggest two important questions that have the potential to unpack new insights in understanding Psalm 87. We will present the questions. Then we will demonstrate how they help us fathom new dimensions of Psalm 87. The questions follow: (1) what happened to the nations in Psalm 87? (2) Is the placement of Psalm 87 significant for its interpretation?

(1) What Happened to the Nations in Psalm 87?

First, is Psalm 87 talking about the nations? The answer to this question depends partly on our understanding of Ps 87:4–6.[16] Verse 4 mentions five labels (*rahav, bavel, pleshet, tsor, kush*). These labels might refer to

11. Terrien, *The Psalms*, 621.

12. Smith, "The Structure of Psalm 87," 357.

13. It is also possible to argue that Ps 87:1 corresponds with the first part of the double superscription in Ps 88:1. The first four Hebrew words in Ps 87 are also mentioned in Ps 88:1, albeit in an inverted order.

14. Tate, *Psalms 51–100*, 389.

15. Some recent insightful Psalm studies emphasize not only its internal coherence but also its purposeful placement within the Psalter. See, e.g., Hossfeld and Zenger, *Psalms 2*, 377–88.

16. All OT references in this essay follow the order of the Masoretic Text.

geographical areas and/or the people of those areas.[17] However, the context of Psalm 87 is not describing geographical locations.[18] It is focusing
on people who are born in Zion (cf. vv. 4 and 6), who are described as
ʾish v ʾish in v. 5 and are included among the nations in v. 6. But are they
Israelites or Gentiles, or a combination?

Kraus argues that Psalm 87 is talking about the members of Israel
in the Diaspora. He sees the aforementioned five Hebrew labels as the
nations in which Israel is dispersed, arguing that surely the ones who
know Yahweh are the Israelites, not the nations. These Israelites were
born in foreign lands and acquired citizenship. He explains that the
Hebrew combination (ʾazkir and l) should be understood in light of a
similar combination of words in Jer 4:16 (hazkiru).[19] There, it translates
"tell the nations." Thus, after reconstructing Psalm 87, Kraus proposes
the following reading, "Yahweh counts up nations in writing them
down: 'This one is born here, that one there. I mention Rahab and Babel
before those who know me; yes, also Philistia and Tyre together with
Cush. But Zion "I call mother," man for man is born there.'"[20] Kraus not
only rearranges the order of the verses, overlooking the final Masoretic
Text and many ancient witnesses as well as the skillful composition of
Psalm 87, but he also adds the word "them" in the first sentence in order
to accommodate his theory (cf. Ps 87:6). He stretches the meaning of
the repeated phrase zeh yulad sham translating it as "this one is born
here, that one there," and translates lyodʿai as "before those who know
me," a very unusual translation.[21] He bases his understanding of Ps 87:4a

17. Although (rahav) usually refers to a mythological creature, its usage in Ps 87:4
is different. Just like Is 30:7, Rahab is connected to Egypt. The word "Rahab" occurs in
Isa 30:7, 51:9; Ps 87:4, 89:11; Job 9:13, 26:12; and possibly in Ps 40:5. See Even-Shoshan,
Konkordantsyah, 1063.

18. This understanding is in agreement with the Septuagint that employs ethnic
terms instead of geographical ones. The Septuagint translates pelshet (Philistia) as
allophuloi (foreigners). The Arabic Polyglotta translates it as "the foreign tribes." See
Walton, *Biblia Sacra Polyglotta*, 225.

19. Dahood rightly argues that it is better to translate the Hiphʿil form (ʾazkir) as
record or inscribe. Tate takes it as "proclaim" based on Jer 4:16 and Isa 12:4. There
(zkr) parallels (ydʿ) and thus resembles Ps 87:4. Dahood, *Psalms*, 298–99; Tate, *Psalms
51–100*, 386.

20. Kraus, *Psalms 60–150*, 185, 187–88.

21. Robert Young clarifies that the Hebrew lamed never means "before." He lists
twenty-eight Hebrew words or combinations that could mean "before" excluding lamed
from his list. See Young, *Young's Analytical Concordance*, 81.

($\check{}$*azkir lyod$\check{}$ai*) on Jer 4:16a (*hazkiru lgoyim*). Although both texts use a Hiph$\check{}$il form of *zkr* + *l*, they are different. One is an imperative, the other is an imperfective; one uses a noun after the *lamed*, the other uses the Qal participle masculine plural with a first-person singular suffix. One means "cause remembrance to the nations" or "remind the nations"; the other means "I cause Rahab and Babel to be remembered."[22] Admittedly, the *lamed* before *yod$\check{}$ai* could be dative; however, it could also fit at least a few other categories: (1) It introduces the result after verbs of esteeming; (2) it could mean "in reference or in regard to";[23] (3) it could mean "as," "in the capacity of," "in relation to," "that is to say," or "in a state of."[24] Consequently, Tate's translation is linguistically possible i.e. *lyod$\check{}$ai* means "among those who know me."[25]

Tate's arguments are more probable than Kraus's. Tate explains that Psalm 87 is talking about Gentiles, not Jews; Tate gives the following reasons: (1) Jewish exiles would not be called Rahab, Babylonians, Philistines, Tyrians, or Cushites; (2) the ethnic identity of Israel was consistently maintained in the Old Testament, regardless of the people's geographical location; (3) Psalm 87 is part of a bigger pattern promoting Zion as the universal center of the world; and (4) Ps 87:5b states that everyone is born in Zion.[26] Tate reads *lyod$\check{}$ai* as "among those who know me," and $\check{}$*ish v $\check{}$ish yulad bah* as "everyone was born in her." Thus, Gentile nations in vv. 4–6 have gone through an identity transformation. They have become children of Zion and are now "Zionites." They are "Zionites" not by force but by birth in the city established by $\check{}$*elyon*, the global God.[27] In short, Tate's suggestion that Psalm 87 is part of a bigger pattern might provide another interpretive framework that has the potential to help us understand Psalm 87 in a better way. Unfortunately,

---

22. For further details, see Brown et al., *Hebrew and English Lexicon* (i.e., BDB), 270b; see also Ps 45:18; 2 Sam 18:18; and Exod 20:24.

23. Gesenius, et al., *Gesenius' Hebrew Grammar*, § 119 t and u.

24. Clines, *The Dictionary of Classical Hebrew*, 479–84, especially nos. 3, 6, 10, and 15.

25. Tate, *Psalms 51–100*, 386.

26. Ibid., 389.

27. $\check{}$*lywn $\check{}$elyon* is mentioned four times in Aramaic and thirty-two times in Hebrew. The Aramaic occurrences (Dan 7:18, 22, 25, 27) refer to a global God and are associated with a global eschatological kingdom including all nations. The Hebrew occurrences are found in the Pentateuch (six times), and mainly in Psalms (twenty-two times). $\check{}$*lywn $\check{}$elyon* is generally a global God and is frequently part of an eschatological picture where the nations are judged (Pss 9 and 46) and transformed (Ps 47).

Tate does not unpack his suggestion. However, we believe that the pertinent pattern can be discovered through intertextual observations related to birth imagery and Zion. This will be the task of the following section.

Birth Imagery and the Eschatological Vision of Zion

The nature of birth imagery must be understood in light of a new vision of Zion. More precisely, it is part of an eschatological vision in which the nations are transformed into the people of God. This vision can be seen more clearly within an intertextual pattern that combines birth images and Zion. Interestingly, the root *yld* is used only nine times in the Psalms: all of them except Ps 7:15 and Ps 90:2 are embedded in eschatological language.[28] The following table should be helpful in classifying some of the relevant data.

Ps 2	Enmity with nations (vv. 1–3) Divine activity in Zion (v. 6) Birth language (v. 7) Eschatological kingdom that includes subduing the nations (vv. 8–12)
Ps 22	Enmity (vv. 12–18) Divine activity (v. 24) Eschatological kingdom that includes the nations (vv. 27–29) Birth language (v. 31)
Ps 87	God favors Zion (vv. 1–2) + Divine activity in Zion (v. 5) No enmity but acknowledgement (v. 4) Birth language (vv. 4–6) Eschatological language that includes the nations (vv. 4–7)
Ps 110	Enmity with the nations is implicit (v. 1) Divine activity in Zion (v. 2) Birth language (v. 3) Eschatological language that includes subduing the nations (vv. 1–2, 5–6)

In light of this table, a few comments are appropriate. First, the above OT examples are not exhaustive but are illustrative of an even bigger pattern.[29] Second, these choices are confined to birth images that

28. Cf. Pss 2:7; 7:15; 22:32; 78:6; 87:4–6; 90:2; 110:3.

29. Other examples include: Isa 9:1–7 (the birth language is embedded in eschatological language); Isa 49 (Zion in v. 14; birth language in v. 21; universal eschatological inclusion of the nations in vv. 22–23); Isa 54 (birth language followed by eschatological language); Isa 66 (enmity with God [vv. 3–4]; divine activity in Zion [v. 6]; birth language [vv. 7–9]; eschatological language that includes the nations [vv. 12–24]); and

use the root *yld* even though the concept of birth is not restricted to one root.[30] In addition, all the chosen texts associate birth images with both Zion as well as with cosmic eschatological language. Third, the pattern in the above table usually includes the following elements: enmity, divine activity in Zion, birth language, and an eschatological image that includes the nations. The exception is found in Psalm 87, in that it does not include enmity. Further, the order of the elements is not fixed; however, the following order has been seen in several places: enmity, divine activity in Zion, birth language, and an eschatological image that includes the nations. Fourth, the birth images in these texts are not identical; however, since they belong to a common pattern, they are useful for understanding Psalm 87 in a better way. With the above in mind, Psalms 2, 22, and 110 will be considered more closely.

Psalm 2 shows us that God will establish his universal rule through the Davidic dynasty, transforming the enmity of the nations into submission. God has chosen a king, proclaiming him as his son whom he has begotten (Ps 2:7). This birth language is used for someone already born. On the one hand, it is intimately associated with inheritance and possession (Ps. 2:8). The nations are the inheritance; the whole earth is the possession of the anointed one, who is born again in the place of the coronation ceremony, i.e., on Mount Zion, God's chosen dwelling place. On the other hand, birth language is relational. It reflects a unique relationship with God. The king, begotten of God, is committed to spreading the fear of the Lord to the ends of the earth (Ps 2:11–12).

Psalm 22 opens with an alienated individual and closes with a universal divine kingdom that includes the nations. It moves from a scene in Zion to the ends of the earth (Ps 22:27–28). Admittedly, the word "Zion" is not mentioned, but we know that the votive offerings "were enjoyed at the temple as a communal meal."[31] The scene moves from Zion to the ends of the earth, back to the place where God is worshiped

---

Mic 4–5 (birth language is embedded in cosmic eschatological language). Further, the following NT references are part of a pattern that associates birth-language with the eschatological kingdom of God: Luke 2:8–14; John 3:1–21; John 16:17–24; Gal 4:21–31; Heb 12:18–29; Jas 1:18; 1 Pet 1:3–5; and Rev 12:1–6.

30. E.g., Isaiah 64 has (a) eschatological language (vv. 1–2); (b) the divine activity element (v. 4); (c) an image where God is the potter and, like clay, the people are formed by his hands (v. 8); and (d) mention of Zion. Note that point (c) could resemble birth imagery, especially in view of Isa 45:9–10.

31. VanGemeren, "Psalms," 210.

(Ps 22:27–28). This psalm emphasizes the universal kingship of God over present and future generations. A nation that proclaims and receives divine righteousness is born.[32] The birth image is associated with worshiping God and proclaiming his redemptive victory and acts of salvation.

Psalm 110 pictures the royal figure as a ruler facing opposition and enmity (Ps 110:1). In Ps 110:2 we observe that the authority of the king of Zion spreads as a result of the divine activity that originates in Zion and reaches into the midst of the enemies. This verse is followed by eschatological language and birth images. The latter could be seen in at least the following Hebrew expressions: *merekhem mishkhhar* and *yaldutekha*. Admittedly, the language is difficult, but the images of birth are dominant.[33] Furthermore, these images of birth are in the context of belonging to God (*'amkha*) and spreading his authority to the ends of the earth. They initiate an eschatological era in which God's people are recruited as his troops.[34] The eschatological language is unmistakable, and the subduing of the nations under the universal rule of God is clear.

In sum, the one who is born spreads the fear of the Lord, his authority over nations, the news of his redemptive victory and acts, and his glory. He or she is involved in spreading God's kingdom to the ends of the earth. Moreover, he or she receives possession and inheritance, the help of the Lord, and the comfort and the joy of the Lord. In light of this understanding, we observe that Psalm 87 shows that those who are born spread the glory of God (Ps 87:3). The glorious things spoken of the city of God could include his redemptive victory and acts (cf. Ps 85:8–13). They receive his joy (Ps 87:7) and receive a "Zionite" status, which might mean that they enjoy a permanent name and ministry before YHWH in the new creation (cf. Isa 66:21–22). Indeed their names are inscribed as "Zionites" (Ps 87:6).

But how are these "Zionites" transformed? What kind of change happens? We know that they are born in Zion, and now, unlike the nations

32. Although the Hebrew text of vv. 30–32 has many textual problems, its sense is clear.

33. VanGemeren explains that some scholars propose different emendations suggesting further birth language. For example, BHS proposes emending (*khelekha*) to (*khllkha*); consequently, NEB reads, "At birth you were endowed . . . since your mother bore you." For a list of proposals that associate this text with further birth images, see VanGemeren, "Psalms," 698.

34. BDB, 378b.

in Ps 79:6, who do not know God, these "Zionites" know God (*yod ʿai*). Out of the 940 uses of the root *yd ʿ*, this is the only time God declares a group of people as those who know him.[35] The book of Psalms informs us that those who know him are those who seek and trust him (Ps 9:11). They are the ones who pursue his lovingkindness and righteousness (Ps 36:11), and enjoy his protection and blessings (Ps 36:8–11). They are associated with a glorious place (Ps 87:3), a multicultural godly community (Ps 87:4, 6), a divinely established Zion (Ps 87:5), and a joyful community (Ps 87:7). They are a community whom God recognizes as part of Zion, and they share a similar distinguished birth.[36]

In consequence, Psalm 87 helps us to hope for an eschatological city that has equality; harmony between the nations; and joyful, active inhabitants who speak of God's glories. The nations are transformed through birth. Unlike fallen Israel, they are not nominal citizens of Zion but a multicultural, godly community who pleases God by upholding his standards of righteousness and justice. They have experienced personal and societal transformation due to their communion with God.

(2) Is the Placement of Psalm 87 Significant for Its Interpretation?

After seeing the transformation of the nations in Psalm 87 through exegetical and intertextual means, one wonders if this reading can be strengthened by recent Psalm studies that read the Psalter as a book. Gerald Wilson is one of the pioneers of this perspective.[37] Based on his

35. Even-Shoshan, *Konkordantsyah*, 432–36.

36. A similar image can be seen in the NT. Those who join the kingdom of God share a common birth experience (John 3). However, the emphasis shifts from the place of their birth to the nature of their birth; their birth is associated with accepting the true light and the logos of God (John 1:12). Further, they are the church of the firstborn who are written in heaven (Heb 12:23—*ai ekklēsia prototokōn apogegrammenōn en ouranois*) and who are part of a multicultural community (Gal 3:26–29; cf. Rev 21:24), a community of Zion, the heavenly Jerusalem, the city of God (Heb 12:22), and a community who are part of an established kingdom (Heb 12:28). The NT community is the children of the heavenly Jerusalem (Gal 4:26). Zion is their mother. This understanding is in exegetical harmony with the LXX, which says in verse 5, "*Mētēr Ziōn erei anthrōpos.*" This is not only a textual possibility, i.e., the *Vorlage* of the Septuagint reads, (*ultsion ʿim yoʾmer ʿish*) arguing either for haplography in the MT or for two different literary traditions, but it is also an exegetical possibility where Zion is metaphorically the mother of those who were born in it.

37. Wilson explains his compositional reading in several publications. See Wilson, *Editing*; Wilson, "Shaping the Psalter," 72–82; Wilson, "King, Messiah, and the Reign of God," 391–406.

biblical analyses of superscriptions, orphan psalms, postscripts, doxologies, and different psalm groupings according to authorship, genre, as well as themes, he argues: "(1) that the 'book' divisions of the Psalter are real, editorially induced divisions and not accidentally introduced; (2) the 'separating' and 'binding' functions of author and genre groupings; (3) the lack of a s/s [superscription] as an indication of a tradition of combination; (4) the use of hllwyh pss [psalms] to indicate the conclusion of segments; (5) the use of hwdw pss to introduce segments; (6) the existence of thematic correspondences between the beginning and ending pss in some books."[38]

The aforementioned compositional reading of the Psalter continues to evoke different reactions.[39] Furthermore, reading Psalm 87 from this perspective opens up new hermeneutical and theological questions, such as, (1) Why did the editors separate the Korah collections (Pss 42–49, 84–85, 87–88)? (2) Why did the editors insert a Davidic prayer in the midst of the second Korah sequence (Pss 84–85, 87–88)? (3) What is the contribution of Psalm 87 to the theological message of Book III (Pss 73–89) and the rest of the Psalter?[40]

In short, Wilson argues that "the Psalter shows a militant messianic view of the Davidic kingship (particularly in Psalms 2–89). And yet . . . the same collection of Psalms offers a subtle alternative emphasizing servanthood subordinated to the rulership of Yahweh."[41] He concludes that "the role of the Davidic [king] . . . recedes in the final form of the Psalter, while David's role as the eschatological Messiah . . . and Servant . . . who ushers in the kingdom and reign of Yahweh moves to the foreground."[42]

Wilson's insights are very helpful, but he overstates his case. His arguments would have been stronger if he had heeded J. Clinton McCann, who had earlier suggested that the first three books have already started answering the problem raised by the failure of traditional Davidic theology.[43] In fact, apart from Psalm 89, the third Book presents a clear image of David as the servant, not the king. Psalm 78:70–72 presents David

38. Wilson, *Editing*, 200.

39. For a helpful survey of recent Psalm studies, see Howard, "Editorial Activity in the Psalter," 52–70.

40. See Katanacho, "Investigating the Purposeful Placement."

41. Wilson, "King, Messiah, and the Reign of God," 404.

42. Ibid.

43. McCann, "Books I–III and the Editorial Purpose," 93–107.

as the servant-shepherd who has a blameless heart, while Psalm 86—the only psalm with a Davidic superscription in the third book—pictures David as the prayerful servant. Furthermore, Rendtorff asks, who is the David of the Psalms?[44] Rendtorff seeks to answer his question through studying the biographical superscriptions as inner biblical exegesis correlated with the books of Samuel, and also through studying the Psalms that mention David (cf. Pss 18, 78, 89, 122, 132, and 144). He concludes that the main image of David appears in the combination of the first three psalms, i.e., David is the Messianic king (Ps 2), the exemplary righteous king (Ps 1), and the powerless fugitive who trusts in God's help (Ps 3).[45] The last component, according to Rendtorff, dominates the second and third books. Rendtorff rightly points out that "it is not the image of the ruling and victorious [David] that is in the foreground."[46]

Looking at the juxtaposition of Psalms 86 and 87 from the aforementioned perspective "reveals an arrangement that serves to assist the community not only to face squarely the disorienting reality of exile, as Wilson suggests, but also to reach a reorientation based upon the rejection of the Davidic/Zion theology that had formerly been Judah's primary grounds for hope."[47] In agreement with McCann, I assert that the traditional hope, embodied by Zion songs, is modified by its literary context, i.e., the juxtaposition of traditional Davidic/Zion theology with laments provides a new understanding of hope. In other words, the placement of Psalm 86 between two Zion songs (Pss 84 and 87) helps the community face the disorienting experience of exile and provides the basis for "a new understanding of the old grounds of hope."[48] The new understanding provides a different view of Jerusalem as well as a different understanding of David. Put differently, the view of Jerusalem corresponds to the view of David. A militant king requires Jewish supremacy, but a servant king requires a multinational, multiethnic Jerusalem that includes equal citizens. Interestingly, Book III presents a reemergence of David in order to present a servant king. After the end of the prayers of David at the end of Psalm 72, David reappears in Psalm 86 as a servant praying for the nations.

44. Rendtorff, "The Psalms of David," 53. See also Rendtorff, *The Canonical Hebrew Bible*, 560–74.

45. Rendtorff, "The Psalms of David," 63.

46. Ibid., 64.

47. McCann, "Books I–III and the Editorial Purpose," 98–99.

48. Ibid., 103.

A NEW DAVID

It is now appropriate to address the reemergence of David in Psalm 86. A study of David will demonstrate the polyphonic depictions of David, whether in the Psalter or in the rest of the Bible.[49] Furthermore, several recent Psalms scholars rightly point out that the Psalter shows editorial activity that reflects an editorial theological conceptual framework in which the identity of David is important.[50] Within this theological framework, Psalm 86 is an important editorial landmark that reflects the transformation in the identity of David and his relationships. The relationship of the Davidic figure and the nations in Psalm 86 is different from Psalm 72. In Psalm 72, the nations should bow down, lick the dust, offer gifts, and serve the king. Unlike the poor who receive gifts, the Gentile kings present gifts. The double royal presentations of gifts and tributes are enveloped within two bowings (Ps 72:9–11). The first bowing is related to defeat and the second to service. In short, although Psalm 72 mentions the blessing of the nations, it still presents a royal ideology that advocates a militant submission of the nations. The vision of a king-centered world perceives the nations as enemies (cf. Ps 72:9) who must submit both to God and to Israel's king. Psalm 86 moves away from this depiction of the nations. The king is no longer the militant figure. He is the poor and needy godly servant.

Psalm 86 has three main self-designations of David: servant, loyal one, and poor and needy one. First, David is a servant. Psalm 86 depicts the servant as a person who trusts Yahweh (Ps 86:2); who has a concern for humanity (Ps 86:8–10); and who takes an interest in fearing God, in learning God's way, and in walking in his truth (Ps 86:11). The David of Psalm 86 relates to humanity in a prayerful way, trusting in the omnipotence of the Creator as well as in his unfailing love (Ps 86:8–10, 13). David is depicted, not as the servant who violently subdues the nations in order to spread God's kingdom, but as the one who trusts God to do wonders, show lovingkindness, and conquer *Sheol*. He is the David of

---

49. In my dissertation I provide a detailed study about David discussing the contributions of many important scholars and the textual data pertinent to David in the Psalter; see Katanacho, "Investigating the Purposeful Placement," 169–240.

50. Auwers, "Le David des psaumes," 187–224; Rendtorff, "The Psalms of David," 53–64; Wilson, "King, Messiah, and the Reign of God," 391–406.

Israel who prays for the nations, serving and representing them before God. David has an intercessory role praying for the ungodly nations.[51]

This David is not only a servant. Second, he is a godly one. At a time when Israel falls into a state of disorientation, David appears to shift the self-centered focus of Israel to a life of prayerful servanthood. Unlike the rest of Book III, which is dominated by national lament and enmity with the nations, Psalm 86 is a prayer full of peacemaking and divine grace. In fact, David becomes identified with and a model for the godly ones of Israel. They too can choose a nonviolent path that is rooted in trusting God. In his prayer, David, the servant of the Lord, combines Zion motifs and Sinai motifs. Zion is supposed to be a point of attraction for all the nations. Indeed, Israel's Torah and life of righteousness should have attracted the ends of the world. However, Sinai theology gives Israel a privileged place since Israel is always the mediator between God and the nations. In his prayer, David engages Zion royal theology with a transformed Sinai theology. Put differently, David employs the grace formula (86:15) that is part of the Sinai covenant in a new sense. He expands the group who might enjoy the lovingkindness and mercy of God. The recipients are not only Israel, but also everyone who calls upon the name of the Lord (Ps 86:5). David becomes a new Moses who intercedes, not for Israel, but for the nations.

The connection between the David of Psalm 86 and Moses has already been asserted by Vorndran, who rightly points out the similarities between Psalm 86 and the Sinai pericope. Both Moses and David are interested in teaching and knowing the way of God.[52] Both employ the grace formula. This connection is further seen by the compositional reading, in which the prayer of David is followed by a prayer of Moses (cf. Ps 90). Comparing the two prayers, we notice the following: Both men are interested in a right heart. David highlights the heart that is devoted to fearing God and to honoring his name (Ps 86:11–12) while Moses emphasizes the wise heart that understands ephemeral human nature (Ps 90:12). Both men seek God's joy (Ps 86:4; 90:15) and divine lovingkindness (Ps 86:5, 13, 15; Ps 90:14). Both show concern for the

---

51. The people of God are called to bless the nations just like their father Abraham was called to be a blessing to the nations. Unfortunately, the holy family (Abraham and Sarah) who lived in the Holy Land failed to bless Hagar, who lived in their own home. Servanthood, not dominance, is the divine means for spreading the blessing. For further details see Katanacho, "Hagar: A Victim of Injustice," 96–100.

52. Vorndran, *Alle Völker werden kommen*, 145–47.

preservation of life (Ps 86:2, 13–14; Ps 90:3–12). Both seek God's compassion for the servant or servants (Ps 86:3, 16; Ps 90:13).[53] While the servant David in Ps 86:17 is comforted, the servants in Ps 90:13 are asking for comfort. The servant David celebrates the works and wonders of God in the pilgrimage of the nations (Ps 86:8–10), but the servants ask that God's works and glory be revealed to them (Ps 90:16). While the servants are seen as the children of Adam, and as a result destined to death (Ps 90:3), the servant David is characterized as the son of God's maidservant and the one who is delivered from *Sheol* (Ps 86:13, 16). In short, David is presented as a Mosaic figure in a Levitical book (Pss 73–89). He asserts the most important commandment in the Mosaic covenant, i.e., there is one God (cf. Exod 20:2–5; Deut 6:4). Like Moses, he uses the grace formula that highlights the basis of the Mosaic covenant. However, he is concerned not with Israel but with the nations—a concern that is elaborated in Psalm 87. David intercedes for the nations, shunning narrow-minded national ideologies. God answers his prayers in Psalm 87. These exegetical perceptions provide a new framework for addressing the Palestinian-Israeli conflict. This leads me to my concluding reflections.

THEOLOGICAL AND ESCHATOLOGICAL REFLECTIONS

As a Palestinian theologian, I am struck by the loud absence of a positive vision for the nations of the Middle East or for its church.[54] This absence is strange especially when many scholars spill a lot of ink on the role of national Israel in God's plan. Herbert Bateman and John Feinberg, for example, discuss important hermeneutical details, struggling over the meaning and role of Israel and the details of her program in God's plan; but they overlook the contemporary needs for prophetic and eschatological voices that promote the divine vision of justice, of the end of evil, of peaceful coexistence between the nations, and of equality in status. One might ask, where are the ethical and eschatological dimensions of love, mercy, and justice for the people of the Middle East? Perhaps it is important to affirm that our eschatological positions influence the daily lives of contemporary Middle Easterners. Unfortunately, addressing the direct implications of our eschatological beliefs on the Middle East and the Islamic world is not given sufficient attention.

53. It is interesting that few manuscripts have the singular "servant" for Ps 90:13.

54. See, e.g., Bateman, *Three Central Issues*; and Feinberg, *Continuity and Discontinuity*.

Those who overlook the needs of the contemporary Middle East will greatly benefit from interacting with Christian Palestinian voices because the emerging Palestinian contextual theology is being shaped by the Arab-Israeli conflict and interreligious trialogue between Muslims, Jews, and Christians. Unlike many Westerners, Christian Palestinians describe the establishment of Israel as "the catastrophe" (*Al-Nakba*) that violated God's standards of love and justice.[55] They are concerned with land, coexistence between radically different groups, justice, and reconciliation.[56] These concerns shape their theology and contributions in the various forms.

Thus, as a Palestinian Christian, I rejoice that Psalm 87 provides a bold voice that stands in tension with many eschatological systems that lead to polarization between Israel and her neighbors. It presents an alternative to God's people in which they are not promoting or asking for revenge and bloodshed (cf. Ps 79:6, 12). Instead, they join the psalmist of Psalm 87 in having a godly vision for the Egyptians, the Philistines, the people of Tyre and Cush. They will be born in Zion. The coexistence of Israel with these nations in Zion reflects a biblical voice that stands against xenophobic and inimical attitudes. No more shouts of "Death for the enemies."[57] No more isolation from the "Other." No more eschatological programs that favor Jewish superiority while ignoring the Jews' calling to be servants of God and a light to the nations.

55. See Katanacho, "Palestinian Protestant Theological Responses," 289–305. Also listen to the story of the State of Israel through the eyes of Christian Palestinians; see Chacour and Hazard, *Blood Brothers* (2nd ed.); Hefley and Hefley, *The Liberated Palestinian*; Rantisi and Beebe, *Blessed Are the Peacemakers*; Raheb, *Bethlehem Besieged*. The first two books focus on the suffering of Palestinians when Israel was established in 1948, while the latter two focus on their experience under Israeli occupation. For a historical presentation of the Arab-Israeli conflict, see Awad, *Through the Eyes of the Victims*.

56. At the cost of oversimplification, Palestinian liberation theologians interpret Christianity in socio-political terms and are concerned about justice and land; see, e.g., Ateek, *Justice and Only Justice*; Raheb, *I am a Palestinian Christian*. Reconciliation theologians are concerned about coexistence, forgiveness, and inter-religious dialogues; see, e.g., Younan and Strickert, *Witnessing for Peace*; Mansour, *Narrow Gate Churches*; Munayer, *Seeking and Pursuing Peace*; Loden et al., *The Bible and the Land*. The first two books present a positive image of Islam, dismissing the need for evangelism and highlighting the need for coexistence. The second two books stress reconciliation, not coexistence. The biblical understanding of reconciliation is the foundation for the future relations of the different people groups in the region.

57. For further discussion on Israel's attitude towards the nations, see "Smith-Christopher, "Between Ezra and Isaiah," 117–42.

Indeed, Psalm 87 puts a vision of equality and an absence of sub-ordination before us. There are no second-class citizens in Zion. This equality is not just civic but is also covenantal. They all share the same God, are born in the same city,[58] and are registered by the same hands. Their linguistic, historical, and military differences are not important. What unites them is God himself. Geography is no longer a point of tension because Zion belongs to God, not Israel. It is the city of God, and he alone can grant citizenship in his city. Citizenship comes by divine declaration, not by biological rights.[59]

This understanding stands in tension with the promotion of a Jewish Jerusalem or a Jewish state, but not necessarily with advocating a truly democratic Israeli state and a shared Jerusalem. Further, even if the Palestinians have their own state, the State of Israel will not become a "Gentile-free" Jewish state, for 20 percent of the current citizens of Israel are Palestinians. The demographic increase of Palestinian Israeli citizens is at a much faster rate than the growth of Israel's Jewish population. In short, instead of promoting a geography that unrealistically calls for isolating the Jews from other ethnic groups, Psalm 87 promotes a new vision of geography in which all who are equally concerned to promote justice and righteousness for all can live as equals.

Last, it is apt to point out that the vision of Psalm 87 is at the heart of the cross of Jesus Christ. Through the Christ-event people can perceive Jerusalem as a mother with many children (Gal 4:26), not as a husband who is torn between two wives. For the Abrahamic promises are for those who belong to Christ (Gal 3:29). Zion is the mother of both Palestinians and Jews who are willing to adopt the divine vision and follow the divine plan. For "there is neither Jew nor Greek, slave nor free, male nor female, for you are all one in Christ Jesus" (Gal 3:27).

BIBLIOGRAPHY

'amru, Yunis. "Al Quds fi al-islam." In *Jerusalem: Palestinian Christian–Muslim Studies*, edited by Geries Khoury et al., 17–26. Jerusalem: Al-Liqa' Center, 1996.

Ateek, Naim Stifan. *Justice and Only Justice: A Palestinian Theology of Liberation.* Maryknoll: Orbis, 1989.

58. For a helpful discussion of the relationship of earthly and heavenly Jerusalem, see Holwerda, *Jesus and Israel*, 106–12.

59. See Katanacho, "Christ Is the Owner," 429–33.

Auwers, Jean-Marie. "Le David des psaumes et les psaumes de David." In *Figures de David à travers la Bible*, by Louis Desrousseaux and Jacques Vermevlen, 187–224. Lectio Divina 177. Paris: Cerf, 1999.

Awad, Alex. *Through the Eyes of the Victims: The Story of the Arab-Israeli Conflict.* Bethlehem: Bethlehem Bible College, 2001.

Bateman, Herbert W., editor. *Three Central Issues in Contemporary Dispensationalism: A Comparison of Traditional and Progressive Views.* Grand Rapids: Kregel, 1999.

Beaucamp, Evode. "Psaume 87." *Laval Theologique et Philosophique 35* (1979) 279–88.

Booij, Thijs. "Some Observations on Psalm 87." *Vetus Testamentum 37* (1987) 16–25.

Brown, Francis et al. *The New Brown, Driver, Briggs, Gesenius Hebrew and English Lexicon: With an Appendix Containing the Biblical Aramaic.* Peabody, MA: Hendrickson, 1979.

Chacour, Elias, and David Hazard. *Blood Brothers.* 2nd ed. Grand Rapids: Chosen, 2003.

Clines, David J. A. *The Dictionary of Classical Hebrew.* Vol. 4. Sheffield: Sheffield Academic, 1998.

Dahood, Mitchell. *Psalm II: 51–100.* Translated by David Eaton. Anchor Bible 16B. Garden City, NY: Doubleday, 1968.

Even-Shoshan, Avraham. *Konkordantsyah Hadeshah le-Torah, Neviʿim, u-Khetuvim.* Jerusalem: Kiryat Sefer, 1982.

Feinberg, John S. *Continuity and Discontinuity: Perspectives on the Relationship between the Old and New Testaments, Essays in Honor of S. Lewis Johnson, Jr.* Westchester, IL: Crossway, 1988.

Freedman, David Noel et al. *The Leningrad Codex: A Facsimile Edition.* Grand Rapids: Eerdmans, 1998.

Gesenius, Wilhelm et al. *Gesenius' Hebrew Grammar.* 2nd ed. Oxford: Clarendon, 1910.

Gruber, Mayer I. *Rashi's Commentary on Psalms (Books I–III): With English Translation, Introduction and Notes.* Edited by Jacob Neusner et al. South Florida Studies in the History of Judaism 161. Atlanta: Scholars, 1998.

Hefley, James C., and Marti Hefley. *The Liberated Palestinian: The Anis Shorrosh Story.* Wheaton, IL: Victor, 1975.

Holwerda, David E. *Jesus and Israel: One Covenant or Two?* Grand Rapids: Eerdmans, 1995.

Hossfeld, Frank-Lothar, and Erich Zenger. *Psalms 2: A Commentary on Psalms 51–100.* Edited by Klauz Baltzer et al. Translated by Linda M. Maloney. Hermeneia. Minneapolis: Fortress, 2005.

Howard, David M., Jr. "Editorial Activity in the Psalter: A State-of-the-Field Survey." In *The Shape and Shaping of the Psalter*, edited by J. Clinton McCann, 52–70. Journal for the Study of the Old Testament Supplement Series 159. Sheffield: JSOT Press, 1993.

Katanacho, Yohanna. "Christ Is the Owner of Haaretz." *Christian Scholar's Review 34* (2005): 425–41.

———. "Hagar: A Victim of Injustice." In *No Going Back: Letters to Pope Benedict XVI on the Holocaust, Jewish-Christian Relations & Israel*, edited by Carol Rittner et al., 96–100. London: Quill, in association with the Holocaust Centre, 2009.

———. "Investigating the Purposeful Placement of Psalm 86," PhD diss., Trinity International University, 2006.

———. "Palestinian Protestant Theological Responses to a World Marked by Violence." *Missiology: An International Review* (2008) 289–305.

Kidner, Derek. *Psalms 73–150: A Commentary on Books III–V of the Psalms*. Tyndale Old Testament Commentaries. London: InterVarsity, 1975.

Koscheski, James R. "An Exegetical Study of Psalm 87." MDiv thesis, Grace Theological Seminary, 1974.

Kraus, Hans-Joachim. *Psalms 60–150: A Commentary*. Translated by Hilton C. Oswalt. Minneapolis: Fortress, 1993.

Leham, Lutfi. "Al Quds fi al-maseehiah." In *Jerusalem: Palestinian Christian–Muslim Studies*, edited by Geries Khoury et al., 47–64. Jerusalem: Al-Liqa' Center, 1996.

Loden, Lisa et al. *The Bible and the Land*. Jerusalem: Musalaha, 2000.

Mansour, Atallah. *Narrow Gate Churches: The Christian Presence in the Holy Land under Muslim and Jewish Rule*. Pasadena, CA: Hope, 2004.

McCann, J. Clinton. "Book I–III and the Editorial Purpose of the Psalter." In *The Shape and Shaping of the Psalter*, edited by J. Clinton McCann, 93–107. Journal for the Study of the Old Testament: Supplement Series 159. Sheffield: JSOT Press, 1993.

Munayer, Salim J., editor. *Seeking and Pursuing Peace: The Process, the Pain, and the Product*. Jerusalem: Musalaha, 1998.

Perowne, J. J. Stewart. *Commentary on the Psalms*. 4th ed. Grand Rapids: Kregel, 1989.

Raheb, Mitri. *Bethlehem Besieged: Stories of Hope in Times of Trouble*. Minneapolis: Fortress, 2004.

———. *I Am a Palestinian Christian*. Translated by Ruth Gritsch. Minneapolis: Fortress, 1995.

Rantisi, Audeh G., and Ralph K. Beebe. *Blessed Are the Peacemakers: A Palestinian Christian in the Occupied West Bank*. Grand Rapids: Zondervan, 1990.

Rendtorff, Rolf. *The Canonical Hebrew Bible: A Theology of the Old Testament*. Tools for Biblical Studies Series 7. Leiden: Deo, 2005.

———. "'The Psalms of David: David in the Psalms." In *The Book of Psalms: Composition and Reception*, edited by Peter W. Flint et al., 53–64. Supplements to Vetus Testamentum 99. Formation and Interpretation of Old Testament Literature 4. Leiden: Brill, 2005.

Smith-Christopher, Daniel L. "Between Ezra and Isaiah: Exclusion, Transformation, and Inclusion of the 'Foreigner' in Post Exilic Biblical Theology." In *Ethnicity and the Bible*, edited by Mark G. Brett, 117–42. Biblical Interpretation Series 19. Leiden: Brill, 1996.

Smith, Mark S. "The Structure of Psalm 87." *Vetus Testamentum* (1988) 357–58.

Tate, Marvin E. *Psalms 51–100*. Word Biblical Commentary 20. Nashville: Thomas Nelson, 1990.

Terrien, Samuel L. *The Psalms: Strophic Structure and Theological Commentary*. The Eerdmans Critical Commentary. Grand Rapids: Eerdmans, 2003.

VanGemeren, Willem. *Psalms*. In *Psalms–Song of Songs*, edited by Frank Ely Gaebelein and Richard Polcyn, 1–880. The Expositor's Bible Commentary. Grand Rapids: Zondervan, 1991.

Vorndran, Jürgen. „*Alle Völker werden kommen*": *Studien zu Psalm 86*. Bonner biblische Beiträge 133. Berlin: Philo, 2002.

Walton, Brian. *Biblia Sacra Polyglotta*. Vol. 3, *Tomus Tertius*. Biblia Sacra Polyglotta. Graz: Akademische Druck-U. Verlagsanstalt, 1964.

Weiser, Artur. *The Psalms: A Commentary*. Translated by Herbert Hartwell. London: SCM, 1962.

Wilson, Gerald. *The Editing of the Hebrew Psalter*. Society of Biblical Literature Dissertation Series 76. Chico: Scholars, 1985.

———. "King, Messiah, and the Reign of God: Revisiting the Royal Psalms and the Shape of the Psalter." In *The Book of Psalms: Composition and Reception*, edited by Peter W. Flint et al., 391–406. Supplements to Vetus Testamentum 99. Formation and Interpretation of Old Testament Literature 4. Leiden: Brill, 2005.

———. "Shaping the Psalter: A Consideration of Editorial Linkage in the Book of Psalm." In *The Shape and Shaping of the Psalter*, edited by J. Clinton McCann, 72–82. Journal for the Study of the Old Testament Supplement Series 159 Sheffield: JSOT Press, 1993.

Younan, Munib, and Frederick M. Strickert. *Witnessing for Peace: In Jerusalem and the World*. Minneapolis: Fortress, 2003.

Young, Robert. *Young's Analytical Concordance to the Bible*. Peabody, MA: Hendrickson, 1992.

❖ 10 ❖

A Palestinian Theology
of the Land[1]

Alex Awad

THE BASIC BELIEFS OF CHRISTIAN ZIONISM

PALESTINIAN CHRISTIANS ARE, FOR the most part, appalled by the great flood of support that numerous Western Christians have poured into the Zionist project during the last 120 years. Sadly, this has turned some Arab Christians in the Middle East and North Africa totally against the Old Testament—the Hebrew Scriptures—and the eternal truths and rich heritage they embody. But other Arab Christians, including this author, have come to a different perspective. They instead determined, through a thorough study of the biblical record in both the Old and the New Testaments, to find out for themselves whether the Bible supports Zionist claims. In the following pages the reader will find the result of my study of Old Testament prophesies about the land in the light of New Testament teachings.

Christians Zionists generally hold to the following doctrines that are also endorsed, either in part or whole, by many Christians who take for granted popular views of prophecy or the covenants:

1. This section originally appeared in Alex Awad's *Palestinian Memories: The Story of a Palestinian Mother and Her People* (Bethlehem: Bethlehem Bible College, 2008), 249–67. The New International Version (NIV) is used for all Scripture quotations.

- Jews have special favor with God, and he gave them the Holy Land. It belongs to them by divine decree and it always will. Neither history, nor the passing of centuries, nor the religious or moral condition of Jews can alter this fact.

- God will bless those individuals and nations who bless the Jews and their State, and God will curse or punish those who do otherwise.

- Jews today are a direct extension of the Israelites in biblical times. Therefore, just as the nations during the Old Testament era were judged as to how they treated ancient Israel, the same is true today.

- Old Testament prophecies, although uttered thousands of years ago, are being fulfilled in Israel today and have been since 1948 when the Jewish state was born.

- God's "end time" plan is directly connected with the modern State of Israel, and Christians can speed up the coming of Christ by helping bring about the fulfilment of prophecies pertaining to Israel.

- The creation of the Jewish state is a miracle of divine intervention on behalf of the Jewish people and a visible sign of the end times and the imminent coming of Jesus Christ.

- The current conflict in the Middle East is caused by Palestinians—Arabs and Muslims—who are out of touch with the will of God as it concerns the land of Israel.

- There will be no peace in the Middle East until Christ comes back. All the efforts of Jews, Arabs, the United Nations, and the United States to broker peace between Arabs and Jews are futile and will not produce peace.

- The Jews will build a Jewish temple in Jerusalem in place of the Al-Aqsa Mosque and/or the Dome of the Rock, where they will resume offering animal sacrifices to God.

- A great (and literal) war, "Armageddon," will break out in the last days between Israel and the surrounding nations. Jesus will come back from heaven to rescue the Jews who now believe in him, after one-third of them get slain in the final war.

The above concepts are held in the hearts and minds of millions of Christians around the world. Some adherents of the Christian Zionist movement have been United States presidents, such as Ronald Regan and George W. Bush. Possibly these politicians embraced the Zionist agenda—or appeared to—in order to win the support and vote of evangelical Christians.

When I speak to groups of Christians from the United States or from Europe, I am often asked: "But what about prophecy? Didn't God give the land to the Jews? Why do Arabs and Muslims want to thwart the plan of God?"

AN ALTERNATIVE BIBLICAL PERSPECTIVE ON THE THEOLOGY OF THE LAND

Many biblical verses in the Old Testament state that God gave the Holy Land to Abraham and his descendents, among whom are the ancient Israelite people. In Gen 12:1–5 God promises Abraham that he will give the land of Canaan to him and his descendents. Similar promises are repeated throughout the Old Testament. The challenge today is to search for answers to the following questions:

- Are God's promises to ancient Israel unconditional?

- Are God's promises to ancient Israel perpetual, i.e., never ending?

- Do Old Testament prophecies relating to "the land" under the old covenant continue to have significance and fulfilment within the framework of the new covenant?

- Does God have a special plan for the Jewish people different from that for other peoples?

Are God's Promises to Ancient Israel Unconditional?

The Old Testament is full of evidence that these promises are conditioned by the faithfulness and obedience of the people of Israel to God. Examine the following references:

- "And if you defile the land, it will vomit you out as it vomited out the nations that were before you" (Lev 18:28).

- "Keep all my decrees and laws and follow them, so that the land where I am bringing you to live may not vomit you out. You must not live according to the customs of the nations I am going to drive out before you" (Lev 20:22).

- "When Abram was ninety-nine years old, the Lord appeared to him and said, 'I am God Almighty; walk before me and be blameless. I will confirm my covenant between me and you and will greatly increase your numbers'" (Gen 17:1).

These and many other verses clearly show that ancient Israel's possession of the land was conditional upon Israel's obedience to God, and when Israel failed to obey God, the people were driven out of the land. The Babylonians exiled the Jews from Israel about six hundred years before Christ, and then in AD 70, the Romans conquered and destroyed Jerusalem and expelled the Jews again. These are two examples of the Jews being removed from the land because of ancient Israel's rebellion against God.

Today the majority of the Jews in Israel and around the world are either secular, or nonreligious traditionalists. Only 20 percent of the Jewish population categorize themselves as religious. Indeed, many leading Zionists who were among the visionaries and founders of the State of Israel were atheists, and modern Israel today is not a nation under God, nor does it claim to be one. The trail of violence and injustice in Israel in the last sixty years is clear evidence that the State of Israel today is not the Israel of the Bible or the Israel of the covenant. Again, God's promise to ancient Israel was conditional upon Israel's obedience. Evangelicals in particular should be concerned that modern Israeli society continues to reject its Messiah, bans missionary activities, and often condemns those who attempt to share the good news of Jesus Christ. To idealize the religious significance of the State of Israel is to close one's eyes to the spiritual, religious, and moral realities of the modern Jewish state.

Are God's Promises to Ancient Israel Perpetual, i.e., Never Ending?

In the past God promised ancient Israel the land, and he gave it to them, thus fulfilling his promises. Some Christians read the Old Testament promises and prophecies that were given three or four thousand years ago, and they strive to find modern fulfillment of those prophecies—prophecies that in actuality have already been fulfilled. Some of the prophecies were given to the Jews when they were living in exile in Babylon. For example, Isaiah promised his exiled contemporaries and those on the verge of exile, that God would have mercy on them and bring them back to the land: "'For a brief moment I abandoned you, / but with deep compassion I will bring you back. / In a surge of anger I hid my face from you for a moment, / but with everlasting kindness I will have compassion on you,' / says the LORD your Redeemer" (Isa 54:7–8).

Indeed, God kept his promises and restored the Jewish people to the land after some seventy years of exile. The prophets preached a message of hope for the exiles, a message that was also a means of preparing them to be restored to the land. But those prophecies do not address today's Arab-Israeli conflict and the current situation in the Middle East. How unfortunate it is that these verses are taken out of their historical context and applied to the present-day conflict between Jew and Arab, because manipulating the word of God in this way is not only unfaithful to the biblical record but is, in its implications, exceedingly harmful to all Palestinians and especially to the Palestinian Christian community. How long will the Bible be used as a manual to promote military occupation? And how often must the Palestinians be subjected to the cruelties and brutalities of military conquests sanctioned by theories of divine involvement?

Do Old Testament Prophecies Relating to the Land under the Old Covenant Continue to Have Significance within the Framework of the New Covenant?

To respond to this question, it is necessary to point out the similarities and differences between the two covenants. Biblical scholars have written volumes on this theme, but to briefly address this question, I will compare six major elements in the two covenants, namely, the nation, the land, the city, the temple, the priesthood, and the sacrifice. The comparison is illustrated in the chart below.

THE TWO COVENANTS—CHART OF COMPARISON		
	Old Covenant	New Covenant in Christ
NATION	Israel	New Covenant in Christ
LAND	Promised Land	Kingdom of God
CITY	Jerusalem	Heavenly Jerusalem
TEMPLE	Temple Mount	Hearts of Believers
PRIESTHOOD	Aaron/Levitical	Christ, Believers
SACRIFICE	Animal	Jesus Christ

According to the old covenant, God chose a specific family to be a light to all the nations: Abraham and his descendants. God created nations from that family and selected one to be used as a vehicle through which all the other nations of the world would be blessed. The people of that nation—Israel, from which the prophets and the law were derived—became known as God's chosen people, as illustrated in the following verses:

- "I will bless those who bless you, and whoever curses you I will curse; and all peoples on earth will be blessed through you" (Gen 12:3).

- "For you are a holy people to the LORD your God. The LORD your God has chosen you out of all the peoples on the face of the earth to be his people, his treasured possession" (Deut 7:6).

- "Yet the LORD set his affection on your forefathers and loved them, and he chose you, their descendants, above all the nations, as it is today" (Deut 10:15).

- "If you fully obey the LORD your God and carefully follow all his commands I give you today, the Lord your God will set you high above all the nations on earth" (Deut 28:1).

With Jesus Christ's death on the cross and the ushering in of the new covenant, the gates of God's grace were opened to the entire human race. Jews and Gentiles now have equal access to all the privileges and responsibilities of being people of God. Who are God's people according to the new covenant? The following verses provide the answer. Consider Paul's declaration to the church in Ephesus:

> For he himself is our peace, who has made the two one and has destroyed the barrier, the dividing wall of hostility, by abolishing in his flesh the law with its commandments and regulations. His purpose was to create in himself one new man out of the two, thus making peace, and in this one body to reconcile both of them to God through the cross, by which he put to death their hostility. He came and preached peace to you who were far away and peace to those who were near. For through him we both have access to the Father by one Spirit. Consequently, you are no longer foreigners and aliens, but fellow citizens with God's people and members of God's household, built on the foundation of the apostles and prophets, with Christ Jesus himself as the chief cornerstone. In him the whole building is joined together and rises to become a holy temple in the Lord. And in him you

too are being built together to become a dwelling in which God lives by his Spirit. (Eph 2:14–22)

In these verses Paul announces to Gentile believers that in Christ they are now:

- One with the people of God
- Citizens with God's people
- Members of the household of God
- Built on the foundation of the apostles and prophets
- A dwelling in which God lives

Believing Gentiles and believing Jews together compose one body—the body of Christ. Paul repeats this same theme when he addresses the Gentiles in the city of Colossi: "Therefore, as God's chosen people, holy and dearly loved, clothe yourselves with compassion, kindness, humility, gentleness and patience" (Col 3:12).

Peter also speaks to both Jews and Gentiles scattered throughout the Roman Empire and announces to them their chosen nationhood established in Christ: "But you are a chosen people, a royal priesthood, a holy nation, a people belonging to God, that you may declare the praises of him who called you out of darkness and into his wonderful light. Once you were not a people, but now you are the people of God; once you had not received mercy, but now you have received mercy" (1 Pet 2:9–10). It is obvious here that the concept of nationhood was modified in the new covenant. Whereas in the old covenant God's people were the Jewish nation, in the new covenant all those who receive the grace of God through Jesus Christ become the people of God. The Apostle John states this fact clearly as well: "He came to that which was his own, but his own did not receive him. Yet to all who received him [Jews and Gentiles], to those who believed in his name, he gave the right to become children of God, children born not of natural descent, nor of human decision or a husband's will, but born of God" (John 1:11–13).

Thus Israel as a nation annulled its privilege as God's chosen nation by rejecting God's ultimate plan for the redemption of humanity in Jesus Christ. Yet God still fulfilled his purpose through them and blessed all the nations of the world through Abraham's seed, that is, Jesus Christ. In calling the old covenant "obsolete" (Heb 8:13), the writer did not mean to imply that God had banned Jews from receiving all the blessing of the new covenant. Rather he meant that God had a greater plan for the Jews, as he had for all people, which was his Son Jesus Christ who by his death redeemed all of mankind, Jews and Gentiles.

THE LAND

In the old covenant the land was important in order to house and shelter God's chosen people and to provide a place for a central temple where the priesthood could function. But, since the basic features of that covenant were changed, there was no longer any need for a specific land or territory to "house" the new covenant. For this reason the concept of a Promised Land was modified in the new covenant to a new reality, a reality that Jesus and his followers called the kingdom of God. When contemporaries of Jesus asked him about the place of the kingdom, he responded by saying, "The kingdom of God is within you" (Luke 17:21). By localizing the kingdom in the hearts of the faithful, Jesus made the kingdom of God both spiritual and global. And a kingdom that is present throughout the world need not—indeed, cannot—be limited to a specific plot of ground. As Luke writes, "Once, having been asked by the Pharisees when the kingdom of God would come, Jesus replied, 'The kingdom of God does not come with your careful observation, nor will people say, "Here it is," or "There it is," because the kingdom of God is within you'" (Luke 17:20–21).

The Samaritan woman who met Jesus at the well also had difficulties with the concept of "sacred" territory. Upon discovering that Jesus was the Messiah, she immediately presented him with a subject that had puzzled Jews and Samaritans for years: "I can see that you are a prophet. Our fathers worshipped on this mountain, but you Jews claim that the place where we must worship is in Jerusalem" (John 4:19–20). Essentially, she had asked, "Which is the right place? Which real estate does God favor?" The reply she received from Jesus is worth examining. He told her, "Believe me, woman, a time is coming when you will worship the Father neither on this mountain nor in Jerusalem. You Samaritans worship what you do not know; we worship what we do know, for salvation is from the Jews. Yet a time is coming and has now come when the true worshippers will worship the Father in spirit and truth, for they are the kind of worshippers the Father seeks" (John 4:21–23).

Jesus' response to this question is of utmost importance to all who continue to be confused about the issue of "the land." First, Jesus did not tell the woman that Jerusalem, where Jews worshipped, or Gerizim, where Samaritans prayed, were exclusively the right places of worship. Second, he directed her attention to a new era in God's dealing with humanity. Jesus said, "Yet a time is coming and has now come." He was referring to the new covenant, a time when God will no longer be concerned about a specific piece of land, territory, or a centralized place of worship but rather about the spiritual attitude of the worshiper.

To overemphasize the importance of the land is to live in the old covenant. God's *terra sanctum* is the human heart! For this reason in reading the Gospels it is clear that significance is given *not* to the land but rather to the kingdom of God. I do not wish to undermine the significance of the Holy Land as a testimony to God's revelation through the Old Testament prophets; as a witness to the acts of incarnation, crucifixion, resurrection, and ascension; and as the place God chose for the birth of the church on the day of Pentecost. I wish rather to emphasize that the land is significant only because God chose it to become the cradle of his acts of salvation to humanity. The Holy Land was God's launching pad for the kingdom of God, a realm that truly has no address and no geographical boundaries.

Jesus also deemphasized the issue of the land in the dialogue that took place between him and his disciples just before his ascension. We read in Acts: "So when they met together, they asked him, 'Lord, are you at this time going to restore the kingdom to Israel?' He said to them: 'It is not for you to know the times or dates the Father has set by his own authority. But you will receive power when the Holy Spirit comes on you; and you will be my witnesses in Jerusalem, and in all Judea and Samaria, and to the ends of the earth'" (Acts 1:6–8). The disciples showed concern over a physical and territorial kingdom of God on earth, with Jerusalem as its capital and Christ as its king. Jesus responded to his disciples' query by telling them it was not needful for them to have this knowledge and only the Father in his authority had access to information of unspecified times and dates in the future. He immediately directed their attention to the task at hand—spreading the good news of the kingdom of God, beginning in Jerusalem and reaching to the uttermost parts of the world. Thus, Jesus deemphasized the territorial concepts of the kingdom of God, while stressing the spiritual and global aspect.

What does all of the above have to do with the current Arab-Israeli conflict? Its connection lies in the fact that the Arab-Israeli conflict is mainly a conflict over land possession. And many Christians, embracing a confused concept of sacred territory in both the old and new covenants, hold that even under the new covenant the land is not only highly significant but belongs exclusively to the Jewish people. Acting out of this mistaken belief, these Christians not only financially and politically support the State of Israel's overriding claim to the land but also refrain from calling Israel to account when it has engaged in acts of terrorism and injustice against the Palestinian population. Sadly, for them certain skewed notions of biblical prophecy such as arcane theories, take precedence over real-world justice and mercy. Consequently, their hearts are not moved with compassion over the plight of millions of Palestinian refugees, the demolition of their homes, the confiscation of their land, the destruction of their lives and economy, and their daily suffering under a brutal occupation.

Should speculative interpretation of prophecy have precedence over the clear teachings of justice and mercy? Perhaps we can deduce the answer to this question from the words of Jesus to the religious folk of his times: "Woe to you, teachers of the law and Pharisees, you hypocrites! You give a tenth of your spices—mint, dill and cumin. But you have neglected the more important matters of the law—justice, mercy and faithfulness. You should have practiced the latter, without neglecting the former. You blind guides! You strain out a gnat but swallow a camel" (Matt 23:23–24).

It is clear that Jesus Christ, as well as Paul and all the other writers of the New Testament, promoted the kingdom rather than the land. Promoting the kingdom of God *brings about* that kingdom and its fruits, whereas promoting the land produces hate, strife, anger, violence, wars, bloodshed, and untold suffering as we have seen in the Middle East in the last one hundred years.

THE CITY

From the time King David moved his capital from Hebron to Jerusalem, the city became a symbol of the spiritual and political life of the nation. As Jerusalem went, so went the fortunes of the Jewish nation. The old covenant underscored the significance of Jerusalem as the spiritual core of the Jewish nation:

- "King Rehoboam established himself firmly in Jerusalem and continued as King . . . and he reigned seventeen years in Jerusalem, the city the Lord had chosen out of all the tribes of Israel in which to put his Name" (2 Chr 12:13).

- "So the name of the Lord will be declared in Zion and his praise in Jerusalem" (Ps 102:21).

- "Pray for the peace of Jerusalem: 'May those who love you be secure. May there be peace within your walls and security within your citadels.' For the sake of my brothers and friends, I will say, 'Peace be with you.' For the sake of the house of the Lord our God, I will seek your prosperity" (Ps 122:6–9).

No doubt Jerusalem had the distinction of being the most prominent city in the old covenant. Although Jesus during his ministry on earth traveled often and ministered to many in Jerusalem, his reflections on the Jerusalem of his day were neither positive nor favorable. Jesus knew that Jerusalem would be the place of his suffering and death: "From that time on Jesus began to explain to his disciples that he must go to Jerusalem and suffer many things at the hands of the elders, chief priests and teachers of the law, and that he must be killed and on the third day be raised back to life" (Matt 16:21).

Jerusalem's tragic history is predicted by Jesus: "O Jerusalem, Jerusalem, you who kill the prophets and stone those sent to you, how often I have longed to gather your children together, as a hen gathers her chicks under her wings, and you were not willing. Look, your house is left to you desolate. For I tell you, you will not see me again until you say, 'Blessed is he who comes in the name of the Lord'" (Matt 23:37–39).

Paul and the other writers of the New Testament did not place the Jerusalem of their day on a pedestal either. Paul wrote: "Now Hagar stands for Mount Sinai in Arabia and corresponds to the present city of Jerusalem, because she is in slavery with her children. But the Jerusalem that is above is free, and she is our mother" (Gal 4:25–26).

The writer of the Epistle to the Hebrews clearly deemphasizes the significance of the earthly Jerusalem as he glorified the heavenly one: "But you have come to Mount Zion, to the heavenly Jerusalem, the city of the living God. You have come to thousands upon thousands of angels in joyful assembly" (Heb 12:22).

The writer of the book of Revelation compares earthly Jerusalem with the wicked city of Sodom: "Now when the [the two witnesses] have finished their testimony, the beast that comes up from the Abyss will attack them, and overpower and kill them. Their bodies will lie in the street of the great city, which is figuratively called Sodom and Egypt, where also their Lord was crucified" (Rev 11:7–8).

The same writer describes the heavenly Jerusalem as the place where God dwells with his people: "I saw the Holy City, the New Jerusalem, coming down out of heaven from God, prepared as a bride beautifully dressed for her husband. And I heard a loud voice from the throne saying, 'Now the dwelling of God is with men, and he will live with them. They will be his people, and God himself will be with them and be their God'" (Rev 21:2–3).

Jesus and his apostles did not sing the praises of an earthly Jerusalem, but they did speak of a heavenly Jerusalem. As we turn our focus on the priesthood, sacrifice, and the temple, we will see that a central city to house a central temple was no longer needed for humans to enjoy the benefit of the new covenant.

I love the city of Jerusalem, my birthplace and the birthplace of my Christian faith. However, the sanctity of Jerusalem and the Holy Land is not contained in the soil, stones, rocks, sand, shrines, churches, mosques, and synagogues that comprise the city. Jerusalem's holiness is contained in its spiritual heritage as the city where God chose to perform his acts of redemption to all humanity. Today, many Muslims, Christians, and Jews have made Jerusalem the greatest obstacle to world peace as a result of too much emphasis on real estate and too little awareness of the spiritual message of peace and reconciliation that Jerusalem has for all humanity.

THE PRIESTHOOD

God instituted the Old Testament priesthood when Aaron, Moses' brother, became the first High Priest. The Pentateuch gives detailed instructions for the management of the institution of the priesthood. The writers of the New Testament, however, described a new type of priesthood, the priesthood of all believers. The Apostle Peter, in his first epistle, addressed new converts—both Jews and Gentiles—and called both of them, "a royal priesthood" when he wrote: "But you are a chosen people, a royal priesthood, a holy nation, a people belonging to God, that you may declare the praises of him who called you out of darkness into his wonderful light. Once you were not a people, but now you are the people of God; once you had not received mercy, but now you have received mercy" (1 Pet 2:9–10).

The writer of the book of Revelation focused on the same theme when he wrote to both Gentile and Jewish believers and referred to all of them as "a kingdom of priests":

"To him who loves us and has freed us from our sins by his blood, and has made us to be a kingdom and priests to serve his God and Father, to him be glory and power forever and ever! Amen" (Rev 1:5–6).

The priesthood in the old covenant was limited to one of Israel's tribes, the Levites. In the new covenant, however, it is clear that all who believe are members of a royal priesthood. In comparing the priesthood of the old covenant with that of the new, the writer of the book of Hebrews explains that the old priesthood must diminish to make way for a new and permanent one, declaring,

- "But because Jesus lives forever, he has permanent priesthood. Therefore he is able to save completely those who come to God through him, because he always lives to intercede for them" (Heb 7:24–25).

- "By calling this covenant 'new,' he has made the first one obsolete, and what is obsolete and aging will soon disappear" (Heb 8:13; see also Jer 31:31).

Clearly, the author of the book to the Hebrews announces that the priesthood of the Old Testament expired, making way for a new priesthood of both believing Jews and believing Gentiles.

THE SACRIFICE

In the old covenant animal sacrifices were an essential part of worship, but in the new covenant, Jesus becomes the eternal sacrifice to atone for all sins. The author of the book to the Hebrews says, "The blood of goats and bulls and the ashes of a heifer sprinkled on those who are ceremonially unclean sanctify them so that they are outwardly clean. How much more, then, will the blood of Christ, who through the eternal Spirit offered himself unblemished to God, cleanse our consciences from acts that lead to death, so that we may serve the living God!" (Heb 9:13–14).

The author continues to add: "Day after day every priest stands and performs his religious duties; again and again he offers the same sacrifices, which can never take away sins. But when this priest [Jesus] had offered for all time one sacrifice for sins, he sat down at the right hand of God" (Heb 10:11–12).

These verses, and many others like them, reflect a dramatic change in the concept of sacrifice as demonstrated in the two covenants. Whereas the sacrifices in the old covenant demand the regular, ritual slaughter of animals, the new covenant presents Jesus as the ultimate and perfect sacrifice to atone for all sins, for all people, and for all times. Thus, the sacrificial order of the old covenant was terminated to make room for the new order. Christians who hope to restore the Jewish sacrificial system should earnestly seek divine understanding to make sure that they are not stepping out of the will of God, as his will regarding sacrifice has been made clear to us in the writings of the New Testament.

THE TEMPLE

Not only did the new covenant terminate the need for animal sacrifices and cancel the Levitical priesthood, but it also abolished the need for a central temple. Instead of the temple in Jerusalem, the church of Jesus Christ—the redeemed from all nations—became the temple of the Holy Spirit. Notice the words of Jesus in response to his disciples' amazement at the grandeur of the Jerusalem temple: "Some of his disciples were remarking about how the temple was adorned with beautiful stones and with gifts dedicated to God. But Jesus said, 'As for what you see here, the time will come when not one stone will be left on another; every one of them will be thrown down'" (Luke 21:5–6).

Paul, in the following three passages, explains to early believers that they themselves are the temple of God:

- "Don't you know that you yourselves are God's temple and that God's Spirit lives in you? If anyone destroys God's temple, God will destroy him; for God's temple is sacred, and you are that temple" (1 Cor 3:16–17).

- "Do you not know that your body is a temple of the Holy Spirit, who is in you, whom you have received from God? You are not your own; you were bought at a price. Therefore honor God with your body" (1 Cor 6:19–20).

- "What agreement is there between the temple of God and idols? For we are the temple of the living God. As God has said: 'I will live with them and walk among them, and I will be their God, and they will be my people'" (2 Cor 6:16).

The above verses contain two messages: First, God's grace period for the temple in Jerusalem expired and the temple was condemned to destruction. In order for a new temple to be established, the old one had to be destroyed. Second, the new temple is no longer a building but is comprised of the body of Jesus Christ, the church.

DOES GOD HAVE A DIFFERENT PLAN FOR THE JEWISH PEOPLE?

Some may say that while the above argument is true for Gentile believers, it is not true for Jews. They may also argue that God has a special plan for the Jews, which differs from God's plan for Gentiles. I do not accept this concept for the following reasons:

1. God's plan in the new covenant includes both Jews and Gentiles, providing salvation and blessing for both. In the new covenant the two are reconciled. To promote an additional plan for the Jews is to contradict the core message of the New Testament. Examine Paul's statement in Galatians: "You are all sons of God through faith in Christ Jesus, for all of you who were baptized into Christ have clothed yourselves with Christ. There is neither Jew nor Greek, slave nor free, male nor female, for you are all one in Christ Jesus. If you belong to Christ, then you are Abraham's seed, and heirs according to the promise" (Gal 3:26–29).

2. There is no mention of a special plan for the Jews in the New Testament, separate from God's redemptive plan for the Gentiles. Those who advocate the concept of a unique plan for the Jews, at the present time or in the future, have to depend entirely on Old Testament references to justify their theory. Paul's discussion in Romans 11–12 highlights the spiritual restoration of the Jewish people through faith in Jesus Christ, not through a physical or territorial restoration. Paul's argument is based on his strong belief that the restoration of the Jewish people depends upon their acceptance of Jesus Christ.

3. To have a special plan for the Jews or any other race is to diminish the power and the effect of salvation that God has provided for all people by the death of Jesus Christ on the cross. The best that God could offer the Jews, he has already provided for them through Jesus Christ. Christ is God's best gift to humanity, including the Jewish people.

4. The eschatological theories that claim a special role for the modern State of Israel in the end times do not make theological sense. Why would God want Jews to be restored to the land and to build a temple where animal sacrifices would be offered? Has not Jesus given his body as the everlasting sacrifice for sins? Why would any Christian support the rebuilding of a temple where animal sacrifices would be offered? Would God be glorified to see Jews practicing animal sacrifices two thousand years after our Lord, the everlasting Lamb of God, gave his life for us on the cross? If such a ritual would not please God, why should any Christian support it or encourage the fringe element few zealously seeking to implement it? Truly, any supposed Christian theology that is not centred in—and does not harmonize with—the cross of Christ is not worth our time and should not have a place in our hearts.

As I lecture in various venues and explain how the old covenant with all its essential components—the nation, the state, the city, the temple, the priesthood, and the sacrifice—have been modified in the new covenant, many ask, "What about God's promises to the Jewish people? Have they expired?"

IS GOD THROUGH WITH THE JEWISH PEOPLE?

With the Apostle Paul, I say, "By no means!" With Paul, I ask them, "Did God reject his people? By no means! I am an Israelite myself, a descendent of Abraham from the tribe of Benjamin. God did not reject his people, whom he foreknew" (Rom 11:1–2).

Paul presents himself as an example of a Jew who is not rejected by God. Throughout the last two thousand years, millions of Jews have experienced the wonderful grace that changed the life of Paul. The gates of God's mercy are wide and ever open to both Jews and Gentiles. In the verse below Paul highlights the fact that God's desire is to bring both

Jews and Gentiles into one kingdom. God does not have one kingdom for the Jews and another for the Gentiles. The covenant was modified, but God's passion to gather Jews and Gentiles to his kingdom has not changed. "As far as the gospel is concerned, they are enemies on your account; but as far as election is concerned, they are loved on account of the patriarchs, for God's gifts and his call are irrevocable. Just as you who were at one time disobedient to God have now received mercy as a result of their disobedience, so they too have *now* become disobedient in order that they too may *now* receive mercy as a result of God's mercy to you. For God has bound all men over to disobedience so that he may have mercy on them all" (Rom 11:28–32, emphasis mine).

I emphasize the word *now* because Paul uses it to refer to the era of the new covenant in Christ. I understand Paul to be saying, now that Jesus has redeemed humanity through his death on the cross, Jews can obtain mercy, grace, and salvation. Therefore the salvation of the Jews can happen now (*i.e., at any time in the present*) as they come to the Savior and not in a far-away future through the establishment of a state or through the building of a temple where animal sacrifices may resume.

God's promises to the Jewish people and to all people are spiritual and do not necessitate occupying a piece of land or forcibly subjugating another nation through superior military might, political maneuvering, and economic manipulation. The promises can be actualized through a humble return of people—both Jews and Gentiles—to God, accepting God's plan for their restoration and salvation. However, the misinterpretation and misapplication of Scripture—granting divine sanction to the Zionist occupation of Palestine—have contributed significantly to the turmoil in the Middle East and, by extension, to wider global unrest. It has brought great suffering, bloodshed, and loss of life to millions, and given fuel to militant groups throughout the world. This manipulation of the Bible has also caused much anguish and frustration to Arab Christians, and it continues to be a stumbling block preventing millions the world over from responding to Christ and embracing his message.

BIBLIOGRAPHY

Awad, Alex. *Palestinian Memories: The Story of a Palestinian Mother and Her People.* Bethlehem: Bethlehem Bible College, 2008.

❖ 11 ❖

Reading the Old Testament in the Palestinian Church Today

A Case Study of Joshua 6

Munther Isaac

INTRODUCTION

PALESTINIAN CHRISTIANS HAVE STRUGGLED for years with the Old Testament (OT) in general and with the theology of the land in particular. The Palestinian-Israeli conflict has had a religious dimension to it from the beginning. The Jews saw Palestine as the land of their fathers, and many saw it as God-given based on God's promises in the OT. In turn, Christian Zionists endorsed and supported this view. Moreover, the rise of the fundamentalist movement in England and then America, with its dispensational theology and strong political influence, played an important role in the creation of modern Israel.[1]

Christian Zionism has created a dilemma for Palestinian Christians. Those Christians in the West who sympathize with Israel, based on their interpretation of the OT and dispensational theology, shock and anger Palestinian Christians when they call on Palestinians to leave the land of their fathers so as not to stand in the way of God's plan.

1. For a detailed discussion of Christian Zionism and the role it played in the creation and support of the modern State of Israel, see Sizer, *Christian Zionism*. All Scripture quotations are taken from the ESV (English Standard Version).

217

As a result, Palestinian Christians have developed a negative attitude towards the OT. Many simply reject the OT and prefer to stay within the boundaries of the New Testament (NT). They see a difference between the God of love in the NT versus the God who gave away their land to the Jews through war and terror. References to "Israel" and "Zion" in the liturgy of the Palestinian church[2] were replaced by terms like "people of God" or "Jacob."[3]

Many Palestinian theologians have described in detail the difficulties they face as theologians and clergy when encountering certain passages from the OT,[4] and many solutions have been offered;[5] perhaps the best known among them is the liberation theology of Naim Ateek. This Palestinian articulation of liberation theology is what Ateek first presented in his *Justice, and Only Justice*, and continues to defend and develop through the work of the Ecumenical Liberation Theology Center, Sabeel.[6]

Palestinian theologian Salim J. Munayer describes the relationship between Palestinian Christians and the OT as one of neglect, rejection, and selectivity.[7] Part of this article shows how I believe Palestinian Christians have become Marcionites both in practice and belief.[8] Whether it is a Palestinian liberation theology or a spiritualization of the OT, the church has fallen prey to misreading or rejecting parts of the

2. I use the term *"the Palestinian church"* as a representation of all the churches and denominations in Palestine today. There are about 45,000 Christians in the West Bank and Gaza, and about 123,400 in Israel, the majority of whom are Greek Orthodox and Catholic, with a few Protestants. See *Sabeel Survey on Palestinian Christians* and *Statistical Abstract of Israel 1998*, No. 49.

3. For a good survey and analysis of how the Palestinian Church has read the OT, see Slajerova, "Palestinian Church Reads Old Testament."

4. See esp. Ateek, *Justice*, 77–79, and Raheb, *I Am a Palestinian Christian*, 55–58. Ateek speaks from his pastoral experience of the Bible becoming part of the problem for Palestinian Christians, whereas Raheb talks about the difficulties he encountered as a seminary student studying in Germany.

5. See, e.g., Sabbah, "Reading the Bible."

6. For more on the work of Sabeel, see http://www.sabeel.org/.

7. Munayer, "Reading the Old Testament in Palestine." Munayer also points out how the relationship is not merely political. The Old Testament brings familiarity with geographical locations and landscape, and with names and cultural patterns of tribal societies, especially for those living in places like Hebron and Bethlehem.

8. Marcionism is a heresy dating from the second century, chiefly espoused by Marcion of Sinope, who rejected the OT and Yahweh, believing that the Hebrew god was different from the God of the NT. For Marcion, the Hebrew god was wrathful, whereas the NT God was all loving and all forgiving. Additionally, Marcion accepted only eleven books from the New Testament, a markedly redacted canon.

OT. This phenomenon is not limited to Palestinian Christians but is also apparent within other Arab Christian communities. Dutch theologian Bernard Reitsma quotes Arab theologians who speak about a "practical type of Marcionitism in the churches in the Middle East," and "a great Marcionite revival in [the] East today."[9] Dr. Riad Kassis from Lebanon wrote a book in Arabic entitled *Why Don't We Read the Book That Jesus Read?*, in which he describes and attempts to deal with a number of reasons why he thinks Arab Christians are not reading the OT.[10]

The purpose of this article is to engage with some of the difficulties that Palestinian Christians have when facing a difficult passage in the OT, and then engage with the text itself as a Palestinian Christian living in the twenty-first century.

JOSHUA 6: A CASE STUDY

I have selected the famous conquest story in Joshua 6 as a case study. Joshua 6 is one of the most challenging chapters in all of Scripture. It has always raised questions not only for Palestinian Christians but also for all Christians. The difficulties in the passage are numerous. In this chapter we encounter holy war and the ban principle (*herem*), a woman prostitute traitor/heroine, miraculously fallen walls, a curse on a town, and, most shockingly, the approval of God for all these things. No wonder some Christians view this story as an embarrassment,[11] problematic, awkward,[12] or offensive[13]—while others have gone as far as to describe the events in the story using terms such as "genocide" and "ethnic cleansing."[14] The story also gives a wealth of material for those who want to attack the OT from outside the Judeo-Christian faith.[15]

9. Reitsma, "Who Is Our God?" 180–202.

10. Kassis, *Limatha La Naqra' Al Kitab allathi qara' hu Yasu'?* The book is an apologetic toward three types of people: Christian Zionists, liberal streams in the Protestant church, and also the Muslim community.

11. Goetz, "Joshua, Calvin, and Genocide," 263–74.

12. Stone, "Ethical and Apologetic Tendencies," 25–35.

13. Epp-Tiessen, "Conquering the Land," 64.

14. Prior, "'Power' and 'the Other'," 27–43.

15. See, e.g., the book by the Palestinian journalist Abdil Majeed Hamdan: *Al Wa'd fil Torah. Al Quds Ard Al Asal Wal Laban*. In this book, Hamdan uses a particular story to illustrate the violent nature of the God of the Torah, and makes a connection with the current Israeli occupation to the Palestinians.

The German theologian Ulrike Bechmann illustrates how Christians have a hard time accepting and relating to Joshua 6. He writes a poem from the perspective of a Jericho woman (not Rahab). For him, the citizens of Jericho are the victims in the story, and God is a butcher! In the poem, the woman of Jericho says: "Tomorrow, when the sun rises, the wall will fall down. The city will be burnt. You know, the God of Joshua has no mercy at all, not even for the old ones or children."[16]

Many Palestinian Christians can relate to this poem. Many would read Joshua 6 the same way. Mitri Raheb remembers when he first encountered this passage as an adult: "The God I had known since my childhood as love had suddenly become a God who confiscated land, waged 'holy wars,' and destroyed whole peoples. I began to doubt this God. I started to hate this God."[17]

Tackling all the theological and ethical difficulties in Joshua 6 in one paper is a very difficult task, and I will not attempt to do so, as many have discussed these issues before.[18] In particular, Bernard Reitsma has done a commendable job of addressing some of the theological issues, like the principle of *herem*, and of interpreting the text especially as it relates to the Palestinian-Israeli issues today.[19]

Instead, I will try to offer a critical theological reading of this story as a Palestinian Christian. I will apply this reading to the Palestinian church today and engage in some self-criticism. In the first part I will discuss four theological "difficulties" that I see in today's Palestinian church as it tries to read this story. Then I will suggest four ways of preaching this text in the Palestinian church today.

I realize that there are many other angles from which we could approach this story, e.g., social and cultural, or exegetical. (There are many interesting views about this chapter of Joshua, including that, perhaps, the text simply exaggerates in order to spread fear in the hearts of the readers.) I also realize that my theological reading will reflect my theological presuppositions and convictions about Scripture, revelation, redemptive history, and the relationship between the Old and New Testaments. My conviction is that Jesus Christ is the Messiah of Israel, the true Israelite,

16. Quoted in Epp-Tiessen, "Conquering the Land," 65.

17. Raheb, *I Am a Palestinian Christian*, 56.

18. See, e.g., Wright, *Old Testament Ethics*, 472–79, and Stone, "Ethical and Apologetic Tendencies," 25–35.

19. Reitsma, "Who Is Our God?"

and a second Joshua, the Savior of the world, and the fulfillment and end toward which the Old Testament and all history are going.

PART 1: FOUR DIFFICULTIES/PROBLEMS IN THE PALESTINIAN CHURCH

1. A Problem of Approach: The Palestinian Church Is Reacting

Everyone brings his or her own background and context to the text. No one reads the text in isolation without being influenced by cultural bias. We all bring our own questions and concerns to the text, and this is legitimate. Of course, many times these questions affect the interpretation.

Palestinian Christians are influenced by their own context in a very unique way. When it comes to reading the OT in general and Joshua 6 in particular, I believe that there is a challenge to how we approach the text. We read the OT *reacting* to Christian Zionism and the new challenges we faced after the *Nakba*[20] and the creation of the modern State of Israel, and so the OT has become a problem for us as Palestinian Christians because our spiritual heritage seems to justify the occupation of our land.

When the Palestinian church studies Scripture, its interpretation is shaped by the fact that it is responding to Zionism and its context. Our theology is thus passive and not active. While it is important to respond to the challenges, we cannot allow the questions raised by Christian Zionism and the politics of our time to determine our interpretation, approach, and theology of the OT. A theology that says what things are *not* is not a holistic theology, though it might contain some truth.

For example, when Palestinian Christians read Joshua 6 they are mainly concerned with questions such as

- *Is God legitimizing/giving our land to our enemies?*
- *Is God for us or against us? Is our God biased towards the Jews?*
- *Does Joshua 6 legitimize the Israeli occupation today?*
- *Are we acting against the will of God when we resist the occupation?*[21]

20. *Nakba* is the Arabic word for "catastrophe," and for Palestinians it marks the destruction of over four hundred Palestinian villages and the expulsion of over seven hundred thousand Palestinians from their homes during the 1948 war that led to the creation of the modern State of Israel.

21. Munayer described how he faced similar challenging questions from his Palestinian Christian students at the Bethlehem Bible College. See Munayer, "The Theological Challenge."

(Inherent in these questions are the presuppositions that Israel of today equals the Israel of the OT, and that the Canaanites of the OT equal the Palestinians of today.)

With regard to the questions raised, we already had our answers before going to the text:

- *No, God cannot be giving our land to the Israelis.*
- *No, God cannot be against us. God cannot be biased.*
- *Joshua 6 cannot be legitimizing the occupation.*

Next, in going to the text, we try to make it answer the questions in the way we want it to answer them. We became victims of doing what we criticized others of doing, viz., using the text to justify an agenda.

It is as if the OT troubles us, and we want to deny its historical and theological validity and authenticity, but we cannot do so because this would be against our tradition. So the best we can do is to make the OT say what we want it to say.

However, we should let the text speak. We are making the text answer our questions, instead of listening to the questions asked by the text. We are theologizing through our eyes, and not through the eyes of the text.

2. A Hermeneutical Problem: What Is the Bible?

Before we speak of a contextual Palestinian Christian theology, we must first seek a *Christian* theology, and then apply it to the Palestinian church. We must read Joshua 6 within the context of the NT and salvation history. We need a complete and holistic view of God, the OT, and salvation history that will help interpret Scripture.

We read the OT in a flat way, and not in a redemptive historical way. I fear that many times we are influenced by systematic theology's approach to Scripture, and we go to the OT asking questions of what is right and what is wrong, before we study the text in its redemptive historical and theological contexts. The grammatical-historical study of any text is only the first step. We must continue and ask how any given text or section in the Bible relates to the grand plan of salvation that is unfolding in history—first in the OT itself and then in the NT.

Before trying to answer the challengers, we must ask ourselves some very basic questions: *What is the OT? Is it a Christian book? And how is it a Christian book? Is it simply a book that contains good lessons and morals from the lives of good people of faith? Is it a book of systematic theology? We need to emphasize the nature of progressive revelation in history, especially in the Palestinian context. The Bible is not the Qur'an. It does not contain eternal doctrines that were created before the foundation of the earth and then dropped down to us from the sky.

Once we answer these questions we can move forward in our task of trying to understand Joshua 6. At the heart of the Joshua 6 problem is the question: *What is the OT?* We must struggle as theologians with this question, which is not a new question, but a question as old as the church itself. This is at the heart of Christianity. If we fail to define the OT with the context of redemptive history, we lose our claim of the OT as a Christian book.

Realizing this problem, the former Latin Patriarch of Jerusalem Michael Sabbah devoted the bulk of his "Fourth Pastoral Letter: Reading the Bible Today in the Land of the Bible" to the question, what is the Bible? This is a very helpful and well-thought-out document for the Palestinian church in all its denominations. Sabbah talks about the Bible as the history of salvation—our own salvation—and he emphasizes the progressive nature of this history. After emphasizing all these, he then proceeds to address difficult issues in the OT, such as violence, the land, and Israel.[22] The particulars addressed in this letter are a clear example of the difficulties faced by Palestinian theologians and lay people.

3. Three Misinterpretations

A wrong approach and a hermeneutical problem will yield poor theology and negative consequences. I will discuss three examples of what I see as deficient theology and the interpretation of Joshua 6 within the Palestinian church: 1) literalism, 2) liberation theology, and 3) spiritualization theology.

1) Literalism

Dispensationalism insists on taking the OT literally. God has two plans: One is earthly, namely, for Israel; the other is heavenly, namely, for the church. The implications are simple: Israel of the OT equals the Israel of today, Canaanites of the OT equal the Palestinians of today, and the Promised Land is the Holy Land of today (modern Israel and the

---

22. Sabbah, "Reading the Bible Today."

Occupied Territories). The events of the twentieth century are proof that God's promises must come true in the end. If the Exodus from Egypt is the greatest miracle in history, the creation of modern Israel in 1948 is the second biggest event in history. (The resurrection is number three on this list.) We read about this all the time, and we see it everyday on Christian television programming. The book of Joshua is a favorite for Christian Zionism.[23] Amazingly, there are Palestinians who believe this as well, and not only among the evangelicals. Many Palestinian Christians read the OT and stumble when reading the word "Israel" or "Philistines,"[24] confusing Israel of today with Israel of the OT. This leads them to think that God favors the Israelis of today over the Palestinians, and that modern Israel is a fulfillment of biblical Israel.

This is a clear illustration of a flat reading of the OT. Joshua 6 is stripped from its place in salvation history. Jesus is not the end (*telos*) of this story, and God is a sectarian God who favors one nation over another.

2) Liberation Theology

The intentions here are good and genuine, and the emphasis on justice by Palestinian liberation theology is crucial for our world today. Naim Ateek, the founder of Palestinian liberation theology, applies a hermeneutical key to reading the OT. This key is that how we understand God is through Christ who is the final revelation. Ateek says, "When confronted with a difficult passage in the Bible or with a perplexing contemporary event one needs to ask such simple questions as: Is the way I am hearing this the way I have come to know God in Christ? Does it fit the picture I have of God that Jesus has revealed to me? Does it match the character of God who I have come to know through Christ? If it does, then that passage is valid and authoritative. If not, then I cannot accept its validity or authority."[25]

---

23. Fr. Jamal Khader talks about the danger of fundamentalism in all religions and shows how certain passages were used in all religions to justify violence. See Khader, "Opportunities and Threats," 141–62.

24. In English, there are two different words: "Palestinians" and "Philistines," but in the Arabic translations the word is the same *Falastin*. The same is true with Israel and Israelites: In Arabic, one word—*Israel*—describes both. Some Arab theologians like the Lebanese Riad Kassis try to solve this by creating new words to describe biblical Palestine and biblical Israel.

25. Ateek, *Justice*, 81–82. It is important to note that I am not making a critique of liberation theology in general, but of Naim Ateek's hermeneutical approach.

When he applied this to Joshua 6, this is the result: "Is such a passage, which is attributed to God, consistent with how God is revealed in Jesus Christ? If not, we must say that it only reveals a human understanding of God's nature and purpose that was superseded and corrected by the revelation in Christ. In other words, such passages are revelatory of a stage of development of the human understanding of God that we must regard, in light of Christ's revelation, as inadequate and incomplete."[26]

Many theologians have criticized Ateek's hermeneutic, and not all Palestinians are pleased by his interpretation. I believe there are serious problems with Ateek's approach, which is labeled by some as Marcionism. Palestinian theologian Yohanna Katanacho critiques Ateek's work as dangerous because "his proposal creates a canon within the canon, rejecting portions of the Old Testament and as a result it deprives Palestinian Christians from seriously considering the whole council of God."[27] I would even go so far as to say that his approach is Darwinistic, when he speaks of "a stage of development of the human understanding of God."[28] Besides, which Jesus are we reading the OT through? A Jesus who is always nice, meek, and all loving? What about the Jesus who emphasized justice and judgment, and who spoke regularly about judgment and hell?

This approach, though wanting to highlight the justice of God, has the potential to yield a view of God as a soft God who always turns the other cheek, who never judges sin but always continues to love unconditionally. A God who never judges is an unjust God.

Though liberation theology has won many mainline denominations to the side of the Palestinians, it continues to push many evangelicals away from it because it is viewed as too liberal.

3) Spiritualization

Before I explain what I mean here, let me say that I do not think that this type of theology is wrong in what it says, but it is wrong in what it does not say, because it does not offer the complete picture. So what do I mean by spiritualization?

The idea in the book of Hebrews that the OT is a shadow or type of the things to come is taken to mean that the OT is physical, and the NT

26. Ibid., 82.
27. Katanacho, "Palestinian Protestant Theological Responses," 293.
28. Ateek, *Justice*, 82.

is spiritual. The task of the preacher is to find spiritual themes in the text and apply them to the modern context of the believer. These spiritual themes include moral exhortations, spiritual lessons that apply to the life of the believer to help him/her grow, and at best provide a pointer to Christ. This type of interpretation of the OT is very common among evangelical Palestinian Christians today.

In this type of interpretation, Joshua 6 becomes a great source of spiritual lessons. It is a story about the power of praise and worship in the life of the church. It is a great example of how obedience brings victory in the spiritual and daily life of the believer and the church. Rahab's faith and her repentance are examples to follow.[29] The crimson rope represents the cross. In evangelical churches today there is even a praise and worship song that celebrates the battle of Jericho and applies it to the spiritual walls in the believer's life, or to the walls hindering the ministry of the church.

Though these things are not wrong in themselves and are very important to the preaching of the church today, they are not the primary content of Joshua. Furthermore, such a reading of the OT fails to answer the questions raised by many about issues like holy war and *herem*, let alone the Palestinian-Israeli issues of today. Are we simply avoiding these questions by focusing on the spiritual nature of the battles?

4. Confusion of Identity

During the war on Gaza in January 2009, Geries Khoury, a prominent Palestinian Christian theologian from the Catholic Church addressed the annual Al Liqa' Center's Palestinian Contextual Theology Conference. In his opening remarks he compared the Israeli military actions in Gaza to those of the Israelites in the book of Joshua when they conquered Jericho. The Jews today, he said, are doing what their "ancestors" did thirty-five hundred years ago when they killed every living creature

---

29. Mitri Raheb recounts how as a child this story was his favorite: "I can still remember the time we children, with bated breath, walked along with Joshua seven times around the city of Jericho. And when we heard about the walls tumbling we cheered, clapped, and danced. We thought that we, the Christian Palestinian children in Sunday school, were truly the conquerors of Jericho." Raheb then explains how this very same story later became a problem for him because of what he thought it said about the Palestinian-Israeli conflict. Raheb, *I Am a Palestinian Christian*, 55–57.

there. Rahab, the prostitute, was compared to the Palestinian collaborators today who help Israel in its actions in Gaza.[30]

This is quite a shocking reading of the events in Joshua. The Israelites in the story are not the people of God. Joshua is not and cannot be a prophet of God. Instead, for Dr. Khoury, the story proves that the aggression and crimes of Israel today are not something new to "Israel."

This is a clear example of the confusion we encounter as Palestinian Christians today. This particular interpretive problem never existed until the *Nakba* and the creation of the modern, secular State of Israel. With this event, terms such as "Israel" and "Palestine" have taken on a double meaning. Ateek speaks of this is his *Justice, and Only Justice*.[31] The confusion also appears when psalms are read or sung in our churches. The reader often replaces words such as "Zion" and "Israel" with, simply, "people of God."[32]

The consequences of this confusion are tragic. Palestinian Christians read passages in the OT such as Joshua 6 and see themselves as the enemy in the story. This was my own personal experience as a child reading the OT. I can still remember reading Isaiah, and cheering God when he declared his judgment on Israel, and then being really disappointed at God when, in the end, God always restores Israel.

Yet we cannot read Scripture in such a way. We—the community of believers in God's Son, Israel's Messiah—are God's people today and in the OT. The OT is *our* story. Joshua is not simply my hero. He is my forefather. The Patriarchs are our ancestors. Israel's victory in the OT is our victory as a community of faith today. N.T. Wright says that the task of the preacher is to "lead our people gently into the fact that the Story of Israel B.C. is part of their family photograph album, and if they want to know who they are now they need to look back even if the photographs are a bit faded and funny and people don't look like that these days."[33]

I am not saying that the church has replaced Israel. Instead, I believe that we joined Israel. We became part of Israel. I believe that Jesus is the

---

30. The papers of this conference can be found in Arabic only, in *Al Liqaʾ Journal* 24:1 (2009).

31. Ateek, *Justice*, 75–77.

32. I experienced this myself when I was once asked to participate in the liturgy of a morning mass in a Catholic church in Palestine while I was a student during the time of the second Intifada. A nun asked that as I read the Psalm, I say "Jacob" instead of "Israel," since "we needed to be 'sensitive' to the congregation."

33. Wright, "New Exodus."

true Israelite (cf. John 15:1; Isa 49:3; 52:13—53:12), and since we are in Christ today, then we are and have always been in Israel. At a certain time in history, we were not part of God's household. Paul speaks of this in detail in Eph 2:11–22 and Rom 11:11–32. But the implications of Ephesians 2 and Romans 11 are that *now* we *are* God's household, and since we are God's household, we claim the history of salvation that started in the OT and found its culmination in the death and resurrection event as *our* history. We share in the nourishing root of the olive tree (Rom 11:17).

Modern Israel not only robbed us of our land and freedom, but it also robbed us of our Scripture and spiritual heritage as Palestinian Christians. In addition, the confusion of identity revealed that when faith is put against nationalism, Palestinian Christians seem to have a hard time accepting that sometimes we are called to choose one over the other, as in the case of Rahab.

Was Rahab a traitor, as Khoury states? Or a heroine, as Hebrews 11:31 states? For a Christian who lives in the West, this is an easy question. Of course, she is a heroine, and the NT speaks of her as such. This is not so for the Palestinian Christian, who is desperate to prove to the Muslims in his country that he is just as patriotic as they are. I believe our reading of this story would have been different if the roles were switched in the story. When Jeremiah warned Judah's king and the Israelites that Jerusalem would fall, and that they should surrender, was he a traitor? Now the issue becomes more intriguing.

The issue of faith versus nationalism is an important issue. I just wonder if we Palestinian Christians are sometimes too Palestinian. We could be better Palestinians if we would take the more difficult route and, like Rahab, choose faith over nationalism.

Conclusion of Part 1

When we understand the OT as the first part of the story of God's redemptive plan in history—a story that progresses until it culminates and finds its completion in the ministry, death, and resurrection of Christ, and then in the establishment of the kingdom (which is taking place today), we will approach Joshua 6 with more confidence. Christopher Wright offers a very helpful treatment of this chapter. He emphasizes that "God's ultimate purpose of blessing all nations does not eliminate his progressive act in judgment on particular nations within history."[34]

---

34. Wright, *Old Testament Ethics*, 473.

Wright believes that there is no contradiction between ultimate blessing and historical judgment. He urges us to read the conquest as a limited event. He then reminds us that God threatened to do the same to Israel—i.e., to punish them—and that he actually did.[35] A reading of the conquest as a limited event is confirmed by the many commandments to Israel in the OT that condemn bloodshed. Was that not the point of God's rejection for David to build the temple (1 Chr 22:9)? Hosea the prophet says, "There is no fidelity, no tenderness, no knowledge of God in the country, only perjury and lies, slaughter, theft, adultery and violence, murder after murder" (Hos 4:1–2).

Furthermore, as Sabbah demonstrates, Joshua 6 shows us the holiness and justice of God. He says, "In the mindset of the times of the sacred writers, the use of violence is related first of all to the concept of God's holiness, and secondly to the concept of justice and the way to preserve it among humankind."[36]

In short, we cannot afford a flat reading of the OT. We must understand God as the Savior, Redeemer, and King of the world. He is an angry and brokenhearted God. *When he looks at our world, he wants to redeem it at all costs—whether be it the herem in Jericho or the blood of his own Son!* We need a complete view of God. We need to read the judgment on the Canaanites in its redemptive historical context.

PART 2: PREACHING JOSHUA 6 IN THE PALESTINIAN CHURCH TODAY

Joshua 6 is a very important epic in redemptive history. We cannot and should not ignore it in our churches today. The OT must be redeemed and returned to its normal position as the church's holy Scripture. As I will attempt to show, Joshua 6 can serve as a weapon in the arsenal of the Palestinian church today in her struggle for peace, justice, and mission.

There are many ways to preach from Joshua 6. I have chosen to highlight four aspects of the nature of God from this chapter that can serve the Palestinian Christian community today. I will not discuss each aspect exhaustively, but each of these four aspects can be developed and unpacked separately.

---

35. Ibid., 476.
36. Sabbah, "Reading the Bible Today," para. 40.

1. God as the Just Ruler of the Universe

In Joshua 6, God used the Israelites as a tool to judge the Canaanites at that time. "And they shall come back here in the fourth generation, for the iniquity of the Amorites is not yet complete" (Gen 15:16).

The Bible is clear that God is the ruler of the universe. He brings the Israelites to judge the Canaanites, and the Babylonians to judge the Israelites. His judgment will come, and we must not think for a moment that sin and injustice can easily get a pass in front of his holy eyes. God is an angry God, and his anger is righteous anger.

I believe this is an encouraging message for Palestinians today. We have been suffering from severe injustice in the last century. We might be tempted to think that God is silent or distant. But perhaps "the iniquity of the Israelites is not yet complete."

Now I must be careful here. We should not be hasty to interpret every natural disaster or war today as God's judgment. We are not God to make such claims. God is the judge, not us. We must "repay no one evil for evil . . . and if possible, so far as it depends on [us], live peaceably with all. [And] never avenge [our]selves, but leave it to the wrath of God, for it is written, 'Vengeance is mine, I will repay,' says the Lord" (Rom 12:17–19). But what we can affirm is that God's judgment of the wicked and the unjust will surely come one day (even if it is after four hundred years, as proven by Joshua 6). The God we believe in is not a powerless, kind, and loving old man who simply harms no one. He is the all-consuming fire (Heb 12:28–29). We must preach this God—this is good news for the victims of this world, the Palestinian Christians included.

Additionally, being the people of God today does not mean an automatic immunity from the judgment of this God. This is clearly seen in the exile. The fate of the Canaanites in Joshua became the fate of the people of God in the exile!

2. God as the Faithful Covenant Keeper

God keeps covenants. In this story God worked against all odds to accomplish an astonishing victory for his people. Today, as a small and weak community, part of the remnant in the land, we must not lose sight of this fact. God has made an eternal covenant with us through the blood of Jesus in the Last Supper. He will never leave us or forsake us, if we hold fast to his promises.

Might, power, tactics, strategies, or anything of that sort did not accomplish victory for the people of God in Joshua 6. Victory was accomplished by faith. The people of God had to believe and trust that once they obey God and do it his way, the walls will fall. And the walls fell.

The Palestinian church faces many challenges today. On top of these challenges is the challenge of survival. Amazingly, we too have a wall around us that needs to fall![37] What is our plan to conquer this wall? What is our strategy to survive in the land? Might? Power? The UN? Foreign support? Obama? International conferences? Alliance with the Muslims in this country? Compromise? Shall we compromise the gospel and keep quiet so as not to disturb others? Or is our strategy one of faith and obedience? Crazy and radical obedience that is ready to bring down the walls in prayer and praise, believing that the walls will eventually fall! The message of Joshua 6 for us today is that with faith and obedience, our God is the God of the impossible.

This God of the impossible brought salvation and victory through a weak, beaten-up, and suffering man on the cross of Calvary, and brought down the walls of death. Can he in the same manner use the small, powerless, and weak minority of Palestinian Christians to bring down the physical walls around us, and the spiritual walls of hatred and revenge? This is the ultimate challenge facing us today.

3. The God Who Welcomes All

Is it not amazing that a Gentile woman and prostitute is the hero of this story? Is it not amazing that Rahab found her way into the genealogy of Jesus? Who said that the God of the OT is the God of the Jews alone? Who said the God of the OT is an exclusive God? Many voices around us today try to tell us Palestinian Christians that we are second class, or somehow inferior to the Jews. I have heard it personally (though indirectly) from Western Christians who come to visit the Holy Land. The OT assures us that this view is misguided. This is also a message to the Palestinian church to be inclusive and not exclusive. We must show and live the message of the gospel that all are welcome in the kingdom of God.

---

37. As of 2002, the Israeli Government started building a projected 703 km (436 mi) wall/fence in Palestinian areas for "security" reasons. The Palestinians view this wall as racist and consider it land theft. In 2004 the International Court of Justice declared that construction of the wall is against international law. Nonetheless, the building of the wall continues to this day.

4. The Suffering God

Joshua 6 points us to the cross and to the crucified one. In Jerusalem, the wrath of God fell neither on the Canaanites nor on the Israelites but on God's Son—the righteous one, the suffering servant. Jesus absorbed this wrath and took the judgment of God upon himself so that we can have life today. There on the cross, Jesus—the new Joshua—accomplished the ultimate victory for the people of God and started a better kingdom, a kingdom of heaven here on earth.

May we all strive to be good citizens in this kingdom today, as we proclaim the whole earth as God's, and Jesus the Jewish Messiah, as the King of kings and Prince of Peace. May it be a kingdom of peace and justice, on earth as it is in heaven.

BIBLIOGRAPHY

Ateek, Naim S. *Justice, and Only Justice: A Palestinian Theology of Liberation*. Maryknoll, NY: Orbis, 1989.

Ecumenical Liberation Theology Center (Sabeel). "2006 Survey on Palestinian Christians in the West Bank and Israel.", 2006. Online: (English) http://www.sabeel.org/pdfs/the%20sabeel%20survey_.pdf; (Arabic) http://www.sabeel.org/pdfs/the%20sabeel%20surveyarabic.pdf.

Epp-Tiessen, Esther. "Conquering the Land." In *Under Vine and Fig Tree: Biblical Theologies of Land and the Palestinian-Israeli Conflict*, edited by Alain E. Weaver, 62–74. Telford, PA: Cascadia, 2007.

Goetz, Ronald. "Joshua, Calvin, and Genocide." *Theology Today* 32 (1975) 263–74.

Israel Central Bureau of Statistics "Statistical Abstract of Israel 1998, No. 49." Online: http://www.cbs.gov.il/archive/shnaton49/shnatone.htm

Kassis, Riad. *Limatha La Naqra' Al Kitab allathi qara' hu Yasu'?* Beirut: Clarion, 2009.

Katanacho, Yohanna. "Palestinian Protestant Theological Responses to a World Marked by Violence." *Missiology* 36 (2008) 289–305.

Khader, Jamal. "Opportunities and Threats for Religions in Time of Conflict and Violence: How (Not) to Use the Name of God." In *Postcolonial Europe in the Crucible of Cultures: Reckoning with God in a World of Conflicts*, edited by Jacques Haers et al., 141–62. Amsterdam: Rodopi, 2007.

Munayer, Salim. "Reading the Old Testament in Palestine." Unpublished article, 2008. Online: http://www.musalaha.netvision.net.il/.

———. "The Theological Challenge the State of Israel Poses to Palestinian Christians." *St. Francis Magazine* 3:4 (March 2008). Online:http://www.stfrancismagazine.info/ja/pdf/2008/The%20Theological%20Challenge.pdf/.

Prior, John M. "'Power' and the 'Other' in Joshua: The Brutal Birthing of a Group Identity." *Mission Studies* 23 (2006) 27–43.

Raheb, Mitri. *I Am a Palestinian Christian*. Minneapolis: Fortress, 1995.

Reitsma, Bernard. "Who Is Our God? The Theological Challenges of the State of Israel for Christian Arabs: Faith and Ethnicity in the Middle East." *Faith and Ethnicity: Studies in Reformed Theology* 6 (2002) 180–202.

Sabbah, Michel. "Reading the Bible Today in the Land of the Bible." (November 1993) Online: http://www.lpj.org/newsite2006/patriarch/pastoral-letters/home-pastoral-letters.html.

Sizer, Stephen R. *Christian Zionism: Road Map to Armageddon?* Downer's Grove, IL: InterVarsity, 2004.

Slajerova, Monika. "Palestinian Church Reads Old Testament: The Triangle of Ethnicity, Faith, Land—and Biblical Interpretation." *Communio Viatorum* 46 (2004) 34–62.

Stone, Lawson G. "Ethical and Apologetic Tendencies in the Redaction of the Book of Joshua." *Catholic Biblical Quarterly* 53 (1991) 25–36.

Wright, Christopher J. H. *Old Testament Ethics for the People of God.* Downers Grove, IL: InterVarsity, 2004.

Wright, N. T. "New Exodus, New Creation, New Humanity." Lecture 2, of 3 parts. From Preaching and Teaching from Romans. Calvin Theological Seminary Continuing Education Conference, January 25, 2003. Online: http://www.calvin.edu/worship/idis/theology/ntwright_romans.php/.

✢ 12 ✢

Theology of the Land

From a Land of Strife to a Land of Reconciliation

Salim Munayer

edited by Joshua Korn

Land is given in covenant. Israel's central task is to keep it so, never
to perceive its land in a social or historical vacuum. In a vacuum all
kinds of coercive deeds are possible and even legitimate. But they
speak no words, give no gifts, keep no promises.

—Walter Brueggemann[1]

W HEN CONSIDERING THEOLOGY OF the land, four important principles are worth keeping in mind.[2] First, God is the creator of the
land, and all creation is sustained solely by him. Second, the land is a gift.
Since God is the creator, the land is his to give as a gift, and not ours to
take or selfishly hold. Third, as God has given us the gift of land, this gift
is given through a covenant. Therefore we have the responsibilities as the
receivers of this gift of land, for our moral and ethical choices and actions

---

1. Brueggemann, *The Land*, 62.
2. For a more detailed analysis of these four principles, see Munayer, *Hosea*, 149–69.

234

affect the land, and there are consequences for our sins. Finally, the land is a gift that has been promised to all people; it is God's blessing to all who are created in his image.

Most conversations dealing with theology of the land begin with Gen 12:1–3.[3] In this passage God promises to make Abraham into "a great nation," through whom "all the families of the earth shall be blessed" if he will only go "to the land that I will show you." Because of eschatological concerns and the way these promises relate to the current political situation, these passages have become very controversial and divisive. In our eagerness to "prove" who is right or wrong, and who has the most justified claim to the land, we often ignore the most fundamental and basic principles concerning the land found in the biblical narrative. In fact, the original covenant concerning the land between God and humanity occurs much earlier in Genesis 1–3, when Adam and Eve are given, and subsequently driven from, the Garden of Eden by God. In the creation narrative we see that God is the creator and keeper of all creation. He has given creation to humanity as a gift, for us to enjoy and to be blessed by, but it is a gift that comes with responsibility. We have to acknowledge him as the creator, and our only provider and sustainer.

We are called to recognize that God is the true and only owner of the land, and we must realize that all of creation belongs to him. The land is a gift from God, given through a covenant and "given by the giver of good gifts and the speaker of faithful words." As God brought the children of Israel into the Promised Land after their wilderness wanderings, the message was clear: In no way have you earned this gift, for "you did not build; you did not fill; you did not hew; you did not plant."[4] The land is a gift, for "the people who are to possess it did not create it."[5]

However, we often forget that the land is a gift and begin to think that we somehow deserve what we did not create. This is because—unlike the years spent wandering in the wilderness, where God was clearly the sustainer and provider—the Promised Land is a land of plenty, and life is easier. "Guaranteed security dulls the memory," and we forget the years of want and dependence. We become arrogant and selfish, unwilling to

3. For a good survey of the available literature on theology of the land and how it relates to the New Testament, see Kohl, "Towards a Theology of Land." All Scripture quotations taken from the (NKJV) New King James Version unless otherwise indicated.

4. Brueggemann, *The Land*, 46.

5. Berry, "The Gift of Good Land," 295.

share the land with others, imagining that we somehow created paradise by our own efforts. Like the children of Israel, we begin "imagining it was always so" and that we made it so. We are "no longer recipient of land but controller, no longer creature of grace but manager of achievement."[6] In the final analysis, the land is not ours; it is his. This is clearly seen when God tells the Israelites not to sell the land permanently, because "the land is Mine; for you are strangers and sojourners with Me." (Lev 25:23).

If the land is a gift from God, we must also remember that this gift comes wrapped in responsibility, and that our actions have an enormous impact on the land. The "Promised Land is not a permanent gift. It is 'given,' but only for a time, and only for so long as it is properly used."[7] The disobedience of mankind led to severe consequences, and expulsion from the garden. In this first exile we see that the relationship between man and God was forever altered. Additionally and significantly, the relationship between man and the land was also changed. As a result of human sin, the ground was cursed, and turned from a fruitful garden to a barren land, which will bring forth "both thorns and thistles," and only provided food by "the sweat of your face" (Gen 3:17–19). From the very beginning, humanity's moral and ethical choices have been inextricably intertwined with the health of the land.

When the land is given, a covenant is made with God. As with any covenant, there are expectations on the part of both parties involved. Obedience was required from Abraham, which he demonstrated by leaving the land of his fathers (Gen 12:4) as well as by willingly offering up his only son Isaac to God as a sacrifice (Gen 22:16). Eugene Korn writes, "The covenant is a holy contract, and as in every contract, each party acquires benefits in return for assuming responsibilities."[8] God's promise of the land to the Israelites is often seen as an unconditional promise, but adopting this attitude is dangerous as well as unbiblical. If the promise is unconditional, any means of claiming and keeping it are acceptable—a disastrous and frightening thought, especially when the Old Testament conquest of the land of Canaan is remembered and seen as an example. "The process of taking possession of the Promised Land, a land flowing with milk and honey, required that it flow also with the

6. Brueggemann, *The Land*, 51–53.

7. Berry, "The Gift of Good Land," 296.

8. Korn, "Land and Covenant."

blood of its indigenous population."[9] The "divinely-mandated shedding of the blood of the natives would be redemptive" and through "this 'ethnic' massacre the land would be cleansed of the defilement with which the native population had polluted it."[10]

This sentiment has found expression in the European colonial and imperial discourse, from the Manifest Destiny of the American westward expansion to the White Man's Burden and *La Mission Civilisatrice*. This perspective has also informed the worldview of some supporters of the modern State of Israel, based on the fulfillment of biblical prophecy. This distortion of the imagery of cleansing the land is interesting, especially in light of the fact that the Scriptures explicitly state that the land is defiled by sin, and is cleansed by righteousness, i.e., the proper treatment of others.

The biblical account is clear that the task given to the children of Israel as they left Egypt and entered the Promised Land was to uphold and observe the Torah. From the outset their presence in the land was contingent on their relationship to God and to the Torah. Walter Brueggemann lists three foundational guidelines to upholding the Torah given to the children of Israel: 1) They were supposed to keep away from any images; 2) they were to observe the Sabbath; and, 3), they were supposed to care for others.

God warns Israel against images and idol worship because he knows that Israel will forget the great works and miracles he performed on her behalf, leading her out of Egypt, and through the wilderness.[11] "Rather, she has preferred to attribute the land's fertility to the Baalim, to pagan gods whose appeasement and worship she thinks will guarantee its bounty. She no longer considers—has indeed forgotten—her true Provider."[12] Speaking through Hosea, God says, "When Israel was a child, I loved him, and out of Egypt I called My son. As they called them, so they went away from me. They sacrificed to the Baals, and they burned incense to

---

9. Prior, "Violence," 129.

10. Ibid.

11. Brueggemann is clear that images are "something other than 'other gods,'" and refer instead to "making controllable representations of our best loyalties and visions. They are efforts to reduce to manageable and predictable form the sources of value and power in our lives" (58). However, there is an obvious connection between the forbidden "images" and our discussion of land and God as the source of all physical blessings.

12. Munayer, *Hosea*, 171.

carved images" (Hos 11:1–2). God very much wants us to remember that it is he who blesses the land and sustains us through it.

This sentiment is also echoed in God's commandment to keep the Sabbath. The children of Israel were given a weekly reminder of the creation narrative, where God is the author of creation, and the whole world is his. It is also found in God's commandment of the Jubilee year, when land was returned to its original owners, "as if to free it of the taint of trade and the conceit of human ownership. But beyond their agricultural and social intent, these sabbaths ritualize an observance of the limits of 'my power and the might of mine hand'—the limits of human control."[13]

The third clause in God's covenant with the Israelites is supremely important in that it relates to the treatment of the poor, the oppressed, and minorities. They are called "brother and sister," but are also "variously characterized: the poor (Exod 23:6; Deut 15:7–11), the stranger (Exod 21:21–24; 23:9), the sojourner (Deut 14:27), the widow and orphan (Deut 24:19–22)," and those "with no standing ground in the community."[14] Significantly, "all these landless poor are redefined as brother and sister, that is, as full participants in the promises of covenant (Lev 25:25–55; Deut 15:11, 12–18; 22:1–4)." Just as they had been strangers in Egypt, God wanted Israel to remember the strangers among them, for "land is for sharing with all the heirs of the covenant, even those who have no power to claim it."[15] God called his people to live in peace with the strangers in their midst, and said, "Woe to you who join house to house; they add field to field, till no place where they may dwell alone in the midst of the land!" (Isa 5:8). These "social virtues" also have "ecological and agricultural implications" that are a result of living in close proximity to others and cannot be ignored.[16]

This last condition is indicative of the nature of God's gift. It is not exclusive, but is a gift intended to be a blessing for all humanity. As shown in Deuteronomy, God gave the gift of land, not only to the children of Israel, but to others as well, such as the Edomites, and the Moabites (Deut 2:5, 9, 19). As we have already seen, when it comes to the strangers dwelling among Israel, God gave very specific instructions on how they were

13. Berry, "The Good Land," 296.

14. Brueggemann, *The Land*, 61.

15. Ibid., 58–62.

16. Berry, "The Good Land," 297.

to be treated. They were to have religious, social, and legal privileges, and were privy to all the blessings God bestowed upon Israel.[17]

Religiously, they were permitted to enjoy the Sabbath rest (Exod 23:12), to make sacrifices at the altar (Num 15:14), to participate in the Jewish festivals in Jerusalem (Num 9:14), and were even granted presence at Israel's holy ceremonies (Josh 8:33). Socially, they were protected from permanent slavery through indebtedness (Lev 25:47–50), received help if needed from the tithes that were collected—akin to welfare (Deut 14:29; 26:12)—and were allowed to take what was left over from the harvest (Lev 19:10; 23:27; Deut 24:19–21). Israelite and foreigner were both under the same legal system and the same laws (Lev 24:22; Num 19:14; 15:16, 27–28). The court system was available to everyone (Deut 1:16; 24:17), and aliens were to be protected from persecution (Lev 19:33–34). Additionally, aliens were to receive fair wages (Deut 24:14), with unrestricted access to the cities of refuge (Num 35:15; Josh 20:9). It is evident that they were to be treated well and partake freely in the gift of land.[18] It is a mistake to interpret the term "strangers" used in this context as referring to either the contemporary Palestinians or Israelis. Our purpose here is to discuss how we are commanded to treat others, not to determine who qualifies as a stranger in the land.

This is also evidenced in the story of Naaman's healing by the prophet Elisha in 2 Kings 5. An enemy of the Israelites, Naaman was still extended grace by God, who healed him with the waters of the Jordan River. It was a gift that was tied to the land, for the Abanah and Pharpar rivers of Syria would not have had the same effect. Here we see a kidnapped girl, enslaved by the enemy, who was still willing to extend help to her master. Through her act of obedience, the name of God was glorified, and the enemy received healing in the land.

When defining the laws God laid down for the children of Israel, it is important to remember that in their scriptural descriptions "all manifestations of holiness are in a social context."[19] God knew that his

---

17. For this analysis, I am deeply indebted to Gary Burge who argues convincingly in *Whose Land? Whose Promise?* (67–93) that any who claim to inherit God's gift and promise are responsible for living by the rigid guidelines that accompany them.

18. While these biblical principles are universally applicable, this "settled vs. stranger" dichotomy is not automatically transferable to the political situation facing the Israelis and Palestinians today, even though both sides often engage in the dangerous game of dismissing the other side as "foreigners," and ignoring or denying their historical narrative.

19. Korn, "Land and Covenant."

people would not be isolated from others, and never intended it that way. Treating your own people well does not require holiness; the true measure is how you treat those who are different or less fortunate than you. "The ideal holy society is not a monolithically Jewish community, but a society where Gentiles are welcomed, where compassion for the 'Other' flows freely and where all respect and protect the dignity of the disadvantaged in their midst."[20]

THE BORDERS OF PROMISE

Much of the modern Israeli-Palestinian conflict revolves around the question of borders, and when concerned with questions pertaining to theology of the land, the issue of biblical borders cannot be ignored. For many, when the topic of borders is broached within this context, the physical, territorial borders of the Promised Land based on God's promises to Abraham are considered to the exclusion of almost everything else. However, recent scholarship has taken great strides toward giving us a fuller, more comprehensive picture by reexamining some basic assumptions, contextualizing the evidence, and offering a more universal reading of the Scriptures that deal with the Promised Land's borders.

Drawing from the work of Nili Wazana of Hebrew University, we are able to make a distinction between the actual territorial borders of the Promised Land, and the other, more symbolic references to the land. Wazana approaches the Scriptures from the perspective of biblical geography, and proposes that we take the images of the Promised Land in the Bible as "literary descriptions," in which case we must view them through the lens of literary analysis.[21] She identifies two qualitatively different ways in which the Promised Land and its borders are described in the Bible.

The first kind of description is dealing with a clearly identifiable and detailed entity. For example, when Abraham is promised the land by God (Gen 12:1–3), the borders are not specifically given: It is referred to simply as the land. A geographical description was not needed because it was understood that God was referencing a "conventional, well-known geographical unit," the land of Canaan.[22] There are only a few instances

20. Ibid.
21. Wazana, "From Dan to Beer-Sheba," 45.
22. Ibid., 50.

in the Bible where God provides a specific map outlining the borders of the Promised Land, and they appear much later, for example in Num 34:1–12. This description is marked by its methodological listing of about twenty geographical landmarks, explicitly making clear what the borders were, what they included, and what they did not. Interestingly, the wording of this description matches contemporaneous Hittite political-legal documents that were used to denote borders.[23] However, the Numbers 34 description—and the few others like it—are the exception, not the rule, and have to be understood within the specific context of the Israelites entering the land from their years of wandering.

Wazana's second category of descriptions is different. Though they do include fixed, geographical borders, she suggests that they belong to a more symbolic, literary kind of description that was common in the ancient world, and do not represent actual or literal borders. The first of these descriptions of the Promised Land, found in Genesis 15, is significant in that it is the only patriarchal narrative that speaks of specific borders. In Gen 15:18–22, God tells Abraham that his descendants will be given the land, "from the river of Egypt to the great river, the River Euphrates." This "from . . . to" phrase—a spatial merism—is common to all the descriptions of the Promised Land in this second category. They also all have borders that are delineated either by the Sea, the Wilderness, or the Mountains. Altogether there are four additional descriptions of the Promised Land that fall into this category (Exod 23:31; Deut 1:7; 11:24; Josh 1:3–4); the Genesis 15 description receives added treatment by Wazana because it is unique and significant for a number of reasons.

This description describes a huge amount of territory, spanning from the river of Egypt to the Euphrates River in Mesopotamia. Aside from being the "foundational text of the concept of Greater Israel,"[24] it is also a somewhat problematic set of Promised Land borders, because it moves a number of Old Testament narratives that clearly took place outside the Promised Land *within* the Promised Land. For example, in Joshua 3–4, the Israelites cross over the Jordan River, and *into* the Promised Land. If the Euphrates River marks the Promised Land's eastern border, the Israelites would have already been in the Promised Land before they crossed the Jordan. The same problem arises when the exodus narrative is considered. God punished the children of Israel

23. Ibid., 51.
24. Ibid., 52–53.

because of their disobedience, condemning them to wander in the Wilderness of Zin for forty years. Aside from the hardships of living a restless, nomadic life in the harsh environment of the desert, this punishment carried particular sting because God had forbidden them from entering into the Promised Land until the disobedient generation had died off (Num 14:30). If the Nile River in Egypt marks the southern border of the Promised Land, God's punishment and prohibition make no sense.

A number of scholars—including Jeffrey Townsend, Moshe Weinfeld, and Zecharia Kallai[25]—have identified the difference between these two categories of descriptions of the Promised Land. On one hand, there are the straightforward border descriptions, typified by the Numbers 34 description, but also found elsewhere, such as in Josh 15:1–12 and Ezek 47:15–20. These descriptions clearly refer to the actual land. On the other hand, there are other kinds of descriptions, explained by Waldemar Janzen as having "originated in the expansive era of the Davidic-Solomonic empire" that were "formulated in grand utopian ancient Near Eastern royal terminology (river to river, sea to sea, etc.), and received their final crystallization by 'the so-called Deuteronomistic author or school' in the Josianic era."[26] However, in Wazana's estimation, calling these latter formulations "boundary descriptions," in the sense that they delineate physical boundaries, is a misinterpretation and a mistake.[27]

Instead, "[t]hese expressions must be studied as literary-ideological phrases, akin to other merism phrases found in the Bible and in ancient Near Eastern literature."[28] This opinion is echoed by many others, including David Holwerda who writes, "Various descriptions [of the borders] were given at various times and under varying historical circumstances. Perhaps one may conclude that the land is not only a territory but an idea as well."[29]

While there are other differences that separate the two categories of descriptions, the most significant is perhaps the use of the merism phrases. Easily mistaken for representing border descriptions, merism

25. See Townsend, "Fulfillment of the Land Promise," 320–37; Weinfeld. *The Promise of the Land*, 52–75; and Kallai, "The Patriarchal Boundaries," 70.

26. Janzen, "Land," 146.

27. Wazana, "From Dan to Beer-Sheba," 55–56.

28. Ibid.

29. Holwerda, *Jesus and Israel*, 89–90.

phrases actually serve a much broader literary purpose. "Merism expressions utilize the prepositions 'from' and 'to' to denote generalizations, presenting a whole (usually abstract) concept, rather than its components." Merisms are meant to indicate the size, scale, and quality of what they are making reference to, and not the literal boundaries or borders. "These merism expressions are not intended to define the extremities of the structure, but to denote its entire magnitude, its extremities determining the whole and characterizing it."[30]

There are numerous examples of merism phrases that do not refer to any kind of borders at all, such as the biblical phrase "from Dan to Beer Sheba," which, as Zecharia Kallai points out, "is not to be taken as an indication of the boundaries of Israel's territories. Dan and Beersheba are sacred centers in the north and south of the country, respectively, and the borders are, of course, beyond them."[31]

It is also important to note that spatial merisms, while making reference to specific physical and geographical locations, are not intended to demarcate borders. If the phrase "from Dan to Beer Sheba" was meant to literally represent the borders of the Promised Land, it would be nonsensical, as it would call for a straight line between the two locations. Obviously, it is not meant to be taken literally. Instead, "spatial merisms express a whole territorial area. They do not refer to a line connecting two places, but designate a whole territorial *concept*, which the representing sites signify."[32] As we shall see, in the ancient Near Eastern context, when the spatial merisms include sites such as the Sea or the Wilderness, the territorial concept being portrayed is universal in scope.

In order to understand the significance of the difference between these two categories of descriptions, it is important to place both categories within their proper context. Whereas the "full border description" given in Numbers 34 is "connected to settlement and inheritance," and is clearly referencing a real place, the other form, with the spatial merisms, is "found in the context of war and conquest, tied up with promises of victories over enemies."[33] Within this context, they are meant to indicate not only the Promised Land but also the whole world. It is a universal claim that encompasses the whole earth. This is seen because of the use

30. Wazana, "From Dan to Beer-Sheba," 56.

31. Ibid., 57.

32. Ibid., 56, emphasis added.

33. Ibid., 63.

of the Sea, the Wilderness, and the Mountains as delineating the "cosmic" borders, because "in ancient Near Eastern traditions these are the areas depicting the very ends of the earth."[34]

Wazana demonstrates how these three areas—the Sea, the Wilderness, and the Mountains—carried connotations of chaotic evil and lawlessness in the literature of the ancient Near East. This usage is evident in Babylonian, Ugaritic, and Hebrew Scriptures. While true that in the biblical account these themes are dealt with in a different way, their influence is still felt even in some of the most well known biblical narratives, such as the story of Jonah, the Israelites' desert wanderings, and the episode atop Mount Sinai. The tumultuous relationship between the ancient Hebrews and these elements of the greater ancient Near Eastern culture does not question the divinely inspired nature of the Scriptures they produced but shows that the writers could not escape the cultural context they dwelt in. That context is reflected in their writings.

It seems safe to assume, with Wazana, that when these spatial merisms are used to describe the Promised Land, they were not intended to indicate the literal boundaries of the land of Canaan. Instead, they were the boundaries of another Promised Land—the whole world. They were used to show the vast magnitude of God's blessings and promise that were to stretch to the ends of the earth. Spatial merisms are also related to the idea of military domination and are similar in many ways to the type of terminology that was typical of Neo-Assyrian imperial propaganda. Thus, the "promise reflected in spatial merisms is not to be understood literally, nor should it be translated and transformed into border lines on maps. It is a promise of world dominion."[35]

Did this mean that God was pledging to Abraham that his descendants would conquer the entire world and rule over them by some imperialistic divine right, based on ethnicity? According to Yohanna Katanacho, this is not the case. He explains that the ancient Near Eastern mentality of empires or global kingdoms was "by nature multiethnic and not tribal or parochial."[36] He draws on the work of Kenton Sparks, who claims that, "[f]or Egyptians and Assyrians, identity was political and cultural, not ethnic, and linked with kingship, the king's relationship to the deity, and the deity's role in extending the national borders and the native empire to

34. Ibid., 64.

35. Ibid., 71.

36. Katanacho, "Christ is the Owner," 438.

the "ends of the earth."[37] God's kingdom, in the context of the promise, is one of justice, peace, and wholeness for the entire world.

FROM JERUSALEM TO THE ENDS OF THE EARTH: THE UNIVERSAL PROMISE OF THE KINGDOM OF GOD

God's true vision becomes clear when he speaks of the inhabitants of the Promised Land. Katanacho says they will be "as numerous as the sand of the sea or the stars of heaven, for God's intentions were not to formulate fixed borders but to unite the ends of the world under the Abrahamic banner."[38] We see evidence for this in Psalm 2:8: "Ask of Me, and I will give You the nations for Your inheritance, and the ends of the earth for Your possession." Unquestionably, "God did not intend to isolate Abraham or his descendants from the rest of the world. On the contrary, he wanted a theocratic kingdom filled with Abraham's children."[39]

Aside from pointing out the differences between the two types of descriptions of the Promised Land, the highly detailed description in Numbers 34, and the largely symbolic spatial merism descriptions, Wazana's research also hints at the universal aspects of the spatial merism promises. When considering theology of the land and bringing New Testament concerns into the picture, the catholic implications of God's promise to Abraham become clear. Katanacho says, "The New Testament demonstrates that Christ is the Abrahamic seed in which and through which all the promises are fulfilled. Through him HaaretzAbrahamic grows into HaaretzGlobal."[40] He quotes Kenneth Bailey, who, when commenting on Romans 4:13, says that "even though Paul knew the Septuagint well, he felt free to replace the word 'ge,' the Greek equivalent of *Haaretz*, with 'cosmos' or the whole world, in order to highlight the cosmic dimensions of the Abrahamic promises; Paul is clearly expanding the promises of land mentioned in Genesis 12:7 and 17:8."[41]

We see in Rom 4:13 the promise that Abraham and his seed will become the "heir of the world," not through "the law, but through the

---

37. Sparks, *Ethnicity and Identity*, 91.

38. Katanacho, "Christ is the Owner," 437.

39. Ibid.

40. Ibid., 439–40.

41. Katanacho, "Christ Is the Owner," 440. Quotation from Bailey, "St. Paul's Understanding of the Territorial Promise," 60.

righteousness of faith." If this promise were to be fulfilled only through the law, then faith would be void and the promise invalid. In v. 16 we see that this promise is not only to those "who are of the law" but also "to those who are of the faith of Abraham, who is the father of us all." Holwerda states, "For Paul, the promise to Abraham had a cosmic sweep, including not just the territory of Canaan but the entire inhabited world."[42]

Given the context of the rest of Romans 4, where Paul is writing about Abraham's faith and about the covenant of circumcision, it is perhaps wise to rethink our traditional interpretation of the promises God made to Abraham, to incorporate all who share the same faith as Abraham. I would like to suggest that in this instance Paul is not bringing anything radically new, but merely giving these promises their proper exegesis. Aside from the few instances of border descriptions, including the Numbers 34 description—set in the context of settlement and where God is giving specifically designated land to a specific people at a specific time—the rest of these passages, commonly taken to be border descriptions of the Promised Land, are actually promises to all the children of Abraham, the "father of us all." For, according to Gal 3:29, "And if you are Christ's, then you are Abraham's seed, and heirs according to the promise."

The arrival of Jesus made this promise available to all. We see it from the very beginning of the New Testament, where Matthew gives the parentage of Jesus and surprisingly includes four women. Not just any women, and not "the four matriarchs of Judaism—Sarah, Rebekah, Rachel, and Leah—but four women who are foreigners and not especially 'holy': Tamar and Rahab the Canaanites, Ruth the Moabite, and Bathsheba, the wife of a Hittite."[43] While Jesus was fulfilling the prophecy concerning his birth, and did come through the Jewish people in a Jewish context, it is clear that "the people of God, Israel was always intended to be and to become a universal people, not limited by racial purity."[44]

The universal implications of God's promise, evident from the start, are often ignored by those who choose to see in the promise an exclusive reading based on ethnicity or religion. However, "[t]he Biblical data demonstrates that the concept of the borders of Haaretz was fluid since

42. Holwerda, *Jesus and Israel*, 103.

43. Ibid., 35.

44. Ibid.

its inception and that God wanted to reach to the ends of the earth. This vision is only possible through Christ, for he alone is the legitimate owner of Haaretz, a place that is not made up of mere dirt but is a locale where righteousness and justice should prevail."[45] Indeed, "[t]he issue for the Bible, therefore, is not about borders, whether the dust of the land of Israel is holy, or whether the land has unique metaphysical properties." The rabbinical tradition in Judaism understands, according to the biblical ideal, "the ascription of holiness to dust and walls as dangerous idolatries."[46] What matters is the way God's people act, not where they act.

According to T. Desmond Alexander, God's plan for the earth from the beginning was to establish a dwelling place where he could commune with his people. Because of mankind's fall, through Adam and Eve, this became impossible. Because of our sin, his method had to change, but his plan remained the same. This is why we see a "fascinating and coherent progression from Eden to tabernacle to Jerusalem temple to church to New Jerusalem" in the biblical narrative.[47] These were all God's means for attaining the end of being with his people, and from the outset he intended for this dwelling place to be universal and extend over the whole earth. For this reason, the tabernacle, God's literal dwelling place on earth, was "linked to both Eden and the cosmos," and "as a model, conveys the idea that the whole earth is to become God's dwelling place."[48] Although Alexander's approach is completely different than Wazana's investigation of the Hebrew Scriptures, they both reach the same conclusion: God's purpose has always been to bless mankind, a blessing which has been expressed by the gift of land—the earth—to all of its inhabitants.

Based on this interpretation of biblical land promises, it is tempting to strip the land of all importance. According to Manfred Kohl, the land is as important in the New Testament as in the Old, but in a radically different way. Because of the universalization of the promises to Abraham, the whole earth is now under promise. Therefore, when the term "the kingdom of God" or "the kingdom of heaven" is used in the New Testament, it is referring to the whole earth, the land of new prom-

45. Katanacho, "Christ Is the Owner," 440.

46. Korn, *Land and Covenant*.

47. Alexander, *From Eden*, 73.

48. Ibid., 41–42.

ise. "Since his father owned all the land in the first place," Kohl writes, "Jesus went far beyond any narrow nationalistic local land concept." Instead he focused on matters of the heart: forgiveness, love, and reaching out to enemies in a transformative way. The Promised Land recedes in importance, for "In God's kingdom nationalism, race, and gender do not matter, as demonstrated numerous times in Christ's ministry, and the local land, as property—even the holy city of Jerusalem as place— becomes secondary."[49]

God's promise has been fulfilled through Jesus, and our understanding of it has shifted from the narrowly defined land of Canaan to the whole world. We find evidence of the universalization of the promises when Jesus tells his disciples that they are to be his witnesses "in Jerusalem, and in all Judea and Samaria, and to the end of the earth" (Acts 1:8). It is significant that this phrase echoes the spatial merisms used in the Old Testament to demark the contours of the Promised Land, which, as we have already seen, were also universal in scope.

This shift is the fulfillment of the promise to bless the whole world found in Gen 22:17–18, when God says to Abraham, "I will surely bless you and make your descendants as numerous as the stars in the sky and as the sand on the seashore. Your descendants will take possession of the cities of their enemies, and through your offspring all nations on earth will be blessed, because you have obeyed me" (NIV). This was Paul's mission, to take the message of God's salvation throughout the world. He demonstrated this in Acts 17:22–32, speaking about God creating "from one blood every nation of men to dwell on all the face of the earth," and the need for "all men everywhere to repent." Paul goes on to indicate that all men—Jews and Gentile–are equal, and all will have to account for their relationship with God through his son Jesus. Significantly, he spoke these words in the literal marketplace of ideas— the Areopagus of Athens.

Because the promise has been universalized to include all the children of God, the responsibilities that accompany it have also become the responsibilities of all who claim God as their father. Paul makes this point in Eph 6:2–3, "'Honor your father and mother,' which is the first commandment with promise: 'that it may be well with you and you may live long on the earth.'" This verse refers to and contrasts with the fifth commandment in Exod 20:12, which commands the children of Israel

49. Kohl, "Towards a Theology of Land."

to honor their fathers and mothers, "that your days may be long upon the land which the Lord your God is giving you." For Paul to quote from this commandment, but to comment on the whole earth, is highly indicative of his theological position concerning the land. Just as the whole earth, including the Promised Land, was part of God's promise, so too is the promise meant for all of God's children.

Many scholars have argued for a renewed reading of the Abrahamic promises, in which the land has importance only insofar as it is important historically, as "the patriarchs, the prophets, and the first Christians—even Christ, the Son of God—walked on it."[50] However, since the promises made to Abraham by God have now been extended to include the whole world, and all believers in Christ the Messiah, continued focus on "obsolete territorial land covenant ignores to a large extent Christ's new covenant of God's Kingdom that through his Spirit encompasses all believers everywhere."[51] Thus, it is understandable that Kohl concludes, "From a biblical perspective (considering both Old and New Testaments), since the Christ event the promise of the territorial land no longer has any significance."[52]

It is true that the promises have been extended. However, it is possible that in saying the actual physical Promised Land has no more significance, we are overstating the case. Rather than completely spiritualizing the process of salvation away from the land, we find the centrality of the land has merely shifted in God's redemptive work. Up until this point, anyone who wanted to worship the God of Abraham, Isaac, and Jacob had to come to Jerusalem, to the temple. However, as Jesus made clear through his talk with the Samaritan woman in John 4:20–24, his coming rendered the physical act of coming specifically to the temple irrelevant. However, this does not lessen the importance of the land. It simply means that *all* land on the whole earth is important, for it all contains the promise of redemptive potential.

It is important to remember that the Samaritans and the Jews considered each other enemies, and disagreed over the location of God's true temple. When the Samaritan woman told Jesus, "Our fathers worshiped on this mountain, and you Jews say that in Jerusalem is the place where one ought to worship" (John 4:20), she was expressing the old

50. Ibid.
51. Ibid.
52. Ibid.

conception of the land, ownership, and right and wrong. However, Jesus told her "the hour is coming when you will neither on this mountain, nor in Jerusalem, worship the Father" (John 4:21). He makes it clear that "the hour is coming, and now is, when the true worshipers will worship the Father in spirit and truth; for the Father is seeking such to worship Him" (John 4:23).

The message is clear: God does not care who you are, or from where you worship him, as long as you worship him in spirit and in truth. This means that we are freed from the obligations of worshiping in Jerusalem at the temple. But we are still bound to this earth, this land, and our worship necessarily reaches God from our terrestrial position.

The trauma of exile from the land was real, and its pain is felt in the prose of the prophets. Yet this was not the end of the story, for the Promised Land was never the final destination for the seed of Abraham. The covenant in Genesis 12 and in subsequent promise passages occurs in a context, within the project to restore humanity back to the garden. We are given a picture of what this will entail in Rev 22:1–3, where the New Jerusalem is described as having a river flowing with the water of life, which feeds into the Tree of Life, which bears fruit all year long and has leaves that bring "healing of the nations." In Hebrews 11, Abraham's faith is contextualized, and he is lauded in verses 9–10, for dwelling in tents in the land of promise, and for waiting "for the city which has foundations, whose builder and maker is God."

This same redemptive future is seen in Mic 4:1–5, when the end of days is described. Micah speaks of peace between all the nations in verse 3, when "They shall beat their swords into ploughshares and their spears in to pruning hooks." And in verse 5, "all people walk each in the name of their gods." This is a "startling claim of theological pluralism," for we see that the kingdom of God "is a place of social and religious diversity, not a monolithic Jewish society where everyone calls God by the same name. Jerusalem is a place where Jews and Gentiles coexist in harmony with each other, respecting each other, and worshiping alongside each other in faithfulness to their respective spiritual traditions."[53]

This wonderful vision is directed towards the future, but there is a very actual and applicable aspect of restoring the kingdom of God that is connected with the land. For the kingdom of heaven is not only concerned with the salvation of souls (though that is a part of it). There is

53. Korn, *Land and Covenant*.

also a very grounded, earthly social dimension, which is connected with humanity's first rebellion. As soon as Adam and Eve leave the Garden of Eden, the first murder takes place when Cain kills his brother Abel. The process of making our way back to the garden, to the kingdom of God, entails reconciliation, living in peace with our neighbors, reaching out to the poor, to the widows and orphans, and even to our enemies. God intended to bless mankind with the gift of land, but when we are unable or unwilling to share it with each other, it becomes a source of strife.

Land still matters! Many believe that the land is no longer a part of our relationship with God, since the promise to Abraham casts a wider net and includes all believers. This is not true. The blessing of the Promised Land has been stretched over the whole earth, stretched far but not thin. The whole earth is filled with promise, and it matters how we handle the gift we have been given. The land itself "eagerly waits for the revealing of the sons of God" when it will be "delivered from the bondage of corruption into the glorious liberty of the children of God" (Rom 8:19–21). In fact, when the Scriptures are considered, the land holds much agency, is hardly objectified, and often takes on anthropomorphic characteristics. The land groans from birth-pains (Rom 8:22), waits eagerly (Rom 8:23), needs rest (Lev 25:5), and vomits out sinners who defile it (Lev 18:25–28). Far from being merely the location upon which humans act, the land is a dynamic entity that responds to our actions and behavior. It is, in fact, a character in the biblical narrative.

We must reverse the trend among certain interpretations of Christianity towards spiritualization "in which we focus on the transcendent Promiser without taking responsibility for the gift given."[54] The moral and ethical behavior of the children of Israel had great influence on the land, and this is no less true for us. If we are willing to repent and humble ourselves, God said, "I will hear from heaven, and I will forgive their sins and heal their land" (2 Chr 7:14).

Even though God's original promise has been extended to include the whole earth, the Holy Land and the holy city of Jerusalem remain important. They are a part of the promise just as is every other spot on the earth, no more important but also no less. The Holy Land and the holy city of Jerusalem remain a highly suggestive and emblematic symbol for the rest of the earth and for all of humanity. For if we are called to reconcile with our enemies, to love God and love truth, to live in

54. Brueggemann, *The Land*, 204–5.

peace and in joy of our deliverance in order to bring about the kingdom of heaven, we can judge how far we are from reaching these goals by observing the Holy Land. That this particular spot of land should be so filled with hatred, violence, and rebellion against God is a telling sign of how far we still have to go, and how vested the forces of evil are in preventing mankind's return to the garden.

FROM EXILE TO THE GARDEN: THE LAND OF MILK AND HONEY

References to the Promised Land in the Bible are many, and as we have seen, while some quantitatively describe the borders, others are more concerned with describing the land qualitatively. For this reason we often see the land promised by God described as a land flowing with milk and honey (Exod 3:8, 17; 13:5; Lev 20:24–26; 22:4; Num 13:27; 14:8; Deut 6:3; 11:8–12; 26:8–9; 27:2–3; 31:20; Josh 5:6; Jer 11:5; 32:22; Ezek 20:5–6, 15). Typically, this phrase is taken to be a description of the land of Canaan, the phrase "milk and honey" as a "metaphor meaning all good things—God's blessings." While some try and draw a literal connection between the land of Canaan and flowing milk and honey, most understand it "to be hyperbolically descriptive of the land's richness."[55]

Throughout the ancient Near East, both milk and honey were symbolic elements, representing fertility in a sensual, erotic way. This is seen in the Song of Solomon, "where the fertility figure of milk and honey suggests the paradise of a woman's body. By extension, a land flowing with milk and honey becomes metaphoric of a divine female figure." Astarte, the Babylonian goddess of sexuality, fertility, maternity, love, and war was often seen as the source of these fertile blessings, and her cult of worship seems to have provided the backdrop to the biblical imagery of milk and honey.[56]

More than simply indicating fertile soil, in the context of the biblical world, milk and honey were also used to describe the otherworldly richness of paradise. Indeed, in many ancient Near Eastern traditions, "the image of an ideal place flowing with milk and honey has long been associated with paradise." Even in Islam we find traces of this association; for example the paradise described by Allah in the Qur'an is depicted

---

55. Cohen, "Why Milk and Honey."
56. Ibid.

as "the eternal garden of joy . . . [and it] possesses not only rivers of pure water and wine, but 'rivers of fresh milk' and 'rivers of pure honey.'"[57]

Given the context from which it arose and what we have learned about merism phrases, there is reason to doubt that mention of a land flowing with milk and honey is making reference to an earthly place at all. The land of Canaan already had certain very specific and known elements associated with it—the famous *Seven Species* of Deuteronomy 8:8, where Canaan is described as "a land with wheat and barley, vines and fig tress, pomegranates, olive oil and honey."

In fact, we find convincing evidence that "flowing with milk and honey" was merely a figure of speech, when the children of Israel rebelled against Moses in the wilderness. Korah spoke out and said, "Isn't it enough that you have brought us up out of a land flowing with milk and honey to kill us in the wilderness? And now you also want to lord it over us! Moreover, you haven't brought us into a land flowing with milk and honey or given us an inheritance of fields and vineyards. Do you want to treat these men like slaves? No, we will not come" (Num 16:13–14 NIV)! Significantly, the phrase "flowing with milk and honey" is used to describe both Egypt *and* the Promised Land. Even Egypt, where they had been slaves, seemed like a Promised Land to them from the perspective of the wilderness.

It makes more sense to think of this phrase as a literary, poetic description of an idyllic paradise, rather than a specific location on earth. There are radical implications to this interpretation when applied to all the many places in the Scriptures where we find this phrase. However, when we remember the universal nature of God's promise, it is clear: The land flowing with milk and honey is not Canaan or Egypt or any other terrestrial place; it is a future return to the garden as the fulfillment of God's promises.

The land that was promised is not only flowing with milk and honey, but it is also unlike "the land of Egypt, from which you have come, where you sowed your seed and watered it by foot, as a vegetable garden" (Deut 11:10). It is reminiscent of the original paradise—the Garden of Eden—before man's relationship with the land was changed by sin and labor was required for the land to be fertile and produce. Although the Promised Land represented a symbolic return to the garden, it was not the final fulfillment of God's plan. For "although the land of Canaan

57. Ibid.

offers the possibility of a return to Edenic fruitfulness (cf. Gen 13:10), it continues as an imperfect environment. At best it is a foretaste of something better still to come."[58] The true return to the garden only becomes possible with the establishment of the New Jerusalem.

THE LAND AS THE LOCATION OF RECONCILIATION

> To live, we must daily break the body and shed the blood of Creation. When we do this knowingly, lovingly, skillfully, reverently, it is a sacrament. When we do it ignorantly, greedily, clumsily, destructively, it is a desecration. In such desecration we condemn ourselves to spiritual and moral loneliness, and others to want.
>
> —Wendell Berry[59]

The land—the whole, physical earth—is a location of reconciliation. This reconciliation is two-fold, as it needs to occur between man and God, and between man and his neighbor. This reconciliation must take place on the land, because this is the precise location where sin came into the world. Land is the scene of the crime of man's rebellion against God. The land must be transformed into a place where atonement and reconciliation happen. If man and God are to be reconciled, the land is where this reconciliation must take place. The restoration of this relationship will also have an effect on the land itself. God says "if My people who are called by My name, will humble themselves, and pray and seek My face, and turn from their wicked ways, then will I hear from heaven, and will forgive their sin and will heal their land" (2 Chr 7:14). It is our duty to submit to God, and to confess to him. This is the only way for true healing to come to the land.

We are also called to reconcile with our fellow man. The example of the prophets is clear: When Amos calls for justice to "run down like water, and righteousness like a mighty stream" (Amos 5:24), he is commenting on how we treat each other. As we have already seen, mistreating each other and engaging in unjust and unrighteous actions have severe consequences for the land. For example, because King Saul tried to annihilate the Gibeonites, even after the Israelites had sworn to spare them, God punished the children of Israel with three years of famine.

---

58. Alexander, *From Eden*, 42

59. Berry, "The Gift of Good Land," 304.

God's punishment was intended for the Israelites, but the land suffered as well, for it became dry and barren. Only when King David restored the relationship with the Gibeonites and gave them justice was the punishment lifted and the land healed (2 Sam 21:1–6).

By his life Jesus made reconciliation possible for mankind. The act of incarnation brought man back into relationship with God and with his fellow man. This act is inseparable from the land, because God became a man, and man comes from the earth. Through Jesus we regain all that we lost through our original sin. Adam, the name of the first man, is closely connected to the Hebrew word for land, *adamah*. Our sin is rooted in the land, but so is our salvation. For Jesus came as the second Adam, and just "as through one man's offense judgment came to all men, resulting in condemnation, even so through one Man's righteous obedience many will be made righteous" (Rom 5:19). While sin brought death to man and to the earth, Jesus brings life. Mankind becomes a "new creation" (2 Cor 5:17), and the land is recast as the "new heaven and a new earth" (Rev 21:1).

The land has felt the consequences of sin over and over, especially in our mistreatment of each other. When Cain killed his brother Abel, God heard Abel's blood "cries out to me from the ground" (Gen 4:10). However, just as the land has seen man shed so much blood through injustice, it was also the place where Christ shed his blood on our behalf. And just as the earth has been the location of so much sin, conflict, hatred, greed, jealousy, and murder, it is also the location of reconciliation. God's vision for us includes the stages of reconciliation, confession, repentance, restoration, and justice, and it takes place within the context of the land. For: "Surely his salvation is nigh them that fear him; that glory may dwell in our land. Mercy and truth are met together; righteousness and peace have kissed each other. Truth shall spring out of the earth; and righteousness shall look down from heaven" (Ps 85:9–11, KJV). Land is the paradoxical location where reconciliation grows in the same ground as conflict.

Of course, the ultimate reconciliation is only to be found in the incarnation of Jesus. He is the Truth and through him all things are possible. He has redeemed mankind, and the earth, through his death, but more importantly, through his life. "For if when we were enemies we were reconciled to God through the death of His Son, much more, having been reconciled, we shall be saved by His life. And not only that, but we also rejoice in God through our Lord Jesus Christ, through whom we have now received the reconciliation" (Rom 5:10–11).

In the context of the Israeli-Palestinian conflict, the need for reconciliation is urgent. Hatred and violence have only grown more intense over the past sixty years of strife. In a significant way this conflict sums up well the destructive result our sin has on each other and on the land. Indeed, the conflict is essentially about who will control the land, and what will be done with the "Others."

Looking forward to reconciliation, one of the most important aspects is repentance/confession. Without first acknowledging our own faults and taking responsibility for them, no progress can be made. Willingly admitting your part in the conflict, taking ownership of the wrong you have done and the pain you have caused, allows the other side to feel that their pain has been acknowledged. They can then offer forgiveness. Chaim Gans puts it well: "Only an understanding of the justice of Zionism that includes a recognition of the right of the Palestinian objection, and only Palestinian recognition of the justice of their opposition to Zionism that also includes recognition of its justified elements, can lead to a stable resolution of the conflict . . . An insistence by either party on only its own right, out of a total unwillingness to also see the justice of the other side, will perpetuate the conflict or cause its resolution to be an imposed and unstable one."[60] In this conflict, there is much wrong that has been done on both sides. The time has come to openly and frankly discuss it, and take responsibility for it.

In order to fully understand the Israeli-Palestinian conflict, an understanding of its origins must first be attained. The Jewish people believe they have a justified claim for establishing their own state, which the Zionist movement based on "the right of every nation to self-determination, on the Jews' historical connection to the land of Israel and, as the tipping point, the persecution of the Jews in the 19th and 20th centuries."[61] The problem is that this expression of national self-determination came at the expense of the Palestinian people. The suffering of the Jewish people was primarily located in Europe, and "since we are speaking of a right that is justified in being realized in the land of Israel because of the persecution of the Jews in Europe, then the relevant European nations should have incurred the lion's share of

60. Gans, "Palestinians."
61. Ibid.

its price. The United Nations Partition Plan did not give expression to this."[62] Instead, the Palestinians were forced to pay the full price for a debt they had not incurred.

Although it began earlier, we can take 1948—the year the State of Israel gained independence—as a starting point of the conflict. The most painful and long-lasting "sin" committed by the Israelis was the expulsion of Palestinians from their homes. Although there has been much debate as to the exact circumstances under which Palestinians came to leave their villages and homes during the war, it is clear that "the refugee problem was caused by attacks by Jewish forces on Arab villages and towns and by the inhabitants' fear of such attacks, compounded by expulsions, atrocities, and rumors of atrocities—and by the crucial Israeli Cabinet decision in June 1948 to bar a refugee return."[63] This first action, based on the premise that Israel must be a Jewish state, has led to other abuses, and "obsessive, excessive, measures about terrorism, the endless fencing in, the interrogations, the legal justification of torture . . . the discriminations against Israeli Palestinians, the fear and contempt, the bellicosity," all aimed at the Palestinians—in Israel and in other countries—who challenge this vision by their very existence.[64]

The list of "sins" is long for the other side as well. The Arab nations have been guilty of perpetuating the conflict in a number of ways, and for using it as an excuse for their own mismanagement. For example, they reason that, "given the perpetual state of emergency caused by Israel, such matters [education, freedom of speech, unpoliticized civil society], which could only be the result of long-range planning and reflection, [are] luxuries that [are] ill-afforded."[65] There is also their "wholesale persecution of communities, preeminently but not exclusively the Jewish ones," whose age-old presence was "suddenly thought to be dangerous." This led to a deluge of Jewish refugees, many of whom ended up in Israel. We must also not forget their "scandalously poor treatment of the [Palestinian] refugees," where they have suffered much persecution and neglect, and have "remained confined in hideous quarantine for almost two generations."[66]

62. Ibid.

63. Morris, *Revisiting the Palestinian Exodus*, 38.

64. Said, "Afterword," 213.

65. Ibid., 208.

66. Ibid., 209.

Even though they have been the victim of tragedy and criminally unfair treatment, the Palestinian people's conduct in the conflict has been far from guilt-free. In addition to accepting the murder of innocent civilians as a legitimate form of self-defense, they have also been guilty of self-pity, victimization, and demonization of the Israeli people. Palestinians have also failed to recognize the very real historical and spiritual attachment the Jewish people have to the land, and they need to find a way to acknowledge the history of Jewish suffering. This issue has usually been completely avoided by Palestinians because they feel as though the Jews have wrongly victimized them as a result of the Holocaust in which they—the Palestinians—had no participation. If Palestinians are to find real reconciliation with Israelis, they have to develop understanding and empathy for the trauma the Jewish people have suffered throughout history. Palestinians also need to realize that just as the traumatic events of the *Nakba* have affected them, the trauma of the Holocaust continues to have a very strong and lasting effect on the collective psyche of the Jewish people.

Unfortunately, there are many instances where both sides have failed to live up to the biblical standards of how to treat the "Other," one of the qualifications for residing on the land. Leviticus 24:22 is explicit: "You shall have the same law for the stranger and for one from your own country; for I am the Lord your God." Israelis and Palestinians have both fallen short of this standard, and the Christian minority has often suffered persecution at the hands of the two majorities, Jewish and Muslim. As we have seen in the Old Testament, there are explicit guidelines detailing the way foreigners should be treated. In the Qur'an we also find *suras* commanding that foreigners be treated fairly and with respect (see 2:62; 3:64; 3:84; 5:48; 4:36–37; 76:8–9). The Qur'an, which places hospitality as a highly important value, also respects the knowledge of the People of the Book, saying of Jews and Christians, "If thou art in doubt as to what We have revealed unto thee, then ask those who have been reading the Book from before thee" (Sura 10:94).[67]

However, in both rabbinical Judaism and Islam, the holy Scriptures are actually less important than oral traditions and interpretations of the law, for all practical purposes, because the Scriptures are seen and understood through the lenses of these interpretive texts. Thus the *Talmud*, the guidelines of *halacha*, the *hadith* and *sharia* law, are often referred to

67. Yusuf Ali, *The Holy Qur'an*, 508.

more than the Tanakh and the Qur'an. This is not intended as a critique of these faith systems; there is much that is good about them, for indeed, "The Orthodox Jew embracing the 'yoke of the law' as being in itself a liberating and fulfilling experience is matched by the Muslim regard for the *Shari'ah*."[68] However when it comes to treatment of the "Other," these guidelines ignore the tolerance and equality found in both the Tanakh and the Qur'an, and in some cases encourage discrimination.

For Muslims the "Holy Land" is important primarily because Jerusalem is Islam's third most sacred city.[69] Once it was conquered, the land became part of the *waqf*—holy Muslim territory. Islam has a specific perspective towards both the *waqf* and non-Muslims. While the latter may live in Muslim countries, they are not considered to be equals and must submit to Islamic authority as *dhimmis*.[70] Non-Muslims contaminate Muslim sovereignty, and under *sharia* law, they are subject to a different court system than Muslims. This was true for Christians and Jews who lived under Ottoman authority, and is also written into the Palestinian National Authority's constitution, or Basic Law, Article IV, "1) Islam is the official religion in Palestine. Respect for the sanctity of all other divine religions shall be maintained. 2) The principles of Islamic Shari'a shall be a principal source of legislation."[71] There is tension in these two statements, for while respect for other religions is found in the Qur'an, it is not found in *sharia* law. These two opposing principles must be reconciled, and Palestinian Christians watch the development of this issue with great interest.

Because of the ethnonational character of the Zionist movement, it has also actively pursued a policy of excluding non-Jews from the national, social, and political life in Israel, a clear violation of the biblical command to treat foreigners with respect. Significantly, this exclusion has taken place through the medium of land. In order to preserve the Jewish character of Israel, the state has placed "severe barriers . . . on Arab acquisition of land." This has been done primarily through "the Jewish National Fund (the JNF is an agency of the World Zionist Organization) [which] established formal standards officially forbidding

68. Brown, *Religion and State*, 25.

69. Hasson, "Muslim Literature," 168–84.

70. Ye'or, *Islam and Dhimmitude*.

71. 2003 Amended Basic Law, Title One, Article 4, Online: http://www.palestinian-basiclaw.org.

the leasing of its lands to non-Jews. Because most lands were actually owned by the JNF, it, in effect, acted as a subcontractor of the state—the Israel Land Authority—for land allocations and leasing."[72] This was only part of the broader Zionist push to legally give "precedence to Jewish immigrants, even Jews who were only potential immigrants, over indigenous Palestinian citizens in almost every sphere." The "apartheid-style system of land transactions" was part of the system of laws that "defined most of the land for sale in Israel as the exclusive and perpetual property of the Jewish people."

This exclusivist land policy is especially problematic when it is remembered that nearly all of the land was confiscated from the Palestinians. Almost "all Palestinian-owned land was taken by the government and turned into state land, to be sold or leased only to Jews. By the end of the confiscation frenzy and the formulation of the policy legalizing it, 92 per cent of the country's land had fallen into Jewish hands."[73] The amount of land confiscated was staggering: the Palestinian owned land within what was to become the State of Israel was around 4.6 million dunams (the Ottoman-era land unit) immediately before the 1948 war and by 1950 this amount was reduced to five hundred thousand dunams.

In spite of the many instances of injustice perpetrated by both sides, as well as the issues separating us, the central question now is not who is right and who is wrong. We cannot ignore history or its consequences; they must be dealt with. We are, however, called to deal with the situation as it is now, and to make peace: "Genuine reconciliation requires facing historic truths, taking responsibility for past injustices, and framing future relations in terms of justice rather than power."[74] As John Paul Lederach states, reconciliation has to be the place where the four elements from Ps 85:10 meet, "Truth and mercy are met together; righteousness and peace have kissed each other" (KJV).

72. Kimmerling and Migdal, *Palestinian People*, 194.

73. Pappé, *A History*, 160–61.

74. Rouhana, "Zionism's Encounter," 127. Rouhana goes on to discuss the asymmetry of the balance of power between the Israelis and Palestinians, which complicates efforts at reconciliation. The imbalance of power also comes into play in discussions on theology of the land, for "the more powerful party does not usually have sufficient incentives to engage in a genuine reconciliation process that would entail painful concessions and painful self-discovery" (127).

First, in an overall sense, reconciliation promotes an encounter between the open expression of the painful past, on the one hand, and the search for the articulation of a long-term, interdependent future, on the other hand. Second, reconciliation provides a place for truth and mercy to meet, where concerns for exposing what has happened *and* for letting go in favor of renewed relationship are validated and embraced. Third, reconciliation recognizes the need to give time and place to both justice and peace, where redressing the wrong is held together with the envisioning of a common, connected future.[75]

This is only possible through Christ, for "He Himself is our peace, who has made both one, and has broken down the middle wall of separation" (Eph 2:14). This wall of separation is both the wall of sin that separates us from God, and the walls we build through our sin, which separate us from each other. Christ has destroyed that dichotomy, and he came to "reconcile them both to God in one body through the cross, thereby putting to death the enmity" (Eph 2:16). Through Jesus, we are all brothers and sisters, and we are important parts of the same body: "Now, therefore, you are no longer strangers and foreigners, but fellow citizens with the saints and members of the household of God, having been built on the foundation of the apostles and the prophets, Jesus Christ himself being the chief cornerstone" (Eph 2:19–20).[76] In this path of reconciliation, we reverse our original disobedience and begin a process of true reconciliation in the land, allowing the earth to "once more become a dwelling place shared by God and humanity."[77]

Having peace and reconciliation here in the Promised Land is important in a symbolic sense, for if it is possible here, then it is possible for the whole earth, "As the dwelling place of God on earth, the temple-city of Jerusalem is in miniature what God intends for the whole world."[78]

75. Lederach, *Building Peace*, 31.

76. Suh makes a number of important and interesting observations on the similarities between Ezekiel 37 and Ephesians 2 in, "The Use of Ezekiel 37." He claims that Paul "may have constructed his argument [in Ephesians 2], based on Ezekiel 37 in that he not only borrowed the material that is found in Ezekiel 37 but that he also applied it to the new community of Christ" (716). This connection gains significance for our conversation here when it is remembered that the famous "dry bones" passage in Ezekiel 37 is frequently used in Christian and secular Zionist circles in connection with the restoration of the Jewish people to the land.

77. Alexander, *From Eden*, 14.

78. Ibid., 45.

We are called to be his witnesses, and proclaim his peace "in Jerusalem, and in all Judea and Samaria, and to the end of the earth" (Acts 1:8). No matter what your view or interpretation of God's covenant, whether you believe that it refers to one group of people, or to all believers in the God of Abraham, there is no way around the moral and ethical guidelines that accompany God's incredible promise. We are instructed to pray to God, asking that his will would be done, "on earth as it is in heaven" (Matt 6:10). With heaven as our model, we strive towards an earth that is a manifestation of the kingdom of God, where all partake in the blessings and promise of God's gifts to mankind.

BIBLIOGRAPHY

2003 Amended Basic Law, Title 1, Article 4. Online: http://www.palestinian basiclaw.org/.

Alexander, T. Desmond. *From Eden to the New Jerusalem*. Nottingham: InterVarsity, 2008.

Abdullah Yusuf Ali, *The Holy Qur'an, Translation and Commentary*. 2nd ed. Indianapolis: American Trust, 1977.

Bailey, Kenneth E. "St. Paul's Understanding of the Territorial Promise of God to Abraham." *Theological Review: Near East School of Theology* 15:1 (1994) 59–69.

Berry, Wendell. "The Gift of Good Land." In *The Art of the Commonplace: The Agrarian Essays of Wendell Berry*, edited by Norman Wirzba. Berkeley: Counterpoint, 2003.

Brown, L. Carl. *Religion and State: The Muslim Approach to Politics*. New York: Columbia University Press, 2000.

Brueggemann, Walter. *The Land: Place as Gift, Promise, and Challenge in Biblical Faith*. 2nd ed. Overtures to Biblical Theology. Minneapolis: Fortress, 2002.

Burge, Gary M. *Whose Land? Whose Promise: What Christians Are Not Being Told about Israel and the Palestinians*. Cleveland: Pilgrim, 2003.

Cohen, Jonathan, "Why Milk and Honey." Online: http://www.umc.sunysb.edu/surgery/m&h.html.

Cryder, Christian. "A Biblical-Theological Context for the Song of Songs: As Seen through the Lenses of Creation, the Fall, and Redemption." *Journal of the American Academy of Religion* 41 (1973) 30–48.

Fretheim, Terence E. "The Reclamation of Creation: Redemption and Law in Exodus." *Interpretation* 45 (1991) 354–65

Freud, Richard A. "The Land Which Bled Forth Its Bounty: An Exilic Image of the Land of Israel." *Scandinavian Journal of the Old Testament* 13 (1999) 284–97.

Gans, Chaim. "Palestinians Were Made to Pay an Unfair Price." *Haaretz*, June 27, 2009. Online: http://www.haaretz.com/hasen/spages/1094908.html.

Hasson, Isaac. "Muslim Literature in Praise of Jerusalem: Fada'il Bayt al-Maqdis." In *The Jerusalem Cathedra*, edited by Lee Levine, 168–84. Studies in the History, Archaeology, Geography and Ethnography of the Land of Israel 1. Jerusalem: Yad Izhak Ben-Zvi Institute, 1981.

Holwerda, David E. *Jesus and Israel: One Covenant or Two?* Grand Rapids: Eerdmans, 1995.

Janzen, Waldemar. "Land." In *The Anchor Bible Dictionary*, edited by David Noel Freedman, 4:143–54. 6 vols. New York: Doubleday, 1992.

Kallai, Zecharia. "The Patriarchal Boundaries, Canaan and the Land of Israel: Patterns and Application in Biblical Historiography." *Israel Exploration Journal* 47 (1997) 69–82.

Katanacho, Yohanna. "Christ Is the Owner of Haaretz." *Christian Scholar's Review* 34 (2005) 425–41.

Kimmerling, Baruch, and Joel S. Migdal. *The Palestinian People: A History*. Cambridge: Harvard University Press, 2003.

Kohl, Manfred Waldemar. "Towards a Theology of Land: A Christian Answer to the Hebrew-Arab Conflict." Originally published (in part) in *Phronesis* 9.2 (2002) 7–26 and in the *International Congregational Journal* 2.2, (2002) 165–78. Also in *The Bible and the Land*, edited by Salim J. Munayer and Lisa Loden. Eugene, OR: Cascade Books, forthcoming.

Korn, Eugene. "Land and Covenant: The Religious Significance of the State of Israel." Revised text of an address given at the International Conference of the International Council of Christians and Jews, Chicago, July 26, 2005. Online: http://www .jcrelations.net/en/index.php?item=2691.

Lactantius. *The Divine Institutes*. Book 7. Online: http://www.newadvent.org/fathers/ 07017.htm

Lederach, John Paul. *Building Peace: Sustainable Reconciliation in Divided Societies*. Washington, DC: United States Institute of Peace Press, 1997.

Morris, Benny. "Revisiting the Palestinian Exodus of 1948." In *The War for Palestine: Rewriting the History of 1948*, edited by Eugene L. Rogan and Avi Shlaim, 37–59. Cambridge Middle East Studies 15. Cambridge: Cambridge University Press, 2001.

Munayer, Salim J. *Hosea*. Asia Bible Commentary. Quezon City: Asia Theological Association, 2010.

Pappé, Ilan, *A History of Modern Palestine: One Land, Two Peoples*. Cambridge: Cambridge University Press, 2004.

Prior, Michael. "Violence and the Biblical Land Traditions." In *Challenging Christian Zionism: Theology, Politics and the Israel-Palestine Conflict*, edited by Naim S. Ateek et al., 127–44. London: Melisende, 2005.

Rouhana, Nadim N. "Zionism's Encounter with the Palestinians: The Dynamics of Force, Fear, and Extremism." In *Israeli and Palestinian Narratives of Conflict: History's Double Helix*, edited by Robert I. Rotberg, 115–41. Indiana Series in Middle East Studies. Bloomington: Indiana University Press, 2006.

Said, Edward W. "Afterword: The Consequences of 1948." In *The War for Palestine: Rewriting the History of 1948*, edited by Eugene L. Rogan and Avi Shlaim, 206–19. Cambridge Middle East Studies 15. Cambridge: Cambridge University Press, 2001.

Sparks, Kenton L. *Ethnicity and Identity in Ancient Israel: Prolegomena to the Study of Ethnic Sentiments and Their Expression in the Hebrew Bible*. Winona Lake: Eisenbrauns, 1998.

Suh, Robert H. "The Use of Ezekiel 37 in Ephesians 2." *Journal of the Evangelical Theological Society* 50 (2007) 715–33.

Tertullian. *Against Marcion*. Book 3. In *The Fathers of the Church*. Online: http://www .newadvent.org/fathers/03123.htm

Townsend, Jeffery L. "Fulfillment of the Land Promise in the Old Testament" *Bibliotheca Sacra* 142 (1985) 320–37.

Wazana, Nili. "From Dan to Beer-Sheba and from the Wilderness to the Sea: Literal and Literary Images of the Promised Land in the Bible." In *Experiences of Place*, edited by Mary N. MacDonald, 45–85. Cambridge: Center for the Study of World Religions, Harvard Divinity School, 2003.

Weinfeld, Moshe. *The Promise of the Land: The Inheritance of Canaan by the Israelis*. The Taubman Lectures in Jewish Studies Berkeley: University of California Press, 1993.

Ye'or, Bat. *Islam and Dhimmitude: Where Civilizations Collide*. Translated by Miriam Kochan and David Littman. Cranbury, NJ: Farleigh Dickinson University Press, 2002.

❖ 13 ❖

Towards a Theology of Land

A Christian Answer to the Israeli-Arab Conflict

Manfred Waldemar Kohl

ABSTRACT: The long-standing Israeli-Arab conflict in the Middle East is based in large part on the rival claims of Jews and Palestinians to the land. According to Scripture, however, all land belongs to God. Moreover, all territorial land promises are negated by God's redemptive plan through Jesus Christ. The fulfillment of every previous covenant lies in the redemption provided in Christ. His new covenant has at its center God's kingdom, which encompasses all believers, for whom earthly possessions—including property—become secondary. Justice and truth, surrounded by mercy and forgiveness, must replace land as the focal point for Jews and Palestinians alike. Kohl argues that a thirty-year old plan for two autonomous nations, Israel side by side with Palestine, is the only—and the correct—solution to the land issue. Jerusalem should be free from all political authority, a holy city belonging to all – Jews, Christians, and Muslims alike.[1]

❝PEACE BE WITH YOU**"**—**"**S*HALOM* alaichem" and "*Salaam aleikum*" in Hebrew and Arabic respectively—is the daily greeting in the Middle

1. Part of this article has been published in *Phronesis* 9:2 (2002) 7–26 and in the *International Congregational Journal* 2 (2002) 165–78. Reproduced here with permission. All Scripture quotations are taken from the New International Version (NIV).

265

East, and yet the lack of peace in the Arab-Israeli conflict is monumental, escalating more and more into an entire Middle East war with global implications. Neither the declarations, mandates, and treaties of the first part of the last century, nor the numerous United Nations resolutions, political conferences, and peace accords of the second half of the century have brought a peaceful solution to the problem, who owns the land? Each side claims, "the land is mine," based on millennia of historical facts on the one side and, on the other, the divine promise spoken by God himself.

The issue of land is fundamental to all humanity and an essential part of all religion. Although the Bible has much to say about "the land," for centuries this topic has been treated rather marginally by both Old and New Testament theologians. Gerhard von Rad's publication on the land in the Hexateuch (Genesis to Joshua) is considered the first major study on the subject.[2] Von Rad's form-critical and traditional-historical study led him to distinguish between the concept of the Promised Land as a gift and the cultural concept of the land as owned by God (Lev 25:23).[3] In this connection the proper translation/interpretation of "inheritance" (*nahalah*) becomes a major issue,[4] as does the proper understanding of sabbatical and Jubilee.[5] One must also point out the very significant differences with regard to the land issue between the first exodus (out of Egypt) and the second (the return from Babylon), as exemplified clearly in the difference between the annihilation language of Joshua and the relationship language of Ezekiel (Ezek 47:22–23).[6] These four specific issues—God as the owner of the land, the right translation/understanding of inheritance, the consideration of Jubilee, and the metamorphosis of language from the Hexateuch to the New Testament period—are still basic to the debate, as is the most fundamental question: how is God to be understood? Or, phrased differently, what were the different understandings of God in the Torah-centered, prophet-centered, and Christ-centered periods?

---

2. See von Rad, "The Promised Land," 79–93.

3. See Wright, *God's People*, 5–43.

4. See Brown, "The Concept of Inheritance." See also Wright, *God's People*, 17–20, with excellent bibliographical references in the footnotes.

5. See Fager, *Land Tenure*; Amit, "The Jubilee Law," 47–59; Weinfeld, "The Sabbatical Year," 39–62; Ringe, *Jesus, Liberation*.

6. See Ateek, "Biblical Perspectives on the Land," 108–16.

In the last few decades the broader studies of Davies[7] and Bruegge-mann[8] have broken ground for excellent new studies and publications in the field,[9] and within the last few years numerous theological consultations have been held on the issue of the importance of the land. These consultations have always included the Israeli-Arab issue.[10] The most recent consultation, sponsored by the Theological Commission of the International Congregational Fellowship, was held at the University of Bangor, Wales, in April 2002.

In biblical terms land as a gift from God began with the Garden of Eden (Genesis 1–2), not with the Abrahamic covenant (Genesis 12). Not only did the fall result in the ejection of humanity from the perfect land and form the basis of all imperfection, misuse, and destruction; it was also, from the beginning, the reason for God's redemptive plan by which he would reestablish a "paradise condition." All God's covenant-commitments with humanity, described and restated throughout the Old Testament (from Abraham to the post-Babylonian captivity period), are overshadowed by his plan for restoring this perfect paradise condition. This plan, through which humanity's fellowship with God is restored, is ultimately fulfilled in the new covenant through Jesus Christ. The Jewish argument that their claim to the land goes back to their patriarch

7. See Davies, *The Gospel and the Land*.

8. See Brueggemann, *The Land*.

9. See Ahituv, "Land and Justice," 11–28; Ateek, "The Earth Is the Lord's"; Bailey, "St. Paul's Understanding of the Territorial Promise," 59–69; and Chacour, *Blood Brothers*; and Chacour, *We Belong to the Land*. See also Chapman, *Whose Promised Land?*; Habel, *The Land Is Mine*, and Habel, "The Suffering Land"; Jeyaraj, "Land Ownership"; Johnston and Walker, *The Land of Promise*; Lilburne, *A Sense of Place*; Lustick, *Arab-Israel Relations*; Maoz, "Jerusalem and Justice"; and Maoz, "A Messianic Jewish Perspective"; March, *Israel and the Politics of Land*; Miller, "Messianic Judaism"; Olson, "Biblical Perspectives on the Land"; Orlinsky, "The Biblical Concept"; Spagnolo, *Problems of the Modern Middle East*; Stevenson, *The Vision of Transformation*; Urbach, "The Land of Israel in Scripture"; Wagner, *Anxious for Armageddon*; Wilken, *The Land Called Holy*; and Zureik, "Palestinian Refugees."

10. In Cyprus (1996 and 1997) and in Bethlehem (1998 and 2000) Jewish, Arab, and Christian representatives gathered to discuss "the Bible and the land." See Loden et al., *The Bible and the Land*. A symposium on Palestinian liberation theology was held in Jerusalem and Bethlehem in 1990. See Ateek et al., *Faith and the Intifada*; and Ateek, *Justice*. The University of Notre Dame sponsored a lecture series called "The Land of Israel in Jewish Thought," published as Hoffman, *The Land of Israel*. The Tyndale Fellowship in England held a theological consultation on the land, published as Johnston and Walker, *The Land of Promise*.

Abraham, and the Arab argument that their claim goes back to Ishmael (who was born before Isaac) and Esau (who was born before Jacob) have both been superseded by God's redemptive plan fulfilled in Christ and have therefore lost their entire significance.

Walter Brueggemann divides his study of the land issue into three parts: the history of promise into the land, the history of management into exile, and the new history of promise, which begins in exile and culminates in kingdom. "Land is a central, if not the central theme of biblical faith," he says. "Biblical faith is a pursuit of historical belonging that includes a sense of destiny derived from such belonging."[11] His statement is correct if he goes beyond his concept of "crucifixion—resurrection through the prism of land"[12] to see the fulfillment of God's land-gift covenant in Christ's kingdom-salvation covenant.

Jews living in the Old Testament era were always looking forward to a more paradise-like land—from the time of Moses, when they were promised "a land flowing with milk and honey" (Lev 20:24); to the promise to David that they would dwell in the land forever (Ps 37:18, 27, 29); to the longing of the pair walking home to Emmaus, who hoped for a redeemed Israel (Luke 24:21). The writer of Hebrews speaks several times of the patriarchs' longing for a "better heavenly country." Beyond the physical land promises, they were envisioning a spiritual reality (Heb 11:10, 16).

O. Palmer Robertson, understanding the Old Testament land promise from a new covenant perspective, states,

> The land which once was the specific locale of God's redemptive work served well within the old covenant as a picture of paradise lost and promised. Now, however, in the era of new covenant fulfillment, the land has expanded to encompass the cosmos . . . Yet, it would be fully in keeping with the new covenant perspective on the land to say that this new covenant 'Israel of God' refers to those who have been 'born from above' by the Holy Spirit sent down from the 'Jerusalem that is above' (John 3:3; Gal 4:26). It is they who are the true inheritors of the promises relating to the land; it is they who, in Jesus' phrase, will 'inherit the earth' (Matt 5:5, referring to Ps 37:11).[13]

11. Brueggemann, *The Land*, 3.

12. Ibid., 180.

13. Robertson, "Leaving the Shadows," 81. For more detail on the entire subject, see Robertson, *The Israel of God*.

One can also point to Paul's statement in this regard. He saw that the original Abrahamic covenant, although it included the promise of land, was not locale-limited. It would become a worldwide covenant through the righteousness that comes by faith (Rom 4:13).

It is always wrong to quote scriptural passages in isolation, making them the only and absolute "God said" and ignoring other scriptural texts pointing to additional aspects of the truth. Scripture must be understood in its linguistic and historic context. One must consider texts from the entirety of Scripture—both the Old and the New Testaments—to obtain a complete understanding of God's past, present, and future plan for humanity. The land issue cannot be seen in isolation, nor can it be interpreted from a self-interested point of view.

> In the realm of biblical interpretation, the danger exists to interpret the Scripture for the benefit of oneself or one's people group without reference to the context and background of the biblical record . . . When dealing with the theology of the land there are many components to be reckoned with: election and calling, prophesy and promise, Israel and the church, millennial questions, eschatology, dispensationalism, the holy land, the promised land, ownership, tendency, covenant, morality, justice, ethical issues and the kingdom of God. These are all subjects that are part and parcel of any comprehensive theology of the land . . . Any less than a full appraisal of the two testaments impoverishes one's understanding of the God of the Bible and will inevitably lead to error.[14]

Land-based issues such as ecology (taking care of the earth)[15] or the evils related to colonialism and human rights[16] can only be addressed if one looks at the entire Scripture from Genesis to Revelation.

Although the land theme appears more than 1,500 times in the Old Testament compared with fewer than fifty references in the New Testament (of which only about a dozen refer to the land of Israel), it is wrong to assume that Christ and the apostles did not care about this issue. Just the opposite is true. For Jesus, the "kingdom of God," or the "kingdom of heaven" (terms used more than one hundred times in the

---

14. Loden, "Knowing Where We Start," 31. On the topic of hermeneutics, see also the excellent paper, Tal, "Contemporary Hermeneutics," 316–38.

15. See Berry , *The Care of Creation*; Bakken et al., *Ecology*.

16. See Prior, *The Bible and Colonialism*; Bakare, *My Right to Land*; Gillan, *Church, Land and Poverty*.

four Gospels alone) was superior to the promised local land. Since his father owned all the land in the first place (Lev 25:23; Ps 24:1), Jesus went far beyond any narrow nationalistic local land concept. The discussion with the Emmaus disciples, whose minds were set on the Israel land issue, clearly indicates that Christ himself and his kingdom had become the fulfillment of all promises. He spoke emphatically when he said to them, "'How foolish you are and how slow of heart to believe all that the prophets have spoken,' and beginning with Moses and all the prophets he explained to them what had been said in all the Scripture concerning himself" (Luke 24:25, 27).

The new land concept, the kingdom of God, has a different presupposition from the old. "The whole spirit of the ministry of Christ in the Gospels puts us on a different ground from that of the Old Testament. Ethnocentricity is opposed, ethnic arrogance is challenged, and any superior feeling is discouraged and shattered (Mark 12:1–12; Luke 20:9–19; Matt 20:1–16)."[17] In God's kingdom nationalism, race, and gender do not matter, as demonstrated numerous times in Christ's ministry, and the local land, as property—even the holy city of Jerusalem as place—becomes secondary.

For Christians, Christ is the central point in history, the heart of Scripture, and the only key to the resolution of conflicting messages or positions. Jesus did not seek power; he rejected kingdoms of the world with all their splendors (Matt 4:8–10). Instead, his preaching focused on the kingdom of heaven (Matt 4:17). In his sermons he repeatedly warned his listeners that possessions and wealth (including land) should have no priority at all; rather, one should seek first and foremost a place in the kingdom of God. "The concept of the kingdom of God shatters any narrow concept of the land. Jesus' frequent use of the term kingdom of God was an intentional way to lift people's ideas and thoughts from a concentration on the land to the universality of God and of God's reign."[18] Although he was born and trained, and although he ministered within, the Promised Land, Jesus' concept of reaching all nations in the world with the love of his father indicates that he did not consider his

17. Ateek, "Putting Christ at the Centre," 58.

18. Ateek, "Biblical Perspectives on the Land," 113. Ateek believes that the kingdom of God becomes for Jesus an inclusive concept, and that the words of Jesus "The kingdom of God is within you" (Luke 17:21) reflect the same view. People carry within them the seed of the kingdom in their faithfulness and obedience to God. It is no more the land as locus but the people.

own homeland superior to or even essential to his ministry (Matt 28:19; John 3:16). Like Paul later, Jesus saw in the Roman Empire—the oppressor—an ally to be used in the expansion of God's kingdom. When challenged by the Pharisees about the Roman taxation requirements, he answered, "Give to Caesar what is Caesar's" (Matt 22:21). He extended genuine help to members of the occupying forces (Luke 7:1–9). It is also important to note that Jesus used the disliked Samaritans as models of charity (Luke 10:33–37), of mission outreach (John 4:39), and of gratitude (Luke 17:16). He emphasized the importance of Jonah, who was sent by God to Nineveh to preach to the worst of the enemies of ancient Israel (Matt 12:41, referring to Jonah 3).

The most disputed piece of land throughout history, the city of Jerusalem—which Jesus knew from childhood—had significance for him primarily inasmuch as it was a pointer to the heavenly Jerusalem. In Jesus' theology, Jerusalem, the physical center of worship, was replaced by non-physical places of worship; the only essential was that God be worshipped in spirit and in truth (John 4:21, 24). Even the sacred temple lost its significance because Christ saw himself as the new temple through which God manifests himself to humanity. The veil separating the most holy place from the rest of the temple was torn at Christ's death (Matt 27:51), bringing to an end the old covenant tradition. Stephen, speaking to the Sanhedrin, made clear that God does not live in houses made by humans (Acts 7:48). For Stephen the temple, Jerusalem, and the Promised Land all culminated in Christ, whom he saw standing at the right hand of God (Acts 7:55–56). Christ is the center of the heavenly Jerusalem (Heb 12:22–24), which is free and the mother of us all (Gal 4:26). He is the replacement for the former local temple.

Messianic Jews, declaring themselves to be one hundred percent Jewish and one hundred percent believers in Christ, claim to be the righteous remnant. Some of them, therefore, claim to be the rightful recipients of the land.[19] Stressing that they are the remnant (Rom 9:6–18) and

---

19. See Stern, "Making the Issues Clear": "Those who insist that all of God's promises to the Jews now apply willy-nilly to all believers in Yeshua, regardless of for whom they were intended, and not to the Jewish people (for whom they were intended) must consider this: there are Jews who are believers, why should not these constitute the present basis for God's continuing to consider the Jewish people the recipients of the promise of the land? Why should the literal meaning of the promise be cancelled and replaced by its spiritual/allegorical application to all believers? Why should this promise apply, in a literal sense, to Gentiles of any kind, whether believers or not? The Messianic Jews are the 'righteous remnant' (Rom 9:6–18) for whose sake God always extends himself"

the first fruits of the Jews (Rom 11:16), they ignore the biblical teaching that in the new covenant the seed of Abraham is Christ alone (Gal 3:16) and that through him the whole world—not just believing Jews—are justified through faith (cf. Gal 3:22–25).

For Paul, God's statement to Abraham that he would be the father of many nations (Gen 17:5) is fulfilled in Christ, whose righteousness—when accepted by faith—transcends both circumcision and national/racial limitations (Rom 4:11–15). The original Abrahamic covenant related to the promised local land now becomes a universal promise related to the cosmos. "In the light of their universal fulfillment in Christ, the narrow Old Testament promises regarding the land take on a very transitory and provisional meaning. They are time-bound and in view of their completion in Christ become theologically obsolete."[20] Ateek goes so far as to state, "The New Testament does not only reinterpret the Old Testament, it de-zionises it."[21]

The early church, following Christ's teaching, emphasized that earthly possessions (including land) might be a hindrance to *diakonia* and the proclamation of the good news to the ends of the world.[22] The followers of Christ saw him as the replacement for the temple, and through their belief in him, they themselves became a temple of the living God (2 Cor 6:16).

Paul, himself a Hebrew and trained in Jerusalem, was well aware of the nationalistic and territorial attitudes of his time. As a follower of Christ, he emphasized to the emerging churches that in his understanding the land had been "christified." Paul's attitude to the land is best summarized by Davies:

> Paul ignores completely the territorial aspect of the promise . . .
> In the christological logic of Paul, the land (like the law, particular and provisional) had become irrelevant . . . The people of Israel living in the land had been replaced as the people of God by a universal community which had no special territorial attachment . . . The land has for him been 'christified.' It is not the

---

(42). According to Stern, in the year 2000, there were about five thousand Messianic Jews in Israel and about 85,000 Arab Christians (49). On the interpretation of Romans, see Shalum and Le Cornu, *Commentary on the Jewish Roots of Romans*.

20. Ateek, "Putting Christ at the Centre," 60.

21. Ibid.

22. There is a need for a theology of possessions and ownership. See Kohl, "Motivation—Designation."

promised land (much as he had loved it) that became his 'inheritance', but the Living Lord, in whom was a 'new creation' . . . To be 'in Christ' . . . has replaced being 'in the land' as the ideal life.[23]

Walker, who has recently done extensive research and writing on the significance of the Promised Land in early Christian thought,[24] saw in the book of Hebrews, written at a time when the destruction of Jerusalem was at hand, "nothing to suggest that the author would have himself maintained any theological attachment to the promised land."[25] Walker also states, "As with Paul, this would only be endorsed by his conviction that Christ had accomplished a new Exodus, hence his comparing his audience to the 'people of Israel' in the desert (Heb 3:7ff) and that Jesus was greater than Moses (Heb 3:3). Jesus was leading his people to a new 'Promised Land,' the place to which he himself had gone ahead as the 'pioneer,' namely the 'heavenly Jerusalem' (Heb 12:22; cf. 12:2). This is the place where God's promises are fulfilled."[26]

John begins his Gospel by saying that Christ came to the world, not to the Promised Land, and concludes, in the book of Revelation, by focusing on the world as cosmos.

> The focus of Revelation is cosmic, not parochial. Jewish apocalyptic is now seen to be the basis for an interpretation of the world as a whole, and imagery that previously related to the Exodus and the deliverance from Egypt is now applied to the deliverance won by Jesus. Once again, this means that Christians are concerned with a quite different "promised land" . . . For the author of Revelation the coming of Jesus signals the end of a narrow focus on the land.[27]

From a biblical perspective (considering both Old and New Testaments), since the Christ event, the promise of the territorial land no longer has any significance. It does have historical significance, and in this sense should be treasured by everyone. Only in a historical sense can one speak of "a Holy Land," since the patriarchs, the prophets, and the first Christians—even Christ, the Son of God—walked on it. For Jews, as well

23. See Davies, *The Gospel and the Land*, 178–79, 182, 213, 217. Cited in Walker, "Listening to the Apostles," 112.

24. See Walker, *Jesus and the Holy City* and *Jerusalem Past and Present*.

25. Walker, "Listening to the Apostles," 119.

26. Ibid.

27. Ibid., 126–27.

as for certain Christian groups who pray daily for the people of Israel and "their" land, to insist on retaining an already-fulfilled and therefore obsolete territorial land covenant ignores to a large extent Christ's new covenant of God's kingdom that through his spirit encompasses all believers everywhere.[28] To consider Galilee the land of salvation, the place of the eschatological fulfillment of the hopes of Judaism (the subject of theological debate beginning in the late 1950s[29]) is equally misleading.

The scriptural understanding of justice and truth (Deut 16:20; John 8:32) must be brought into focus and must replace any territorial land promise concept. Justice and truth—for Jews, Arabs, and Christians; for believers and nonbelievers; for politicians and any person in authority— should be upheld. Truth, based on fact, is liberating. To minimize or ignore the terrible plight of the Jews throughout the past two thousand years is to ignore the truth. How can any human being feel untouched by the indescribable atrocities of the Holocaust? Equally, no one should ignore the historic fact that after the destruction of Jerusalem millions of people lived between the hills of Lebanon and Mount Sinai and established a right to call this area their home. Both Jews and Palestinians have a right to exist on the land.

The truth is that Jews, Muslims, and—perhaps most of all— Christians have all in the past committed uncountable evil acts of every kind. If ever there was a need for reconciliation, forgiveness, and love, it is now—by everyone and for everyone, but first and foremost for those whose focus is on the Middle East. Justice must be surrounded by mercy. For someone to take away any land, without permission and proper compensation, from people who for generations and millennia have possessed it, is grossly unjust and must be corrected.

If Reinhold Niebuhr is correct in saying that love, forgiveness, and compassion are possible only between individuals (political communities being motivated only by power and self-interest),[30] then any efforts

28. Robertson, in "Leaving the Shadows," writes: "In this age of fulfillment, therefore, a retrogression to the limited forms of the old covenant must be neither expected nor promoted . . . By claiming the old covenant form of the land-promise, the Jews of today may be forfeiting the greater new covenant fulfillment of the land-promise . . . How sad it would be if evangelical Christians who profess to love the Jewish people should become a primary tool in misdirecting their faith and expectation" (82).

29. Stemberger, "Galilee—Land of Salvation?" Stemberger's argumentation refers primarily to Lohmeyer, *Das Evangelium des Markus*; and Marxsen, *Der Evangelist Markus*.

30. See Niebuhr, *Moral Man*.

to bring about change must begin on a grassroots level, dealing with individuals, the most promising of which may be the upcoming generation of leaders.[31]

At the consultations on the Bible and the land held in Cyprus, Bethlehem, and Jerusalem, intense arguments followed the presentation of papers by Christian theologians of Arabic, Jewish, and Western backgrounds. The real breakthrough in communicating their respective views of justice and truth came when participants, primarily the younger among them, began to share personal testimonies of experiences of being hurt, ignored, misunderstood, forgiven, liberated, or loved. In his summary of one of the consultations Robertson stated, "It has brought together members of the body of Christ that have lived long with the deepest division. It has allowed the basic realities of the kingdom of Christ to be brought to bear on a circumstance that has resisted human solution for decades. The end is not in sight. But the beginnings of the end are already present in principle."[32] The credo of that same consultation stated, "[We] call upon all concerned with the Middle East conflict to act justly and righteously toward one another. We repudiate violence and injustice, from any quarter, toward people or property and we call upon all believers in Christ to discuss their differences within the framework of the Word of God."[33]

A unique rabbinic interpretation of Deut 16:20 (where justice is mentioned twice)—that the first mention of justice applies to the Jews, while the second applies to other people[34]—could also be understood to state that the first justice applies to me (and everything that encompasses my life), while the second justice applies to my neighbor (and everything that encompasses his or her life). This same concept is expressed throughout the preaching of Jesus, culminating in the greatest commandment: "Love the Lord your God . . . and your neighbor as yourself" (Matt 22:37–39). Paul says that the entire law is summed up in this single commandment: "Love your neighbor as yourself" (Gal 5:14).

31. It is encouraging that analysts of today see in Generation X a shift from concern for possessions to a greater focus on nonmaterial values.

32. Wood, "Pointers for the Future," 187–94.

33. Ibid., 194.

34. Ateek, *Justice*, refers to this interpretation by Reuven Moscovitz, who used it at a conference in Jerusalem in 1977 (177). Ateek gives several other references to rabbinic literature on this passage in Deuteronomy (212).

God is known by his justice (Ps 9:16; Isa 30:18), God loves justice (Ps 11:7), and justice should be foundational to his people (Ps 106:3). Justice is the measuring line (Isa 28:17) and is seen as a flowing river (Amos 5:24). Being just and loving are inseparable (Luke 11:42), and the basis of justification by faith (Rom 3:26). If true justice is upheld, peace will follow automatically.[35]

Being a just and loving God includes being a God of forgiveness, and faith in God without forgiveness of fellow human beings is impossible. In a chapter entitled "'Never Again' or 'Yes, Again?'"[36] Naim Ateek quotes a description by the Austrian Jewish psychiatrist Viktor Frankl, a survivor of the death camps of Nazi Germany, of fellow survivors: "Now, being free, they thought they could use their freedom licentiously and ruthlessly. The only thing that had changed for them was that they were now the oppressors instead of the oppressed. They became instigators, not objects, of willful force and injustice. They justified their behavior by their own terrible experience."[37]

Numerous Palestinians have experienced untold injustices and persecution under the Israeli occupation of the past fifty years, and in many cases the Palestinians of today have also fallen into the trap described by Frankl, seeking revenge, ruthlessly, at any cost. Both Jews and Palestinians have to be reminded of these moving words of Frankl: "Only slowly could these men be guided back to the common-place truth that no one has the right to do wrong, not even if wrong has been done to them."[38]

Ateek, himself a Palestinian, closes his chapter titled "Justice, and Only Justice: A Final Plea," with a challenge: "Do not destroy yourself with hate. Maintain your inner freedom; insist on justice, work for it and it shall be yours," and adds the prayer of St. Francis, "'Lord, let me be an instrument of your peace . . .'"[39]

An essential part of the Christian answer to the Middle East conflict is forgiveness. Hate can be changed to love through forgiveness. Jesus tells us, "Love your enemies and pray for those who persecute you"

35. This issue has recently been dealt with in Tambasco, *Blessed are the Peacemakers*; and Desjardins, *Peace, Violence*. However, this is a topic that needs much more attention and study.

36. Ateek, *Justice*, 178–87.

37. Frankl, *Man's Search for Meaning*, 143.

38. Ibid., 144.

39. Ateek, *Justice*, 187.

(Matt 5:44). God's kingdom, the new Christ-centered covenant, promotes forgiveness based on love, and this forgiveness generates peace. This is what the New Testament understands as justice.

In the early 1970s George Hunston Williams, then Hollis professor at Harvard University (the oldest academic chair in America), was asked by the leadership in Washington DC for advice on the Middle East dilemma from a Christian point of view. After spending weeks in theological discussion with colleagues and students, Professor Williams personally advised the president of the United States that the United States should continue to support the new State of Israel and should also help to create and support a new, independent State of Palestine. Both peoples could, he said—even *must*—exist side by side.[40] Unfortunately, this advice was never officially documented or taken seriously. I believe that this approach, suggested thirty years ago, is still valid today, and my voice is only one of many encouraging this line of action.

"Israeli Jews must come to accept the fact that, in order to live their religious faith, they do not have to have an exclusive political control of the whole of Palestine."[41] Jews, Palestinians, and even Christians "can achieve a full expression of religious life by sharing the land. Once this principle is affirmed, justice is not far off, and peace and reconciliation will become a welcomed reality."[42]

As a group of rather naïve young theologians at one of Professor Williams's colloquia, we simply designed two independent, autonomous states, Israel and Palestine, each having access to the sea and equal rights to the resources of the land. We hoped that the world would support both countries equally financially, thus avoiding strife and jealousy. We saw Jerusalem as a historic, holy city belonging to all—Jews, Christians, and Muslims alike—and free from any political authority. Today, I believe, even more than at any other time, these simple dreams are the solution. Such an arrangement would surely please God, the owner of all the land. Such an arrangement would be the best demonstration to the entire world that God, the creator and sustainer of humanity, honors justice, love, and forgiveness.

---

40. As a teaching fellow under Professor Williams at the time, I organized several colloquia on the topic and was present when Professor Williams announced that these were the points he had personally made to the president.

41. Ateek, "Biblical Perspectives on the Land," 115.

42. Ibid., 115.

On another personal note, a few weeks prior to the writing of this paper I visited the Middle East. In Bethlehem I was asked to speak at the theological school located only a few yards from Israel's checkpoint with all its violence, shooting, and stone throwing. It was in Bethlehem that the Prince of Peace was born, and where shepherds received the angelic proclamation, "Glory to God in the highest, and on earth peace to men on whom his favor rests" (Luke 2:14). Bishara Awad, founder and president of the Bethlehem Bible College, a partner school of Overseas Council International, is a Palestinian Christian who loves his land, as has his family over many generations. Speaking from his heart, Awad simply said that for him the Christian answer to the Arab-Israel land conflict lies in the fact that Jesus our Lord did not die on the cross to redeem a land. He died to redeem a lost humanity, "to rescue us from the domain of darkness and to bring us into the kingdom of the Son he loves" (Col 1:13). He quoted Paul's statement, "You are no longer strangers and foreigners, but fellow citizens with the saints and members of the household of God" (Eph 2:19–20), and concluded with the reassuring statement given by the Apostle Peter: "You are a chosen generation, a royal priesthood, a holy nation, his own special people, that you may proclaim the praises of him who called you out of darkness into his marvelous light" (1 Pet 2:9).[43]

POSTSCRIPT

Carl Armerding is correct in stating that a contemporary theology of land is long overdue.[44] A comprehensive theology of possessions/materialism and a theology of conflict resolution are equally lacking. Hopefully some of the emerging biblical scholars will work on these themes. To be effective, however, in any of these studies the term *"theology"* needs to be seen as a verb, and not just as a noun.

BIBLIOGRAPHY

Ahituv, Shmuel. "Land and Justice." In *Justice and Righteousness*, edited by Henning Graf Reventlow and Yair Hoffman, 11–28. Sheffield: JSOT Press, 1992.

Amit, Yairah. "The Jubilee Law: An Attempt at Instituting Social Justice." In *Justice and Righteousness*, edited by Henning Graf Reventlow and Yair Hoffman, 47–59. Sheffield: JSOT Press, 1992.

43. Awad, "Speaking from the Heart," 177–85.
44. Armerding, "Stewardship of the Land," 220.

Armerding, Carl E. "Stewardship of the Land: A Christian Mandate." In *The Land of Promise*, edited by Philip Johnston and Peter W. L. Walker, 215–31. Downers Grove, IL: InterVarsity, 2000.

Ateek, Naim S. "Biblical Perspectives on the Land." In *Faith and the Intifada: Palestinian Christian Voices*, edited by Naim Ateek, Marc H. Ellis, and Rosemary Radford Reuther, 108–16. Maryknoll, NY: Orbis, 1992.

———. "The Earth is the Lord's: Land, Theology and the Bible." *Mishkan* 27 (1997) 75–80.

——— et al., editors. *Faith and the Intifada*. Maryknoll, NY: Orbis, 1992.

———. *Justice, Only Justice*. Maryknoll, NY: Orbis, 1989.

———. "Putting Christ at the Centre: The Land from a Palestinian Christian Perspective." In *The Bible and the Land*, edited by Lisa Loden, et al., 55–63. Jerusalem: Musalaha, 2000.

Awad, Bishara. "Speaking from the Heart: The Palestinians and the Land of Their Fathers." In *The Bible and the Land*, edited by Lisa Loden et al., 177–85. Jerusalem: Musalaha, 2000.

Bailey, Kenneth E. "St. Paul's Understanding of the Territorial Promise of God to Abraham: Romans 4:13 in Its Historical and Theological Context." *Near East School of Theology Theological Review* 15 (1994) 59–69.

Bakare, Sebastian. *My Right to Land in the Bible and in Zimbabwe: A Theology of Land for Zimbabwe*. Harare: Zimbabwe Council of Churches, 1993.

Bakken, Peter W. et al., editors. *Ecology, Justice and Christian Faith: A Critical Guide to the Literature*. Bibliographies and Indexes in Religious Studies 36. Westport, CT: Greenwood, 1995.

Berry, R. J., editor. *The Care of Creation: Focusing Concern and Action*. Leicester: Inter-Varsity, 2000.

Brown, Arthur M. "The Concept of Inheritance in the Old Testament." PhD diss., Columbia University, 1965.

Brueggemann, Walter. *The Land: Place as Gift, Promise, and Challenge in Biblical Faith*. Overtures to Biblical Theology 1. Philadelphia: Fortress, 1977.

Chacour, Elias. *Blood Brothers: A Palestinian's Struggle for Reconciliation in the Middle East*. Eastbourne: Kingsway, 1985.

———. *We Belong to the Land: The Story of a Palestinian Israeli Who Lives for Peace and Reconciliation*. San Francisco: HarperSanFrancisco, 1992.

Chapman, Colin. *Whose Promised Land?* Tring, UK: Lion, 1983.

Davies, W. D. *The Gospel and the Land: Early Christianity and Jewish Territorial Doctrine*. Berkeley: University of California Press, 1974.

Desjardins, Michael. *Peace, Violence and the New Testament*. The Biblical Seminar 46. Sheffield: Sheffield Academic, 1997.

Fager, Jeffrey A. *Land Tenure and the Biblical Jubilee: Uncovering Hebrew Ethics through the Sociology of Knowledge*. Journal for the Study of the Old Testament Supplement Series 155. Sheffield: JSOT Press, 1993.

Frankl, Viktor E. *Man's Search for Meaning: An Introduction to Logotherapy*. Newly revised and enlarged. New York: Washington Square, 1963

Gillan David S., editor. *Church, Land and Poverty: Community Struggles, Land Reform and the Policy Framework on Church Land*. Johannesburg: Progress, 1998.

Habel, Norman C. *The Land Is Mine: Six Biblical Land Ideologies*. Overtures to Biblical Theology. Minneapolis: Fortress, 1995.

————. "The Suffering Land: Ideology in Jeremiah." *Lutheran Theological Journal* 26 (1992) 14–26.

Hoffman, Lawrence A., editor. *The Land of Israel: Jewish Perspectives.* University of Notre Dame Center for the Study of Judaism and Christianity in Antiquity 6. Notre Dame: University of Notre Dame Press, 1986.

Jeyaraj, Jesudason. "Land Ownership in the Pentateuch." PhD diss., University of Sheffield, 1989.

Johnston, Philip, and Peter Walker, editors. *The Land of Promise: Biblical, Theological and Contemporary Perspectives.* Downers Grove, IL: InterVarsity, 2000.

Kohl, Manfred. "Motivation—Designation: Historic Glimpses into Donations and Fund Raising for Christian Ministry." In *The Contentious Triangle: Church, State, and University. A Festschrift in Honor of Professor George Hunston Williams*, edited by Rodney L. Petersen and Calvin Augustine Pater, 319–37. Sixteenth Century Essays & Studies 51. Kirksville, MO: Thomas Jefferson University Press, 1999.

Lilburne, Geoffrey R. *A Sense of Place: A Christian Theology of the Land.* Nashville: Abingdon, 1989.

Loden, Lisa. "Knowing Where We Start: Assessing the Various Hermeneutical Approaches." In *The Bible and the Land*, edited by Lisa Loden et al., 15–35. Jerusalem: Musalaha, 2000.

Loden, Lisa et al., editors. *The Bible and the Land.* Jerusalem: Musalaha, 2000.

Lohmeyer, Ernst. *Das Evangelium des Markus 1.* Kritisch-exegetischer Kommentar über das Neue Testament, I/2:15. Göttingen: Vandenhoeck & Reprecht, 1959.

Lustick, Ian S., editor. *Arab-Israel Relations: Historical Background and Origins of the Conflict.* New York: Garland, 1994.

Maoz, Baruch. "Jerusalem and Justice: A Messianic Jewish Perspective." In *Jerusalem: Past and Present in the Purposes of God*, edited by Peter W. L. Walker, 151–73. Grand Rapids: Baker, 1992.

March, W. Eugene. *Israel and the Politics of Land: A Theological Case Study.* Louisville: Westminster John Knox, 1994.

Marxsen, W. *Der Evangelist Markus. Studien zur Redaktionsgeschichte des Evangeliums.* Forschungen zur Religion und Literatur des Alten und Neuen Testaments 49: 67 Göttingen: Vandenhoeck & Reprecht, 1956.

Miller, David. "Messianic Judaism and the Theology of the Land." *Mishkan* 26 (1997) 31–38.

Neibuhr, Reinhold. *Moral Man and Immoral Society: A Study in Ethics and Politics.* Scribner Library. New York: Scribner, 1960.

Olson, Dennis T. "Biblical Perspectives on the Land." *Word and World* 6 (1986) 18–27.

Orlinsky, Harry M. "The Biblical Concept of the Land of Israel: Cornerstone of the Covenant between God and Israel." In *The Land of Israel: Jewish Perspectives*, edited by Lawrence Hoffman, 27–64. University of Notre Dame Center for the Study of Judaism and Christianity in Antiquity 6. Notre Dame: University of Notre Dame Press, 1986.

Prior, Michael. *The Bible and Colonialism: A Moral Critique.* The Biblical Seminar 48. Sheffield: Sheffield Academic, 1997.

Rad, Gerhard von. "The Promised Land and Yahweh's Land in the Hexateuch." In *The Problem of the Hexateuch and Other Essays*, 79–93. London: SCM, 1966.

Ringe, Sharon H. *Jesus, Liberation and the Biblical Jubilee: Images for Ethics and Christology.* Overtures to Biblical Theology 19. Philadelphia: Fortress, 1985.

Robertson, O. Palmer, "Leaving the Shadows: A New Covenant Perspective on the Promise of the Land." In *The Bible and the Land*, edited by Lisa Loden et al., 65–82. Jerusalem: Musalaha: 2000.

————. *The Israel of God Yesterday, Today and Tomorrow*. Nutley, NJ: P & R, 2000.

Shalum, Joseph, and Hilary Le Cornu. *A Commentary on the Jewish Roots of Romans*. Baltimore: Messianic Jewish Publishers, 1998.

Spagnolo, John P., editor. *Problems of the Modern Middle East in Historical Perspective: Essays in Honour of Albert Hourani*. St. Anthony's Middle East Monographs 26. Reading, UK: Ithaca, 1992.

Stemberger, Günter. "Galilee – Land of Salvation?" In *The Gospel and the Land*, edited by W. D. Davies, 409–39. Berkeley: University of California Press, 1974.

Stern, David H. "Making the Issues Clear: The Land from a Messianic Jewish Perspective." In *The Bible and the Land*, edited by Lisa Loden et al., 37–54. Jerusalem: Musalaha, 2000.

Stevenson, Kalinda Rose. *The Vision of Transformation: The Territorial Rhetoric of Ezekiel 40–48*. Society of Biblical Literature Dissertation Series 154. Atlanta: Scholars, 1996.

Tambasco, Anthony J., editor. *Blessed Are the Peacemakers: Biblical Perspectives on Peace and Its Social Foundations*. New York: Paulist, 1989.

Tal, Uriel. "Contemporary Hermeneutics and Self-Views on the Relationship between State and Land." In *The Land of Israel: Jewish Perspectives*, edited by Lawrence A. Hoffman, 316–38. University of Notre Dame Center for the Study of Judaism and Christianity in Antiquity 6. Notre Dame: University of Notre Dame, 1986.

Urbach, Chaim. "The Land of Israel in Scripture." *Mishkan* 26 (1997) 21–30.

Wagner, Don. *Anxious for Armageddon: A Call to Partnership for Middle Eastern and Western Christians*. Scottdale, PA: Herald, 1995.

Walker, Peter L. W. *Jesus and the Holy City: New Testament Perspectives on Jerusalem*. Grand Rapids: Eerdmans, 1996.

————, editor. *Jerusalem: Past and Present in the Purposes of God*. Carlisle, UK: Paternoster, 1994.

————. "Listening to the Apostles: An Interpretation of the Land in the New Testament." In *The Bible and the Land*, edited by Lisa Loden et al., 107–35. Jerusalem: Musalaha, 2000.

Weinfeld, Moshe. "The Sabbatical Year and Jubilee in the Pentateuchal Laws and the Ancient Near Eastern Background." In *The Law in the Bible in Its Environment*, edited by Timo Veijola, 39–62. Publications of the Finnish Exegetical Society 51. Göttingen: Vandenhoeck & Ruprecht, 1990.

Wilken, Robert L. *The Land Called Holy: Palestine in Christian History and Thought*. New Haven: Yale University Press, 1992.

Wood, Michael. "Pointers for the Future: A Summary of Outstanding Issues." In *The Bible and the Land*, edited by Lisa Loden et al., 187–94. Jerusalem: Musalaha, 2000.

Wright, Christopher J. H. *God's People in God's Land: Family, Land, and Property in the Old Testament*. Grand Rapids: Eerdmans, 1990.

Zureik, Elia. "Palestinian Refugees and Peace." *Journal of Palestine Studies* 24 (1994) 5–17.

❖14❖

A Biblical Perspective on Israel/
Palestine

Colin Chapman

INTRODUCTION

The Significance and Seriousness of this Question

I HOPE I HARDLY need to point out that we are dealing here with one of the most complex, bitter, and longstanding conflicts in the world in the last hundred years, and that this conflict has far-reaching implications for the peace of the world. The creation of the State of Israel in 1948, the Six Day War in 1967, and Israel's continuing occupation of the West Bank have profoundly affected the lives of every single person in this region for the last sixty years. These are the huge stones that have been thrown into the pool, and the ripples go on affecting us all day after day.

Western support for the State of Israel has often been unquestioning, and Christians—especially evangelical Christians, and especially evangelical Christians in the United States—have played a highly significant role in strengthening this instinctive sympathy for Israel.

This support for Israel, however, combined with all the different policies of Western powers in recent years (including the war in Iraq), is probably at the top of the list of grievances that fuel the anger of Arabs and Muslims. I might even go as far as to suggest that if the West after 1967 had dealt with the Israeli-Palestinian conflict in a more even-handed way and pressed both sides hard and consistently towards a peaceful resolution on the basis of international law, the events of 9/11 might have never happened.

My Personal Pilgrimage

My first introduction to the Middle East was in 1968 when I went to work in Egypt, which was still recovering from the disaster of 1967. I first began to understand what the Palestinian problem was all about through my wife, Anne, who before our marriage in Jordan, had been working as a nurse among Palestinian refugees in Zarqa, Jordan, and had been caught up in the Jordanian civil war in September 1970 (also called "Black September").

In 1977 I wrote an article about the Israeli-Palestinian conflict for a popular Christian monthly magazine in the UK because I could not reconcile the attitudes of many Christians in the West to the conflict with what I could see was happening on the ground in the Middle East. The angry letters I received in the subsequent months forced me to do further research both into the history of the conflict and into biblical interpretation and eschatology, culminating in writing the book *Whose Promised Land?* I wrote it in Beirut during the difficult days of the Lebanese civil war when there was often the sound of gunfire in the streets; it was first published in 1983.

I have spent seventeen years working in different places in the Middle East in three separate spells (the latest until 2003), and have therefore tried to keep in touch with how Christians in the West perceive the conflict, and how it has been working out on the ground. I quickly realized that the conflict has enormous implications in many different areas because it touches on biblical interpretation, theology, contemporary international politics, interfaith relations, and the proclamation of the gospel. And I have come to believe what is at stake over this issue is nothing less than our understanding of God, our witness to the gospel, and the credibility of the Christian church—especially in the Middle East—in relation to the Jewish people and the House of Islam throughout the world. The stakes are very high!

Relating the Bible and Theology to History and Politics

When I wrote *Whose Promised Land?*, I was aware that most Western Christians knew very little about the history of the land since biblical times. The first third of the book was therefore simply trying to tell that story, explaining in particular the origins of the conflict since the rise of the Zionist movement and the return of Jews to the land after 1880. The second part traced the theme of the land from Genesis to Revelation. The final section explored other ways of using the Bible in relation to the conflict over the land.

Although we cannot explore the history and politics here, I want to emphasize the point that what we understand *from Scripture* is likely to profoundly affect the way we think about the conflict playing out before our eyes at the present time. We cannot keep our interpretation of the Bible and our theology in one compartment and our understanding of the conflict in another. We desperately need to be able to bring the two together so that we can live with the practical implications and the out-working of our biblical interpretation.

TWO RADICALLY DIFFERENT BIBLICAL AND THEOLOGICAL STARTING POINTS

We need to recognize that there are at least two radically different approaches among evangelical Christians: the restorationist and dispensationalist approach, and the approach from covenant theology. I describe and evaluate both below.

Restorationism and Dispensationalism

These are not the same, but I suggest that they have the same starting point. I am using "restorationism" to describe the belief of many Puritans and many evangelicals from the eighteenth century to the present day that God would one day *restore* the Jewish people to the land. In the American context these ideas were generally summed up under the term "premillennialism." Dispensationalism, first developed by John Nelson Darby in the 1840s and popularized in the United States by people like William Blackstone and D. L. Moody, takes restorationism as its starting point and builds a complete eschatological system on this foundation. So while restorationism and dispensationalism are not the same, they do seem to start from the same assumptions, which I would summarize as follows:

Although Jesus as the Messiah is the fulfillment of all the promises and prophecies of the OT, the *promises and prophecies about the land and about biblical Israel remain the same* even after his coming, and *need to be interpreted literally.* Because of the promise to Abraham, therefore, the *Jewish people have a special, divine right to the land for all times.* And even if the prophecies about a return to the land were fulfilled in a limited way in the return from the exile in Babylon in 539 BC, they have been *fulfilled once again in recent history* in the return of Jews to the land since the 1880s, the establishment of the State of Israel in 1948, and the capture of East Jerusalem in 1967. These events are signs pointing to the Second Coming.

Evaluation of This Approach

I recognize that many of you are probably starting from this kind of position. And even if you do not share these views yourself, I think you would agree that this is the starting point of many of the churches from which you come, and the majority of evangelical Christians, not only in the United States, but throughout the world.

I have to say, however, that this is not my starting point. But instead of challenging this approach point by point, what I want to do at this stage is simply to indicate very briefly what I see as its most significant weaknesses. I want to spend most of my time putting forward a positive, coherent, and convincing alternative.

1. The insistence on literal interpretation. The famous Cyrus Scofield of the *Scofield Reference Bible* wrote, "Not one instance exists of a 'spiritual' or figurative fulfilment of prophecy . . . Jerusalem is always Jerusalem, Israel is always Israel, Zion is always Zion."[1] And Hal Lindsay wrote, "If you take the Bible literally, then you will come up with the premillennial point of view . . . I *hate* those who read their ideas into scripture by using allegory."[2]

This insistence on literal interpretation is seen most clearly in the assumption that the thousand years described in Revelation 20 must be

---

1. Scofield, *Scofield Bible*, 45–46.
2. Lindsay, quoted in Gorenberg, *The End of Days*, 121 (emphasis added).

understood as a literal period of a thousand years when Christ will rule the earth.

2. *The distinction between biblical Israel and the church.* John Hagee writes, "Scripture plainly indicates that the church and national Israel exist side by side and that neither replaces the other—not yesterday, not today, not tomorrow . . . Scripture describes and defines two Israels: one is a physical Israel, with an indigenous people, a capital city called Jerusalem and geographic borders plainly defined in Scripture. Yet there is also a spiritual Israel, with a spiritual people and a spiritual New Jerusalem. Spiritual Israel, the church, may enjoy the blessings of physical Israel, but it does not replace physical Israel in God's plan for the ages."[3]

3. *Sympathy for one side in the conflict.* For the last one hundred years this starting point has inevitably led many Christians to have an instinctive sympathy for the Jewish people and for the whole Zionist project. "If what we have been witnessing is the fulfillment of biblical promises and prophecies," they say, "then surely we must see the hand of God in the establishment of the State of Israel and therefore be critical of the Arabs, who seem to be trying to thwart or even destroy the Jewish state." Much, if not most, of what evangelical Christians know about the conflict comes from popular Christian sources (like *The Late Great Planet Earth* a few decades ago or, more recently, the Left Behind series, as well as from the teachings of televangelists and personalities hosted on Christian radio networks), and there seems no need to study the history of the conflict in any objective way. Questions of justice, human rights, and international law become totally irrelevant.

Let me go on now to attempt to summarize an evangelical approach that is an alternative to restorationism and dispensationalism, which I am calling "covenant theology."

Covenant Theology

The promises given to Abraham and all the prophecies in the OT have to be interpreted *in the light of the coming of the kingdom of God in Jesus.* The OT must therefore be read through the spectacles, the glasses, of the NT. Because OT promises and prophecies (*including those about the land and about biblical Israel*) have been fulfilled in the coming of the kingdom in Jesus, the return of Jews to the land and the establishment

3. Hagee, *The Final Dawn*, 97.

of the State of Israel have taken place under the sovereignty of God, but have *no special theological significance.* They are not to be seen as signs pointing forward to the Second Coming. *All believers in Jesus inherit all the promises made to Abraham.* They are "a chosen people, a royal priesthood, a holy nation" (1 Pet 2:9; cf. Gal 3:26–29) and enjoy their spiritual inheritance, which is "kept in heaven" (1 Pet 1:4; Hebrews 4; 12:18–24).[4]

If this is the starting point, let me try to elaborate this approach in the following ten stages:

1. *The covenant promise to Abraham about the land (in Genesis 12, 15, and 17) is* unconditional. *But the promise about the land needs to be seen as one strand of the covenant and interpreted alongside the promises about the nation, the covenant relationship, and blessing for all peoples of the world. A Christian interpretation of the land promise must therefore be closely related to the interpretation of the other three promises.*

In the book of Genesis the covenant with Abraham has four strands: 1) the nation, 2) the land, 3) the covenant relationship, and 4) blessing for all peoples of the world. These four strands need to taken together as a kind of "package deal" in which all of the strands are bound together and are interdependent. Our interpretation of each one is therefore tied up with our interpretation of the other three. As Christians we have no difficulty in seeing the promises about the nation, the covenant relationship, and blessing for all peoples of the world as fulfilled in Christ. And I suggest that we have no reason to put the promise *about the land* in a special category, insisting that it must be fulfilled literally and that it cannot be related in any way to Christ.

So, for example, when Peter is writing to Jewish and Gentile Christians in Asia Minor, he uses titles which earlier had been reserved exclusively for the Jewish people: "You are a chosen people, a royal priesthood, a holy nation" (1 Pet 2:9). And writing to the Galatians, Paul says to Jewish and Gentile Christians: "If you belong to Christ, then you are Abraham's seed, and heirs according to the promise" (Gal 3:29). It is inconceivable to me that Paul would have thought that these Gentile Christians inherit *all* the covenant promises made to Abraham *except those about the land.*

2. *In the OT continued possession of the land is* conditional. *Disobedience to the law of the covenant means that the people forfeit the right*

---

4. All Scripture quotations are taken from the New International Version (NIV).

to live in the land and will be expelled from the land (Lev 18:24–28; Deut 4:25–27). The promise of restoration to the land is also conditional on repentance (Deut 30:1–5). Because there is some kind of repentance during the exile (e.g. in Daniel and Nehemiah), God brings the people back to the land in faithfulness to his promise to restore them after repentance. If the return of Jews to the land since 1880 is to be seen as a fulfillment of prophecy, how does it fit the terms of Deuteronomy 30? After the coming of Christ, repentance would mean recognition of Jesus as Messiah.

In passages like Deut 4:25–27, God says to the children of Israel through Moses, "If you are obedient, you can live in the land. But if you are disobedient, I will throw you out of the land." Leviticus 18:28 says that the land "will vomit you out as it vomited out the nations who were before you." The land does not belong to the children of Israel, but to God: "the land is mine, and you are but aliens and my tenants" (Lev 25:23). While the land has been given to them as a gift, therefore, they can continue to live in the land *only* if they are faithful to the covenant.

When God brings the people back to the land after the Babylonian exile, he does so in accordance with the terms of Deuteronomy 30: "If you return to the Lord your God . . . even if you are exiled to the ends of the world, from there the Lord your God will gather you, and from there he will bring you back" (Deut 30:2–3). But how can we say that the same pattern has been repeated in the Zionist movement of the nineteenth and twentieth centuries? Restorationists and dispensationalists say that God has brought the Jews back to the land "in unbelief," and point out that many who have returned to the land in recent years have come to believe in Jesus as Messiah. We must, of course, rejoice that this has been happening. But the fact that the condition of repentance that is taught in Deuteronomy 30 has not been fulfilled in this recent return makes it difficult to assert with confidence that the events of the last 120 years must be seen as a further fulfillment of OT prophecies about a return to the land.

3. The tabernacle and the temple in Jerusalem are signs of God living among his people (Exod 25:8; 1 Chr 23:25) and point forward to the incarnation. Christians have no difficulty in seeing everything associated with the tabernacle and the temple as being fulfilled in Christ (e.g. John 1:4; 2:18–22; Hebrews 4–10). It is therefore unthinkable that the rebuilding of the temple should be seen as a significant event in God's plan of salvation for the world.

When John says, "The Word was made flesh and lived [*eskenō sen*; literally, "tabernacled"] among us; and we beheld his glory" (1:14), he is saying in effect, "We have seen the glory of God not on the tabernacle in the wilderness nor on Solomon's temple, but on the person of Jesus." For John, therefore, Jesus is the fulfillment of Ezekiel's vision of the glory of God returning to a restored temple in Jerusalem. In John 2:18–22, Jesus speaks of himself as the fulfillment of everything that the temple had stood for: "Destroy this temple, and I will raise it again in three days." John comments, "The temple he had spoken of was his body."

4. *Prophecies of a return to the land are linked with spiritual renewal of the nation and God's plans for the nations (e.g. Ezek 36–37). Since these prophetic dreams were fulfilled in a very limited way after the return from exile, the people continued to look forward to a future national and spiritual restoration (Hos 6:1–3; Zech 14:9).*

In Ezekiel 36–37 many different themes and images like these are woven together to depict the glorious future that God has in store for his people when they are restored to the land:

- "Like dry bones coming to life, I will bring you back to the land . . ."
- "I will sprinkle clean water on you, and . . . I will cleanse you from all your impurities."
- "I will give you a new heart and put a new spirit in you . . ."
- "I will put my Spirit in you and move you to follow my decrees and be careful to keep my laws."
- "You will live in the land I gave to your forefathers."
- "I will call for the grain and make it plentiful . . . the desolate land will be cultivated."
- "Then the nations . . . will know that I the Lord have rebuilt what was destroyed."
- "I will make their people as numerous as sheep."
- "I will make them one nation in the land . . . Judah and Israel will be reunited."
- "There will be one king over all of them . . . my servant David will be king over them . . . forever."
- "They will all have one shepherd."
- "I will make a covenant of peace with them . . . an everlasting covenant."
- "I will put my sanctuary among them forever . . . my dwelling-place will be with them."

Like Ezekiel, all the other prophets are looking forward to the time when God will establish his sovereignty over the whole world, when in the words of Zechariah, "The LORD [Yahweh] will be king over the whole earth" (Zech 14:9).

And Hosea, in some important words to which we shall return later, expresses the hope that God will one day revive and restore the whole nation of Israel: "After two days he will revive us; on the third day he will restore us, that we may live in his presence" (Hos 6:1–3).

These, then, were the hopes and expectations of the Jewish people that built up over the centuries before the coming of Christ, and they included both national and spiritual restoration and renewal.

5. *The* Torah, *the* land, *and the temple were fundamental themes in Judaism at the time of Christ. Jews looked forward to the coming of the Messiah, who would enable the Jews to drive out the Romans and establish an independent Jewish state in the land, so that the Jews could obey the* Torah *in the land (e.g., Luke 2:25, 38; 24:21).*

Luke tells us, for example, that Simeon was looking forward to "the consolation of Israel" (Luke 2:25), and Anna spoke about Jesus to all who were looking forward to "the redemption of Jerusalem" (Luke 2:38). These expressions sum up the hopes of the Jewish people as they had developed since the time of the prophets, and Simeon and Anna believed that they were going to be fulfilled in Jesus. This was the worldview of the disciples of Jesus, and their expectations therefore included all these dreams and centered round the establishment of a sovereign, independent Jewish state in the land in which the people of Israel would live in obedience to the *Torah.*

6. *Jesus had little or nothing to say about the land; the only clear reference is Matt 5:5 (cf. Ps 37:11). The reason for this silence is not that Jesus took traditional Jewish hopes for granted and affirmed them, but that the fulfillment of all these hopes is now to be understood in the context of the coming of the kingdom of God in and through Jesus (Mark 1:15). Jesus predicted the destruction of the temple; but instead of speaking about its restoration, spoke about the coming of the Son of Man (Mark 13; Matthew 24; Luke 21:5–36).*

Restorationists and dispensationalists argue that if Jesus said little about the land, it is because he did not need to say anything about it and could take traditional Jewish teaching for granted. The other possible explanation, which I find much more convincing, is that Jesus could not affirm all the nationalistic expectations of the Jewish people. In his teaching about the kingdom of God there was no place for traditional Jewish ideas that the kingly rule of God revolved around the Jewish people and the Promised Land. In Mark's summary of the message of Jesus (Mark 1:15), he says, in effect, *The time that the prophets looked forward to—when they said "In that day . . ."—has at last come! The kingly rule of God is just about to come and God is about to establish his kingly rule on the earth.*

Here I would strongly commend W. D. Davies' magisterial study *The Gospel and the Land: Early Christianity and Jewish Territorial Doctrine*, which attempts to demonstrate how the teaching of Jesus challenged and changed the expectations of the Jewish disciples about the kingdom of God as they related to the land. This is how Davies summarizes the way Jesus transformed traditional Jewish ideas about the land: "In the last resort this study drives us to one point: the person of a Jew, Jesus of Nazareth, who proclaimed the acceptable year of the Lord only to die accursed on a cross and so pollute the land, and by that act and its consequences to shatter the geographic dimension of the religion of his fathers. Like everything else, the land also in the New Testament drives us to ponder the mystery of Jesus, the Christ, who by his cross and resurrection broke not only the bonds of death for early Christians but also the bonds of the land."[5]

Recent studies of the eschatological discourses suggest that the main thrust in what Jesus says in these passages concerns the immediate future and the events leading up to the destruction of Jerusalem in AD 70, and that it is only in the last section of the discourses, when he speaks about "that day," that he is speaking about the end of the world. This interpretation helps to resolve a major difficulty frequently recognized in the traditional interpretations, namely, that Jesus seems to be jumping from the immediate future to the end of the world and then back again to the immediate context. In Daniel's vision, the coming of the Son of Man is not a coming *to earth* but a coming *into the presence of God* to receive kingship and kingly authority. In this interpretation, therefore, the whole sequence of events, including the death and resurrection of the Jesus, the ascension, the giving of the Spirit, and the destruction of Jerusalem in AD 70, are to be taken together as a series of events in

5. Davies, *The Gospel and the Land*, 375.

which Jesus is seen to be entering into his kingly rule. Sayings about the coming of the Son of Man can still be related to the Second Coming, but their primary reference in the context of these discourses is to the events leading up to the destruction of Jerusalem. This interpretation then helps us to make sense of Jesus' saying that "There are some standing here who will not taste death until they see that the kingdom of God has come with power" (Mark 9:1).

7. *The disciples began with typical Jewish ideas about the land and the kingdom of God; but the teaching of Jesus, in the period between the resurrection and the ascension, gave them a new understanding of the kingdom. The meetings with the risen Jesus recorded in Luke 24:13–27 and Acts 1:1–8 marked a turning point in the thinking of the disciples. There is nothing in the NT to suggest that they continued to look forward to restoration to the land or the establishment of a Jewish state as part of God's plan for the Jews or for the world.*

When the two disciples on the road to Emmaus say, "We had hoped that he [Jesus] was the one who was going to *redeem Israel*," they are expressing the hopes of all first-century Jews. But in his response, Jesus says, in effect, "Don't you realize that *Jesus* has *redeemed Israel—but not in the way that you expected*" (cf. Luke 24:13–27)?

Similarly, in Acts 1:1–8, when the risen Jesus is speaking to the disciples about the kingdom of God, and the disciples ask him, "Are you at this time going to restore the kingdom to Israel?," they are expressing the same hopes of a restored Jewish state in the land. There are two significantly different interpretations of Jesus' reply to the disciples' question (1:7–8). According to the first interpretation, given by restorationists and dispensationalists, Jesus accepts the *idea* that this will one day happen, but simply tries to correct their understanding about the *timing* of when it will take place: "It is not for you to know" (1:7). According to the second interpretation (which I follow), Jesus is correcting not only their understanding about the *timing* of it all but also *the idea itself*. He is trying to show them that the kingdom of God is not something literal and physical, that it is not related only to the Jews, and that it is not tied to the land. He then goes on to speak about his disciples taking the gospel to the ends of the earth, helping them to see that this is what the coming of the kingdom of God is about. I believe that at this point the disciples at last begin to understand the nature of the kingdom of God. I cannot find a single verse in the NT that suggests that the disciples continued to hold on to traditional Jewish expectations about an independent Jewish state in the land.

8. *NT writers continued to use OT terminology about the land and the temple, but reinterpreted them in different ways in light of the incarnation (e.g., John 1:14; Acts 20:32; 1 Cor 6:19; Eph 1:14; 1 Pet 1:3–5). Their interpretation of the OT is not always literal (e.g., Luke 1:29–33, 22:28–30; 1 Cor 15:3–4).*

The word "inheritance" [*klēronomia*], for example, is often associated with the land. Here are three examples of this land terminology being given a new interpretation in the NT:

- Peter says that all believers are given new birth into a living hope, and into *an inheritance*. There is a clear reference here to the land, since Peter describes our inheritance as one that—unlike the literal, physical land—"can never perish, spoil or fade" (1 Pet 1:2–5).

- Paul's address to the Ephesian elders contains clear echoes of Joshua's farewell address. Thus, whereas Joshua was enabling the people to enter the inheritance of the land, Paul says: "I commit you to God and to the word of his grace, which can build you up and give you *your inheritance* among all who are sanctified" (Acts 20:32).

- In Ephesians Paul writes of the Holy Spirit as the one "who is a deposit guaranteeing *our inheritance*" (Eph 1:14).

I am often told that my argument is based on silence—on the fact that the NT has so little to say about the land. My answer is that the argument is *not* based on silence, since NT writers *do* use land terminology. They use words like "inheritance," which are associated with the land (e.g., 1 Pet 1:3–5), but they always interpret the theme of the land in spiritual ways (e.g., Hebrews 4).

We have already seen how John speaks of Jesus describing himself as the one who fulfills everything that the temple had meant (John 1:14). And Paul is extremely bold when he compares individual believers with the temple in which God lives: "Do you not know that your body is a temple of the Holy Spirit?" (1 Cor 6:19).

If we ask how NT writers interpret the OT, we can hardly say that their interpretation is always literal. Luke, for example, in his account of the annunciation to Mary in 1:29–33 sees no problem in seeing Jesus as the fulfillment of all the promises made to David in 2 Sam 7:11–16. Of course, Luke knows that Jesus never sat on David's throne in Jerusalem and ruled over his people in the way that David had done. But he has no difficulty in claiming that Jesus of Nazareth, the crucified and risen Messiah, is the fulfillment of OT promises and prophecies. This is not simply a spiritualizing of the OT. In Luke's mind the kingly rule into which Jesus has entered through his incarnation, suffering, death, resurrection, and ascension *is the real and substantive fulfillment* of what God had promised in the OT about the kingly rule of the Messiah.

Paul's reference to the resurrection of Jesus "on the third day according to the scriptures" in 1 Cor 15:3–4 is another example of how OT expressions and ideas are interpreted in the NT. In speaking about Jesus being raised "on the third day according to the scriptures," there must be a clear echo of Hos 6:1–3, which, as we have already seen, expresses the hope of the revival and restoration of the nation of Israel. In this way the resurrection of Jesus is seen as the beginning of the revival and restoration *of the nation of Israel*. These, therefore, are examples of how NT writers understand and interpret the OT. It is hard to see how we can possibly insist that their interpretation is always literal.

9. *The church is not "the new Israel"; it does not replace Israel (replacement theology or supersessionism). The church is Israel renewed and restored (1 Pet 2:9–10; John 15:1–4 [cf. Ps 80:8–18]). Gentile believers are grafted into Israel (Romans 9–11) and inherit all the promises made to Abraham. In these chapters Paul looks forward to a brighter future for the Jewish people, but this is related to the Messiah, not to restoration to the land.*

Along with many others, I am often accused of teaching "replacement theology" or "supersessionism," the idea that the church has taken the place of, or "superseded," Israel. But this is not my understanding. The NT never speaks of the church as "the new Israel," and it was therefore most unfortunate that theologians in the second century started using this expression to speak about the church, implying that God had finished with "the old Israel"—the Jewish people. Paul clearly says in Romans 9–11 that "God has not rejected his people" (11:1), and that "they are loved on account of their forefathers" (11:28). But he also says that when they fail to believe in Jesus as Messiah, they are "broken off because of unbelief" (11:20), and therefore fail to benefit from the covenant promises. In Paul's terminology, therefore, every Gentile believer is grafted into Israel, and *the church is Israel—but Israel renewed and restored in Jesus the Messiah.*

These ideas are also clearly implied in John 15 when Jesus claims to be "the true vine" (John 15:1–11). In Ps 80:8–18 the vine is a symbol of Israel: "You brought a vine out of Egypt . . . and planted it and it took root and filled the land" (80:8–9). So when Jesus says, "I am the vine . . . I am the true vine . . . ," he is identifying himself with Israel, as if saying, "I am Israel; I am the true Israel . . . and all who believe in me are the branches of the true vine, the true Israel." So John 15 can be the basis for a challenging devotional message about "abiding in Christ." But it has deeper levels of meaning and application than this!

In this context let me add that Ezekiel's vision of the valley of dry bones (Ezek 37) can be seen as looking forward to the resurrection of Jesus. Ezekiel is told, "These bones are the whole house of Israel." And if Jesus *is* Israel—if he *sums up* Israel—it is the resurrection of Jesus and not the return of Jews to the land since 1880 that is the fulfillment of Ezekiel's prophecy which goes beyond the immediate context of the prophet himself.

10. *The reign of Christ in Revelation 20:1–7 has to be interpreted in the context of the whole book of Revelation, and hardly provides an adequate basis for all the ideas associated with the Millennium—a literal reign of Jerusalem for a thousand years.*

I realize that we are embarking here on one of the most sensitive, controversial, and divisive issues of all; and in many ways I would prefer to say nothing about the subject. But I know from previous experience that if I do not say anything, the very first question afterwards will be, "What about the Millennium?" So let me summarize very briefly five reasons for challenging views about the Millennium that are so widely accepted among evangelical Christians:

1. Revelation 20:1–5 is the *only* passage in Scripture that speaks about the Millennium.

2. This passage must be interpreted in the context of the book that is full of symbols that need to be interpreted. It was not meant to be seen as a video of future history.

3. There is nothing in the passage that relates the Millennium to the Second Coming of Jesus.

4. There is nothing in the passage that suggests that the Millennium is on earth.

5. The main focus in this passage is on the martyrs, not on the whole church.

I suggest that for these reasons, and no doubt many others, the idea of a literal Millennium—a literal reign of Jesus on earth—based on this one passage cannot be used as the main hermeneutical key for constructing our eschatology.

Evaluation of this Approach

In evaluating this approach I hope that some of you will tell me what mistakes, weakness, and limitations you see in this approach. But let me end by pointing out briefly what I see as the *strengths* of this approach in relation to the Israeli-Palestinian conflict:

1. It is based on a *thoroughly evangelical view of the authority and inspiration of Scripture.* It cannot be rejected out of hand on the grounds that it is "liberal."

2. It is *thoroughly Christ centered* because of its emphasis on how much of the promises and prophecies in Scripture have already been fulfilled in Jesus. My personal testimony would be that study in these areas has enriched and deepened my understanding of the incarnation and the finished work of Christ.

3. Instead of giving us tidy answers on a plate, it *gives us the responsibility of interpreting and understanding recent history.* It enables us to recognize that while there is much in biblical prophecy still to be fulfilled, the Bible may not be able to help us to understand the complexities of this particular conflict. We will need to study history and international relations if we want to understand the roots of the conflict and its development over so many years.

4. It enables us to see *how to address the political and justice issues in practical ways.* There is no suggestion that we can find a simple formula from the prophetic writings, that will enable us to understand and resolve the conflict between Israel and the Palestinians. It therefore encourages us—dare I say it?—to put our theology to one side and to attempt to understand the conflict in its own terms—as a clash of nationalisms, with two peoples claiming the same piece of land for different reasons. Political problems require political solutions; and the conflict over the West Bank and East Jerusalem, for example, cannot be resolved by pointing to biblical proof texts, but only through face-to-face negotiation on the basis of international law and with the encouragement and help of the watching world.

5. It enables us to *proclaim the gospel clearly to Jews and Muslims*. Many Jews will no doubt be disappointed when Christians do not support their claims to hold onto the West Bank and when Christians even want to ask awkward questions about the very concept of a Jewish state. But instead of encouraging Jews to see the State of Israel as *a* fulfillment or *the* fulfillment of Jewish hopes, our message to the Jewish people should be that it is in the person of Jesus the Messiah that the hopes of their nation have been fulfilled—not in their return to the land and the creation of the State of Israel. Similarly, in speaking with Muslims, I find myself constantly needing to distance myself from Christian Zionism, which has become an enormous stumbling block for the gospel in the minds of Muslims.

In short, this way of interpreting Scripture enables us to read the OT through the eyes of Jesus, to read the OT through the spectacles, the glasses, of the NT writers. When we see how Jesus *has already fulfilled* so many of the hopes and dreams of Israel in the OT, we can see how, in addressing this particular conflict at this particular time in history, the followers of Jesus today can, in the spirit of the Beatitudes, *both* hunger and thirst after righteousness/justice *and* be genuine peacemakers.

BIBLIOGRAPHY

Burge, Gary M. *Whose Land? Whose Promise?: What Christians Are Not Being Told about Israel and the Palestinians.* Cleveland: Pilgrim, 2003.

Chapman, Colin. *Whose Promised Land? The Continuing Crisis over Israel and Palestine.* Oxford: Lion, 2002.

———. *Whose Holy City? Jerusalem and the Israeli-Palestinian Conflict.* Oxford: Lion, 2004.

———. *"Islamic Terrorism": Is There a Christian Response?* Grove Ethics Series. Cambridge: Grove, 2005.

Davis, W. D. *The Gospel and the Land: Early Christianity and Jewish Territorial Doctrine.* Berkeley: University of California Press, 1974.

Fisk, Robert. *The Great War for Civilisation: The Conquest of the Middle East.* London: Fourth Estate, 2005.

Gorenberg, Gershom. *The End of Days: Fundamentalism and the Struggle for the Temple Mount.* Oxford: Oxford University Press, 2002.

Hagee, John, *The Final Dawn over Jerusalem*, Nashville: Nelson, 2000.

Morris, Benny. *Righteous Victims: A History of the Zionist-Arab Conflict, 1881–1999.* London: Murray, 2000.

———. *The Birth of the Palestinian Refugee Problem Revisited.* 2nd ed. Cambridge Middle East Studies 18. Cambridge: Cambridge University Press, 2004.

Pappé, Ilan. *The Ethnic Cleansing of Palestine.* Oxford: OneWorld, 2006.

Scofield, Cyrus. *Scofield Bible Correspondence Course*, 45–46. 19th ed. Chicago: Moody Bible Institute, n.d.

Shlaim, Avi. *War and Peace in the Middle East: A Concise History*. Revised and updated. New York: Penguin, 1995.

Sizer, Stephen R. *Christian Zionism: Road Map to Armageddon?* Downer's Grove, IL: IVP Academic, 2004.

———. *Zion's Christian Soldiers? The Bible, Israel and the Church*. Nottingham, UK: InterVarsity, 2007.

Wagner, Donald E. *Dying in the Land of Promise: Palestine and Palestinian Christianity from Pentecost to 2000*. London: Melisende, 2003.

Weber, Timothy P. *On the Road to Armageddon: How Evangelicals Became Israel's Best Friend*. Grand Rapids: Baker Academic, 2005.

❖ 15 ❖

Israel

Land and People

Malcolm Hedding

"I will establish My covenant between Me and you and your descendants after you throughout their generations for an everlasting covenant, to be God to you and to your descendants after you. I will give to you and to your descendants after you, the land of your sojournings, all the land of Canaan, for an everlasting possession; and I will be their God." (Gen 17:7–8)[1]

THE DEBATE THAT RAGES over Israel's modern-day restoration is undoubtedly a heated one, and there are good, honest Christians on both sides of "the divide." It is crucial for us to make this observation because it is highly dangerous to treat each other with disdain and disrespect because we do not agree on this issue. Our salvation is not regulated by issues like this, but instead by our personal repentance and acceptance of Jesus as Lord and Savior, all based on his finished work on the cross.

THE HEART OF THE MATTER

Some Christians see no biblical significance in the modern-day restoration of Israel. For them the State of Israel is just like any other. The

1. All Scripture quotations are taken from the New King James Version (NKJV).

national destiny of the Jewish people in the Promised Land has been lost since the time of Christ because of their rejection of his messianic credentials. They believe this even though the Scriptures affirm that the promise to them in this regard is an everlasting one! Consequently, the church is exclusively the "New Israel of God," and the only hope for all men—be they Jew or Gentile—is the acceptance of the gospel.

From a certain perspective I must say that the latter statement is true. There is indeed "no other name given among men, under heaven, by which we can be saved" (Acts 4:12). We are not dual covenant by belief!

But is this the whole truth? I think not. The heart of the matter, or the real issue, is, has the everlasting promise of God in the Abrahamic Covenant, bequeathing the land of Canaan to the Jewish people, been revoked? And if so, what evidence of this "revoking" is in the Bible? In other words, the debate is about what one thinks of the Abrahamic Covenant. This alone is the heart of the matter!

THE NATURE OF THE COVENANT

First mentioned in Gen 12:1–3 and reinforced time and again through-out all of Scripture (mostly, in fact, in the New Covenant Scriptures), the Abrahamic Covenant sets aside a people and a land for the blessing of the nations: "In you all the nations of the earth will be blessed . . ." (Gen 12:3). For the Apostle Paul this was one of the earliest proclama-tions of the gospel (Gal 3:8). Thus, the Abrahamic Covenant is that great covenant of the Bible that promises salvation to a world lost in sin. It is made with Abraham and his descendants after him (Gen 17:7). It is, therefore, "the covenant of decision," and all the other great covenants of the Bible flow out of it. So, John the Baptist and even Jesus come into the world because of the promise made to Abraham in this covenant (Luke 1:54–55, 72–75). The Jewish people, as Abraham's descendants, are chosen as the servants of the covenant. In other words, the nation of Israel is not brought into existence as an end itself, but as a means to an end—the salvation of the world. They are the means by which God delivers his redemptive initiative to the world.

Jesus said, "Salvation is of the Jews" (John 4:22). Paul said, "They are the custodians of the oracles of God" and from them come the prophets, the giving of the law, the covenants and the Messiah who God blessed forever" (Rom 3:1–2; 9:1–5).

It is truly hard to believe that the covenant has been replaced in the light of all this, because if it has, then the decision to bless the whole world with salvation has also been replaced!

THE NATURE OF THE DEBATE

The debate over Israel's modern-day restoration is over the continuing power and existence of the Abrahamic Covenant. In other words, has this covenant been abolished or reconstructed, and if so, what biblical evidence is there for it?

First, the abolitionist theory—the total removal of the covenant—is not possible because of the new covenant. For instance, in Galatians 3 we are told, "if we are Christ's, then we are Abraham's children according to the promise" (Gal 3:29) Moreover, Christ redeemed us from the curse of the law "so that the blessing of Abraham" might come upon us by faith. The writer of the book of Hebrews insists that the wavering believers can trust God and his promises in the new covenant because he is faithful, completely, to his promises made in the Abrahamic Covenant (Heb 6:13–20). Hence, there is absolutely no indication that this covenant has been disempowered, replaced, or reconstructed. On the contrary, it is affirmed and established, and this after Israel's rejection of Jesus' messianic credentials! Indeed, Paul argues that it cannot be annulled (Gal 3:17), and in Romans 11 he argues that Jewish unbelief has not removed them from God's calling and purpose (Rom 11:11, 29).

Second, the more popular reconstructionist theory states that the Abrahamic Covenant has been altered or adjusted. This is also not possible. This is an argument from silence, but those who see no significance in Israel's modern-day restoration must make it. Given the overwhelming evidence in the NT, they inadvertently accuse God of lying! A covenant that promises the world salvation and promises everlasting possession of the land of Canaan to the Jewish people is not trustworthy! This is truly amazing when one considers that John the Baptist and Jesus came into the world because of this covenant and that our embracing of the Lord Jesus as Lord and Savior locates us in the promises made in it. The God we serve does not lie (Num 23:9; Titus 1:2)! Actually, according to Rom 15:8, Jesus came to confirm the promises made to the fathers, and not to reconstruct or replace them.

THE NATURE OF EVIDENCE

It has to be acknowledged by all in this debate that Jesus returns to Jerusalem (Acts 1:11). Indeed, in a mysterious way, he links this return to Jewish acceptance of his messianic credentials (Matt 23:39). As Jesus himself stated in his Olivet Discourse, one of the signs of his return is the return of the Jews to East Jerusalem (Luke 21:24). When we add to this the interesting conversation that he had with his disciples on the Mount of Olives concerning the restoration of the kingdom to Israel (Acts 1:6),[2] the picture becomes clear: that a latter day return of the Jews after AD 70 to Jerusalem is expected! On what grounds? Clearly as the NT everywhere affirms, on the grounds of an everlasting promise made to them in Abraham (Heb 6:13–20).[3]

Those embracing the reconstructionist, or replacement, view of the Abrahamic Covenant have to grapple not only with the weight of evidence in the NT, but also with the weight of evidence in the OT. Exile and correction are always followed up with a promise of restoration (Amos 9:9–15). On what grounds? The Abrahamic Covenant (Deut 30:1–10; Ps 105:7–15; Hag 3:14–15).

It is precisely here that the reconstructionists misuse Scripture. In contradiction of the context of OT Scripture, which in all cases concerning the covenant is literal, they affirm that these passages have to be read allegorically! In short they wrest from Scripture its own authority, and they assume for themselves this authority. They will decide what Scripture means. This is totally unacceptable as a method of exegesis. The truth is we are not literalists or spiritualists (subscribers to the allegorical method of interpretation) but contextualists. The context of Scripture will alone decide our exegesis of it. If we follow this erroneous method of exegesis to its logical end, we can equally assume that Jesus' death on the cross was not literal! In fact an early church heresy did precisely this. This is nothing new.

2. The theological gymnastics that some theologians perform in the quest to negate the plain meaning of this text are indeed nothing short of bizarre. When Scripture obviously and plainly challenges our "water-tight" positions, our response should be to honor it; not attempt to negate it, but rather to readjust our thinking. Scripture does not contradict itself, and when we imply that it does, we are always wrong.

3. Mainstream Christian Zionists do not support the modern-day restoration of Israel because of eschatological considerations, but because of a promise made to Abraham four thousand years ago. They are not thirsting for Armageddon, as some assert, but rather affirming the efficacy of a covenant that dominates all of Scripture.

THE NATURE OF THE DIVIDE

While the Abrahamic Covenant promises salvation to the world (Gal 3:8) and land to Israel as an everlasting possession, the Mosaic Covenant that flows out of it, demands from Israel that

1. She live out the light and blessing of God that she gives to the world (Exod 19:1–6).

2. She live out the heavenly demands of justice and righteousness (Mic 6:5–8; Exod 23:11; Isa 5:7).

Failure in these two areas would lead to correction, judgment, and exile; but not loss of possession, only loss of domicile! In all honesty, Christian Zionists fail in these areas. That is, they stress the promises of the Abrahamic Covenant but ignore the commands of the Mosaic Covenant.

How sad it is that the church can never find balance. We always think that "the other side" is wrong, when in reality we are both wrong and both right. Scripture is therefore clear that Israel's possession of the land of Canaan is unconditional and everlasting (Exod 32:13), but her domicile—i.e., privilege of living on the land of Canaan—is conditional. That is, conditional upon her righteous behavior. This includes treating the stranger with respect and justice. In this regard the church and the Christian Zionist world should find its voice. For Arabs, Palestinians, Christians, and other minorities living in the Holy Land, this is the issue. The failure of Christian Zionists to address these issues has prevented these minority groups from hearing their message. But equally, the failure of Christians who champion these issues to address the consequences of the Abrahamic Covenant adequately has diminished their voice in the Jewish world. The truth is we all need to "grow up" and be more balanced.

IN THE END

In the end Scripture affirms that Israel will exist forever as a nation before God, and he will not cut her off because of all that she has done (Jer 31:35–37). It is deeply troubling when Christians use Scripture as a weapon against each other.[4] I do not write in this way. I believe that in

---

4. A theologian that spends his life and ministry seeking to debunk the position of Christian Zionists recently stated, regarding Israel's modern day restoration, that the

the end we must all acknowledge that there are great Christians on both sides of this debate. I have set forth my position in this paper—a position I believe to be true. Truer than all of this however, is faith, hope, and love; but the greatest of these is love.

"jury is still out" concerning whether this restoration has biblical significance or not. He should stay out of this area of ministry altogether because if the "jury comes in" and affirms the biblical significance of Israel's modern day restoration he will be caught out resisting God himself. This is a highly challenging theater of ministry and we should all remember that we who have mounted this stage, as teachers, will incur a greater judgment (Jas 3:1).

❖ 16 ❖

Where Is the Promised Land?

A Covenantal Perspective

Stephen R. Sizer

THE SUBJECT OF THE land is deeply controversial and highly politicized. Even its name—Canaan, Israel, Palestine, the Promised Land—says as much about our presuppositions as our knowledge of Middle East geography: Promised Land? Promised to whom? Under what terms? For what purpose?

Let's cut to the chase. The thesis of this chapter is that the Jewish people today are not the inheritors of the land promises originally made to Abraham. This fallacy is based on a misreading of Old Testament (OT) promises without any regard to their New Testament (NT) fulfillment. Those who embrace this view today—typically called Christian Zionists—fail to recognize the continuity between God's people in the old covenant and in the new covenant. Under both covenants, membership has always been on the basis of grace and faith, not race or works. The notion that God has two "chosen" peoples, or that God has purposes for the Jewish people apart from faith in Jesus Christ, is at best deeply flawed and at worst heretical because it ignores the progressive revelation of Scripture and undermines the finished work of Christ.

Of course, God has a continuing purpose for the Jewish people; in every generation he is grafting some back into the one people of God as they come to recognize Jesus as their Lord and Savior. That is what Romans 9–11 is all about. Of course, we should pray that their eyes are opened and that in God's time he will ensure that "all Israel" is saved, for everyone who calls on the name of the Lord will indeed be saved (Rom 10:13, 11:26).[1]

In this chapter we are going to consider what the Bible actually says about the significance and purposes of the Promised Land. We will show that the land was never intended as an "everlasting possession" exclusively for the Jewish people. We will see that they were only ever, at best, temporary residents. Then we will examine the terms under which they were allowed to return from exile, and who was entitled to citizenship in the kingdom. Finally, we must, of course, consider what the Lord Jesus and the apostles have to say about all this.

But before we can turn to the Bible, we need to deal with a red herring and some most unhelpful, pejorative terms. Those who identify with Zionism and contemporary Jewish claims to the land (the borders of which they do not usually define, rather conveniently) often accuse their opponents of what is called "replacement theology." This is the idea that the church has somehow "replaced" Israel. This they claim led to all manner of evil, including the Crusades, the Spanish Inquisition, Soviet pogroms, the Nazi Holocaust, as well as contemporary anti-Semitism. Now imagine this next sentence written in capitals and in bold: The Church has not replaced Israel! I have been writing on this subject for about twenty years, and I have yet to meet anyone who believes that nonsense. It is just as absurd to believe that all who call themselves Christians are "born again," as it is to believe that all Israelites were God's "chosen people." If you are in any doubt, read Rom 2:28–29 and 4:16, where Paul addresses that question authoritatively.

The Bible actually teaches that there is a direct continuity between the remnant of Israel and the remnant of the church of Jesus Christ (Eph 2:14–18; Heb 11:39–40). If, as Paul says, Gentile believers in Jesus "though a wild olive shoot, have been grafted in among the others" (Rom 11:17), it begs the question, grafted into what? Israel of course! The church is not the "New Israel"—it is Israel. The remnant of Israel and the church are one and the same. They always have been and always will be (Rev 7:9). God has only ever had one people. God's people have never been exclusively defined in racial terms. Those who insist that this is

---

1. For what Paul means by "all Israel," see Stott, "The Place of Israel," 164–72.

the case do not know their New Testament. Worse, they are no different from white South Africans who still try to justify apartheid on biblical grounds. Zionism is just another form of racism. When Isaiah was prophesying these words, he was referring to Gentiles like me (praise God): "Let no foreigners who have bound themselves to the Lord say, 'The Lord will surely exclude me from his people' . . . And foreigners who bind themselves to the Lord to minister to him, to love the name of the Lord, and to be his servants, all who keep the Sabbath without desecrating it and who hold fast to my covenant—these I will bring to my holy mountain and give them joy in my house of prayer. Their burnt offerings and sacrifices will be accepted on my altar; for my house will be called a house of prayer for all nations" (Isa 56:3, 6–7).[2]

The promises made to Abraham are fulfilled only in those who recognize Jesus as their Lord and Savior, whether Jewish or Gentile.

> Is God the God of Jews only? Is he not the God of Gentiles too?
> Yes, of Gentiles too . . . It was not through the law that Abraham
> and his offspring received the promise that he would be heir of
> the world, but through the righteousness that comes by faith. For
> if those who depend on the law are heirs, faith means nothing
> and the promise is worthless, because the law brings wrath. And
> where there is no law there is no transgression. Therefore, the
> promise comes by faith, so that it may be by grace and may be
> guaranteed to all Abraham's offspring—not only to those who are
> of the law but also to those who have the faith of Abraham. He is
> the father of us all. As it is written: "I have made you a father of
> many nations." He is our father in the sight of God, in whom he
> believed—the God who gives life to the dead and calls into being
> things that were not. (Rom 3:29; 4:13–17; see also 1 Pet 2:9–10)

Ironically, some Zionist Christians seem to subscribe to a "replacement theology" of another kind. They believe that Israel has replaced, or soon will replace, the church. That was J. N. Darby's view: The church, he said, is merely a "parenthesis" to God's continuing purposes. His views have been popularized through the Brethren and the *Scofield Reference Bible*.

Here's a far more profound question that will test your presuppositions. Keep this in mind as you read this chapter as well as the other chapters in this book: Was the coming of the Lord Jesus Christ—his life, death, resurrection, and ascension—the fulfillment of the promises made to Abraham, or merely their postponement? You work it out. Do

---

2. All Scripture quotations are taken from the New International Version (NIV).

you see the implications? Was the mission of Jesus central or peripheral to God's continuing purposes for the Jewish people? If the promises God made to Abraham apply exclusively, unconditionally, and eternally to Jewish people, then why on earth did Jesus die on the cross? Now let us look at the Bible together.

THE SIGNIFICANCE AND PURPOSES OF THE PROMISED LAND

It is ironic that God chose a Gentile called Abram, from what is Iraq today, to be the father of his people: "I will establish my covenant as an everlasting covenant between me and you and your descendants after you for the generations to come, to be your God . . . The whole land of Canaan, where you are now an alien, I will give as an everlasting possession to you and your descendants after you; and I will be their God" (Gen 17:7–8).

Fast-forward a few centuries, and the hope of a land of their own remained strong, as God's people languished as slaves in Egypt and then during their long wilderness travels. The realization of the promise of land with definite boundaries demonstrated that God was trustworthy, and that he cared for those who called upon his name (see Gen 26:3–5; Exod 6:1–8; Josh 24:11–27). Psalm 105 is an example of where God's promises concerning the land were remembered:

> O descendants of Abraham his servant, O sons of Jacob, his
> chosen ones.
> He is the LORD our God; his judgments are in all the earth.
> He remembers his covenant forever,
> the word he commanded, for a thousand generations,
> the promise he made with Abraham,
> the oath he swore to Isaac.
> He confirmed it to Jacob as a decree,
> to Israel as an everlasting covenant:
> "To you I will give the land of Canaan as the portion you will
> inherit." (Ps 105:6–11)

WHAT THEN ARE THE BOUNDARIES OF ISRAEL?

Zionists invariably claim considerably larger borders for Israel than those presently under military occupation in the Golan and West Bank.

The boundaries of the land God promised to Abraham and his descendents are mentioned in Genesis 15: "On that day the LORD made a covenant with Abram and said, 'To your descendants I give this land, from the river of Egypt to the great river, the Euphrates'" (Gen 15:18). If these boundaries were applied today, parts of Egypt, Lebanon, Syria, Jordan, Palestine, Iraq, Kuwait, and Saudi Arabia would be incorporated.

While most secular Israelis today would not insist on these "biblical" borders, the founders of Zionism, including Theodore Herzl and David Ben-Gurion, certainly did. Perhaps that is why, after more than sixty years since the foundation of their state, every single Israeli government has avoided becoming tied down to any particular borders. This is the principal reason for the ongoing Arab-Israeli conflict. Until Israel withdraws from land stolen in 1967, it will never enjoy peace with its neighbors. And yet, under King Solomon, the boundaries of Israel did indeed extend from Egypt to the Euphrates. The book of First Kings uses the metaphor of sand on the seashore from Genesis 22:17 to show that the boundaries of Solomon's kingdom were the fulfillment of the promises made to Abraham (1 Kgs 4:20–21, 24). The question remains: Was that promise ever intended to be everlasting?

WAS THE LAND AN EVERLASTING POSSESSION?

God brought the Israelites into the land of Canaan to further his redemptive plan for the world, not because of their size or significance. Neither was the land a reward for good behavior (Deut 7:7). Just the reverse is true. God describes them as a "stiff-necked people" (Deut 9:5–6). He repeatedly insisted that continued residence was conditional because, ultimately, they and the land belonged to God. For example, "The land must not be sold permanently, because the land is mine and you are but aliens and my tenants" (Lev 25:23). Notice the intensity of Jeremiah's prophecy: "I brought you into a fertile land to eat its fruit and rich produce. But you came and defiled my land and made my inheritance detestable" (Jer 2:7). It is God's land, not theirs. Because the land belongs to God, they could not buy or sell it permanently. That was the purpose of the year of Jubilee. "The earth is the Lord's and everything in it" (Ps 24:1). The Scriptures are very clear: Residence in the land was always conditional: "If the LORD your God enlarges your territory, as he promised on oath to your ancestors, and gives you the whole land he promised them, because you carefully follow all these laws I command you today—to love the LORD your God and to walk always in obedience to him" (Deut 19:8–9).

Did you notice the "ifs" and the "because"? The promises concerning the land were never unconditional. True, in Gen 17:8 the land is described as "an everlasting possession," but in the very next verse the Lord adds a conditional clause—circumcision. Other conditions are attached by Joshua. In his final speech he warns, "If you violate the covenant of the LORD your God, which he commanded you, and go and serve other gods and bow down to them, the LORD's anger will burn against you, and you will quickly perish from the good land he has given you" (Josh 23:16).

The prophets reinforce this same message of conditionality. Jeremiah, for example, warns, "Through your own fault you will lose the inheritance I gave you. I will enslave you to your enemies in a land you do not know, for you have kindled my anger, and it will burn forever" (Jer 7:4).

Thankfully, God's anger did not literally "burn forever" against the Jewish people. He sent Jesus to take their punishment and ours upon himself (Isa 53:4–6). Faith in Jesus now becomes the sole criterion for receiving the inheritance promised (John 15; Acts 3:22–25: Heb 11:13–16). While the boundaries of the land given to Abraham in Genesis 15 are clear, as are the conditions given for residence, the question remains, for whom was the land intended?

TO WHOM WAS THE LAND ENTRUSTED?

The myth of racial purity is nothing new, nor is the desire to exclude those deemed inferior. This is particularly true today in Israel, which is being increasingly redefined as a Jewish state. The rights of Arab-Israeli citizens are being eroded. Surprisingly perhaps, the Old Testament anticipates and repudiates the racist assumptions inherent within Zionism. Israel as a nation was never narrowly restricted to those who were the physical descendants of the twelve sons of Jacob. Israel always incorporated people of other races and this extended, not just to their identity and right of residence, but also to the inheritance of land. Moses, for example, warned against racial exclusivity: "Do not abhor an Edomite, for he is your brother. Do not abhor an Egyptian, because you lived as an alien in his country. The third generation of children born to them may enter the assembly of the LORD" (Deut 23:7–8).

The Edomites were descended from Esau and lived in what is today the Negev and Southern Jordan. King David, similarly, looked forward to the day when other races including Egyptians (from Rahab), Iraqis (from Babylon), Palestinians (from Philistia), Lebanese (from Tyre), and Africans (from Cush) would have the same identity and privileges as the Israelites: "I will record Rahab and Babylon among those who acknowl-edge me—Philistia too, and Tyre, along with Cush" (Ps 87:4). The only criterion for citizenship is faith. Scripture is clear: God welcomes people of all races into his family, all "who acknowledge me." Under the Second Exodus, which was considered greater than the first, interestingly (Jer 23:7–8), when God's people returned from exile in Babylon, God specif-ically instructs them to share the land and give an inheritance to people of other races who trust in him: "'You are to allot it as an inheritance for yourselves and for the aliens who have settled among you and who have children. You are to consider them as native-born Israelites; along with you they are to be allotted an inheritance among the tribes of Israel. In whatever tribe the alien settles, there you are to give him his inheritance,' declares the Sovereign Lord" (Ezek 47:22–23). Those of other races, therefore, had the same rights as "native Israelites." God's people have always been inclusive—never based on race. The Promised Land under the old covenant was intended by God to be shared.

WHAT IS THE NEW TESTAMENT PERSPECTIVE?

Clearly the aspirations of those seeking a Messiah had political overtones. The Jews longed for a Messiah to liberate them from the humiliation of foreign domination (Luke 1:68–79; John 6:14–15). This is why, not know-ing it was Jesus they were talking to, the disciples embarrass themselves by lamenting his failure to restore political sovereignty to the Jews: "we had hoped that he was the one who was going to redeem Israel" (Luke 24:21). And even after they recognize the risen Lord Jesus, they are still hanker-ing for a political solution, "Lord, are you at this time going to restore the kingdom to Israel?" (Acts 1:6) It is interesting that in this question, the Apostles at least see "Israel" as having a separate existence as a people apart from political sovereignty. John Calvin comments, "There are as many mistakes in this question as there are words."[3] John Stott elaborates why. He points out the catalogue of errors their question contains and lays to rest the silly notion that Jesus was ambiguous or sympathetic to their political aspirations.

> The mistake they made was to misunderstand both the nature of the kingdom and the relation between the kingdom and the Spirit. Their question must have filled Jesus with dismay. Were they still so lacking in perception? . . . The verb, the noun, and the adverb of their sentence all betray doctrinal confusion about the kingdom. For the verb *restore* shows they were expecting a political and territorial kingdom; the noun *Israel* that they were expecting a national kingdom; and the adverbial clause at this time that they were expecting its immediate establishment. In his reply (7–8) Jesus corrected their mistaken notions of the kingdom's nature, extent and arrival.[4]

Pentecost was still a few weeks away. The Holy Spirit had not been given. So the disciples could be forgiven for aligning themselves more with the contemporary Zealots than with the Old Testament covenants.

In their shoes we too might have longed for the reestablishment of the monarchy and liberation from Roman occupation. But the fact is that Jesus repudiated the notion of an earthly and nationalistic kingdom on more than one occasion (see John 6:15; 18:36). No, Jesus has a very different assignment for them: "It is not for you to know the times or dates the Father has set by his own authority. But you will receive power when the Holy Spirit comes on you; and you will be my witnesses in Jerusalem, and in all Judea and Samaria, and to the ends of the earth" (Acts 1:8). To borrow from John Stott, the kingdom that Jesus inaugurated would be instead spiritual in character, international in membership, and gradual in expansion. To realize their mission, the apostles must literally turn their backs on Jerusalem and become exiles from the land in order to be Christ's ambassadors to the world (Matt 20:20–28; 2 Cor 5:20–21). While the Lord Jesus promised to be with them, they were never instructed to return.

No, the New Testament knows nothing of the contemporary preoccupation, common among Christian Zionists, with exclusive claims to real estate; least of all with land that has been stolen from others.

---

3. Calvin, *Acts*, 29.

4. Stott, *The Message of Acts*, 40–41.

As John Stott says, "Christ's kingdom, while not incompatible with patriotism, tolerates no narrow nationalisms."[5] Instead, Jesus redefines the boundaries of his kingdom to embrace the entire world. In the Sermon on the Mount, for example, Jesus takes a promise made to the Jewish people concerning the land, in Ps 37:11, and applies it to his own followers living anywhere in the world. "Blessed are the meek, for they will inherit the earth" (Matt 5:5). Although the word can indeed mean "soil" or "the whole earth," by citing Psalm 37, Jesus is clearly referring to the land of Israel. This is not replacement theology but fulfillment theology. The promise of Psalm 37 is interpreted and applied by the Lord Jesus to his own followers.

THE LAND PROMISES FULFILLED IN THE CHURCH

And this is not a case of "pleading from silence;" just the reverse. From Pentecost onwards, Old Testament language concerning the land is invested with new meaning and applied to the church. For example, Peter explains how the covenantal promises made to Abraham (Gen 12:3; 22:18) and reiterated by the Prophets were being fulfilled among those who recognized God's redemptive plan in the Lord Jesus: "Indeed, all the prophets from Samuel on, as many as have spoken, have foretold these days. And you are heirs of the prophets and of the covenant God made with your fathers. He said to Abraham, 'Through your offspring all peoples on earth will be blessed'" (Acts 3:24–25).

There could be no going back. In his First Epistle, Peter describes Christ's followers as, "God's elect, strangers in the world, scattered" (1 Pet 1:1), evoking memories of Abraham's journeying (see Gen 23:4) and the Jewish exiles in Babylon (see Ps 137:4). He assures them that their inheritance, unlike the land, "can never perish, spoil or fade" (1 Pet 1:4). Paul asserts the same understanding when he insists, "If you belong to Christ, then you are Abraham's seed, and heirs according to the promise" (Gal 3:29).

WHERE THEN IS THE PROMISED LAND?

The Bible predicts a glorious future for the Jewish people, but not back in the land. God's plan is to bring people of all nations, Jews and Gentiles,

---

5. Ibid., 43.

into one people of God through the new covenant achieved in the death and resurrection of the Lord Jesus Christ. Frequently, Christian Zionists refer to Romans 9–11 as if these chapters warrant Zionism or predict the contemporary State of Israel. True, Paul insists that God has not rejected the Jewish people or the covenant promises. On the contrary, says Paul, they have and are being fulfilled. But notice the criterion: "It is not the natural children who are God's children, but it is the children of the promise who are regarded as Abraham's offspring" (Rom 9:8). In the next chapter he reinforces this conviction: "For there is no difference between Jew and Gentile—the same Lord is Lord of all and richly blesses all who call on him, for, 'Everyone who calls on the name of the Lord will be saved'" (Rom 10:12–13). The children of Abraham, therefore, are those Jews and Gentiles who through faith in Christ have been made righteous. Together, they have been made "heirs of God and co-heirs with Christ" (Rom 8:17). The kingdom that Jesus heralded is now internal not territorial. It is universal, not tribal. When the Pharisees asked Jesus when the kingdom of God would appear, he replied, "The kingdom of God does not come with your careful observation, nor will people say, 'Here it is,' or 'There it is,' because the kingdom of God is within you" (Luke 17:20–21).

Jesus shatters the racial straight jacket of Zionism today and liberates the real meaning of the covenant made with Abraham. The inheritance of the saints was and remains ultimately never an "everlasting" share of territory in Palestine but an eternal place in heaven. The book of Hebrews shows that even Abraham, the Patriarchs, and later Hebrew saints looked beyond Canaan to "another" country, a better one, where all the covenant promises of God will finally be fulfilled:

> For he was looking forward to the city with foundations, whose architect and builder is God . . . And so from this one man, and he as good as dead, came descendants as numerous as the stars in the sky and as countless as the sand on the seashore. All these people were still living by faith when they died. They did not receive the things promised; they only saw them and welcomed them from a distance, admitting that they were foreigners and strangers on earth. People who say such things show that they are looking for a country of their own. If they had been thinking of the country they had left, they would have had opportunity to return. Instead, they were longing for a better country—a heavenly one . . . These were all commended for their faith, yet none of them received what had been promised. God had planned

something better for us so that only together with us would they be made perfect. (Heb 11:10–16, 39–40)

Like an old wineskin, or a temporary landing strip, the land has served its purpose: It provided a specific location where God could enter space time history; a place where God could reveal himself progressively and prophetically; a place in which he could nurture a people for his own to be a light to the other nations; a setting for the life, death, resurrection, and ascension of the Lord Jesus Christ; a base for the training, then commissioning of the apostles; and from Pentecost, a strategic launch pad for God's rescue mission to the whole world.

As the apostles were scattered, exiled from the land, ambassadors to the whole world, the land itself became irrelevant to God's ongoing redemptive purposes.

The Promised Land
Like an airport runway

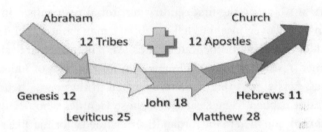

So where then is the Promised Land? Simple: Wherever God's people now dwell (John 4:23–24; Acts 20:32), and it is ultimately being prepared for us in heaven (Heb 11:16; Rev 21:1–4)!

BIBLIOGRAPHY

Burge, Gary M. *Jesus and the Land.* London: SPCK, 2010.

Calvin, John. *The Acts of the Apostles 1–13.* Calvin's Commentaries 6. Edinburgh: St Andrew's University Press, 1965.

Johnston, Philip, and Peter Walker, editors. *The Land of Promise.* Downer's Grove, IL: InterVarsity, 2000.

Sizer, Stephen R. *Christian Zionism: Road Map to Armageddon?* Downer's Grove, IL: IVP Academic, 2004.

———, editor. *Zion's Christian Soldiers? The Bible, Israel, and the Church.* Nottingham: InterVarsity, 2007.

Stott, John R. W. *The Message of Acts.* Bible Speaks Today. Leicester: InterVarsity, 1990.

———. "The Place of Israel," In *Zion's Christian Soldiers? The Bible, Israel, and the Church,* edited by Stephen R. Sizer, 164–72. Nottingham: InterVarsity, 2007.

❖ 17 ❖

Jesus and the Land[1]

Gary M. Burge

IN THE MID-40S OF the first century, territorial nationalism in Judea began to boil over. Josephus tells us about a man named Theudas who lived under the Roman Procurator Fadus. And Theudas had decided to wed armed resistance to a religious vision for the land of Judea (*Ant.* 20:5.1; cf. Acts 5:33–39). This land belonged to the Jews, Theudas argued, and it needed to be cleansed of those Gentiles who occupied it. Theudas took 400 men to the Jordan River, claimed a Joshua-like reentry that would reconquer the land, and decided he would defeat Rome as if they were the new Canaanites. The Procurator Fadus would have none of it. His cavalry met the Jewish rebels in the desert, killed them, captured Theudas, and brought his head to Jerusalem as a trophy.

Two years later Rome's next Procurator, Alexander, began re-registering Judea for tax purposes. Again, violent resistance erupted. Josephus describes a man named Judas the Galilean who saw this act as so offensive, he was willing to die in war to stop it (*Ant.* 20:5.2; cf. 18:1.6). *If the land were to provide revenue, it belonged to Israel and the temple, not a Gentile occupier. God was the only ruler of the land, and any who claimed sovereign rule usurped his role.* The Romans quickly and

---

1. This chapter is excerpted from Gary Burge, *Jesus and the Land: The New Testament Challenge to "Holy" Land Theology* (Grand Rapids: Baker Academic, 2010) 25–40. Used by permission. All Scripture quotations are taken from the New Revised Standard Version (NRSV) unless otherwise indicated.

easily killed Judas as well as his sons, and this stood as a second warning to the Jews about who owned the land.

These two stories provide a convenient window into the nationalistic tensions at work in first-century Judea. Ownership and control of the land by the Jews had been frustrated since the Roman conquest in 63 BC. The great accomplishments of the Maccabees in the second century BC, driving Greek occupiers from the Judean mountains and establishing a Jewish kingdom, had now been lost to Rome. Theologies of land restoration—yearnings for a new and successful era of Jewish sovereignty over its ethnic heritage—were everywhere in the wind.

Even the NT points to these aspirations. In Acts 1:6 the apostles ask Jesus a seemingly innocent question: "Lord, will you at this time restore the kingdom to Israel?" Now that the power of Jesus has been seen in his resurrection, their assumptions are clear. *This messianic power must conclude with the fulfillment of Israel's national vision.* Jesus had spoken about the kingdom; did this not include the kingdom of Israel? The land would be returned to its rightful owners. The current exile, a Gentile exile as dreadful as that in Babylon, should end. A Jewish kingdom would prevail, and Rome would leave.

The same frustrated hope is recorded in Luke 24:21. In despair the disciples at Emmaus tell the unrecognized resurrected Jesus that their dreams had been dashed at the cross: "We had hoped he was the one to redeem Israel." This desire fits well with the stresses felt throughout the country. Redemption would come only when the land itself would be returned to the Jews and the foreign occupation ended. "Redeeming Israel" does not refer to the salvation of souls but to the restoration of the nation, the cleansing of the land, and a divinely endorsed inheritance of the Holy Land that was deeply woven into the fabric of Israel's religious life.

If such concerns about Jewish identity and the land were widespread in early first-century Judea, Jesus was surely aware of these debates and their competing visions. A faith centered on Torah, temple, and land could not ignore the problem of occupation. Jesus' contemporaries knew three alternatives that witnessed regular debate: cooperation, separation, or resistance. One could cooperate with the occupation and hope that Rome would ease its control and the imperial demands would relax over time. And who knows, perhaps the province could even benefit from Augustus's *Pax Romana*. Why not try to make it work? Herod and his dynasty had pursued this model fully. Any Roman ship arriving at the famed port of Caesarea Maritima in Judea was greeted not only by state-of-the-art anchorage with marble quays and tapestry awnings, but also by an expansive marble temple for Augustus that loomed over the breakwater. Roman public architecture, a theater seating thirty-five hundred, and a hippodrome hosting twenty thousand spectators for horse or chariot racing confirmed loudly that this was a *Roman* port. Judea had never seen anything like this. Herod modeled the cooperative outlook on the Roman occupation. Even two of Herod's sons, Herod Antipas and Philip (by his wife Cleopatra), were educated in Rome (*Ant.* 17:20).

On the other hand, one could separate from this wretched occupation and build an alternate community where believers could pray for relief and await God's intervention. The sectarians of Qumran near the Dead Sea pursued this course. Jerusalem and the land had become intolerably unclean not only through the Romans, but also through those Jews who were running Jerusalem and flirting with the occupiers. Life in the land had become impossible. In the wilderness where purity was still possible, they prepared a place for the Lord. And for them an eschatological solution brought resolution. Qumran's *War Scroll* outlined how God would bring about his own intervention and the task of the believer was waiting and preparing. Its opening lines (1QM 1:1–7) lay out the contours of the final battle between the "sons of light" and the "sons of darkness." The opponents are the *Kittim* (a frequent code for the Romans) and Jews who have ignored the life of righteousness by aligning themselves with the "sons of darkness."

Or one could resist by refusing to pay taxes or even by taking up the sword. If Judas Maccabeus had done it in the second century BC, why could not Israel be successful again? We might call this a reborn "Maccabean Vision"—a religiously fired Jewish nationalism that saw its first order of business as the cleansing of the land. This was no doubt the vision of Judas the Galilean and Theudas. And it is echoed in the messianic *Psalms of Solomon*: "Wisely and righteously let him [messiah] expel sinners from *the inheritance*, and destroy the sinner's pride as a potter's vessel. With a rod of iron may he break in pieces all their resources. Let him destroy the lawless gentiles by the word of his mouth" (17:21–24, emphasis added). But this was a dangerous vision that ultimately led to the destruction of Jerusalem and the devastation of the nation by war. Indeed, the land was "cleansed," but Rome did the cleansing with its own legions by devastating Judaism beyond repair.

Do the gospels give us any insight into Jesus' attitudes?

LAND AND POLITICS IN JESUS' WORLD

In the volatile climate of first-century politics, among a people living under the harsh realities of the Roman military occupation, we should not expect a public teacher like Jesus to speak explicitly about the land and its rightful owners. To exhibit resistance to Rome is to run up against a skilled army that is watching for signs of subversion. To show cooperation with Rome is to run up against fellow Jews for whom such sympathies are intolerable. In every explosive political context—both today and in antiquity—people with opinions must remain opaque to the many listeners standing in the shadows who are choosing sides.

When W. D. Davies wrote *The Gospel and the Land* in 1974, he was keenly aware of the old thesis that had been renewed by S. G. F. Brandon in 1967.[2] In *Jesus and the Zealots*, Brandon argued, not only that Jesus objected to the political occupation of Rome, but that he was publicly sympathetic with a movement called the Zealots, who advocated open resistance. However, the evangelists who wrote their Gospels following the war of 66–70 were eager to cooperate with the empire, disassociate themselves from recalcitrant Judaism, and tame Jesus' image as a political activist. Thus Brandon discerned multiple layers in the Gospel tradition that betrayed not only the evangelists' correction, but also the truer, authentic portrait of a fully political Jesus.

Since 1967, Brandon's thesis has not won the day despite efforts of scholars such as J. D. Crossan.[3] His critical reconstruction of Jesus may owe as much to the political and social upheavals of the 1960s as it does to an honest exegesis of gospel texts. From the early work of Davies to the more recent efforts of N. T. Wright,[4] a new portrait has emerged that has added nuance and complexity to Jesus' view of the land. Indeed politics and land claims were a potent religious force in the first century, but Jesus' relationship to them held an allusive subtlety that requires close examination.

Two initial observations deserve attention. First, Jesus is surprisingly silent with regard to the territorial aspirations and politics of his

2. See Brandon, *Jesus and the Zealots*.

3. Crossan, *The Historical Jesus*.

4. Wright, *Jesus and the Victory*, 83–91; see also Horbury, "Christ as Brigand," 183–95.

day. The national ambitions of Judaism under Rome constantly pressed Jewish leadership to respond. Either Judea was capitulating to the occupation or Judea had to organize to defeat it. However, Jesus is oddly silent about the debate. Moreover, Jesus is curiously receptive to contact with the occupiers. In Matt 8:5–13, he responds to the request of a Roman centurion whose valued servant was ill. Here we find no repulsion of the soldier, no condemnation of Gentiles, but rather we find receptivity and welcome. He says of the Roman: "Not even in Israel have I found such faith" (8:10). What emerges is a general impression that Israel's national ambitions tied to reclaiming the land live on the margin of Jesus' thinking.

There was a Roman law (now well known) that if a Roman soldier wanted a defeated subject to be his porter, he could demand it. This rule included use of the person's donkey and cart as well. But the law limited this service to one (Roman) mile. Although this provision for forced labor was deeply resented, in Matt 5:41 Jesus announces that if you are told to go one mile in such a situation, *go two miles*! And he says more. In Matt 5:44 he commands his followers to love "their enemies" and pray for those who persecute them. These are certain allusions to the Roman occupation that not only deny political resistance but also were no doubt inexplicable to Jesus' followers. In a word, Jesus is strangely unsympathetic with attitudes that would demand resistance to Rome and the struggle for the land as religious duties.

However, in an important passage, Jesus is tested by those who chose aggressive resistance.

Following the removal of the corrupt and violent Archelaus (son of Herod I) in AD 6, the subsequent political disruption that brought direct Roman rule to the land inspired new forms of Jewish resistance. Instability and reorganization in AD 6 presented an ideal opportunity for this agenda.

For many Jews, Roman taxation had become a burdensome symbol of Israel's enslavement, and it was widely believed that it was the basis of Judea's financial value to the empire. In AD 6, tax revolts sought to lessen this value. Mark 12:13–17 records Jesus confronted by "Pharisees and Herodians," two groups with deep, though different, concerns about the occupation. Their question concerning taxes ("Should we pay taxes to Caesar or not?") is not innocent but a veiled, opaque public test. When Jesus inspects a coin, sees Caesar's image, and directs them to "render to

Caesar what is his," we can fairly interpret this as a refusal to support the tax revolt. Some scholars see this revolt as the beginning of the Zealot movement (*Ant.* 18.1) and this passage as Jesus' explicit denial of their agenda. The kingdom he advocated could not be co-opted by a nationalistic movement that sought to win back the land by force.[5]

Matthew records an even more direct test. In Matt 17:24–27 tax collectors ask Jesus' disciples if he "pays the tax." In this case it is the annual temple tax, an entirely different matter from the tax revolt against Rome. Nevertheless the half-shekel tax was controversial and denied by some (including Qumran) as an invention of the Pharisees. Jesus acknowledges that such taxes are the prerogative of kings, who place these burdens particularly on those who are not their sons. Jesus suggests that sons (of kings) do not pay such taxes, but he will pay so as not to bring offense. Jesus then performs a miracle where Simon Peter finds a coin in a fish's mouth and pays up. Once again Jesus does what is required, conforming to those "kings" who would levy taxes. Cooperation is chosen above resistance; compliance is endorsed over refusal.

CONTINUITY AND DISCONTINUITY

Aside from the explicit question of resistance, there are signs in Jesus' ministry where he shows genuine continuity with the Jews' strong identity with the land.[6] His life begins and ends within the ancient inheritance treasured in Judaism's Scriptures. His birth in Bethlehem evokes memories not only of David and his history there (1 Sam 17) but also the many OT references to the historic Judean village south of Jerusalem. In the Hebrew Scriptures Bethlehem is mentioned forty times. Jesus is also known as a Nazarene, from the city of Nazareth in southern (lower) Galilee, his childhood home, and while the OT does not refer to this village—and it is also absent in Josephus and the Talmud—still, excavations suggest that an obscure village did exist in the city's current location with a population of perhaps 500 to 1,500. From here, Jesus moved to Capernaum, a well-known fishing village on Galilee's northwest shore and a crossroads for much east-west traffic in the north. Excavations in the last twenty-five years have uncovered the remains of the first-century

5. See the classic treatment of Stauffer, "Christ and the Story of the Tribute Money," 112–37.

6. See Marchadour and Neuhaus, *The Land, the Bible, and History*, 61–77.

basalt walls of the community that lived at the site. And after Galilee, his life ended in Jerusalem, Israel's most sacred city. This has left many NT scholars with an interesting question: Did Jesus envision a mission to the Gentiles, or did he see his work as permanently limited to Judaism?[7]

His public story began at the Jordan River, moved into the wilderness, and then began in earnest in Galilee. This movement beginning at the Jordan evoked memories of Israel's beginning with Joshua. (The name "Jesus" stems from the Hebrew "Joshua.") Was this Israel begun anew? Was this a revived Jewish claim on the land? Jesus' continuation into the wilderness further provoked this parallel with Israel. His selection of *twelve* apostles pushed it yet further. *Were these the newly imagined twelve tribes?* In some manner Jesus was reliving Israelite history, restoring Israelite hope for a new life in the Land of Promise. And all of this would take place within Israel's ancient borders. From Capernaum Jesus launched his public ministry in Galilee and with very few exceptions, he worked within the *sacred geography* of Israel's Promised Land. Therefore we might say that Jesus' identity and outlook were formed in the land (not the Diaspora or land outside Israel); and he sought to realize his mission within the land (not within the empire).

Jesus' continuity with Israel's geographical consciousness can also be found in his command to the Twelve when they are sent out: "Go nowhere among [Gk: *in the way of*; *eis hodon*] the Gentiles, and enter no town of the Samaritans, but go rather to the lost sheep of the house of Israel" (Matt 10:5–6; cf. Mark 6:7–11; Luke 9:1–5; 10:1–12). Therefore their efforts must be limited to the cultural perimeters of Judaism, no doubt as it was located in the land. Jesus' instruction may be an order to remain in Galilee, avoiding the south (Samaria) and the perimeters of the region where concentrations of Gentiles would be found. Nevertheless, it is clear that the full embrace of Gentile work beyond the boundaries of the land will not happen until following the resurrection (Matt 28:19). This was a vision that was realized in the efforts of the early church.

While Jesus lived his life fully respecting Israel's geographical location, there are also signals that he would not be limited to the national constraints that this entailed. In other words, there was also *discontinuity* with the Israelite commitment to the land. In Matthew, non-Jewish magi

---

7. Schnabel, *Early Christian Mission*, 327–82. Schnabel rejects the critical consensus and argues that Jesus was indeed convinced that mission must go beyond the confines of traditional Judea.

welcome the Messiah (2:1–12), Galilee is "Galilee of *the nations*" (4:15), Jesus is greeted and followed in Syria as well as in the Decapolis (4:24–25), and he ministers on the east side of the Sea of Galilee, where the Gentile demoniac was healed (8:28–34, possibly from Gentile Gerasa or Gadara).[8] According to Mark, Jesus' feeding miracle (Mark 6:30–44) is duplicated on the lake's east side among Gentiles (Mark 8:1–10). Among the Jews (on the west side) he feeds five thousand; among the Gentiles of the Decapolis (on the east side), he feeds four thousand.

One striking aspect of Jesus' ministry is that he even locates it in Galilee at all. This region in the far north was considered *different* from Israel's Judean heartland. During the eighth century BC, the Jewish population there had been deported by the Assyrians only to be replaced by foreigners who had been resettled themselves (2 Kgs 15:29). During the Maccabean era (the second century BC), the region was so Hellenized that the Jewish army in Judea sent three thousand troops north to "purify" the land, kill thousands of Gentiles, and transfer the remaining Jews to the south "with great rejoicing" (1 Macc 5:23). By the NT era Hellenization only increased—witness new Greek cities in Ptolemais, Scythopolis, and Sepphoris—and this fueled suspicion about Jewish life there. These cities were mirrored by great Hellenistic cities further east: Gadara, on the Yarmuk River; Pella, facing Scythopolis; and Gerasa, on the high eastern desert plateau. Every fisherman on the Sea of Galilee could see Hippos poised on a prominent shore-side eastern hill. As Matthew reminds us (citing Isaiah), this was a land of "darkness," a region in the "shadow of death," a place of Gentiles (Matt 5:16–17). Why does not Jesus work from Jerusalem? Why not devote himself to Judea? Why launch his efforts from the questionable geographic margin?

One story in Luke illustrates well the tensions inherent in Jesus' willingness to consider favorably those outside Israel's geographic parameters. Jesus' inaugural presentation in the Nazareth synagogue began when he read messianic texts from Isaiah (Luke 4:16–30). And yet, the resistance of the town to his ministry led to a startling warning. In Elijah's day there was a famine and Elijah was sent exclusively to Zarephath, *a widow in the land of Sidon*. In Elisha's day when leprosy threatened Israel's life, Elisha was sent exclusively to Naaman, *a man from Syria.* That day the reaction of the crowd was swift and sure; they attempted to kill Jesus not because of his claim to messianic status through Isaiah,

---

8. See France, *The Gospel of Matthew*, 381.

but due to his seeming disregard for the exclusivity of Israelite privilege in their land.

We find therefore both surprise and reassurance in the conduct of Jesus' ministry as it regards the land. No record gives us an account of Jesus crossing the Mediterranean to enter Jewish communities in places like Alexandria, Egypt, or traveling north to Antioch, Syria. No record tells us that he entered Gentile enclaves within the land such as Caesarea-Maritima, Scythopolis, Sepphoris, Tiberius, Ptolemais, Gadara, or Hippos. (His arrival in Bethsaida and Caesarea-Philippi may be the sole exception.) He remains in Galilee rather than the Jewish heartland, yet he comes to Jerusalem, respecting its festivals. He appears to respect the territorial limits to Jewish life in the land. And yet, having said that, Jesus was willing to step outside those limits in ways that both surprise and disturb his audiences.

This is also true of Jesus' central message: the kingdom of God. While he announces the kingdom's arrival within the land, in no manner is the kingdom linked to the territorial aspirations of Judaism as were the "kingdom aspirations" of the Maccabean era. Jesus' kingdom cannot be nuanced into a political movement that might reflect Jewish nationalism. And yet the kingdom belongs first to the Jews. Similarly Jesus shows utmost respect for Jerusalem, the city at the center of Jewish territorial commitment. And yet he can still call for its severe cleansing (Mark 11) and talk about its destruction stone by stone (Mark 13:2). The call from the popular territorial theologies was for the recovery of the temple not its destruction. Jesus is at odds with the "land theologies" of his day.

CRITICAL PASSAGES IN THE GOSPELS

But can we find explicit passages in the gospels where Jesus and the Gospel writers exhibit an obvious consciousness of the land and an awareness of what the religious and political climate called for? For some scholars the land itself has become a literary metaphor in the Gospels for how the spiritual formation is perceived. James Resseguie has argued that for Luke, the desert, the inland sea (Galilee), and the mountains each symbolize some feature of connection with God. They are—respectively—a place of testing, a place without control (which God may control), and a place of refuge. And above all, the Jordan

River is a boundary that separates the desert from the Promised Land itself.[9] Seven passages deserve note.

1. Matthew 5:5

In the well-known Sermon on the Mount (Matt 5–7), Jesus describes a radical inversion of religious values. Enemies should be loved; mourners comforted; and the persecuted vindicated. Luke distributes these themes elsewhere: losing life will save it (9:24); the first will be last (13:30); the humbled exalted (14:11). This reversal of religious priority is the key to understanding Matt 5:5, "Blessed are the meek, for they shall inherit the earth." Here Jesus is echoing Ps 37:11 (which Matthew shapes using the Greek Old Testament, LXX Ps 36:11) where the land, inheritance, and the "meek" are placed in juxtaposition.[10]

Psalm 37 describes the reversal of fortunes that will accompany God's activity within Israel. Those who are wicked and angry represent the unrighteous, who will share little of Israel's inheritance. They employ the sword and aggression in order to take what they think is theirs. And yet, God is not on their side. He will give the land to those who trust in him (37:3), who delight in his ways (37:4), remain patient (37:7), and are righteous (37:29). Those who are *meek* will be delighted when they gain the land (37:11) because they are the ones who least expect it, and who have been defeated by the strong and the powerful. Psalm 37 describes those who are greedy and those who are generous (37:21); those who grasp after what they want and those wait for God to supply it. The land will belong to the latter.

The Greek term *praus*; (here *hoi praeis*) refers to those who are humble and unassuming, and it is used both in Matt 5:5 as well as the Greek version of Psalm 37. And yet the context in the psalm does not refer to submissiveness as a temperament but to those who have been humbled by the circumstances of their lives and do not react in anger. "In view are not persons who are submissive, mild, unassertive, but those who are humble in the sense of being oppressed (hence, 'have been humbled')."[11] In Matthew's only other two uses of the adjective, this describes the ministry of Jesus himself (11:29; 21:5). First Peter 3:4 applies

---

9. Resseguie, *Spiritual Landscape*.

10. France, *The Gospel of Matthew*, 166.

11. Hagner, *Matthew 1–13*, 92.

this to Christians. In later Christian literature it should be an attribute of Christian leaders (*Didache* 15:1).

The gift such people receive is the land [Gk, *gē*]. This flexible word (used 250 times in the NT alone) can refer to the soil (Matt 13:5), a region—"land of Judea" (Matt 2:6), the earth itself (Matt 5:18, 35), or the inhabited world (Luke 21:35). It can also refer to the land of Israel (Luke 4:25). But since its use here in Matthew 5 springs from Psalm 37, Jesus' reference would have gained immediate notice among his listeners as a reference not to the entire *earth* but to the Land of Promise, the Holy Land. Moreover Jesus refers to these recipients as *inheritors* of this land. This is yet another potent term for Jesus' audience. This word [*klēronomeo*, to inherit; *klēros*, inheritance] was commonly used to refer to the assignment of land in the OT promises.[12] When "inheritance" is joined to "land," the allusion is unmistakable: this is the *land of inheritance*, the land of promise. "Blessed are the meek for they shall inherit the land."[13]

This leads to a scandal at the heart of Jesus' pronouncement.[14] In a world where the powerful were ready to make bold political and military claims on the land; where the strong assumed that they had the right, thanks to their position or privilege to take what was theirs, Jesus appears as "the re-arranger of the land."[15] Meekness leads to inheritance— the strident will walk away empty-handed. The great reversal keenly felt throughout Jesus' ministry—*the last will be first!*—has now been applied to the land, this land of inheritance, the land of Judah, no doubt the most precious commodity fought for in Jesus' day.

Does this mean that Jesus here offered a territorial promise to his followers? This is not likely. For as we shall see, and as commentators regularly show, while the land itself had a concrete application for most in Judaism, Jesus and his followers reinterpreted the promises that came to those in his kingdom. Their kingdom is in heaven (Matt 5:3, 10); they shall see God (5:8); and their rewards will be counted in heaven (5:12). Still, Jesus exploited one of the most potent images of his day—the land —and refused to offer it to those who demanded to have it.

---

12. Herrmann, *klēros*, TDNT, 3:759–61.

13. For some interpreters, the term *gē* should remain "earth," and refer to the Jewish hope of a regenerated world. See Rom 4:13.

14. Brueggemann, *The Land*, 164.

15. Ibid., 162.

2. Luke 13:6–9

In this parable, Jesus describes a man who planted a fig tree in his vineyard. Yet when he came seeking fruit from it, there was none. The caretaker then proposes to the owner that since the tree remained fruitless for three years, it should be cut down. The owner refuses but instead orders that the tree be given one more year of good care and fertilizer, and if it fails after another year, it should be removed.

For some scholars this parable was later historicized in the cursing of the fig tree found in Mark and Matthew (Mark 11:12–21; Matt 21:18–22). While certain literary sharing may have occurred between the two narratives as they were formed in the tradition, many reject this interpretation, seeing the parable as source for the cursing because of their different emphases.[16] In Matthew and Mark, judgment on Israel is immediate and certain; Luke's parable urges forbearance.

The parable includes one vital line (here in italics): The caretaker argues, "For three years now I've been coming to look for fruit on this fig tree and haven't found any. *Cut it down! Why should it use up the soil*?" The final phrase uses the Greek term *gē*, which we met in Matt 5:5. It may refer to the soil (NIV) or the ground (RSV); but it may refer to the land. Its use here is suggestive because it is linked to a potent symbol for Israel: a vineyard holding a fig tree. And if this link is maintained, an echo of passages in the OT comes to mind, where the land itself has an independent life in relation to Israel. The land can either spit out its residents (Lev 18:28; 20:22) or withhold its goodness.[17]

Judgment on Israel for its lack of fruit may lead to its removal *from the land*. It may be cut away. This is a prophetic critique of Israel: the land cannot be possessed without reference to righteousness. Living in the land comes with preconditions of fruitfulness. The land therefore is not a place of security unless those within it maintain some relation to God. Marshall comments, "Is there a hint that another vine will be planted in its place?"[18] This idea of land that fails to be fruitful—used as a metaphor—was common in Judaism. The later apocryphal story of Ahikar does this to a palm tree that lived along a river and tossed its fruit into the water. The owner is eager to cut it down but the dresser begs to

16. See Davies, *The Gospel and the Land*, 355.

17. For the many ways the fig served as a Jewish symbol, see Snodgrass, *Stories with Intent*, 259–60.

18. Marshall, *The Gospel of Luke*, 555.

save it (8:35). Such metaphors were commonplace in antiquity: lack of productivity leads to loss.[19]

3. Mark 11:12-14; 20-22 (Matt 21:18-19)

While the well-known cursing of the fig tree does not refer to the land per se, nevertheless it evokes the same motifs embedded in Luke 13:6-9. Its setting strongly reinforces the parable: Mark "sandwiches" the story with three main elements: (a) the initial cursing (11:12-14), (b) the cleansing of the temple (11:15-20), and (c) the final withering of the tree (11:20-22). This is an interpretative schema designed to tell us that the cursing is a prophetic act meant to symbolize what is taking place in the temple: *it is judged for its failure to produce the fruit of its purposes.* "My house shall be called a house of prayer for all nations; but you have made it a den of robbers."

This scene puts Jesus at odds with those who held confidence in the success of Israel's national ambitions for the land, its most important city (Jerusalem), and the temple. These things were not sacrosanct, not above critique or criticism. Once again, residence in the land was contingent upon fruitfulness—righteousness, no doubt—and the temple had been found wanting. Trees and nations planted in the land will wither (or, in Luke 16, be cut down) should they fail to do what God desires. Being anchored in the land is no guarantee of security.

4. Mark 12:1-12 (cf. Matt 21:33-46; Luke 20:9-19)

Each of the Synoptic Gospels records a major narrative parable at the close of Jesus' public ministry. And in some respects, it may rightly be viewed as the signature parable of Jesus' climactic relationship with Israel or Jerusalem. Extensive studies have probed the parable and discovered numerous debated ideas. Here we can only give a concise summary.[20]

Jesus describes a vineyard and its recalcitrant, difficult renters. The owner, now absent, had taken good care of the vineyard: it was walled, protected, watered, and pruned. His only request was that the tenants would pay him with some of the fruit that came from the vineyard. When the owner sends his servants to collect they are shunned and in

19. Snodgrass, *Stories with Intent,* 256–57. Snodgrass provides examples from early Judaism, Greco-Roman writings, early Christian apocrypha, and later Jewish writings.

20. For a review of discussion and literature, see Snodgrass, *Stories with Intent,* 276–99, and his earlier, "Recent Research," 187–215.

some cases, beaten or killed. Finally the owner sends his son, thinking that his stature would be persuasive. However, the tenants hatch a sinister plot: they decide to kill the son and thus leave the vineyard without an heir, hoping all along to gain the land in the owner's absence.

This parable is vital for our discussion since it is certainly Jesus' variation on Isaiah's well-known parable of the vineyard in Isa 5:1–7. The preparation and care of the vineyard is described (5:1–2), its failure to produce good fruit outlined (5:3–4), and the judgment of the owner (God) proclaimed (5:5–6). Then Isaiah makes the parallel explicit: "For the vineyard of the LORD of hosts is the house of Israel and the people of Judah are his pleasant planting" (5:7). The vineyard then is a potent metaphor for Israel *in the land*. And Israel's lack of "fruitfulness" is reflected in how it has lived in "the land" (5:8). The signature sin of these people is greed as they consume the land for their own interests.

The vine metaphor was not unique to Isaiah. As a symbol for Israel and its life in the land, it was used by Jeremiah (2:21; 8:13; 12:10), Ezekiel (7:6; 17:6; 19:10), and Hosea (10:1). The luxuriant vineyard is likewise a metaphor for the blessing of life in the land (Mic 4:4; Zech 3:10, 8:12). But most important, Israelites can be described as vines that have been transplanted out of Egypt and replanted in God's vineyard, the Land of Promise (Ps 80:8, 14; Isa 5:2). Ezekiel used the vine/vineyard image for the transplanting of Israel to Babylon in the exile (19:10–14).

These background images enrich the meaning of Jesus' parable in Mark 12. If the vineyard is the land (and its people), *Jerusalem's refusal to accept the vineyard owner's son will lead to its judgment*. Thus Jesus ends the parable with a surprising announcement: The owner will come and "destroy those tenants and *give the vineyard to others*." Matthew adds, "therefore the kingdom will be taken away from you and given to a nation producing fruit" (21:43).

By speaking about the vineyard—which alludes directly to Isaiah's pregnant metaphor—Jesus is making a direct comment about the contingency of life in the land. Possession of the land is not a human prerogative. There is another owner—God—and the vineyard's tenants are accountable to him.

5. Matthew 19:28 (cf. Luke 22:30)

Jewish eschatology looked forward not simply to a renewal of Israel's national life, but to a renewal of its life *in the land*, a renewal that included a transformation of the land itself. Its crops would give enormous yields (Amos 9:3) and the land would be transformed (*1 En.* 62:5). Judgment would ensue on this day of renewal as every tribe on earth stood before God (*Ps. Sol.* 17:28).[21]

In Matt 19:28 Jesus reassures Peter and his followers, pointing to the promises of his kingdom, which they will inherit. The Twelve will sit in judgment on the twelve tribes of Israel (just as in the Jewish eschatology), and this will occur "in the new world" (RSV). Literally Jesus refers to "the regeneration" or "rebirth." Greek-speaking Jews might use this term to describe the land following the flood (e.g. Philo; Josephus, *Ant.* 11.3.96). Hence Jesus looks forward, not simply to the dawning of God's eschatological rule from heaven, but to the land itself experiencing renewal and transformation just as in the Jewish expectation. Jesus' interest here in the land is in how it will undergo change and rebirth.

6. Matthew 25:14–30

For some scholars, this parable about risk, investment, and accounting may refer to the land. Here a wealthy man is departing for a journey and he entrusts various sums to his servants. Two of the servants use the money creatively and gain a profit. But a third buries it. When the master returns, the first two servants are commended, but the third is judged in no uncertain terms.

The instinct to bury money was completely understandable in the first century. In a world without secure public banking, burying money was often the best way to guarantee it would not be stolen. For this reason, it is not unusual for archaeologists to uncover "treasures" buried in floors, villa courtyards, even fields. Jesus is aware of the threat of money theft (Matt 6:20) and even tells a story about finding treasure that has been buried (Matt 13:44).

In the story the man buries his money in the "ground" [*gē*]. This is the term we encountered in Matt 5:5, which has a variety of meanings. In this parable, it could refer to the soil or the ground; but for some, it may refer to the land. If this is the case, it refers to the cautious, preservationist instinct in first-century Judaism to preserve the land in a world rapidly overwhelmed by pagan life. Rather than risk investments, the third servant hides his money *inside the land*.

21. These thematic connections and their application to Matthew 19 are outlined in Davies, *The Gospel and the Land*, 363–65. See also Wright, *Jesus and the Victory*, 320–68.

Such an interpretation is far from certain since it requires an allegorizing of the story that is foreign and arbitrary to the story itself. This may be an innocent account of a man putting money in the ground.

7. Luke 12:13–21

Rabbis were known to arbitrate domestic conflicts in villages. And since Jesus is reputed to be a rabbi, he is approached by a man who is struggling with his brother over their inheritance. As we have seen, this term —"inheritance"—may well have an innocent connotation, but it also was one more synonym for the land inherited by Israel. Thus in the parable of the vineyard (Mark 12), the tenants hope to kill the son and thereby gain "the inheritance," the land (the vineyard).

In the present story Jesus refuses to arbitrate between the two brothers. Instead he takes advantage of the opportunity to talk about the foolishness of fighting for an inheritance that is temporal, which can be taken away in a moment by death. He tells the parable of the Foolish Barn Builder to underscore the point. After his estate is prosperous beyond measure, God visits him to say, "Fool! This night your soul is required of you." The upshot of Jesus' instruction to the men is simple: This inheritance is not as important as the inheritance you have in heaven.

For those who were struggling to hold the land and fight for it at all costs, the parable is provocative. It is a warning not unlike Jesus' relocation of his kingdom: His will not be a kingdom that values struggle and conflict but will be anchored to heaven. And Jewish identity that struggles solely to hold the land may miss the more important place God holds for us with him.

SUMMARY

We began by underscoring the dramatic and intense interest Judaism had in the land during the first century and argued that this atmosphere of political struggle must be assumed behind most of Jesus' teachings. Reference to the land—a subject of extreme contention—would have to be veiled and nuanced very carefully, or else a public teacher would be drawn into the competing agendas of the activists of his day.

Jesus clearly respects the uniqueness of Israel's location in the land. He limits his ministry and that of his disciples to geographic Israel with very few exceptions. We have no record of Jesus working within the major Hellenistic regions of his world despite the fact that they surrounded and penetrated Galilee. For him, both Judea and its great city, Jerusalem, were sacred locales with unparalleled theological roles to play in history.

But this ushers in a surprise. Jesus is reticent with regard to debates about the land. He expresses no *overt* affirmation of first-century territorial theologies. He does not repeat Judaism's call to land ownership, nor does he express criticism of the foreign occupation. He never elevates Jerusalem to such a degree that it becomes a focal point of Jewish nationalism. He even anchors his work in Galilee, a region looked upon with scorn by Judeans.

Jesus seems to follow a different tack. In his theological outlook, blessings do not simply accrue to those Jews living in the land. He points to Damascus and Sidon and the stories of Elijah and Elisha as models of *distributed blessing* for nations outside the land. But it is not simply foreign lands that might be blessed; it is *the poor and the landless*. Surprising reversal was a hallmark of Jesus' teaching. Those who are last will become first; those who are rich will become poor. Those who fight to possess the land will be trumped by the meek. In his most explicit saying about land and inheritance, Jesus says that *the meek will inherit the land.*

Walter Brueggemann describes this as a poignant scandal at the heart of Jesus' land theology. Those who possess the most and who have the most to lose by a revision of Jewish territorialism resist Jesus forcefully.[22] Jesus in this respect is the great "re-arranger" of the land. And his opponents know it.

Brueggemann anchors in the Old Testament a theme he now locates in the Gospels. The land itself presented Israel with a devastating challenge to faith. One could *grasp with courage* or one could *wait in confidence* for the gift of land. One could seize the land or one could wait for land. The prophets consistently urged Israel to choose the latter. And here Jesus does the same.

Brueggemann finds moving symbols of these choices in modern Israel. There is Masada and there is the Western Wall (formerly called the Wailing Wall). The first represents militarism, the second patient longing and prayer. As symbols they represent timeless choices that pertained to Israel in the first century, the Middle East today, indeed to each of us. We may grasp, or we may wait; we may seize those places we claim to be ours by divine—or racial or national—right, or we can suspend our desire in faith. Sufficient evidence in the Gospels makes

22. Brueggemann, *The Land*, 164.

clear that Jesus echoed the sentiment of the prophets that a messianic reversal was afoot, a reversal that Jesus' mother Mary once offered when she recalled the sentiments of Hannah (1 Sam 2:1–10), who said,

> The LORD sends poverty and wealth;
> he humbles and he exalts.
> He raises the poor from the dust
> and lifts the needy from the ash heap;
> he seats them with princes
> and has them inherit a throne of honor. (1 Sam 2:7–8)

In these verses we find a theological inversion that would bring land loss to land graspers and land receipt to those who bear promises but lack power.[23] Mary exclaimed at the birth of Jesus that in her family's loss and poverty and landlessness, she was witnessing something parallel:

> He has performed mighty deeds with his arm;
> He has scattered those who are proud in their inmost thoughts.
> He has brought down rulers from their thrones
> but has lifted up the humble.
> He has filled the hungry with good things
> but has sent the rich away empty.
> He has helped his servant Israel,
> remembering to be merciful
> to Abraham and his descendants forever, just as he promised our
> ancestors." (Luke 1:51–55)

BIBLIOGRAPHY

Brandon, S. G. F. *Jesus and the Zealots: A Study of the Political Factor in Primitive Christianity*. Manchester: Manchester University Press, 1967.

Brueggemann, Walter. *The Land: Place as Gift, Promise, and Challenge in Biblical Faith*. 2nd ed. Minneapolis: Fortress, 2002.

Burge, Gary M. *Jesus and the Land: The New Testament Challenge to "Holy" Land Theology*. Grand Rapids: Baker Academic, 2010.

Crossan, John Dominic. *The Historical Jesus: The Life of a Mediterranean Jewish Peasant*. San Francisco: Harper, 1991.

France, R. T. *The Gospel of Matthew*. The New International Commentary on the New Testament. Grand Rapids: Eerdmans, 2007.

Hagner, Donald. *Matthew 1–13*. Word Biblical Commentary 33A. Dallas: Word, 1993.

Herrmann, J. "*klēros*." In *Theological Dictionary of the New Testament* 3:759–61, edited by Gerhard Kittel and Gerhard Friedrich. Translated by Geoffrey W. Bromiley. 10 vols. Grand Rapids: Eerdmans, 1964.

23. Ibid., 161

Horbury, William. "Christ as Brigand in Ancient Anti-Christian Polemic." In *Jesus and the Politics of His Day*, edited by Ernst Bammel and C. F. D. Moule, 183–96. Cambridge: Cambridge University Press, 1984.

Marchadour, Alain, and David Neuhaus. *The Land, the Bible, and History: Toward the Land That I Will Show You*. The Abrahamic Dialogues Series 4. New York: Fordham University Press, 2007.

Marshall, I. Howard. *The Gospel of Luke: A Commentary on the Greek Text*. The New International Greek Testament Commentary. Exeter, UK: Paternoster, 1978.

Resseguie, James L. *Spiritual Landscape: Images of the Spiritual Life in the Gospel of Luke*. Peabody, MA: Hendrickson, 2004.

Schnabel, Eckhard J. *Early Christian Mission*. Downer's Grove, IL: InterVarsity, 2004.

Snodgrass, Klyne. *Stories with Intent: A Comprehensive Guide to the Parables of Jesus*. Grand Rapids: Eerdmans, 2008.

———. "Recent Research on the Parable of the Wicked Tenants: An Assessment." *Bulletin for Biblical Research* 8 (1998) 187–216.

Stauffer, Ethelbert. "Christ and the Story of the Tribute Money." In *Christ and the Caesars: Historical Sketches*, 112–37. London: SCM, 1955.

Wright, N. T. *Jesus and the Victory of God*. Christian Origins and the Question of God 2. Minneapolis: Fortress, 1997.

❖ 18 ❖

Summarizing the Points
of Dispute

Peter Walker

I T WAS A GREAT privilege to be involved in each of the four consultations—held between 1996 and 2000—that focused on the "theology
of the land." These consultations, first in Cyprus and then in Bethlehem,
brought together Bible-believing Christians on both sides of the debate,
both Messianic and Palestinian, together with those from Europe and
North America with a desire to see appropriate reconciliation between
these two viewpoints. So I am delighted that now, ten years later, there is
an opportunity to update the original volume of essays, produced in the
light of the first three consultations in early 2000, by adding significant
contributions to this debate that have been articulated in the last decade.

What was not included in the first volume, however, was a snap-
shot summary of the major sticking points that we had encountered
in the midst of our debates. This short epilogue now seeks to provide
this. It is based on notes taken after the second consultation in 1997,
when it was becoming clear that we were revisiting some of the same
unrecognized differences we had touched on the year before. This summary acted as a framework for our subsequent consultation, giving us a
fruitful agenda for those later meetings. As a result, it may well be that
some of the essays eventually included in the two volumes cover the
same ground and reconcile some of the differences noted here. Yet we

thought readers might still benefit from seeing the sticking points listed here in the format in which we ourselves encountered them in the midst of our discussions. To keep this brief, the points of dispute will be listed under the original six headings.[1]

1. INHERITANCE

This key biblical word in the Old Testament is sometimes used of Israel (with the nation being seen as God's inheritance) but is also used of the physical land that Israel inherited.[2] Used in this way, it reminded the Israelites that they were strictly "tenants" (with God himself as the prime owner of the land), but equally that they had received an undeserved gift of grace.[3] But how does the New Testament use this word "inheritance" and who can claim to be its true inheritors?

The Palestinian viewpoint would note how the New Testament now applies this language of "inheritance" not to a land but to that which all believers graciously receive through Christ (1 Pet 1:4). They would also highlight Paul's insistence that all believers, both Jew and Gentile, are now equally "heirs" of God's promises in Christ (Rom 8:17). Paul is adamant on this point in Galatians 3, where he builds his argument on the idea that Christ himself is ultimately the true "seed" (singular) who is the inheritor and guarantor of the divine promises.[4] Thus, on this view, the notion of an "inherited land" has been transformed in the New Testament era. Moreover, if there were any continuing sense in which the "seed of Abraham" still inherited the physical land, then arguably the implication of Galatians is that the true inheritors of this land promise

1. For the sake of simplicity, I highlight the differences between the "Messianic" and "Palestinian" viewpoints, but this terminology necessarily hides the fact that these are generalizations, that the nuanced position of any individual normally associated with that label is not truly represented here, and also—of course—that there were "Westerners" present in the consultations who might well have adopted a mixture of these positions without themselves being, strictly, either "Messianic believers" or "Palestinian Christians." All Scripture quotations are taken from the New International Version (NIV).

2. For the land as Israel's "inheritance," see Num 26:53; 36:2; Deut 4:21, 38; 15:4 etc; Josh 11:23; Pss 105:11; 135:12; 136:21; Isa 58:14; Jer 3:19; Ezek 45:1; 48:29.

3. See Lev 25:23 ('the land is mine'). It also undergirded the prophetic concern that no Israelite should be sold into slavery and thereby disinherited or removed from his ancestral connection to the Promised Land: see e.g., 1 Kgs 21:1–16 (Ahab's attack on Naboth's "inheritance").

4. For other relevant NT texts, see Eph 2:11–23; 1 Pet 2:9–10.

are not those physically descended from Abraham, but rather those who by faith have been incorporated into Israel's Messiah.

A Messianic viewpoint, however, would see the promise of this land inheritance in the Old Testament as not being overthrown by the New, but rather as continuing (parallel to the "spiritual inheritance" now enjoyed by Gentile Christians): The promise still stands and those of Jewish descent are the rightful "heirs." They would also highlight that, even within the Old Testament, there are several instances—principally during the exile—when the Israelites were not strictly in active "possession" of the land, but nevertheless were still its rightful "owners" by divine promise. This distinction between "possession" and underlying "ownership" then explains how the promise of their inheritance has not been broken through nearly 2,000 years of not "possessing" the land of Israel. Jewish descendants of Abraham have always been its rightful owners, even though "dispossessed," and this applies to the present day—even if some parts of the land are currently "occupied" or administered by others.

2. COVENANTS

The Bible is a book based on God's covenant promises. There are several episodes in biblical history where God makes such covenant promises (e.g., Noah, Abraham, Moses, David) and the promises of a "new covenant" (as found in Jer 31:31) give rise to the second half of the Bible being described in toto as the "New Testament" (or "New Covenant"). Yet this then gives rise to much dispute as to whether these apparently successive covenants are all aspects of but one overarching divine covenant promise, or whether there are several covenants, which then relate to each other in various ways, perhaps by contrast or perhaps with a later covenant superseding an earlier covenant. In particular, were the important covenants (to Abraham and again to David) strictly unconditional, or were they conditional in some way? Could the recipients of the promise eventually lose out on that which was promised? Indeed, could the promise effectively be terminated—and thus totally removed from divine consideration—or is there something about them that is "eternal" and lasts "forever," come what may?

A Messianic viewpoint would focus on the eternal and unconditional nature of these covenants. In particular, the divine promise of the land, an integral part of the covenant with Abraham, was explicitly stated to be "forever" (Gen 17:17–18). This cannot be revoked—neither by the passage of time nor by the dawning of a "new covenant" nor by the disobedience of the descendants of Abraham. The Israelites would eventually go into exile (the curse of the covenant for such disobedience), but they were "restored" to the land precisely because the gift of the land was itself unconditional.

A Palestinian response would highlight that there are other divine promises that, though explicitly stated as being "forever," do not appear to have been fulfilled.[5] So perhaps, the Hebrew word "forever," *le-olam*, does not mean literally "to the end of the eternity" but only "for a very long time." Alternatively, if David was promised that there would always be a descendant on his throne and that his dynasty would last "forever" (2 Sam 7:12–16), then there is a manifest problem in Old Testament history when the kings of Judah are taken into exile, never to return. This dashing of the divine promise evidently causes much heart searching for subsequent biblical writers (e.g., Pss 74 and 79). The solution to this dilemma, however, is given in the New Testament when the angel announces at Jesus' birth that he "will sit on the throne of his father David and his kingdom will have no end" (Luke 1:32–33); this then is underscored when the apostles proclaim Jesus as Israel's Messiah, as the true Davidic King (cf. Acts 2–3). So here is an instance of an "eternal" promise continuing over into the New Testament era—and indeed, into eternity—but, crucially, in a form or mode which is not literal or "political" in the same way as the original promise sounded.

Therefore, this suggests by parallel reasoning that the divine promise of the land also might continue into the present but in a different mode. Hence we see the New Testament references to the "ends of the earth" now coming within God's kingdom-rule under Christ (Acts 1:8) and to Abraham's "inheriting the world" (Rom 4:13), indications that the apostles saw the land-promise as now fulfilled in a maximalist and global fashion; hence, too, the references in Hebrews to the enduring "Sabbath-rest" for God's people which is the ultimate fulfillment of the Promised Land as established under Joshua (Hebrews 3–4). Thus, Hebrews' portrait of the temple, the city of Jerusalem, and the land as all being viewed differently in the light of the coming of Jesus, needs to be heeded today, not least by Messianic believers, the contemporary equivalent of the first-century "Hebrew" believers. In the days of the "new covenant" (Heb 8:7–10; 9–10;

---

5. A small but interesting example is that of the Recabites, whose tribe, according to Jer 35:19, will last "forever."

12:22–24), believers are to focus elsewhere, not on the original physical form of the promise, but on what they eternally signified; and they must not be tempted back into merely Jewish ways of seeing matters, ignoring the divinely intended fulfillment of those realities as now revealed in Jesus.

3. THE ROLE OF JESUS IN FULFILLING THE COVENANT

Within this framework of covenant fulfillment, there is then much dispute concerning the role of Jesus himself. As Israel's Messiah, he presumably came to fulfill the Abrahamic and Davidic covenants in some way, but how did he do so? The questions we have just raised can also be phrased like this: Does the fulfillment Jesus accomplished cause the covenants to continue after him in much the same way as before, only deeper (as might be argued from a Messianic position)? Or instead, does his fulfilling them somehow bring their original shape to an end, with their now being supplanted by something slightly different which yet reflects God's original and eternal intention (as might be argued from a Palestinian position)? Thus a Messianic believer might argue that even if Jesus is the true Davidic king in a nonpolitical sense, the original promise suggests that we might still expect a king over Israel in a more obviously literal sense. Or again, Jesus may have come as a fulfillment of God's promise to Abraham, thus bringing God's blessing to "all nations." But surely that does not annul the promise within that Abrahamic covenant concerning his descendants' ownership of the land?

This same point might be construed diagrammatically as follows. For the Messianic position, the covenant promises in the Old Testament are like a straight line that then is supplemented by extra aspects of fulfillment brought about by the coming of Jesus. For the Palestinian position, however, those covenant promises are funneled down onto Jesus and then reemerge in the New Testament in a new form. In the former scheme there is an emphasis on continuity, but with additions; in the latter, there is a greater note of discontinuity, pointing instead to what might be termed "intentional transformation." The latter scheme seems to work well for a biblical theme like the temple, for the New Testament clearly teaches that we no longer need a physical temple because Jesus himself is the true temple, and because he has offered the ultimate sacrifice for sin.[6]

---

6. See John 1:14; 2:21; Heb 10:10–22; for Christian believers constituting a new temple in Christ, see also 1 Cor 3:16–17; 6:19; Eph. 2:21–22; 1 Pet 2:4–8.

However, the former scheme seems to work better for a biblical theme like the land, for at first sight there does not seem to be any substantial New Testament teaching that overturns the Old Testament's perspective on this key topic. The Palestinian position (indebted to Hebrews) might therefore more frequently talk in terms of typology—where the reality revealed in the New Testament is God's intended pattern or "type," which has been preceded or foreshadowed by an Old Testament "antitype" that might (outwardly) appear quite different. The Messianic position would use this category more sparingly, fearing that such typological fulfillment might effectively undermine the Old Testament promises or seemingly render them null and void.

These differences, located at the level of how we construct our overall biblical framework, are then matched by differences at the more detailed level—namely, when we look at Jesus' public ministry and try to assess his attitude to the Abrahamic promises concerning the land. The Messianic position would highlight that Jesus' teaching seems to pass over this topic in silence (thus presumably leaving the promise "unchanged" in the New Testament era). The Palestinian position would argue that in his one explicit reference to the "land issue" (in Matt 5:5), Jesus is universalizing its scope from the Promised Land to the whole "earth." Moreover, he clearly was opposed to the nationalistic desires of his fellow Jews (and the "Zealots") for political independence, warning instead that fighting Rome would only bring down God's judgment upon Jerusalem.[7] If so, then he must have disagreed with the Zealots' interpretation of these Old Testament land promises that inspired them to hope for Israel's independent kingdom. Jesus did not see those promises being fulfilled in that way and, arguably, through his own ministry, was revealing quite a different way in which they were being fulfilled. To this the Messianic position might reply: "Yes, Jesus in his own day was not working for a 'political' or physical fulfillment, but that may simply be for reasons of timing. Now, two thousand years later, it is God's time for those land promises to come back into play." In other words, the land promises were not transformed—still less, annulled—by Jesus in the first century; they were simply left untouched. Our diagram thus extends into the present era by showing how the promises were perhaps "put on hold" for many centuries (the dotted line) but have recently come back into operation.

7. See *e.g.* Luke 13:35; 19:41–44; 21:20–24; 23:28–31.

A key text at this point in the discussion is Acts 1. The risen Jesus answers the disciples' insistent question about the "restoration of the kingdom to Israel" with: "It is not for you to know the seasons . . . but you will be witnesses . . . to the ends of the earth" (Acts 1:7–8). A Messianic reading of this text would see Jesus here as saying this political restoration has simply been delayed: It will come about in the future but only after the disciples have first gone out to the world in evangelism. A Palestinian response, by contrast, might be: "Jesus' own teaching (in v. 3) had an expressly different emphasis—being focused on the 'kingdom of God,' not on 'Israel'—and thus his reply offers a redefinition of their misguided restoration-hope: the kingdom will come and Israel will truly be restored by the very means of their going out to the world with the news of Jesus as Israel's true King and Messiah. When the 'ends of the earth' come under the rule of Jesus as Lord, that will be the true fulfillment of God's promises to restore his people."

These two quite different interpretations of Jesus' understanding of Israel's restoration then come to the surface in other places within the Gospels and Acts. In each case the essential dispute is, was Jesus leaving the restoration hopes of Israel to one side and focusing on fulfilling other aspects of Old Testament prophecy? Or was he claiming that his ministry was the surprising fulfillment of those hopes, and that he was indeed restoring Israel but at a deeper level—inaugurating her true return from exile, redeeming her from sin, and regathering her around himself as the true center of God's people? The former (Messianic) view then opens the door to see the establishment of the modern State of Israel as a fulfillment of those Old Testament hopes of restoration; but the latter view questions whether we can apply these "restoration" categories to this modern event because, on this view, Jesus and the New Testament writers have given a definitive reinterpretation of this restoration theme—a reinterpretation that is authoritative and thus disallows us from seeking fulfillment of these promises in these ways that seem to undermine the reality of the fulfillment offered by Jesus.

4. OTHER NEW TESTAMENT QUESTIONS

The shape of the debate is gradually becoming clear. Within this framework we can now list more briefly some other points of dispute in interpreting the New Testament:

- What is the significance of the New Testament's teaching about the redundancy of the Jerusalem temple? Can that rightly be used to set up a paradigm of "fulfillment by transformation," which can then be applied (as above) to other Old Testament realities (i.e., the city of Jerusalem, the land of Israel, the people of Israel)? And within this, how do we interpret those more positive references to the temple in Acts, where the apostles still use it for worship and teaching (e.g., Acts 3:1)?[8] Was this merely an interim necessity, or should we receive this as somehow potentially "normative," such that a rebuilt temple today would still be compatible with Hebrews' teaching about its redundancy?[9]

- What are the implications of the widespread teaching in the New Testament that Jesus is a New Moses who has performed a new "exodus" for God's people?[10] Does this imply that there is effectively a corresponding new "Promised Land" towards which this new Moses figure is leading us?

- When Paul uses his frequent tag "in Christ," is he using this in a locative sense—seeing it as the new covenant equivalent of "being in the land" as the sphere of God's blessing? Why are there so few references to the land in his writings? Does this reflect his lack of interest in this nonissue? Or was he an ardent Jewish nationalist before his conversion (even a "proto-Zealot"?) that has now consciously abandoned this "political" interpretation in the light of Christ?[11]

- If the New Testament writers all assert that Gentiles are now included within God's people as Gentiles, does this necessarily mean that all Jewish distinctive has to be abolished? Would Paul have discouraged

8. Acts 3:1; 21:26.

9. This raises a key historical question about the book of Hebrews: was it written before the destruction of the temple (such that its teaching proactively dismisses the temple's significance in the light of Christ)? Or was it written in the aftermath of AD 70, thus being merely a reflective interpretation of how to live in a post-temple world (which could thus be ignored if a new temple were built)? The majority viewpoint is for a date in the 60s AD: see Bruce, *Epistle to the Hebrews*; Guthrie, *The Letter to the Hebrews*; and Lane, *Hebrews 1–8*; for a post-70 reflection, see e.g., Isaacs, *Sacred Space*. See further Walker, *Jesus and the Holy City*, 227–32.

10. See e.g., Luke 9:29–30; Matt 2–5; John 6–8; 1 Cor 10:1–4; Heb 3:1–6; Rev 15:3.

11. Paul's references: he twice uses the word "zeal" to describe his pre-Christian stance (see Gal 1:14 and Phil 3:6).

Jewish believers in Jesus from circumcising their sons? Can Jewish practices (e.g., in regard to Sabbath and dietary regulations) be observed without countermanding Paul's desire that such things not erect a barrier between Jew and Gentile, or encourage a "two-tier" element within God's one people in Christ (as encouraged in Eph 2:11–22)?[12] If they can, then presumably the Jewish privilege of being "owners" of the land can continue in the new covenant era without disposing Gentile believers? But, if they cannot, then the converse may be true.

- In particular, how are we to understand Jesus' teaching about Jerusalem being "trampled upon until the times of the Gentiles are fulfilled" (Luke 21:24)? Is this a long-term future prophecy, suggesting a nearly two-thousand-year period of Gentile rule over Jerusalem, viz., until 1967, matching in some way Paul's references to the "fullness of the Gentiles" (Rom 11:25)? Or is it simply the Lukan parallel to the verses found in Matthew and Mark that speak about God's mercifully limiting (or "cutting short") the length of those days "for the sake of the elect" (Matt 24:22; Mark 13:20)? In other words, the force of the phrase is that the "times of the Gentiles"—when they besiege the city and then gloat over its defeat—will actually be kept short; the severe trauma will not last more than a few years (perhaps matching AD 67–72?).

- This raises the multiple questions relating to Romans 11, a text that can often dominate the entire proceedings! In sum, is Paul predicting a distinctive end time scenario when God will "save Israel," either through Christ or in some other distinctive and "mysterious" way? Or is he advocating that Israel will be saved—in some smaller, less spectacular way—through the normal process of Jewish people responding to the Good News of their Messiah Jesus? If there is such a distinctive "end times" period, then special rules might apply to that season in God's purposes (e.g., God fulfilling prophecies literally that previously had been fulfilled in Christ in a different way). If there is not, however, then we must be careful not to be led astray from the norms laid down by the apostles.

---

12. See also Rom 3:29–30; Phil 3:2–9; 1 Pet 2:9–10.

5. THE RETURN TO THE LAND

This last point leads on to dispute about how to evaluate the return of Jewish people to the land of Israel in our own day. Is this a straightforward fulfillment of OT prophecies (e.g., Ezekiel 36–39), showing the enduring nature of the promise in Genesis 12? Or is it an event that, while under the providence of the God of the Bible, is not strictly a fulfillment of those passages (their having been fulfilled either in the sixth or fifth centuries BC, or through the "restoration" accomplished in Messiah Jesus)? If the latter, what might these deeper providential purposes of God be? (For example, might it be a means of God showing the descendants of Abraham that their ultimate salvation and *shalom* is precisely not to be found in the land, but only in their Messiah as revealed in Jesus?)

Yet even if it were granted that this return is indeed a fulfillment of Old Testament prophecy, there would then be a subsequent series of disputed points:

- If Israel has been returning to the land, why are we not seeing the parallel movement of a "returning" to the Lord (which is what Ezekiel's prophecies were primarily about)? What is the relationship of these two "returnings"? Why was nineteenth-century Zionism principally espoused by secular Jews? And what are we to make of this secular atheism continuing to be the majority position within contemporary Israeli society? Thus, if there has been only a minimal "returning to the Lord," does that begin to throw back questions as to whether this is indeed a fulfillment of Ezekiel?

- In this period of supposed prophetic fulfillment, how much is strictly the work of God alone, and how much is the responsibility of human beings to bring about? Should we be actively encouraging *aliyah*, enabling the "returning" to the land, and be proactive in evangelism (enabling the "returning" to the Lord), or should believers adopt a more passive stance? In particular, since witnessing to Messiah Jesus among Jewish people is historically so complex, should believers simply adopt an acquiescent and uncritical role of "loving Israel" in the hope that through this loving support God will do his work of bringing them to himself?

- Above all, even if we are in prophetic times, what are the biblical mandates for justice that still remain? Does the "prophetic" right to return to the land trump and render irrelevant the bracing demands for justice and righteousness, expressed so forcefully by those same OT prophets? Do Israel's prophetic rights to the land somehow excuse them from moral and social righteousness in the land? Just because something has been prophesied, this does not mean we are locked into a deterministic sequence of events, where we are absolved of our human responsibilities to "seek justice, love mercy and walk humbly with our God" (Mic 6:8).

- Following from this: If Ezekiel himself acknowledged the political and social rights of those who had come to live in the land during the period since Israel's deportation into exile, then equally God has a concern for the Palestinians who, in our own day, are residents in this Promised Land. If the models of conquest espoused uniquely in the days of Joshua were not consciously invoked by Ezekiel, then presumably they should not be invoked today. In theory, of course, it should be possible to adhere to a belief in the land as being rightfully "owned" by Israel, without equally desiring to expel all non-Jewish residents from its borders. In practice, however, this conviction about ownership can all too easily fuel an inhospitable exclusivism. The biblical mandates for the "alien in your midst" then become even more important (e.g., Num 15:15).

6. MISSION ISSUES FROM THE WIDER MIDDLE EAST

Finally, these disputes over detail reflect some wider differences of perspective with regard to mission. How does our "theology of the land" affect the wider Christian community in its promotion of the gospel in the Middle East, both amongst Jews and Muslims?

(A) Relating to Judaism

With regard to Judaism, when Christians adopt a positive and "prophetic" interpretation of Israel's return to the land, this presumably is seen positively among many Israeli Jews. Even if they themselves do not read the Old Testament with an attitude of faith in the God of Israel, presumably they are grateful for this Christian support of Israel—this expression of solidarity after a long period when relations between church and synagogue have been historically sour. By contrast, were Christians to take a more negative view (especially if they become pointedly critical of Israel's political and moral stances), this might well have the effect of undermining the promotion of the gospel—not least because criticism of Israel so often is perceived as an expression of "anti-Semitism."

Yet, there remains the key point, alluded to above, that this stance of support for Israel can easily become, in the minds of many Christians, not a means to an end, but a sufficient end in itself. In other words the goal of evangelistic mission is effectively forgotten in the bid to "comfort Israel"—seemingly at all costs. This then effectively begins to undermine and work against the gospel of Jesus—with Israelis gratefully taking the Christian support offered in the name of Jesus but "digging in their heels" in response to the Christian claims that this Jesus is their Messiah.

(B) Relating to Islam

With regard to Islam, of course, the issues largely work in entirely the opposite direction. Missionaries working in the wider Middle East are constantly aware of the negative effect for mission and outreach among Muslims that results from Christian support for Israel. This support can easily be seen by Muslims as support for their "enemies" in the region and, indeed, as a modern-day outworking of a Crusader mentality within Western Christendom. This is deeply resented. There is then a strong incentive for Christians in Arab countries to distance themselves from Christian Zionist groups, whose advocacy for Israel has such unfortunate effects within this local context.

There is also an urgent need for such Christians to offer an intelligent approach to the Old Testament; for in the eyes of the Muslims, it is this portion of the Christian Bible that has encouraged this undesired support of Israel. Thus the divine promises to Abraham, the conquest narrative under Joshua, and the later prophecies about a "return" all need to be interpreted sensitively in this context. No wonder there can be a strong temptation for Christians in the wider Middle East to downplay their commitment to the Old Testament. Certainly they find they have an urgent task of interpreting the Old Testament "Christianly" (rather than in a merely "Jewish" fashion), developing a truly Jesus-centered biblical theology.

All this is driven by the missionary imperative and by the desire to promote the gospel of Jesus—demonstrating how the Christian faith offers a coherent and distinct "middle ground" between Judaism and Islam—but there are real dangers of dismissing the Old Testament too much, or of becoming overly critical of Israel. For, just as Christians who are seeking to witness among Jewish people can end up supporting Israel too easily, so Christians working among Muslims can end up being too uncritical of Islamic fundamentalism or some of the extreme positions found within Palestinian nationalism.

CONCLUSION

So the sticking points, as outlined above, evidently revealed disagreement on matters both large and small: both "big framework" ideas and points of exegetical detail on particular words. We also discovered there were other issues rumbling underneath the surface. For example, we discovered that in wanting to affirm the reality of divine judgement at work within Israel's biblical history, it was too easy to fall ourselves into judgmental responses to contemporary situations.

Getting all these issues out onto the table proved very valuable. In order to bring this about, we needed to exercise the discipline of not interrupting each other (for example, disagreeing vehemently on a point of detail, and thereby never hearing the underlying, deeper point) and to develop a "charitable presumption" towards each other. Yet the results of this godly patience towards one another were invaluable at the time. So we hope those who read these reflections many years later will be able now to enjoy the fruit of our discoveries and to take the debate forward in further creative ways which foster both biblical faithfulness and Christian charity, to the glory of Jesus.

BIBLIOGRAPHY

Bruce, F. F. *Epistle to the Hebrews*. New International Commentary on the New Testament. Grand Rapids: Eerdmans, 1964.

Guthrie, Donald. *The Letter to the Hebrews*. Tyndale New Testament Commentaries. Leicester: InterVarsity, 1983.

Isaacs, Marie, E. *An Approach to the Theology of the Epistle to the Hebrews*. Journal for the Study of the New Testament Supplement Series 73. Sheffield: Sheffield Academic, 1992.

Lane, William W. *Hebrews 1–8*. Word Biblical Commentary 47A. Dallas: Word, 1991.

———. *Hebrews 9–13*. Word Biblical Commentary 47B. Dallas: Word, 1991.

Walker, Peter. *Jesus and the Holy City: New Testament Perspectives on Jerusalem*. Grand Rapids: Eerdmans, 1996.